AGAINST THE GREAT RESET

EIGHTEEN THESES CONTRA THE NEW WORLD ORDER

Edited by Michael Walsh

BOMBARDIER BOOKS

Published by Bombardier Books
An Imprint of Post Hill Press
ISBN: 978-1-63758-630-3
ISBN (eBook): 978-1-63758-631-0

Against the Great Reset:
Eighteen Theses Contra the New World Order

Cover Design by Matt Margolis

Post Hill Press
New York • Nashville
posthillpress.com

Published in the United States of America
1 2 3 4 5 6 7 8 9 10

To the memory of Angelo Codevilla (1943–2021)
Author, comrade, teacher, friend

CONTENTS

Part I: The Problem

Part II: The Political

Part III: The Economic

Part IV: The Personal

Part V: The Practical

Part VI: The Ineffable

PART I: THE PROBLEM

INTRODUCTION: RESET THIS

BY MICHAEL WALSH

What is the Great Reset and why should we care? In the midst of a tumultuous medical-societal breakdown, likely engineered by the Chinese Communist Party and abetted by America's National Institutes of Health "gain of function" financial assistance to the Wuhan Institute of Virology, why is the Swiss-based World Economic Forum (WEF) advocating a complete "re-imagining" of the Western world's social, economic, and moral structures? And why now? What are its aspirations, prescriptions, and proscriptions, and how will it prospectively affect us? It's a question that the men and women of the WEF are hoping you won't ask.

This book seeks to supply the answers. It has ample historical precedents, from Demosthenes's fulminations against Philip II of Macedon (Alexander's father), Cicero's *Philippics* denouncing Mark Antony, the heretic-hunting Tertullian's *Adversus Marcionem*, and the philosopher Friedrich Nietzsche's *Nietzsche contra Wagner*. Weighty historical issues are often best debated promptly, when something can yet be done about them; in the meantime, historians of the future can at least understand the issues as the participants themselves saw and experienced them. Whether the formerly free world of the Western democracies will succumb to the paternalistic totalitarianism of the oligarchical Resetters remains to be seen. But this is our attempt to stop it.

So great is mankind's perpetual dissatisfaction with its present circumstances, whatever they may be, that the urge to make the world anew is as old as recorded history. Eve fell under the Serpent's spell, and with the plucking of an apple, sought to improve her life in the Garden of Eden by becoming, in Milton's words, "as Gods; Knowing both Good and Evil, as they know." The forbidden fruit was a gift she shared with Adam; how well that turned out has been the history of the human race ever since. High aspirations, disastrous results.

The expulsion from the Garden, however, has not discouraged others from trying. Indeed, the entire chronicle of Western civilization is best regarded as a never-ending and ineluctable struggle for cultural and political superiority, most often expressed militarily (since that is how humans generally decide matters) but extending to all things both spiritual and physical. Dissatisfaction with the status quo may not be universal—timeless and static Asian cultures, such as China's, have had it imposed upon them by external Western forces, including the British and the Marxist-Leninists—but it has been a hallmark of the occident and its steady civilizational churn that dates back at least to Homer, Plato, Aeschylus, Herodotus, Pericles, and Alexander the Great, with whom Western history properly begins.

The philosopher Friedrich Nietzsche, assaying the inelegant Koine, or demotic, Greek of the New Testament in *Beyond Good and Evil*, observed: "*Es ist eine Feinheit, daß Gott griechisch lernte, als er Schriftsteller werden wollte—und daß er es nicht besser lernte*": "It's a particular refinement that God learned Greek when he wanted to become a writer—and that he didn't learn it better." Nietzsche, the preacher's son who became through sheer willpower a dedicated atheist, was poking fun at the fundamentalist belief that the Christian scriptures were the literal words of God himself (Muslims, of course, believe the same thing about the Koran, except more so). If something as elemental, as essential to Western thought as the authenticity of the Bible, not to mention God's linguistic ability, could be questioned and even mocked, then everything was on the table—including, in Nietzsche's case, God Himself.

With the death of God—or of a god—Nietzsche sought liberation from the moral jiu-jitsu of Jesus: that weakness was strength; that victimhood was noble; that renunciation—of love, sex, power, ambition—was the highest form of attainment. That Nietzsche's rejection of God was accompanied by his rejection of Richard Wagner, whose music dramas are based on the moral elevation of rejection, is not coincidental; the great figures of the nineteenth century, including Darwin and Marx, all born within a few years of each other, were not only revolutionaries, but embodied within themselves antithetical forces that somehow evolved into great Hegelian syntheses of human striving with which we still grapple today.

Wagner, the Schopenhauerian atheist who staggered back to Christianity and the anti-Semite who engaged the Jew Hermann Levi as the only man who could conduct his final ode to Christian transfiguration, *Parsifal.* Charles Darwin, ticketed for an Anglican parsonage but mutating into the author of *On the Origin of Species, The Descent of Man*, and all the way to *The Formation of Vegetable Mould through the Action of Worms*. Karl Marx, the scion of rabbis whose father converted to Lutheranism and, like Wagner for a time, a stateless rebel who preached that the withering away of the state itself was "inevitable"—and yet the state endures, however battered it may be at the moment.

It's fitting that the "Great Reset of capitalism" is the brainchild of the WEF, which hosts an annual conference in the Alpine village of Davos—the site of the tuberculosis sanatorium to which the *naïf* Hans Castorp reports at the beginning of Thomas Mann's masterpiece, *The Magic Mountain*.[1] Planning to visit a sick cousin for three weeks, he ends up staying for seven years, "progressing" from healthy individual to patient himself as his perception of time slows and nearly stops. Castorp's personal purgatory ends only when he rouses himself to leave—his *Bildungsreise*[2] complete—upon the outbreak of World War

1 *Der Zauberberg* (1924). The title might also be translated as *The Enchanted Mountain*, which is perhaps more descriptive and evocative of the novel's mood.

2 "Journey of education."

I, in which we assume he will meet the death, random and senseless, that he has been so studiously avoiding yet simultaneously courting at the Berghof.

Central Europe, it seems, is where the internal contradictions of Western civilization are both born and, like Martin Luther at Eisleben, go home to die. And this is where the latest synthetic attempt to replace God with his conqueror, Man, has emerged: in the village of Davos, in the canton of Graubünden, Switzerland: the site of the annual meeting of the WEF led by the German-born engineer and economist Klaus Schwab, born in Ravensburg in 1938, the year before Hitler and Stalin began carving up Poland and the Baltics.

Ah, but carving things up is so last century. Hitler may have proclaimed the New World Order back in 1941, with all "*Neuropa*"[3] at his feet, a phrase and sentiment echoed by George Herbert Walker Bush's inarticulation of the same concept just short of half a century later, but today's benevolent progressives—the bastard offspring of Mrs. Jellyby and Sir Oswald Mosley via the British royal family (Prince Charles, a title without a job, is of course fully on board with the Reset), with contributing DNA from Rousseau, Marx, and Alinsky—have bigger fish to fry.

In an age of atheism and disbelief, note the religious fervor of neo- and cultural-Marxism and the messianic quality of Schwab's anti-humanistic Great Reset. If the God of Abraham is dead, and the Judeo-Greco-Roman Christ—however transitionally triumphant during two millennia of Christianity—reduced to a sacred avatar of weakness and failure, what is there left but Man? Man the accident, Man the despoiler, Man the biological sport, Man the intruder? Wagner, in his "Bühnen-Weihfestspiel" (sacred stage play) *Parsifal*, hailed *die Erlösung dem Erlöser*, the Redemption of the Redeemer: the negation of the negation become a transfiguring positive. But who is this redeemer? The incarnation of scripture's Second Coming, bringing a

3 In W. E. B. Du Bois's famous neologism, written that same year in *The Journal of Negro Education.*

glorious end to the human comedy? Or the worm Ouroboros, forever devouring its tail?

If we have reached the end of history, the final casting off of the Rousseauvian-Marxist chains of the clergy and the *bourgeoisie*, what future prospect stands before us? Caspar David Friedrich's *Wanderer above the Sea of Fog* is the German Romantic pictorial epitome of the conundrum of existence: to admire the view or jump? The wild, smoky mountain we have climbed affords us a breathtaking vista, but atop it we find not a quantum of solace but yet another, higher peak. And who dwells atop that Olympus? The oldest gods in the Western canon, Zeus & Co.? Or is it, still far from heaven, the realm of Mephisto and his damnable *Walpurgisnacht*?

Between the Homeric Greeks and the German Romantics—a walk through Goethe's house in Weimar illustrates the cultural cord that binds Germany's greatest poet and Greece's—what is there for us moderns to discuss or argue that the nineteenth century has not bequeathed? Our Jewish-Christian-Islamic faiths, however derivative of each other, and originating in nearly the same place, are both complementary and antagonistic, affording us thousands of years of contention and disputation, but it was Nietzsche and his fellow central-European intellectual radicals, operating on high emotions, who demanded that we imagine a world altogether devoid of them.

Thus do we come back to Man. In the motion picture *2001: A Space Odyssey* (1968), writer Arthur C. Clarke and director Stanley Kubrick envisioned the transition from ape to man beginning not with the discovery of fire, much less the notion of a deity but, adumbrating the biblical Samson, with the jawbone of a felled animal, thus identifying essential human nature with war and weaponry. The black monolith that subsequently appears is neither Pallas Athena nor the burning bush, bent on matters martial or the imposition of arbitrary moral and dietary strictures; indeed, it demands neither fealty nor fidelity and threatens no punishment. In its impersonal, irresistible attraction, it resembles nothing so more than Goethe's apotheosis at the end of

Faust, Part II, the pull of the life-giving, eternal-feminine principle that draws us ever forward: *Das Ewig-Weibliche*.

Alexander Pope, the great eighteenth-century poet, philosopher, and translator of Homer, famously remarked in *An Essay on Man* (1733–34) that "the proper study of mankind is man." What precedes that line, however, is also of contextual interest: "Know, then, thyself, presume not God to scan / the proper study of mankind is man." Pope wrote just half a century short of the French Revolution, which elevated Man and dethroned both Louis XVI and God himself in a land that had been for more than twelve hundred years "the eldest daughter of the Church." In so doing, the French propelled Europe headlong—or headless, as the case may be—into the calamitous[4] nineteenth century.

Perhaps the language Schwab and his *Kameraden* habitually use in describing their ambitious project offers us a clue to its origins and their intentions, as in this excerpt from the WEF's Great Reset website [emphasis added]:

> The Covid-19 crisis, and the political, economic and social disruptions it has caused, is *fundamentally* changing the traditional context for decision-making. The inconsistencies, inadequacies and *contradictions* of multiple systems—from health and financial to energy and education—are more exposed than ever amidst a global context of concern for lives, livelihoods and the planet. Leaders find themselves at a historic crossroads, managing short-term pressures against medium- and long-term uncertainties.
>
> As we enter a unique *window of opportunity* to shape the recovery, this initiative will offer insights to help inform all those determining the *future* state of global relations, the direction of national economies,

---

[4] *Pace* historian Barbara Tuchman and her essential study, *A Distant Mirror: The Calamitous 14th Century* (1978). The nineteenth century outdid even its illustrious forebear half a millennium earlier in both triumph and tragedy.

> the *priorities* of societies, the nature of business models and the *management* of a global commons. Drawing from the vision and vast expertise of the leaders engaged across the Forum's *communities*, the Great Reset initiative has a set of dimensions to build a new *social contract* that honours the *dignity of every human being*.

The viper tongue of totalitarianism is most often bathed in palliatives before it strikes. Appeals to the "social contract" take us at once back to Rousseau, abandoning the five bastard infants he had with his mistress Thérèse Levasseur—as it happens, one of Boswell's round-heeled conquests as well—on the steps of the nearest foundling hospital. The idea of "contradictions" instantly transports us to the Great Freeloader, Marx himself, and the "internal contradictions" of capitalism, while the words "fundamentally," "communities," and "opportunity" evoke the still-potent shade of former president Barack Obama, a disciple of Saul Alinsky. With such a powerful threat to Anglo-Western notions of individual liberty and personal freedom emerging again from the bowels of central Europe, the time has come no longer to simply "stand athwart" but to combat the hunnish-Marxist tide, as we have had to do at least since 1870–1871 and the Franco-Prussian War.

Once more into the breach, then: behold the present volume. In commissioning sixteen of the best, most persuasive, and most potent thinkers and writers from around the world to contribute to our joint venture, my principal concern has been to offer multiple analyses of the WEF's nostrums and in so doing to go poet Wallace Stevens's "Thirteen Ways of Looking at a Blackbird" a few better. Then again, given the surname of the WEF's chief, perhaps a better, more potent literary citation might be Margret's little ditty from the Büchner/Alban Berg expressionist opera, *Wozzeck* (1925): *In's Schwabenland, da mag ich nit*—"I don't want to go to Schwab-land." Nor, as Hans Castorp's journey illustrates, should anyone wish to visit Davos-land if he prizes his freedom, his possessions, and his sanity. To the Great Resetters, we are all ill, all future patients-in-waiting, all in dire need of a drastic corrective regimen to cure what ails us.

In these pages, we shall examine the Great Reset from the top down. The eminent American historian Victor Davis Hanson begins our survey with "The Great Regression," locating Schwab's vision within its proper historical context. He is followed by Canada's Conrad Black and America's Michael Anton and their views of capitalism and socialism, with not a few attacks on conventional, osmotic wisdom that will both surprise and enthrall. Britain's Martin Hutchinson outlines the contours of the Reset's "Anti-Industrial Revolution," even as the American economist David Goldman confronts both Schwab's notion of the "Fourth Industrial Revolution" and China's immanentizing its eschaton in real time, along with the Red Dragon's commitment to the upending of Western civilization and its own Sino-forming of a post-Western world.

American writer, editor, and publisher Roger Kimball tackles the implications of a neofascist Reset in his essay, "Sovereignty and the Nation-State," both of which concepts are under attack in the name of "equality," its totalitarian successor "equity," and the political consequences of our re-embrace of Rousseauvian concepts as applied to governments. British historian Jeremy Black discusses the misuses toward which the study of history has been and will be put to by the Resetters. The late Angelo Codevilla contributes what alas became his final essay, "Resetting the Educational Reset," to sound the tocsin about the dangerous left turn of the once-vaunted American educational system, now reduced to a shrill, sinistral shell of its former dispassionate glory.

From Down Under, the Philippines-born Richard Fernandez twins two eternally competing faiths, religion and science; the American-born, Australian-based political sociologist Salvatore Babones contributes a remarkably clear explication of the kinds of transportation feasible under the "green energy" regimen the Reset seeks to impose upon us, and its practical and social implications. Writing from Milan, Alberto Mingardi, the director-general of the *Istituto Bruno Leoni*, gets to the heart of the Great Reset's deceptive economic program with an essay concerning faux-capitalist "stakeholder capitalism" and its surreptitious replacement of shareholder capitalism in the name of "social justice."

The Great Reset, however, is not strictly limited to matters financial, pecuniary, or macroeconomic. Social and cultural spheres are of equal importance. James Poulos looks at the Reset's unholy relationship with the predatory Big Tech companies that currently abrogate the First Amendment by acting as governmental censors without actually being commanded by an act of Congress or, increasingly, an arbitrary presidential mandate. From British Columbia, noted Canadian author and academic Janice Fiamengo weighs in on the destructive effects of feminism upon our shared Western culture while, on the lighter side, Harry Stein examines the history of American humor—which in effect means worldwide humor—and how the leftist takeover of our shared laugh tracks has resulted in a stern, Stalinist view of what is and what is not allowed to be funny.

The British writer Douglas Murray has a go at the permissible future of *Realpolitik* under the panopticonic supervision of the Reset, the Chinese Communist Party, and the Covid hysterics, while the American journalist John Tierney lays out the road to civilizational serfdom that the unwarranted panic over the Covid-19 "pandemic" has triggered during its media-fueled run between 2019 and 2022. My contribution, in addition to this Introduction, is an examination of the Reset's—and, historically, elitist tyranny's—deleterious effects on Western culture: the very thing that gave birth to our notions of morality and freedom.

At its heart, the Great Reset is a conceited and self-loathing central-European blitzkrieg against the cultural, intellectual, religious, artistic, physical, and, most of all, moral inheritance we have received from our Greco-Roman forebears. This has been latterly shorthanded, with the rise of "wokeness," to "white" culture. Typically racialist, if not outright racist, the cultural Marxists behind wokeness insist on reducing humanity to its shades of skin color and then claiming that although all skin colors should achieve in exact same proportions to their share in a given population, some skin colors are better than others and any skin color is preferable to white. It's a deeply repellent principle that masquerades as a perversion of Jeffersonian democracy but is in fact a simultaneous attack on individuality and merit that seeks to roll back the scientific and cultural advances of the past two millennia, wielding both science and culture as weapons against our shared technological and moral heritage.

The goal, as always, is power—the eternal fixation of the socialist Left. As Professor Codevilla, to whose memory this book is dedicated, noted in one of his last published essays:

> "Totalitarian," to Westerners, describes a ruler's attempt to exert control over someone's rightful autonomy, regardless of the power grab's success, because we assume that we have rights that natural law forbids be taken from us. Property may be the most obvious of these. Your life, liberty, and pursuit of happiness are also naturally, inalienably your own. Mussolini first used the term *totalitarismo* in reference to his boast of "everything within the state, nothing outside the state, nothing against the state," even though his regime's aims were hardly as ambitious as the goals of those who have sought to remake humanity—such as the perpetrators of the French Revolution and those inspired by Marxism-Leninism. We Westerners believe that any uninvited attempt to control what is ours is inherently unlawful and illegitimate.

Such power grabs are generally undertaken under a cloak of beneficence—of redemption. Caesar acted on behalf of the people, not the Optimates, in provoking the civil war with Pompey in order to "save" the Republic; his successor, Augustus, eschewed the title of Emperor in favor of First Citizen, but the Roman Empire in fact began with him. The French Revolution is the beginning of the modern Promethean ideal of political rebirth and renewal, but it ended in the slaughter of both aristocrats and clergymen until it was finally brought to a halt by Napoleon's daring seizure of power in 1799, dubbing himself First Consul in an homage to Rome, thus directing the nineteenth century along the bloody dialectical road to 1914 and into the present day.

The goal then as now was to make the world anew, a task undertaken once more by the Soviets in 1922 upon their ascension to power in Russia. The French revolutionaries had established a new Year One, starting at the fall equinox and marked by Roman numerals, and although they kept the traditional twelve months, they decimalized them (as well as, briefly, the hours of the day) into three ten-day weeks, adding extra days as needed at the end of the year to make things come out right. The months themselves got a makeover as well, being renamed, most famously Brumaire (thanks to Marx[5])—analogous to the Zodiac sign of Scorpio—and Thermidor ("thermal," since it ran from July 19 to August 17, roughly corresponding to Leo).[6]

For their part, the Bolsheviks were dead set on creating the New Soviet Man (новый советский человек), a Marxist-Leninist superman who would cast off the Mephistophelian bands of illusion of the West and propagate a new species of physically fit, clear-minded, selfless socialists, fit and bred for the task before them: the triumph of the proletariat and the withering away of the state. Once again, high aspirations, disastrous results.

Such siren songs, when briefly heeded, inevitably end with a crash upon the rocks, their irresistible beauties in reality strange, impossible hybrids: bare-breasted women with the voices of angels and lower bodies of birds. Think Waterloo in 1815, Berlin in 1945, and Moscow at Christmas 1991, when the Soviet Union collapsed in a heap of its own internal contradictions. The fate of Mao's China will be much the

---

5 In his 1852 essay, *The Eighteenth Brumaire of Louis Bonaparte.*

6 Thermidor didn't last long as a new month but it did achieve a kind of immortality thanks to the French playwright Victorien Sardou, who in an 1891 drama of that name commemorated the execution of Robespierre. The play, in turn, gave its name to the famous lobster dish.

same. A nation of intellectual thieves, shameless imitators, dishonest businessmen, and physical cowards is unlikely to withstand any serious engagement with even a decadent and corrupt West temporarily ruled, in accordance with the late Robert Conquest's third law of politics, by a cabal of its enemies.

Over the long haul, however, the Western world has proven stubbornly resistant to officially mandated unreality. Not even the prolonged intellectual quackery of Sigmund Freud and his followers (whose "science" was happily adopted and weaponized by Marxist societies) has been able to shake the Western fondness for dogged empiricism; flights of fancy and fantasy are more properly the realm of artists, whose material is not the universe, nor even the mind, but the human soul. And soulcraft cannot be written into statecraft, no matter how diligently its proponents try.

We, the inheritors of Greco-Roman civilization, have rejected or repelled repeated philosophical, religious, and military incursions from North Africa, the Arabian Peninsula, the steppes of Central Asia, and even all-out war with the Empire of Japan. This is not to say we haven't learned from history and, often, improved ourselves via our syncretic way of accumulating and employing knowledge and insight. Alexander sought to meld Achaemenid Persian civilization with that of the Macedonian Greeks; today this is derisively known as "cultural appropriation." In reality, it is a typically creative dialectic that lies at the heart of Western cultural dominance. Despite the pressure by the modern Left to acknowledge such chimeras as meaningful manmade global warming, "climate change," fundamental sex reassignment, and other fashionable and transient falsehoods that lately plague us, most sane people reject them out of hand and remain irremediably, traditionally human.

But the modern Left's standard tactic is first to propose a transparent counterfactual (men becoming women being perhaps the most egregious), act on it as if it were real, and then demand that we all do the same. They never stop, they never sleep, they never quit. The Great Reset proposes to command by fiat what Nature and Nature's

God has thus far refused to countenance. Just surrender your freedom; your mobility; even your diet—eat more bugs! they sing—and heed us. But the sirenic Alemannis and the Davoisie have poultry legs, and the Chinese relish for chicken feet ought to give us pause.

In the second epistle of *An Essay on Man*, referenced above, Pope weighs Man in the balance, and finds him…human, all too human.

> Plac'd on this isthmus of a middle state,
> A being darkly wise, and rudely great:
> With too much knowledge for the sceptic side,
> With too much weakness for the stoic's pride,
> He hangs between; in doubt to act, or rest;
> In doubt to deem himself a god, or beast;
> In doubt his mind or body to prefer;
> Born but to die, and reas'ning but to err;
> Alike in ignorance, his reason such,
> Whether he thinks too little, or too much:
> Chaos of thought and passion, all confus'd;
> Still by himself abus'd, or disabus'd;
> Created half to rise, and half to fall;
> Great lord of all things, yet a prey to all;
> Sole judge of truth, in endless error hurl'd:
> The glory, jest, and riddle of the world!

How can any sentient being, thus described, be certain of anything? Trapped temporally on middle-earth, pragmatic Man cannot doubt the evidence of his senses, yet he must in order to reach beyond the quotidian to the celestial. In our weakness for leadership, we harken to those who would order us, decide for us, provide for us, command us. It is the world of Orwell's *1984* that the WEF offers us, but spiced with the soma of Huxley's *Brave New World* and the totalitarian conformity of Yevgeny Zamyatin's *We*. No wonder licentious sex and untrammeled pharmacology, commingled with brutal physical punishment, have loomed so large in the leftist pantheon; the lust comes naturally.

But at the same time there appears to be in the West some sort of self-correcting mechanism, a desire to cast off indolence as the old order changeth and danger looms. As the great circle from Romulus and Augustus closed on the western Roman Empire in 476 A.D. in the person of the boy emperor Romulus Augustulus, along came the barbarians from the Celtic, Gallic, Suebi, and Saxon lands to replace it with the nascent nation-states of modern Europe. Good from evil, evil from good and still, like Adam and Eve, we haven't quite been able to distinguish between them. Some gods we are.

Instead, the proper study of mankind being man, Pope exhorts us to locate our strength in our origins, always mindful of our deficiencies, and our inevitable failures:

> Go, wondrous creature! mount where science guides,
> Go, measure earth, weigh air, and state the tides;
> Instruct the planets in what orbs to run,
> Correct old time, and regulate the sun;
> Go, soar with Plato to th' empyreal sphere...
> Go, teach Eternal Wisdom how to rule—
> Then drop into thyself, and be a fool!

Eve and Adam, history's original chumps, were deceived. No matter how much we taste of the Tree of Knowledge, how much we pant after it, we cannot become as gods. That is the satanic temptation. It may be that no religion yet invented and established has got it right, that as the Greek and Roman deities gave way to Yahweh and Jesus the Christ and Allah, other, more potent gods may emerge and cast down the idols that came before them.

The only thing that is certain is that man cannot and will never replace his gods as an object of veneration, and all such previous efforts have ended in failure. Even the French Revolution was forced to institute the Cult of the Supreme Being to supplant the Cult of Reason, before that cult, too, fell to the temporary restoration of Christianity. For reasons presented herein, the proposed Cult of the Great Reset is unlikely to fare any better—but in the meantime its danger is present, and the damage it can do is incalculable.

The satraps of Davos don't want to simply reset a post-Covid world. Or a post-fossil fuels world. Or even a post-racial world. They want to run it, forever, and while they no longer have need of a god, they'll always need an enemy. They may not believe in a power higher than themselves, but they certainly believe in demons, and their most irksome devil is you.

THE GREAT REGRESSION

BY VICTOR DAVIS HANSON

Orwellian Philology

The Great Reset was first concocted at the WEF in Davos by its founder Klaus Schwab as a way to assemble together global success stories like himself. His idea apparently was that grandees who have done well for themselves could do even better for the rest of us—*if* these anointed could just be unbound and given enough power and authority to craft rules for nearly eight billion of the planet's ignorant.

A word of caution is needed about the pretentious and supposedly benign signature title of the Great Reset project. Assume the worst when the adjective "great" appears in connection with envisioned fundamental, government-driven, or global political changes. What was similar between Lyndon Johnson's massively expensive but failed "Great Society" and Mao's genocidal "Great Leap Forward" was the idea of a top-down, centrally planned schema, cooked up by elites without any firsthand knowledge, or even worry, how it would affect the middle classes and poor. So often, the adjective "*great*" is a code word of supposed enlightened planners for radical attempts at reconstruction of a society that must be either misled or forced to accept a complete overhaul.

When "*great*" is applied to a proposed transnational comprehensive revolution, we should also equate it with near religious zealotry.

"The *Great* Reset," after all, in all its green and "woke" glory, with all of its credentialed and "expert" devotees, is still a faith-based rather than scientific effort. Its spiritual predecessor was perhaps the eighteenth-century "*Great* Awakening" of Protestant evangelicalism that swept the eastern seaboard of colonial America in reaction to the secularism of the Enlightenment. But this time around the frenzy is fueled more by agnostics who worship secular progressive totems such as Al Gore or Greta Thunberg.

Given the Davos elite's cosmic ambitions, "*great*" also conjures up a messianic reference to God's "*Great* Plan" that should from on high reorder earthly life under a few trusted religious authorities. It recalls the notion of Alexander the "*Great*" of a brotherhood of man, which supposedly was to fuse conquered peoples into one vast and enlightened east-west, Persian-Hellenistic empire—albeit *after*, rather than before, eastern tribes were conquered, and sometimes slaughtered, in efforts to achieve a common, centrally planned purpose.

To reassure a shared brighter post-Covid-19 path ahead, Schwab drops most of the familiar globalist names that resonate power, money, seriousness, and wisdom. And the Great Resetters are now quite familiar: the world's third or fourth richest man, Bill Gates, coming off his denials of palling around with the late Jeffrey Epstein; Jack Ma, the Chinese multibillionaire and Alibaba CEO apparently now "forcibly disappeared" by the Chinese communist government for too many candid speeches; the septuagenarian Prince Charles whose long anticipated monumental accomplishments apparently must still await his ascension to the British throne; the polymath Dr. Anthony Fauci who has laced his 2020 "noble lie" assessments of wearing and not wearing masks or achieving and not achieving herd immunity in terms of climate change, race, Chinese cooperation, and global progressive expertise; John Kerry, one of the multilateralist architects of the Paris Climate Accord and Iran Deal; and the usual rotating leaders of the U.N., IMF, World Bank, and the European Central Bank.

In its post-Covid-19 global comprehensiveness, the Great Reset has ambitions to be our greatest "woke" project yet. On examination, it is a kitchen-sink mishmash of agendas that incorporate the U.N.'s long stale "Sustainable Development" plan ("Agenda 21"), the Green New Deal, tidbits of Black Lives Matter sloganeering, critical race theory, "stakeholder" capitalism that often champions ESG, or forced corporate embrace of "environmental and social governance" over shareholder profitability, open-borders rhetoric, and boutique redistributionism dumbed down from Thomas Piketty's *Capital in the Twenty-First Century*. Reset offers us a global Fabian socialist future, repackaged as a European Union-like top-down diktat. But above all, the agenda incorporates the pop insights of various half-educated corporate billionaires. All now find themselves in a secure enough position to dabble with Trotskyite ideas—to be foisted upon others not so fortunate and lacking their own exemptions from the toxicity of the elite's theories.

The same linguistic suspicions hold true of the use of the noun "Reset." It assumes a year-zero arrogance that all that came before was flawed. And all that will follow, we are assured, will not be so defective. Such absolutism is reminiscent of former President Barack Obama's grandiose promise on the very eve of the 2008 election: "We are five days away from fundamentally transforming the United States of America"—a transformation that birthed the Tea Party revolt just two years later, during the 2010 midterm elections, one of the greatest conservative political pushbacks of the past seventy years.

We remember that just four months after Obama's promises of transformation, the romance of fundamental change went international with the idea of a foreign policy "reset" that focused on a new détente with Vladimir Putin. The idea was inaugurated in 2009 by Secretary of State Hillary Clinton on the assumption that Putin's past territorial aggressions had arisen from an absence of dialogue and ecumenical outreach from the prior "unilateralist" George W. Bush administration. Bush supposedly had wrongly sanctioned Putin for his 2008 miniature war with Georgia that resulted in the Russian absorption of South Ossetia. And the go-it-alone "cowboy" Bush apparently had also unduly polarized Putin and thus wet the ex-KGB operative's beak for additional irredentist acquisition.

The reactive makeover that followed from the Obama-Clinton "reset" was unfortunately an utter failure. Its pompous declarations and talk of "listening" and "outreach" ended in fresh Russian aggressiveness, most notably in the 2014 Russian invasions of both Crimea and eastern Ukraine. Such appeasement created the original seeds for Putin's eventual spring 2022 catastrophic Russian invasion of most of Ukraine and attack on Kyiv. In addition, Russia earlier in 2013 had reentered the Middle East, on Secretary of State John Kerry's 2011 invitation, after a three-decade hiatus. Then followed Russia's informal partnerships with both Iran and China, and Moscow's much greater and more comprehensive crackdowns on internal dissidents. In all talks of the Great Reset, we should then recall that Vladimir Putin apparently interpreted "reset" as American laxity to be leveraged rather than as magnanimity to be reciprocated. In cruder terms, Americans speaking loudly while carrying a twig was no way to "reset" Putin.

The telltale noun "Revolution," of course, also makes its appearance frequently in Great Reset rhetoric, specifically in connection to Klaus Schwab's 2017 bestselling book, *The Fourth Industrial Revolution*. In it, Schwab makes the now familiar argument that the internet, computers, electronic communications, artificial intelligence, and the new global interconnectedness of the prior "Third Revolution" have at last synchronized into wonderful harmony.

The supposedly never-before-seen, never-imagined fusion of the paradigms of economic, social, cultural, and political life offers us a once-in-a-lifetime—or, rather, last—chance to exploit them—even if most of us are not sufficiently equipped to appreciate the opportunity. Yet Schwab makes the fundamental error that these new technologies act as independent drivers of the way people behave and think, rather than as accelerants that nonetheless have not changed ancient fixed and predictable human behavior.

In Schwab's way of thinking, imagine that a modern computerized high-tech pump sends forth two thousand gallons of water a minute, and therefore its essence, "water," is now likewise "new" and different from what emerged for millennia at a rate of a gallon a minute from preindustrial hand pumps. Again, we fools outside the Davos agenda would apparently mistakenly believe that greater volume had not much altered from antiquity water's molecular structure, chemical properties, and use in the natural world.

A glimpse of the idea that Davos-like elites can gather to discuss reset planning in an age of paradigm-changing technology is popular at the national level. A good example is the invitation-only conference on entertainment, technology, finance, and communications held each summer in Idaho at the Sun Valley Resort, hosted by the investment bank of Allen & Company. In 2021, the usual corporate and media globalist suspects showed up, among them Facebook's CEO Mark Zuckerberg, Amazon founder Jeff Bezos, Apple CEO Tim Cook, Microsoft cofounder Bill Gates, Netflix co-CEO Reed Hastings, ViacomCBS (now Paramount) chairwoman Shari Redstone, Disney chairman Robert Iger, New York City's former mayor Michael Bloomberg, GM CEO Mary Barra, WarnerMedia CEO Jason Kilar, Discovery CEO David Zaslav, CNN anchor Anderson Cooper, and film and television producer Brian Grazer. The premise was Platonic. A meritocracy—chosen by the metrics of either acquired or inherited wealth, influence, celebrity, or a corporation's ability to influence millions—immune from private bias and guided by reason, should be given latitude to override the dangerous emotions of the masses.

So there are plenty of linguistic reasons alone to be suspicious of the grandiose notion of a top-down, international, and fundamental transformation of the way the world is supposed to work. Much of the Great Reset's vocabulary is honed by Schwab, its architect, an eighty-four-year-old German author, academic, scholar—and the founder and godhead of the WEF that meets annually in Davos. And Schwab is not really new to this reset business. In fact, his entire life has been one quixotic effort to create all sorts of mini-Great Reset organizations—the WEF, the Schwab Foundation for Social Entrepreneurship, the Forum of Young Global Leaders, the Global Shapers Community, and on and on.

Never Let a Plague Go to Waste

Yet what is different this time around is twofold: one, Schwab now has global ambitions to reset the entire world, not just one discipline or one country or even one continent; and two, he plans to do so under the pretense of a 2020–2021 pandemic "urgency." That is, the Covid-19 outbreak—and its near endless SARS-CoV-2 mutant sequelae—seem to him to offer a singular opening for transnational elites to reset a frightened and insecure world, even as it thinks it is reemerging from a global quarantine. And this time around, we are supposed to be confronted with a permanent and existential threat far more serious than past fears of the Spanish flu, a "nuclear winter," or climate change. Until Covid-19, the latter crises were still not scary enough reasons for the world's best and brightest to assume stewardship of our collective future.

Schwab's team also seems energized that the Joe Biden administration may well offer a third term of the internationalism of the Obama years of 2009–2017. Biden's slogan, after all, is "Build Back Better." Does "better" mean apparently superior to America's 2019 pre-Covid-19 open society, secure borders, declining crime, low minority unemployment, near record overall peacetime unemployment, unmatched energy production, strong economic growth, low inflation and interest rates, and the first substantial gain in middle-class income in over a decade?

Nonetheless, after the Trump years, a leftist U.S. government seems to look favorably upon subordinating national sovereignty to international overseers, in such agendas as rejoining the Paris Climate Accords, the Joint Comprehensive Plan of Action (or "Iran Deal"), or the Trans-Pacific Partnership (TPP). Secretary of State Antony Blinken has even welcomed in the United Nations to probe whether the United States was guilty of systemic racism, apparently on the premise that membership of that body might have insights lacking in a constitutional America.

More specifically, many on the American Left have already adopted Schwab's Great Reset notion of leveraging the Covid-19 crisis (spelled out in detail in his 2020 coauthored book with Thierry Malleret, *COVID-19: The Great Reset*) to push policy implementations that otherwise Western publics in time of calm and security admittedly would reject. This idea is now a gospel of elites. In late May 2021, ex-President Obama himself pontificated about financially leveraging the crisis, "There's a teachable moment about maybe this whole deficit hawk thing of the federal government. Just being nervous about our debt 30 years from now, while millions of people are suffering—maybe that's not a smart way to think about our economics."

Translate Obama's "teachable moment" incoherence into English, and he seemed to suggest that borrowing trillions of dollars in a pandemic does not require worrying too much about how it is to be paid back—especially if such negation helps to spread the wealth. In Obama's reset vision of a new, better economics, the fixed idea of debits and credits on a balance sheet are simply a deficit hawk's ossified construct. Printing more money is to be synonymous with making more of the deserving better off. We note, however, that pandemic economics does not always apply to the investment strategies of those who in live in the Kalorama district of Washington, D.C. and vacation in a seaside estate on Martha's Vineyard.

Earlier, on April 20, 2020, California Governor Gavin Newsom likewise had joined the pandemic-reset fad. He boasted similarly about leveraging his own statewide quarantine in hopes of a new economic "era." "There is opportunity for reimagining a progressive era as it pertains to capitalism, a new progressive era and opportunity for additional progressive steps," Newsom babbled on about his planned reset. "So yes, absolutely," he added, "we see this as an opportunity to reshape the way we do business and how we govern." Over the ensuing year, Newsom proposed record California state tax increases, more green subsidies and regulations, more rent extensions and eviction prohibitions, and hundreds of millions of dollars in transfers to illegal aliens residing in his state, while clamping down on personal freedoms of millions of Californians. By mid-July 2021, despite a resurgence of the Delta variant, thousands of well-trained and vaccinated Californians were driving alone in their cars—wearing masks—while deaths attributed to Covid-19 in a state of over 40 million had decreased to about twenty to thirty per day.

Newsom himself only resonated what Hillary Clinton herself gushed at about the same time of the then two-month-old pandemic: "That this would be a terrible crisis to waste, as the old saying goes. We've learned a lot about what our absolute frailties are in our country when it comes to health justice and economic justice." Clinton's "old saying" was actually a recycled quote from her former associate Rahm Emanuel, who was also Obama's chief of staff. He too bragged of the 2008 panic that would supposedly empower the Obama transformation project: "You never want a serious crisis to go to waste." Later Emanuel clarified that crises allow radical changes that were before never even considered—or rather always considered crackpot.

Apparently, without catastrophe, no one in his right mind would vote for far-left agendas—as Clinton knew from her own earlier failed experiences in pushing single-payer healthcare. Or as multimillionaire Jane Fonda, in an unguarded moment, gushed of the coronavirus, "I just think Covid-19 is God's gift to the Left." The occasional Davos attendee then elaborated how the pandemic had prepped Americans for new horizons: "We can see it now. People who couldn't see it before. You know, they see it now. We have a chance to harness that anger and make a difference. So, I'm just so blessed to be alive right now."

With rare neosocialist friends like these in the United States, a new Biden administration, and the world shell-shocked by the pandemic, the artist of globalism, Schwab, finally had found the ideal canvas for his final masterpiece. "There are many reasons to pursue a Great Reset," Schwab reminded us, "But the most urgent is Covid-19. Having already led to hundreds of thousands of deaths, the pandemic represents one of the worst public-health crises in recent history. And, with casualties still mounting in many parts of the world, it is far from over."

Note the lack of any Schwab optimism regarding the current use of efficacious and generally safe vaccines, new treatment protocols and pharmaceuticals, and greater knowledge of the epidemiology of Covid-19 that all had radically curtailed the virus's lethality. But then again, an element of the world's weird reaction to the pandemic was nonstop pessimism. Statisticians and "modelers" warned of several million dead to come in major countries, of a disaster something along the lines of or worse than the so-called Spanish flu of 1918–1919, and of the draconian measures required to save us from a medieval plaguelike fate.

In such surreal times, Schwab, then, sees few dangers of an obstructionist China silencing all international queries about the relationship between Covid-19 and its Wuhan virology lab; unaccountable technocrats; antidemocratic bureaucrats; emergency measures to override constitutional freedoms; overreaching elected officials who all were as eager to exploit the pandemic as they were incompetent in stopping its spread; and their hypocrisies of violating the very quarantine mandates they ordered for others.

Galvanizing the "international community" is the approved course to rethink and recalibrate the entire way the entire world is organized. As Fonda hinted, the virus apparently has done us a favor by reminding us that our previous trajectories were leading to global perdition, until we were in a sense warned, liberated, and then saved by the Level-Four-Wuhan lab-spawned coronavirus. Or again, as Schwab put the reset:

> As we enter a unique window of opportunity to shape the recovery, this initiative will offer insights to help inform all those determining the future state of global relations, the direction of national economies, the priorities of societies, the nature of business models and the management of a global commons. Drawing from the vision and vast expertise of the leaders

> engaged across the Forum's communities, the Great Reset initiative has a set of dimensions to build a new social contract that honors the dignity of every human being.

How Will Davos Save Us?

In this regard, Schwab and the Davos community envisioned a rare chance to renegotiate for the people their ancient Lockean social contracts between the governed and their government. And in this context, he outlined three main Great Reset agendas, all of such magnitude as to divide the world into two great year-zero eras of before and after Covid-19.

The *first* is to "steer the market toward fairer outcomes." Such redistributive efforts would include "changes to wealth taxes, the withdrawal of fossil-fuel subsidies, and new rules governing intellectual property, trade, and competition."

In this first step, Schwab envisions an international consortium of corporate magnificoes, government officials, bureaucrats, activists, and progressive oligarchs who would in concert lobby to change nations' laws to regulate and tax international capital and income, with enough power to monitor and correct the internal decision-making of more than 190 sovereign nations and millions of private businesses worldwide. Imagine such regulatory ambitions as going well beyond international rules governing trade, navigation of the seas, or the use of air spaces. A cynic might observe that the world's richest citizens who made their fortunes due to mostly unfettered transnational global capitalism have at this point in their multimillion- and multibillion-dollar careers decided to pull up their attic ladders while they are on top.

Such grandiose talk is not just idle narcissism "of the vision and vast expertise of the leaders engaged across the Forum's communities." Instead, these people are deadly serious. In the June 2020 meeting of the G-7—a sort of "little" reset—heads of seven major Western countries agreed in principle to the Biden administration's post-Covid-19 "Build Back Better" plan to harmonize global tax rules in multilateral fashion.

The Western leaders' aim was to ensure that individual nations did not compete with each other in offering singular financial incentives to lure multinational corporate investment. By globally establishing uniform rates of taxation, these overseers would then discourage corporations from relocating to countries with lower tax rates—effectively institutionalizing the current status quo of relative E.U. nations' economies, or ending any country's idea of creating a more free-market environment to attract job-creating industries.

The old corporation's duty to its stockholders to protect and increase their investments by wise and efficient management would begin to be redefined by how much they paid in taxes to governments who could redistribute such profits more responsibly. In some sense, talk of a distinct corporate world and government is anachronistic under the Great Reset, since the two would be fused into one entity. Indeed, the Biden administration has offered a paradigm in its efforts to partner with Silicon Valley social media companies to monitor and censor individual citizens' supposedly incorrect if not dangerous views on vaccinations and mask-wearing.

So the Biden international tax proposals are just a start. Recently, the 140-country Organization for Economic Cooperation and Development (OECD) believed the G-7 preliminary agreement was a "landmark step towards the global consensus necessary to reform the international tax system." Again, the subtext is that individual nations eventually should not have the innate rights to set their own tax and regulatory structures. In this regard, the Reset idea of uniform international taxation mirrors the Biden administration's domestic efforts to reinstate the so-called state and local tax (SALT) uniform income tax deduction. It was repealed by the Trump administration in 2017 to discourage blue states from using federal deductions to subsidize their always-rising state income taxes.

Indeed, the idea that residents of high-tax states could no longer deduct their state and local taxes reduced the incentives of so-called blue states to steadily increase taxes, given residents now understood the full cost of their SALT bite, and thus might even more exercise their free will to migrate to low-tax states. In both the foreign and domestic cases, the rationale is to prevent competitive tax and regulatory climates through centralized rules. And the net effect would be to discourage more free-market nations and states that apparently wrongly believed that less regulation and taxation, coupled with more competition, translated into greater national wealth and opportunity. The overarching theme is to stifle individualism and free choice, whether at the international, national, or state level.

The meaning of Schwab's idea of "fairer" would be adjudicated apparently by selected Great Reset bureaucrats and advisors—perhaps we should call them "steerers"—who would set income goals necessary for correct expenditures and investments. Nearly eight billion global citizens, then, would not just harmonize their entrepreneurial behavior, but also would be directed on how the resulting windfall income should be properly spent. The G-7 (the Western European and North American club of major consensually governed nations) June 2021 meeting, for example, produced a twenty-five-page blueprint on just what those investments would entail. Forced and rapid phaseouts of natural gas, oil, and coal were thematic throughout the agenda.

In California "fossil-fuel subsidies," to the extent they still exist, pale in comparison to the billions of dollars in subsidies for wind and solar. Yet the result is the highest gasoline, natural gas, and electricity prices in the continental U.S.—and periodic black- and brownouts during high summer temperatures to prevent massive grid failures. And these costs and disruptions fall most heavily on the middle and lower classes.

When Schwab waxes on about "new rules governing intellectual property, trade, and competition," we suspect that he is either not referring to systematic Chinese violations of copyright and patent laws, currency manipulation, technological appropriation, product dumping, and institutionalized industrial espionage, or that he has no clue how any international agency could stop such banditry even if it wished. In other words, is the subtext of these utopian bromides that because the current global community cannot enforce existing and less encompassing international laws, it wants additional coercive authority to force recalcitrant nations to follow its envisioned far more sweeping rules?

In the June 2021 summary document of the G-7, China and Russia are cited frequently, but largely in the context of gentle Western remonstrations to better adjust their international behavior to the norms of international citizenship. Given that none of the current internationalized agencies has either the will or ability to confront China—the world's greatest polluter, the world's most egregious violator of human rights, and its current most flagrant transgressor of global commercial rules—it is ironic how often the Reset instead scolds Western publics. But then again, it is a symptom of inert Western bureaucracies that to justify their inability to address the felonies of the guilty, they square the circle of their impotence by fixating on the misdemeanors of the innocent. Or put in simpler terms, how can the Great Reset have the vision, authority, and power to establish "new rules governing intellectual property, trade, and competition" when no one can enforce such existing international laws, given not just China's serial cheating, but its boasting that no one or nothing can curb such behavior?

Here we enter the most frightening aspect of the Great Reset: the assumption that Western elite architects of Reset are so compromised by Chinese financial influences that they cannot discuss rationally Beijing's culpability for the origins and acceleration of the pandemic; the internment camps of the Chinese communist government; its systematized global hacking; its constant bullying of Taiwan, Japan, Australia, and other neighbors; its neocolonialist Belt and Road Initiative; its illegal occupation and militarization of the Spratly Islands; and its systematic racism and religious intolerance.

Berkshire Hathaway Inc. vice chairman Charlie Munger has praised the Chinese Communist Party for shutting down the initial public offering planned by Jack Ma of Alibaba. The latter seems to have vanished from public view after criticizing China's government regulators. Yet as Munger put it, "Communists did the right thing. They just called in Jack Ma and say, 'You aren't gonna do it, sonny,'" And the multibillionaire investor seems to see China as a model, at least in some aspects, for America: "I don't want the, all of the Chinese system, but I certainly would like to have the financial part of it in my own country." Translated into Davosese, there is a certain grudging admiration for Chinese authoritarianism that can green-light needed Western public policy without the messy give-and-take of American constitutional government.

Billionaire businessman, former New York mayor, communications titan, and Chinese investor Michael Bloomberg is on record contextualizing the Chinese communist dictatorship as somehow attuned to public opinion, as if it were almost a Western-style consensual government: "The Communist Party wants to stay in power in China and they listen to the public... Xi Jinping is not a dictator. He has to satisfy his constituents, or he's not going to survive... he has a constituency to answer to." Does Xi's constituency include Muslim Uyghurs?

Microsoft founder and one of the richest men in the world, Bill Gates matches his business interests in China with frequent praise of the communist government. In April 2020, Gates ignored all the early reports of connections between the Wuhan virology lab and ground zero of SARS-CoV-2—and the Chinese disinformation campaign to hide information about the relationship. Although the Chinese government ordered a complete lockdown on Wuhan and forbade travel to or from the city, it nevertheless allowed residents of the infected region to fly all over the Western world. And what was Gates's reaction to China's handling of the virus? "China did a lot of things right at the beginning." He went on to praise Beijing and deprecate the American response, even though the American Operation Warp Speed delivered the world's first effective vaccinations a mere ten months after the onset of the pandemic, saving hundreds of millions of lives the world over—in contrast to China's ineffective and sometimes dangerous immunizations.

Of course, it is unfair to single out international captains of industry, financiers, and corporatists for envisioning globalism as by necessity appeasing the Chinese communist government. Nearly a decade and a half ago, liberal *New York Times* columnist Thomas Friedman was giddy over the efficiency of Beijing's Mussolini-like focus on rebuilding Chinese infrastructure. He summed up the progressive consensus of admiring China's unique ability to enact by fiat good and correct public policy. Friedman gushed that China was "led by a reasonably enlightened group of people." And why did he offer such an upbeat assessment of the ruthless communist apparat? In Friedman's words, they were doing the proper things by "boosting gasoline prices" and "overtaking us in electric cars, solar power, energy efficiency, batteries, nuclear power and wind power." And he sighed of American constitutional republicanism: "our one-party democracy is worse."

The Reset's de facto policy of turning a blind eye to Chinese outlawry is now ossified and discredited. No matter: we still should assume that the Great Reset is impossible without the participation of China's nearly 1.5 billion population, and thus the West must extend to Beijing blanket exemptions. Or, the architects of the Reset quietly believe that the coddling and appeasing of the Chinese government will accelerate its historic international profiteering and internal modernizing, and thus the resulting greater wealth and prosperity will ensure that China, by fits and starts, completes its Western circle of matching supposedly free-market capitalism with consensual government.

The Great Reset's *second* component "would ensure that private investments advance shared goals, such as equality and sustainability." In fact, the current ESG—"Environmental, Social, and Governance" fad criteria—predate the Great Reset. It is a creed that threatens to redefine free-market capitalism in quasi-religious terms, perhaps not unlike orthodox Islamic countries that profess that charging interest is antithetical to Koranic tenets and seek to deny the realities of the free market and indeed human nature itself. In the Western case, ESG ratings follow from a set of standards for corporations' operations that are not market driven or aimed at increasing shareholder profitability. In turn, environmentally and socially conscious investors are supposed to use ESG guidelines to screen their likely portfolio strategies. Companies thus will supposedly use racial and gender quotas to appoint officers and board members on the basis of their appearance and contextualize their profitability on the criteria of not just competitive returns on investment but also on corporations' supposed global commitments to green and diversity agendas. One can envision mediocre CEOs pointing to their diversity portfolios for exemption from being fired for investment incompetence. Or, in the words of the Great Reset dogma:

> Here, the large-scale spending programs that many governments are implementing represent a major opportunity for progress.... Rather than using these funds, as well as investments from private entities and pension funds, to fill cracks in the old system, we should use them to create a new one that is more resilient, equitable, and sustainable in the long run. This means, for example, building "green" urban infrastructure and creating incentives for industries to improve their track record on environmental, social, and governance (ESG) metrics.

Translated to the American experience, the public side of the Great Reset's politically correct agendas is to build upon the massive multitrillion-dollar annual deficits ("large scale-spending programs that many governments are implementing") by ensuring not just up-to-date freeways, bridges, and airports but rather effective next-generation infrastructure, redefined by the degree to which it can be adjudicated as equitable and meeting correct green standards.

Ironically, the Reset push coincides with the 2021 American debate over borrowing somewhere in the neighborhood of $2 trillion to $3 trillion, in an age of $30 trillion in aggregate national debt, to invest in infrastructure. But the very word "infrastructure" no longer implies rebuilding or expanding roads, bridges, ports, or water and sewage plants. Only somewhere between 6 and 17 percent of America's massive proposed spending bill would go to improving transportation, communications, and utilities. Instead, the vast majority of federal dollars is envisioned to promote various entitlements and new federal regulatory social programs. So even the idea of building and repairing concrete "things" is highly politicized, shorting roads for visions of mass transit, green energy, and high urban density projects. We should assume the architects of Reset will not be taking trains to work from their urban high-rise apartments any more than they would be flying to Davos on commercial airlines.

Indeed, this dream of internationalized politically correct "green" and "urban" infrastructure seems the most antiempirical of the Reset's commandments. I live ten miles from the unfinished, now graffiti-tagged "first link" of California's fourteen-year, multibillion, and, so far utterly failed, mass-transit project—a dystopian warning of what could happen on an international scale. Yet to the east and just three miles distant from my farm is the busiest and most dangerous "freeway" in the nation: the north-south 99 freeway that runs lengthwise from the Oregon border to Los Angeles.

Highway 99 in too many places is still unchanged from its last update sixty years ago, due to Sacramento's neglect to maintain and expand this critical longitudinal link. Instead, the state and federal governments have chased the fantasies of mass transit. So far, a decade of work has not resulted in a foot of rail laid on this first leg—a bizarre 113-mile high-speed rail line "to nowhere" from Merced to Bakersfield, California. That corridor currently enjoys a fraction of the daily commuter road traffic of the San Francisco Bay Area or Los Angeles basin.

Note that the supporters and architects of high-speed rail were originally Bay and Los Angeles commuters. However, once the project was to begin and the costs, disruption, and timetables were announced, local and almost always liberal elected officials nixed the project. In exasperation, the California High-Speed Rail Authority then turned to the less populated, far poorer and more conservative Central Valley. It sold the project as a WPA-like jobs program that would infuse state and local dollars into a depressed economy.

By late 2021 the quarter-built skeleton of the state high-speed rail project still looked like a Daliesque version of Stonehenge, while the nearby chaos and carnage of the 99 seems like something out of an apocalyptic *Road Warrior* film. The rail's original completion date of 2018 has been pushed back to 2033—a distant target that still no one believes is credible. The original price tag of $33 billion has ballooned to $98 billion, again a figure likely to be vastly underestimated. In human terms, people die weekly on a vital but antiquated freeway—one easily expanded and repaired for a fraction of the costs of an unproved, stalled mass transit line.

Again, one also wonders about the consequences that follow from the Great Reset promise of "creating incentives for industries to improve their track record on environmental, social, and governance (ESG) metrics." California's experience once more offers some hint. Its green incentives, from carbon offsets to hyper-regulation of agriculture, construction, and manufacturing, have ensured that California is an increasingly moribund state. It is often held up as the model of America's reset future, even as its business climate, for example, sits near dead last in many rankings, such as those of the 2020 *State Business Tax Climate Index* compiled by the Tax Foundation.

California suffers from one of the largest population exoduses of any state. It is a medieval society of the nation's richest zip codes juxtaposed with the highest poverty rates in the United States, the largest number of residents on state assistance, among the highest gas and energy prices in the country, along with nearly the worst-ranked schools and infrastructure, topped off with the largest homeless population. Twenty-seven percent of Californians were not born in the United States, and it has the largest population of illegal aliens. In some sense, California has adopted the conquistadors' hacienda system of two rather than three classes in which a coastal elite ensures open borders and entitlements in exchange for the service and fealty of a subservient peasantry—without much worry about an autonomous, bothersome, and obstreperous middle class.

Yet of all fifty states, California's policy and governance most likely would synchronize with the aims outlined by the Great Reset—in terms of green energy, government "investments" in infrastructure and schooling, woke corporate monopolies in Silicon Valley, efforts to increase taxation, and regulation, and the imposition of racial, gender, and environmental targets to adjudicate corporate governance.

Again, this Great Reset is an effort to harmonize mandates across national boundaries. In part, the cosmopolitanism is a result of observing in horror the unfettered federalism of the United States. Globalists are not fond of models in which states set their own tax and regulatory climates. The result is too uncontrollable, as Americans react accordingly to individual state idiosyncrasies. And increasingly, they vote with their feet by moving to regions of less government, more liberty and free will, more dynamic free enterprise and fewer regulations—all popularly considered synonymous with much better schools, superior infrastructure, less crime, and more effective social services.

While globalization is seen as a gift horse for the Great Reset, worldwide harmonization also could pose risks that such uniformity might mean population outflows, especially within Europe, from high-tax, highly regulated "blue nations" to low-tax, less regulated "red" nations. And that is why G-7 protocols, Great Reset agendas, and ESG criteria all seek to enforce uniformity, stifle dissent, and indeed wish to outlaw any noncompliant party.

Not surprisingly absent in the published synopses of the Great Reset, and in the books of Klaus Schwab, is any sensitivity to the cares and preferences of the billions on the planet subject to the dictates of a select few. So what is clear about the ESG agenda, the plans of the Great Reset, and the experience of California is a shared distrust of individualism, a fear of competition, the elevation of "equity" above freedom and liberty, and the desire for supra-political authority to implement policies that otherwise have no popular support.

The Great Reset agenda's *third* and final priority is to:

> harness the innovations of the Fourth Industrial Revolution to support the public good, especially by addressing health and social challenges. During the COVID-19 crisis, companies, universities, and others have joined forces to develop diagnostics, therapeutics, and possible vaccines; establish testing centers; create mechanisms for tracing infections; and deliver telemedicine. Imagine what could be possible if similar concerted efforts were made in every sector.

Again, translate that mishmash and we are left trusting our collective future to select government-approved technocrats, academics, and properly woke CEOs who will more intimately control our private lives "in every sector." How ironic that the Great Reset manipulates the chaos and fears of Covid-19 to push through its otherwise apparently inert agenda, and yet remains oblivious to the true and frightening lessons of the pandemic.

Companies such as Walmart, Amazon, and Target have already seen "what could be possible" when government picks and chooses quarantine winners and losers on the basis of size, profits, and insider influence. As hundreds of millions of Americans were by edict shut in their homes, huge international corporations became even more monopolistic at the expense of small businesses. Government policy all but ensured that Doug McMillon of Walmart, Jeff Bezos of Amazon, and a woke Mark Zuckerberg would spike their already massive profits and use their virtual monopolies to massage the dissemination of information, whether by Facebook or the *Washington Post*. Schwab seems clueless that the role of the media, corporations, government, and universities during the Covid-19 crisis has become downright scary. As they fused, they more effectively curtailed free expression, weaponized oversight, cancelled free thinkers, and exercised a level of ideological censure rarely seen in the west. In the end, we were left with the former president of the United States (but not Taliban leaders) banned from Twitter.

In addition, many who read Schwab's gush might counter that they have already seen what was once deemed unimaginable from health agencies during the pandemic. Often, racially calibrated considerations determined the queues of the vaccination eligibility. In June 2020, ideologies trumped science when medical experts issued blanket exemptions to the followers of Black Lives Matter (BLM), who marched en masse without criticism and in violation of all edicts concerning face masks, social distancing, and sheltering in place. Currently, Americans witness woke open-borders policies in which thousands at the southern border enter the U.S. in the midst of a pandemic without either vaccinations or even Covid-19 testing while the Biden administration promises to go door-to-door to urge American citizens to be vaccinated and has virtually closed the northern border with Canada.

More specifically, the international medical-political-industrial complex never presented clear cost-to-benefit analyses in its strategies of conquering the virus. That is, Western publics were never fully apprised of the costs entailed by national shutdowns and quarantines versus commensurate losses from the virus. The missed medical procedures, greater mental and familial abuse, the billions of hours of lost schooltime, the increases in suicides, the psychological damage of forced confinement among 330 million people, and the spikes in violent crime, as well as a genuinely self-created recession that destroyed the livelihoods of millions in the United States all might well in the long run have led to more death and depression than the toll from the virus.

In his coauthored book and a series of editorials and essays, Schwab and his associates have filled in a great deal of detail about the Great Reset's particulars. But the general assumption that pervades all the three foundational principles of the Great Reset is the supposed inability of elected leaders and legislatures of Western constitutional governments to solve problems independently and in concert with and on the directive of their own voting citizenry.

Schwab apparently believes new solutions became viable only during the global Covid-19 pandemic, suggesting he assumes that Covid provides a needed corrective to Western popular skepticism of internationalism as expressed in the 2016 American presidential and British Brexit votes. In this sense of history and contemporary events, we should offer a final warning of *what the Reset is not.*

Our Passé Constitution

The Great Reset is *not* historically minded. It seems oblivious to previous unimpressive transnational efforts at world governance, from the League of Nations to the United Nations, that never met the expectation of their idealistic creators. In the case of the former, its laxity may well have fueled the fascist forces that triggered World War II, and in the latter, it has never really prevented a major war. And as currently constituted, the U.N. usually has obsessed over tiny, democratic Israel when it was not weighing in on the side of nondemocratic and often corrupt states that claimed they were victimized postcolonial revolutionary regimes, such as Iran, Cuba, and Venezuela.

The United States that pulled out of the Paris Climate Accord far better met that consortia's targeted reductions in carbon emissions than most of its remaining members. International efforts to "solve" the Israeli-Palestinian "crisis" met mostly with seventy years of failure. The much-derided unilateral American-sponsored Abraham Accords under Donald Trump led to calm—even as they were largely ignored or despised by the "international community."

More specifically, one of the chief lessons of the Covid-19 pandemic is that international and transnational bodies such as the World Health Organization (WHO) are often incompetent police that need policing. They become corrupt and cower before the power and money of communist China or a perceived progressive "global consensus." On almost every key Covid-19 question, from travel bans to the role of the Level-Four virology lab in Wuhan, to the origins, transmissibility, and treatment of the disease, the WHO and its director, the former Ethiopian health minister Tedros Adhanom Ghebreyesus, were either wrong or contradictory to the point of incoherence. In terms of the vaccinations, the Operation Warp Speed paradigm of incentivizing private pharmaceutical companies to compete for government contracts resulted in the most rapid appearance of efficacious and generally safe vaccines, in a way far superior to the more statist European Union, Chinese, and Russian competitors.

In truth, the "international community" has very little control over the behavior of the Chinese communist government. Beijing lied about the origins, nature, and danger of SARS-CoV-2. It leveraged the reputations of international investigatory teams and individual scientists to lead them to maintain the farce that the pandemic jumped from bats or pangolins into the human population, without any role at all of the Wuhan lab that was engaged in "gain-of-function" coronavirus research. Few wished to note the lab's past sloppy safety protocols, or that it was partially or fully under the control of the Chinese military, or that its own researchers had fallen severely ill by what turned out likely to be their own gain-of-function and engineered coronavirus.

The strange career of the once-sainted Dr. Fauci is emblematic of the dangers of government-corporate fusion, a favorite of the WEF crowd at Davos. Fauci has gone from saintly status as an international medical icon to a rank politico. His continually changing edicts and deceptions on the wearing of masks, the likely date of a rollout of the vaccine, the nature of herd immunity, and the connections he green-lit and weaponized between the Wuhan lab and the National Institutes of Health and the National Institute of Allergy and Infectious Diseases exposed him not just as an insider bureaucratic functionary, but one granted near-dictatorial powers to control the lives of millions on the basis of his alleged superior "scientific" expertise.

The centralization of public policy in a few select bureaucracies ensured little audit of nationalized health policy—to the point that the Center for Disease Control was finally adjudicating when and if millions of American landlords could collect contracted payments from their renters. What was terrifying about Covid-19 was not the lack of international cooperation. It was the manner in which internationalists deliberately first circumvented their own nations' laws forbidding dangerous gain-of-function research to both fund and collaborate with what turned out to be a renegade and reckless Chinese medical establishment—and then lied about it to the point of warping international teams tasked with investigating the Wuhan origins of the virus.

To this day, neither Dr. Fauci, his Chinese counterparts, nor the research intermediaries that he empowered, can explain to the global community why in a cost-benefit analysis such apocalyptic research is worth the dangers. Nor can Ghebreyesus, the director-general of the WHO, explain why he was quiet in the critical days when the Chinese government was shutting all domestic travel to and from Wuhan, China, but allowing flights from Wuhan to Europe and the United States. Nor can the WHO director-general account for his verbatim parroting of Chinese deceptive talking points about the origins, transmissibility, and lack of international dangers from the Wuhan outbreak.

One day, historians may well conclude that many of Dr. Fauci's gyrating directives were intended to divert attention from his own role in sending American government money to agencies circumventing bans of gain-of-function viral research—in collaboration with the Wuhan virology lab. And they may cite the WHO as culpable for allowing China to hide critical information about Covid-19 when transparency and accountability might have saved thousands of lives.

Intellectuals and the elite in general are especially prone to the globalist virus, at best from concern for global well-being amid local intractable pathologies, at worst out of an end-of-history, megalomaniac impulse to solve innate problems on a grand scale, once and for all. The biographer and moralist Plutarch (c. 100 A.D.) claimed in his essay "On Exile" that Socrates had once asserted that he was not just an Athenian but instead "a citizen of the cosmos"—a kosmopolitês. In later European thought, communist ideas of universal labor solidarity drew heavily on the idea of a world without borders. "Workers of the world, unite!" exhorted Karl Marx and Friedrich Engels. Or as Eugene V. Debs, the American socialist, in 1915 put it, "I have no country to fight for; my country is the earth; and I am a citizen of the world."

Wars broke out, in this thinking, only because of needless quarreling over obsolete state boundaries when the real conflict was between uniform global capitalists and a worldwide exploited underclass. The solution to this state of endless war, some argued, was to eliminate borders in favor of transnational governance and policing. H. G. Wells's prewar science fiction novel *The Shape of Things to Come* (1933) envisioned borders eventually disappearing as elite transnational polymaths, in the manner of League of Nations grandees, enforced enlightened world governance. Norman Angell's earlier *The Great Illusion* (1909) argued that war between blinkered nationalist states had become so destructive and irrational in the Western industrialized world that it would gradually disappear, as transnational elites would certainly discover more civilized ways of resolving conflicts—as if they had done so in their own private or professional lives.

On the urging of President Franklin Roosevelt, defeated 1940 Republican presidential candidate Wendell Willkie in 1942 went on a seven-week, thirty-one-thousand-mile tour of the world. He concluded from his travels and meeting with wartime allies the need for one-world government. His manifesto, *One World*, published in 1943, quickly hit the bestseller list. Indeed, the book sold 1.5 million copies in just four months, the greatest rapid nonfiction sales up to that time. Willkie met with Stalin and came home advocating more military aid to the Soviet Union. Had he not died at fifty-two, many considered Willkie likely to become the first secretary-general of the United Nations.

President Obama did not think he meant to deprecate America when early in his first term he said at an April 2009 press conference, "I believe in American exceptionalism, just as I suspect that the Brits believe in British exceptionalism and the Greeks believe in Greek exceptionalism." To Obama, it was not controversial to suggest that his own country was typical, like every other nation, in thinking it was more exceptional than others, rather than believing that by some disinterested standard it actually was. America was, in fact, demonstrably "exceptional" by any metric, but to Obama such recognition might have seemed counterproductive to his agenda, parochial, and chauvinistic.

Obama earlier as a candidate in 2008 went to Berlin and declared himself both an American and a "world" citizen ("Tonight, I speak to you not as a candidate for president, but as a citizen—a proud citizen of the United States, and a fellow citizen of the world."). He added that Germans and Americans were united by the "burdens of global citizenship." Obama seemed to suggest that borders, walls, and boundaries would fall and be absorbed into a new enlightened transnationalism. Americans would recalibrate their norms to align them with global standards, whose nature has never been quite spelled out. Indeed, it was quite striking how often U.S. leaders emphasized, often in clumsy fashion, how they saw themselves as internationalists and felt their own Americanism was in some sense no big deal.

Or as then-Vice President Joe Biden put it to a questioner in a 2014 town hall at Harvard University:

> America's strength ultimately lies in its people. There's nothing special about being an American. None of you can define for me what an American is. You can't define it based on religion, ethnicity, race, culture.

Biden may have been trying to define, correctly, Americanism as more of an idea than a status rooted in blood and soil, but for that very rare reason there *is* something special about the American system that is not found abroad.

Citizenship by definition asks of the resident certain responsibilities in exchange for delineated rights. But who or what would dispense such *global* gifts? And what do citizens of the world ask in return? How do eight billion get along as a global commonwealth under a shared protocol of values, when there is no message of ecumenicalism that would dare to transcend race, religion, and gender, especially akin to the Western tradition of personal freedom, consensual government, and human rights?

In other words, under Great Reset globalism, the standard criteria of human rights, free choice, and consensual government would not be found in the U.S. Constitution but rather through the aggregate of the values of most countries in the world. Unfortunately, all too many are illiberal, opposed to freedom, and often deeply antithetical to the ideals and laws of the United States.

In sum, the same old, same old Great Reset is better envisioned as the Great Regression.

CHINA, COVID-19, *REALPOLITIK*, AND THE GREAT RESET

BY DOUGLAS MURRAY

It is a good rule of thumb that one should become skeptical—and perhaps also concerned—whenever everyone in a position of authority starts to say the same thing. Particularly when they also all do so at the same time.

Such a moment arrived in 2020 when nearly every Western statesman, and a few others who might aspire to that role, began to use the phrase "Build Back Better." Boris Johnson claimed that he might have used it first. Joe Biden seemed to believe that he had. But they were hardly the only people to use it from the early days of the Covid-19 crisis onwards. Almost overnight, it seemed as though absolutely everyone was using the same words. Prime Minister Jacinda Ardern said it down in New Zealand. Prime Minister Justin Trudeau used it in Canada. Bill Clinton used it as he was campaigning for Joe Biden. And the mayor of London, Sadiq Khan, used it as he was campaigning for himself. Even minor royals could be heard parroting the same alliterative pleasantry. According to Prince Harry, speaking from his self-imposed exile in California, the Covid pandemic "undoubtedly" presents "an opportunity for us to work together and build back better."

The prince is no stranger to political cliché, as he showed there, managing to pack in two of them into just half a sentence. Yet nor did people far more self-aware than him at any stage seem to realize that the phrase sounded strange in the first place, never mind that they should all also be using it at the same time. A year and a half after the phrase was first being used, President Joe Biden was still struggling to get his Build Back Better bill through the U.S. Senate. The phrase became so ubiquitous that almost no one in a position of power stopped to ask the question that ought surely to have loomed.

Why should a global pandemic be seen as simply an opportunity? In the immediate aftermath of the coronavirus leaking out from Wuhan, China, millions of people around the world died from the effects of contracting that virus. The global economy contracted at an astounding rate. Government borrowing soared to rates unknown outside of wartime in order to furlough millions of people who would otherwise have been destitute. Entire economies—including a U.S. economy that was roaring in an election year—were suddenly forced to a halt. None of this looked like a source of optimism. Ordinarily, the mass laying off of the workforce, the racking up of unprecedented peacetime debt, and the ordered shuttering away of the citizenry in their houses would be a source of concern and fury before it was a cause for optimism and opportunity.

But with only a couple of notable exceptions, during the Covid era, Western politicians skipped the rage stage. Indeed, they even skipped over the blame stage. Just as the WHO and other compromised international bodies failed to get to the roots of the source of the virus, so most Western politicians spent zero time or political capital on the question of why the virus had been unleashed on the world in the first place. Instead, they jumped straight to the question of just how much could be achieved by the unparalleled opportunity that the virus had allegedly gifted us.

Within a little over a year, politicians themselves seemed to be laughing at the phrase, even as they could not stop using it. In October 2021, Boris Johnson's office seemed to imagine that the British public had become so thrilled by the "build back better" tagline that it was time for some riffs on the theme. At this stage, somewhere between lockdowns umpteen and nineteen, Johnson released a number of videos on his social media pages in which the slogan build back better was posted on the screen. Johnson seemed to imagine that the British public was in a playful mood around the theme. The videos included one of him spreading butter on some pieces of toast and looking at the camera and saying "build back butter." In a second video, with the build back better motif over it, the Prime Minister could be seen unrolling a packet of fish and chips. "Mmm" he says appreciatively, before looking at the camera and saying "Build back batter." Terms like "pathetic" and "inadequate" would fail to do justice to such political moments.

The obvious comparison to make at this stage is with great plagues in history. And though most were of a degree of seriousness that far outweighs the effects of Covid, it is a sobering consideration. Who, for instance, viewed the so-called "Spanish flu" of a century ago as an opportunity? Who would have dared in the early months or years after that pandemic ravaged the planet to see it as an opportunity to rebuild the global economy in a different way?

There are two things that are most visibly disturbing about the political reaction to all of this. The first is the desire to leapfrog over the most obvious stage in the post-pandemic era. Which should have been a clinical, careful and failsafe analysis of how this novel coronavirus managed to come out of Wuhan. The second disturbing thing is that the leap should have immediately moved on to a restructuring of the global economy and of free societies that seemed already to be sitting there, ready-made.

The extent to which that first stage was leaped over has many reasons. But one of these undoubtedly had much to do with the incumbent in the White House when the "China virus" first came into the world. President Trump was in an election year and was understandably intent on not shuttering the U.S. economy ahead of an election. He was also keen to attribute blame towards the place where he saw the virus originating. Whether the cause of the leak was a Wuhan wet market (as was early on deemed the only permissible explanation) or the Wuhan Institute of Virology (as soon seemed likelier), Trump was keen that China got the blame for releasing the virus into the world. And there was much to be said for this. Even if the leak had been an accident, it was one that the Chinese authorities did nothing to contain, allowing flights out of the region even as the first knowledge of the virus made the Chinese Communist Party (CCP) shutter flights and regions within Chinese borders.

But keen observers will have noticed that Trump was a divisive president and that what he said was the case was strenuously pushed back against by his critics when it was true as well as when it was not. Early in 2020, as Trump continued to talk about the source of the virus, his political opponents decided to claim that identifying China as the source of the virus would lead to an upsurge in anti-Chinese racism. And so Democrat Speaker of the House Nancy Pelosi, for instance, not only deplored the president's language but also implored Americans to demonstrate their contempt for the president's "racism" in a practical way. Speaker Pelosi implored people to visit their local Chinatown and show solidarity with Chinese people. In Florence, Italy, the mayor went one better in the global game of grandstanding against Trump. On February 1, 2020, Dario Nardella urged Florentines to "hug a Chinese" person to combat racism. It is not known how many Italians contracted the virus through this demonstration of Sino-fraternalism.

The point is that from the earliest stage of the virus, the opportunity to point fingers appeared to have been queered by the fact that one of the only people in the world pointing fingers was a person who most of the political class around the world were ostentatiously opposed to. Even to speak of lab leaks or Chinese culpability in those days was to sound Trump-like, a fact that played very well indeed into the public relations campaign orchestrated by the CCP.

The effectiveness of that PR campaign was visible from the very start of the virus, and showed the extent to which a swathe of the scientific, media, and political establishments in the West were already literally or figuratively in the pocket of the CCP.

As early as February 2020, *The Lancet* was publishing a letter signed by twenty-seven prominent virologists saying "We stand together to strongly condemn conspiracy theories suggesting that Covid-19 does not have a natural origin." One of the signatories of that letter, Peter Daszak, was the president of EcoHealth Alliance, a nonprofit that has received millions of dollars in grants from the U.S. government and has subcontracted hundreds of thousands of dollars of its work to the Wuhan Institute of Virology. Assertive condemnations and joint statements such as this effectively shut down the lab leak theory and labelled it a conspiracy throughout most of 2020. The virus was apparently to be seen as something as unavoidable as a tsunami or other natural disaster. If it happened to take down the global economy, then so be it. Nothing to be done. These things happen.

Whenever anybody stepped out of line from this attitude, even when that anybody was a Western government, the CCP proved itself typically adept at a form of punishment: beating. In April 2020, it was revealed in Australia's *Daily Telegraph* that the Five Eyes intelligence network (consisting of the U.K., U.S., New Zealand, Canada, and Australia) was looking seriously into the question of the origins of the virus. In particular, it was reported that the Five Eyes were investigating whether the virus had in fact been released from the Wuhan laboratory. That same month, the Australian government came out ahead of the rest of the international community and called for a full investigation into the origins of the virus. For this, the Australian government received a textbook CCP lashing.

China's ambassador to Australia told the Australian *Financial Review* that the Chinese public were "frustrated, dismayed and disappointed with what you are doing now. If the mood is going from bad to worse, people would think why we should go to such a country while it's not so friendly to China. The tourists may have second thoughts." The message—or rather threat—was clear. Chinese students, parents, and consumers were all said to be on the verge of boycotting any and all Australian products, from education to beef and red wine. The

CCP's tactic was the familiar mob one: nice little country you've got there. Shame if anything were to happen to it.

The editor of the state-run *Global Times*, Hu Xijin, went one further, proving to be even less diplomatic than the CCP's diplomats. Hu took to Weibo (China's answer to Twitter) to describe Australia as a piece of "chewing gum stuck on the sole of China's shoes." He continued, "Sometimes you have to find a stone to rub it off." Perhaps this was another reason why the rest of the world was so slow to ascribe even the merest claim about China: not just association with President Trump, but incurring the likely wrath of the CCP in Beijing, with all the real-world economic consequences such a move can have.

But the Australian government was right, of course. For whether the virus came from a lab or a wet market, was deliberately leaked or accidentally leaked, the behaviour of the CCP in the aftermath of the world shutting down was both sinister and suggestive enough to warrant serious investigation. For instance, in February 2020, the Chinese authorities disappeared a citizen journalist named Chen Qiushi. His work had been focusing on the outbreak of the virus and it took a full half a year for his whereabouts to become known. In September of the same year, Qiushi's friends revealed that he had been "found." He was apparently "quarantined by force" and while in good health was living under CCP government supervision. So far, so new normal.

Scores of other Chinese citizens who were believed to have some knowledge of what went on at the laboratory in Wuhan were similarly treated. For instance, Huang Yanling, who worked at the Wuhan Institute of Virology and was believed to be "patient zero" in the coronavirus outbreak, was just one of dozens of doctors, scientists, and others whom the CCP disappeared once the world's attention was turned on them. If the CCP had nothing to hide, then it was going about it in a very strange way.

Yet what options did the rest of the world have, even with such a minimalistic aim as trying to work out how a similar outbreak might be avoided in the future? Ordinarily, it might have looked to fall back on respected and agreed-upon international bodies. But the main such body—the WHO—was shown to be unfit for purpose from the very outset of the virus. When the WHO finally carried out a four-week investigation into the source of the virus a year after it first spread, the conclusions were foregone. Dr Peter Ben Embarek of the WHO told the world at a press conference in Wuhan that it was "extremely unlikely" that the virus had come from the Wuhan laboratory. After returning from the press conference, Embarek had the decency to admit that "politics was always in the room" during his investigations. As well they might have been, given the fact that the CCP comprehensively arranged, structured, and curtailed WHO's investigations during their visit, deciding who the WHO could and could not meet, where they could meet, and where they could not. To take just one example, the members of the WHO investigation committee were not allowed to meet Chinese patients who were among the earliest patients to develop respiratory and other symptoms of Covid-19.

It is impossible to consider the world's response to the events ignited by the Covid crisis without facing up to this singular political reality. Knowingly or through a laxness, which is as bad, China managed to unleash a virus on the world in 2020 which threw the globe into turmoil and happened to leave China as the only major economy in the world exiting 2021 with economic growth. And yet to date there has still been no reasonable suggestion or estimation of how the CCP might be made to pay, or even be blamed, for this fact.

This stark political reality put me in mind of the response I noticed last decade over the slow but comprehensive snuffing out of democracy in Hong Kong. When I was last there in the 2010s, the umbrella protests were still going on. These were the aftermath of the movement that had once burned strong, where predominantly young Hong Kong citizens gathered with umbrellas to protest the CCP's ever-increasing grip on the former British territory. It was a sad and pitiful sight, the end of this movement, with the remaining protestors sitting in the underground passes of the city as the rain poured down outside. The dejected end of a movement that had once demonstrated enormous hope.

In the immediate aftermath of that trip, I happened to be, in short order, in Paris, London and Washington and in each place, I described to various officials the sad sight of the end of this prodemocracy movement. Back then (in 2014/2015) I was struck by the response in both London and Paris. In the French tongue, the response spoke for London as well: it was, essentially, "Bah, but what are you going to do? It is China." Only in Washington, I noticed, did officials and politicians not take this fatalistic approach. There, people asked follow-up questions. Questions I was all too ill-equipped to answer. "What could we do to help these people" for instance. And the reason I raise this is because this to me already seemed symptomatic. In most of the developed countries, the rise of the CCP was seen as inevitable and unstoppable—whether it was desirable or not. Countries like Britain and France had effectively conceded that the CCP era was going to be upon us at some point soon, if not already. And in this situation, it was important to do what you could to fit in with the new reality.

This was not only a geostrategic calculation. It was also becoming increasingly clear that this was a personal calculation for many people in the West. In a pattern that has still received far too little media or other attention, when politicians stood down from office—as for instance they did with great regularity in Britain in the last decade—a place, if not sinecure, could apparently always be found for them somewhere within the warm embrace of the CCP's front organizations. After he stepped down from office in 2016, one of the roles that former prime minister David Cameron first took on was a position as head of a major Chinese investment fund. His former partner in the Conservative–Liberal Democrat coalition government of 2010–2015, Danny Alexander, went one further.

During the coalition government, Alexander had been chief secretary to the Treasury, one of the most important positions in government. Before his elevation to parliament, his most prestigious role was as head of communications for the Cairngorms National Park Authority. While in government, Alexander once had the honesty to admit that being chief secretary to the Treasury in the aftermath of a global financial crisis was his toughest job to date. As well it might have been. But it was perhaps inevitable that after losing his parliamentary seat in the 2015 election, Mr. Alexander would not be content with returning to the Cairngorms National Park Authority. Other entities clearly noticed that a former chief secretary to the Treasury in search of work is a useful asset to vacuum up. Chief amongst these was the CCP. And so it was that Mr. Alexander soon found himself rejoicing in the title of vice president and corporate secretary of the Asian Infrastructure Bank in Beijing. An immensely prestigious position, and a well-remunerated one at that—certainly when compared with any competing compensation packages in the Cairngorms.

But this process—what one might call "elite capture"—has been happening in all of our countries for the best part of twenty years and more. Ever since China was allowed into the World Trade Organization (WTO) in 2001, it has managed to buy up vast swathes of Africa and the Far East as well as ports from Europe to Israel. It has also managed to buy up vast swathes of the political and ex-political classes in Europe and the rest of the world. When, at the start of the Covid era, some of the few CCP hawks in Washington and elsewhere talked of a new Cold War with China, it always had to sidestep this central political reality, which was that the reality of Western-Chinese entanglement by 2020 was such that the Cold War analogy simply did not hold.

As the U.S. Secretary of State Mike Pompeo reminded me during an interview at the U.S. embassy in London during the summer of 2020, during the Cold War, American and other Western businesses had absolutely negligible financial or other business ties with the U.S.S.R. "Decoupling" from the U.S.S.R. was never a problem during the Cold War. The few people who did try to couple with it are now household names because of their efforts. By contrast, the prospect of "decoupling" the West's financial prospects with those of Communist China now appears to be a labyrinthine, perhaps impossible, task. What are the real prospects of American and European banks decoupling, even if ordered to do so, from their Chinese markets? What are the chances that even if the worst-case scenario were to emerge—such as an event that shut down the global economy—that Western businesses would be able, even if they were willing, to turn away from the Chinese market? Would Barclays? Would HSBC? Would any number of other banks and financial institutions? As the reactions of such institutions to the security laws introduced in Hong Kong have shown us, the answers are already in on that one.

Given this situation, even before you come to the question of what could be done with a situation such as the coronavirus crisis, you have to confront this question of reality. Even if the worst-case scenario was proven. Even if it was proven beyond all reasonable doubt that the CCP had deliberately released a bioweapon into the world in the early weeks of 2020, what would the rest of the world be willing to do about it? What could it do about it? Would the markets urge revenge or caution? Would the political class around the world call for reparations or for a steadying of the global economic ship? Would it be easier to focus on what the fruits, as well as the roots, of the rotten tree happened to be? Or would it be easier to focus on some other matter that could conveniently come along to make everyone focus their attentions on things that were less undesirable?

Happily for those in charge of most of the world's democracies in 2020, such a ready-made, oven-ready change of focus did indeed exist.

For more than a generation, the West had been fomenting a new view of capitalism and the modern economy. Though it originated on the Left, this interpretation owed more to a paleoconservative, agrarian, almost Tolkienesque dream than almost anyone was willing to concede. It viewed almost every piece of technological progress since the Industrial Revolution as effectively disastrous. The spread of capitalism round the globe had, in the twenty-first century alone so far, led to the raising of more than a billion people out of absolute poverty. Many of these people happened to have been in China. But what was clearly true was that countries like Germany and the U.K. that had benefited from the postindustrial era had by the late twentieth century decided that they could afford to change their ways having acquired the benefits. Having once fueled these countries' economic progress, fossil fuels in particular were now identified as the source of the planet's woes.

Although China, India, and other emerging economies were increasingly reliant on fossil fuels (China alone building more than one hundred new coal-fired power plants in recent years), the Western economies were, by the 2020s, in the process of a difficult political and energy turn. Having decided that their own future should be green, they had to find a way to persuade the developing world that they should make their future green as well. The more polite among the developing nations decided to go along with the formalities of this dance. Prime Minister Narendra Modi of India, for instance, committed at the Cop26 climate conference in Glasgow in 2021 that he would make India carbon-neutral by 2070. A promise I am certain that the world will be able to hold India, and Prime Minister Modi, to with enormous care.

But there is something undeniably awkward about this particular turn in the global order. And it included an inbuilt hypocrisy that the emerging economies were all too pleased to point out. Why should countries like India, and indeed China, not be permitted to enrich themselves and raise the living standards of their populations in the twenty-first century in the same way as the West had throughout the nineteenth and twentieth centuries? At all global conferences, on climate change or anything else, this glaring problem continually asserted itself. The Western powers could afford to preach the virtues of decarbonization because they had benefited from the era of carbonization. Countries such as India and China, intent on raising the world's largest populations out of absolute poverty, were in a different situation.

And so the behaviour and aspirations of the West began to look like a first-world luxury. The West could afford to go green—possibly—because it had spent two centuries not doing so. And perhaps the calculation would work. In the meantime, as the West was attempting to get off carbon, its lectures to the rest of the world looked unimaginative if not selfish. Western countries were effectively in the position of advising the rest of the world not to do as they had done. More specifically, they were in the position of a gentleman in a Tesla telling a person on a motorcycle that he should consider walking.

But for a certain type of Western politician—including the Democratic Party in the U.S. and the Conservative Party of Boris Johnson in the U.K. (not to mention Justin Trudeau's Liberal Party in Canada and many others)—the world had been too slow to wake up to their warnings on carbon and the environment. The public in each country had become all too familiar with dire economic warnings about the imminence of the climate apocalypse. They had even drafted in and made a global celebrity of a Scandinavian truant with a disorder that specifically makes her incapable of listening to points of view or evidence that counters what she believes. At the Cop26 climate conference in Glasgow, Prime Minister Boris Johnson, who had throughout his career as a newspaper columnist been a climate sceptic, claimed that the world had just "one minute" left to save the planet.

Of course, in this scenario the shuttering of the world's economies, the grounding of all commercial airline flights, and more was a dream that even the extremists of groups like Extinction Rebellion could hardly have imagined might occur in their lifetimes. As the world was locked in its houses and all (even essential) travel was curtailed, the populations got a taste of what the future being planned for them might look like. And for most people—especially those young people who were meant to be studying or were paying for claustrophobic accommodation that they could not afford or leave—this was a deeply unpleasant experience.

And yet at exactly this moment, the world's leaders seemed all to agree that this was a great moment. A great opportunity. A moment for a Great Reset.

Since that phrase has become bandied around with considerable laxness in the last couple of years, perhaps it is worth highlighting the fact that as far as I can count, the Great Reset now consists of at least three different things. Or at least it means around three different things to different groups of people.

The first thing that the Great Reset means is what Klaus Schwab and Thierry Malleret described in their 2020 book *COVID-19: The Great Reset*. Since everything to do with the Great Reset has now joined phrases like "the Great Replacement"[7] as being deemed by many to be an unadulterated "conspiracy theory," it is worth pointing out the simple reality of what Schwab, the founder and Executive Chairman of the World Economic Forum, described in his book. For the book is real, it is easily purchasable, less easily readable, and completely open about what the authors describe as the changes that are needed "to create a more inclusive, resilient and sustainable world." According to them, "a new world will emerge" after the pandemic, "the contours of which are for us to both imagine and to draw."

The book is a list of attempts to address every modern clichéd obsession of the globalist mainstream. It seeks to address the environment, obviously. But it also has sections on how the Great Reset might be used to address "inequality," which is, throughout, agreed to be solely a bad thing. It also seeks to address "mental health and well-being," Schwab and Malleret incidentally have almost nothing to say on some of these matters. On the matter of mental health, for instance, all they can recite are the banalities of the age—the importance of mental health, the way in which it has been underplayed in the past, and the extent to which people's mental health is both important to them and likely to undergo stress during a period of lockdown. But with their constant desire to be upbeat and come up with answers, what can Schwab and Malleret suggest? Why, they can suggest that all of this means that Covid-19 provides a great opportunity to accelerate awareness of an issue that "was already on the radar screen of policy-makers. In the post-pandemic era, these issues may now be given the priority they deserve. This indeed would constitute a vital reset." So there's a positive of coronavirus right there.

---

7 A phrase first coined by the French writer Renaud Camus [b. 1946] to describe demographic change in Europe.

On other issues, their suggestions are more concrete. For instance, Schwab and Malleret say that on the issue of the environment "the moment must be seized to take advantage of this unique window of opportunity to redesign a more sustainable economy for the greater good of our societies." On the subject of "inequality" Schwab and Malleret are reduced to citing the socialist filmmaker Ken Loach whose "most recent work" is described as a film that portrays the plight of delivery drivers who are self-employed and do not necessarily receive holiday pay or sick pay. Elsewhere, they talk about the death of George Floyd and the success of the Black Lives Matter movement.

No cliché is left unturned. The authors claim, erroneously, that Margaret Thatcher said that "there is no such thing as society" and praise the return to an era of big government to tackle inequality. About the details of this, the authors are characteristically vague. All they can suggest to deal with these challenges is that there should be "a broader, if not universal, provision of social assistance, social insurance, healthcare and basic quality services." Secondly that there should be "enhanced protection for workers and for those currently most vulnerable."

So far, so banal. But I cite these excerpts, and could cite plenty more, simply because it is a matter of record that Schwab, the chairman of the WEF, reacted swiftly to the Covid-19 pandemic by saying that what it most presented was a set of opportunities. The Great Reset then, is first and foremost a book. A matter of record. And available to be waded through by anybody who has the patience to do so.

But the Great Reset is also a second thing, which is what politicians around the world started to take it to mean and started to use it to mean. This is the set of blandishments embedded in such phrases as the demand that we "build back better." In the hands of politicians, the Great Reset became the great opportunity to use the virus to do things that they had already long wanted to do or claimed that they had long wanted to do.

At the G-7 summit in Cornwall in June 2021, this was the main upbeat subject of discussion among world leaders. There was no discussion of the source of the virus. No serious discussion about the possibility that the CCP ought to be held to account for what it had allowed to be unleashed on the world. No calls for the CCP to be held to account for crashing the global economy. Instead, the leaders of the world's leading democracies focused solely on the great opportunity that now allegedly lay in front of them. From the point of view of the host country—the U.K.—the prime minister's most important role was to woo his American rival and persuade Joe Biden that he was not (as Biden had once said of Johnson) "a physical and emotional clone" of Donald Trump.

Johnson hates this comparison, made when Biden was running for the presidency, and perhaps he chose to overegg the pudding when, during Biden's early months in office, Johnson stressed again and again his commitment to the green agenda. But regardless of all the banalities uttered in Cornwall, few could have beaten the love letter that Johnson clearly intended to wing directly at Biden, albeit in front of the free world's other leaders and the world's media.

In Cornwall, when Boris Johnson announced the importance once again of "building back better," he stressed that this meant that we should also be "building back greener, building back fairer and building equally and—how should I put it?—in a more gender-neutral and perhaps a more feminine way."

What did any of this mean? Other than that Johnson wanted to be close to Biden. It appeared to mean that Johnson—a longtime opinion writer for the *Daily Telegraph* in the U.K.—had decided simply to succumb to every shibboleth of the new era. That included the presumption that the economy will be more successful if it is more equitable and "fair." And that an economy that is more "feminine" is likewise an economy that is more likely to roar (see also Christine Lagarde's famous comments on "Lehman Sisters").[8] All of this, and much more, is seriously contestable. But it remains remarkable that senior politi-

8 "As I have said many times, if it had been Lehman Sisters rather than Lehman Brothers, the world might well look a lot different today," Lagarde said in 2018.

cians should have found that this ready-made set of political banalities and unproved assumptions were in place and ready to be accelerated now that the CCP had done the world the favour of unleashing a pandemic upon us all.

If the first vision for a Great Reset was Schwab's and the second was politicians using the pandemic to accelerate policies and prejudices that they already held, then it is also true to say that a portion of the public took the Great Reset to mean a third thing. And this one requires unpacking with a certain degree of delicacy.

This is because the Great Reset has now been framed as a political conspiracy theory whenever it is cited, thanks to a particular political spin cycle it has been put through in the age of the internet. It need hardly be said that a global pandemic is a disorientating thing to live through at any stage in history. During the Spanish flu, people dropped dead on buses in capital cities of the developed world. Great swathes of the rich and famous as well as the poor were swept away by it. But Covid-19 happened at a different stage in information technology: an age in which populations were ordered to isolate but still had access to reams of information unequaled in human history.

The fact that sources of information have become more diffuse in the multimedia era is a cliché. The fact that it has allowed people to pursue totally different avenues of facts as well as opinions presents a challenge that our societies have barely begun to grasp. But from the beginning of the coronavirus era, it was perhaps inevitable that a reliance on certain agreed-upon forms of news information ("trusted sources" like the BBC and the *New York Times*) would start off relatively high and swiftly diminish. This was because the official narrative that these organs of opinion put out shape-shifted in real time. In large part, this was because the narrative of the scientists and other government advisers shifted as well.

In the era of information and disinformation, even before this crisis, there had been a generally agreed-upon view that perhaps the last realm in which expertise was respected was the scientific realm. In recent decades, each other source of information had been provably corrupted one by one, with the public seeing through their sense-making apparatuses sector by sector. The corruption of the media had been documented from the 1990s onward. The corruption of the banking system had been demonstrated when elements of that system almost crashed the global economy in 2008, paying no real price for doing so. Perhaps science was the last remaining magisterium in which people had not previously chosen their own path through the varieties of expertise on offer and agreed instead on the concept of a broadly settled consensus.

From the earliest days of the Covid pandemic, democratic governments stressed their reliance on this one remaining, respected group of people: scientists. It was on the advice of the scientists that populations were locked into their houses, deprived of the most basic liberties, and subjected to punishments for infringement that would have been previously unimaginable outside of some dystopian novel.

Yet the populations put up with this until the magisterium of the scientists also began to erode. Figures like Professor Neil Ferguson from the faculty of medicine at Imperial College London turned out to have gotten all of their modeling predictions of likely deaths off by many times. Soon the public learned that the same Professor Ferguson (not to be confused with the distinguished Scottish historian Niall Ferguson) had a career track record of similar exaggeration. In previous scares, such as the foot-and-mouth outbreak in the U.K. in 2001, it was Ferguson's erroneous predictions that led to the slaughter of millions of the nation's perfectly healthy cattle.

At one stage of the coronavirus, Ferguson told the BBC that it was "almost inevitable" that daily infection rates of Covid in the U.K. would hit a record of one hundred thousand and peak at over two hundred thousand after any restrictions were relaxed. As it happened daily cases hardly topped thirty thousand. And of course, he himself was caught breaking a lockdown by which he had helped insist that everyone in the nation must abide. Still, despite being wrong on almost everything, often by several orders of magnitude, these were the sorts of experts upon whom the British government drew. In America, the same story was replayed with Dr. Fauci, who began the pandemic a hero and ended as one of the most divisive figures in the country. In part, again, this was because of shifts in expertise and opinion that happened in real time. Masks were at first useless at preventing the spread of the virus, then absolutely essential. People were meant to not congregate, then the good doctor would say young people could get frisky with each other on a date.

All the time the public could see events that shifted the whole narrative without any real-world recognition of the fact. For instance, when the Black Lives Matter protests began in the early summer of 2020, they came at a time when the public worldwide had been told not to congregate even with close family members outside of their own households. Then along came protests in America but also in London and other major cities around the world in which tens of thousands of people crammed together in support of the cause. And not only did dozens of health professionals justify this, such as one joint letter from American professionals supporting the breaking of lockdowns because racism was also a public health crisis. The public noted such contortions and contradictions. But a population that had been told not to even sit near friends on a park bench also noticed that the predicted "spikes" in Covid infections mysteriously did not occur when thousands of protestors gathered together—or indeed raided various retail stores—in the name of BLM.

And so the last magisterium also began to fall. And people understandably looked around for answers to all of this. What was really going on? Who was orchestrating all of this? And what was the aim?

The vaccines era threw up similar contortions. While she was running for vice president, Kamala Harris said that under no circumstances would she take a vaccine shot. Only a matter of months later, as vice president, she implored everyone in the country to take it. It turned out that there were good vaccines and bad vaccines, and that they all depended on whether a Democrat or a Republican was in the White House. Just as vaccine suspicion during Trump's presidency was rife on the Left, so during the Biden presidency it became rife on the

Right. And the claims of newscasters and politicians that the vaccines were the way out of the virus began to take hit after hit. The first hit came when it became clear that one, two, or even three doses of the vaccine did not make a person immune from contracting the virus. More importantly, it became clear that those people who were not vaccinated, or chose not to be vaccinated, were in significant part to be turned into some variety of second-class citizens.

In countries like Austria and Germany, the authorities made it clear that life for unvaccinated people would be made effectively impossible. Almost no activity could be taken part in outside of the house. In Britain, a prime minister who twenty years earlier had vociferously opposed the introduction of identity cards to work out who was actually in Britain made it de rigueur for people to be asked for their vaccination papers before entering public venues. And even in the country where skepticism towards all such government-paper demands has historically been highest—the United States—city after city turned in no time from insisting that vaccine mandates would never come into place to them coming into place and becoming a normal part of life.

All this is fertile ground for the most obvious fomenting of actual conspiracy theory. The idea that the vaccinations are part of a push by a global elite to do anything from implanting microchips to killing the populations of entire countries. What is a population to think when it is locked in its homes for months on end, including through the winter, told things that repeatedly turn out to be untrue, and then made to do things which only a few months earlier they were told would never happen? Often by the very same people.

At such moments, one has to remember that most people have had zero up-close, let alone consistent, contact with politicians and have little or no idea of the way in which decision-making occurs. My own observation is that as a result, most people have an exaggerated belief in the capabilities of those in power to effect change on matters large or small. When things go wrong, it is assumed that there must be a reason or a motivation. The cock-up or the muddling-through theories of history might tend to be the interpretation of those who have seen close-up the sausage of politics being made. But outside of that realm of direct experience, it is highly common to view great designs having been put into place to explain real-world events.

And that is where the third interpretation of the Great Reset comes into play. For what Schwab and Malleret did in their book turns out not just to have been banal, largely undesirable, and aspirational beyond their reach, but also severely unwise. They have given rise to a third interpretation of the term they have coined that now sees the Great Reset as a real thing happening in real time, being forced upon the public by a highly coordinated elite, from the WEF down, and intended to fundamentally and indeed permanently alter the relationship between citizens or subjects and those in positions of power. It is, in my view, a mistake to view it in this way. But it is hardly surprising that it should have happened. At a time at which bewildering things have been occurring, the desire to find an overarching plan in place to explain it, and for that plan to be openly spelled out by a nefarious and aloof collection of elites, is a formidably strong potion to be playing with.

To the extent that a Great Reset is happening, it is happening because even the combined democracies of the world under their current leadership do not have the will or desire to punish or even admonish China for what it allowed to come out of Wuhan in 2019–2020. Rather than depress their populations or demonstrate their own weakness in the face of the world's rising power, they have decided to put a positive spin on this most nonpositive of turns. They have decided to skip the blame stage, or even the discovery stage, and pretend that Covid is just the thing we needed to put our houses in better order. To behave more fairly, more gender-neutrally, more femininely, and of course more greenly. They have decided in short to use a crisis as an opportunity: an opportunity to embed a set of banal ambitions, the efficacy of which has yet to be proven, in order to demonstrate that they are the ones taking the initiative. In reality, they are the ones dodging the greater questions—including the geostrategic questions—of the era.

Those who follow the third interpretation of the Great Reset as listed above see a global elite with unrivaled power able and willing to force itself upon the populations of the world. I depart from this interpretation for many reasons. Not least of these reasons is that everything in the programme seems to me to be a demonstration of unparalleled weakness by those forces of alleged power. If the unimaginative global class wanted to find an alliterative phrase to respond to the rise of Chinese power, it would not be the one that they have landed on. And it would not be the crass jokes that Boris Johnson imagines still entertain a weary public. The phrase one would use to face down what China has done and what China is doing might start with "Build Back Bitter" and move on to the only thing that matters in the race of the twentieth century: the need for the West to build back bigger. Much bigger.

There is no way around this challenge. The only way is through. Which means focusing not on self-defeat, or self-defeating policies, but on victory. A victory that will come about only by a set of means: by exposing those members of the Western elites who have been subjected to elite capture by China; by shaming those companies who choose business with China over even some residual loyalty to the countries and societies that made them; by reforming or removing ourselves from international organisations that are in hock to the CCP; and by disentangling free societies from the Chinese Communist experiment as much as we can.

To the extent that it is a policy, the Great Reset attempts to avoid that unavoidable conclusion. It aims to replace national government with world government, and in an increasingly CCP-dominated world, that would lead in only one direction: against the cause of democratic and financial freedom. The Great Reset is an attempt to duck a challenge. It is better by far to recognize the challenge and accept that the experience of the Corona era is not an opportunity. It is a warning.

PART II:
THE POLITICAL

SOVEREIGNTY AND THE NATION-STATE

BY ROGER KIMBALL

I think I know man, but as for men, I know them not.
—Jean-Jacques Rousseau

In a memorable passage at the beginning of *The Critique of Pure Reason*, Immanuel Kant evokes a soaring dove that, "cleaving the air in her free flight," feels the resistance of the wind and imagines that its flight "would be easier still in empty space." A fond thought, of course, since absent that aeolian pressure, the dove would simply plummet to the ground.

How regularly the friction of reality works that way: making possible our endeavors even as it circumscribes and limits their extent. And how often, like Kant's dove, we are tempted to imagine that our freedoms would be grander and more extravagant absent the countervailing forces that make them possible.

Such fantasies are as perennial as they are vain. They insinuate themselves everywhere in the economy of human desire, not least in our political arrangements. Noticing the imperfection of our societies, we may be tempted into thinking that the problem is with the limiting structures we have inherited. If only we could dispense with them, we might imagine, beating our wings, how much better things might be.

What a cunning, devilish word: "might." For here as elsewhere, possibility is cheap. Scrap our current political accommodations and things might be better. Then again, they might be a whole lot worse. Vide the host of tyrannies inspired by that disciple of airy possibility, Jean-Jacques Rousseau. "Man was born free," he declaimed, "but is everywhere in chains": two startling untruths in a single famous utterance. Rousseau was keen on "forcing men to be free," but we had to wait until his followers Robespierre and Saint-Just to discover that freedom in this sense is often indistinguishable from what Robespierre chillingly called "virtue and its emanation, terror." Something similar can be said about Karl Marx, that other acolyte of possibility. How much misery have his theories underwritten, promising paradise but delivering tyranny, oppression, poverty, and death?

It wasn't so long ago that I had hopes that the Marxist-socialist rot—outside the insulated purlieus of humanities departments at Western universities, anyway—was on the fast track to oblivion. Has any "philosophy" ever been so graphically refuted by events (or the number of corpses it created)?

Maybe not, but refutation, like reason, plays a much more modest role in human affairs than we might imagine. In fact, the socialist-inspired utopian chorus is alive and well, playing to full houses at an antidemocratic redoubt near you. Consider the apparently unkillable dream of "world government." It is as fatuous now as it was when H. G. Wells infused it with literary drama toward the beginning of the twentieth century.

All human children need to learn to walk by themselves; so, it seems, every generation needs to wean itself from the blandishments of various utopian schemes. In 2005, the political philosopher Jeremy Rabkin published a fine book called *Law Without Nations? Why Constitutional Government Requires Sovereign States*. Rabkin ably fleshes out the promise of his subtitle, but it would be folly to think this labor will not have to be repeated. The temptation to exchange hard-won democratic freedom for the swaddling comfort of one or another central planning body is as inextinguishable as it is dangerous. As Ronald Reagan memorably put it,

> Freedom is never more than one generation away from extinction. We didn't pass it to our children in the bloodstream. It must be fought for, protected, and handed on for them to do the same, or one day we will spend our sunset years telling our children and our children's children what it was once like in the United States where men were free.

The late English philosopher Roger Scruton made the connection between this insight and the bulwark provided by the nation-state. "Democracies," he wrote, "owe their existence to national loyalties—the loyalties that are supposedly shared by government and opposition." Confusing national loyalty with nationalism, many utopians argue that the former is a threat to peace. After all, wasn't it national loyalty that sparked two world wars? No, it was that perverted offspring, *nationalism*, which at great cost was defeated only by the successful mobilization of national loyalty. Scruton quotes G. K. Chesterton on this point: to condemn patriotism because people go to war for patriotic reasons is like condemning love because some loves lead to murder.

It is one of the great mysteries—or perhaps I should say it is one of the reliable reminders of human imperfection—that higher education often fosters a particular form of political stupidity. Scruton anatomizes that stupidity, noting "the educated derision that has been directed at our national loyalty by those whose freedom to criticize would have been extinguished years ago, had the English not been prepared to die for their country." This peculiar mental deformation, Scruton observes, involves "the repudiation of inheritance and home." It is a stage, he writes,

> through which the adolescent mind normally passes. But it is a stage in which intellectuals tend to become

> arrested. As George Orwell pointed out, intellectuals on the Left are especially prone to it, and this has often made them willing agents of foreign powers. The Cambridge spies [Guy Burgess, Kim Philby, and others] offer a telling illustration of what [this tendency] has meant for our country.

It is also telling that this déformation professionelle of intellectuals encourages them to repudiate patriotism as an atavistic passion and favor transnational institutions over national governments, rule by committee or the courts over democratic rule. Rabkin reminds us of the naïveté—what others have called the "idealism"—that this preference requires. In order to believe that international bodies will protect human rights, for example, you would have to believe

> that governments readily cooperate with other governments on common projects, even when such cooperation promises no direct exchange of benefits to each side. In the end, you must believe that human beings cooperate easily and naturally without much constraint—without much actual enforcement, hence without much need for force.
>
> To believe this you must believe that almost all human beings are well-meaning, even to strangers. And you must believe that human beings have no very serious disagreements on fundamental matters.

The persistence of such beliefs is no guide to their cogency or truth. What another Jeremy, Jeremy Bentham, long ago called "nonsense on stilts" presents a spectacle that is perhaps unsteady but nonetheless mesmerizing. And when it comes to the erosion of the nation-state and its gradual replacement by unaccountable, transnational entities such as the E.U., the U.N., or the so-called "World Court," the results are ominous.

The political tendency of such institutions was brilliantly captured by John Fonte's coinage "transnational progressivism." As Fonte explains in his book *Sovereignty or Submission: Will Americans Rule Themselves or Be Ruled by Others?* (2011), "transnational progressivism" describes the antinationalist impulse that seeks to transfer political power and decision-making "from democratic nations to supranational authorities and institutions" such as the European Union, the United Nations, the World Bank, the International Monetary Fund, and kindred organizations ("judges from the European Court of Human Rights and the International Criminal Court; career officials in the U.S. State Department, the British Foreign Office, and the German Foreign Ministry; American CEOs of major global corporations; NGOs such as Amnesty International, Human Rights Watch, and Greenpeace"; and so on and so forth).

A sterling contemporary example is the Great Reset recently proposed by the Davos-based WEF, which seeks "to revamp all aspects of our societies and economies, from education to social contracts and working conditions." Exploiting the panic caused by the Covid-19 crisis, the WEF demands that "every country, from the United States to China, must participate, and every industry, from oil and gas to tech, must be transformed" in its socialist scheme to bring about a "Great Reset of capitalism."

The true political ends of such elite enterprises are generally swaddled in emollient rhetoric about freedom and democracy. Thus the PR surrounding the WEF's Great Reset is festooned with talk of "stakeholder capitalism," "equality," "sustainability," and other items in the lexicon of socialistically oriented political obfuscation.

The real agenda, however, is revealed in its call for "changes," i.e., increases in taxes on wealth, a turn away from reliance on fossil fuels, and "building 'green' urban infrastructure and creating incentives for industries to improve their track record on environmental, social, and governance (ESG) metrics." Stepping back, John Fonte uncovered some revelatory gems that speak candidly about what's really at stake. For example, Robert Kagan of the Brookings Institution put it with all possible clarity when he declared in 2008 that the "United States... should not oppose, but welcome a world of *pooled and diminished national sovereignty*" (my emphasis). "Pooled and diminished national sovereignty." At least we know where we stand.

The question of sovereignty—of who governs—is at the center of all contemporary populist initiatives. It has been posed with increasing urgency as the bureaucratic burden of what has been called the "deep state" or administrative state has weighed more and more forcefully upon the political and social life of Western democracies.

The phenomenon is often identified with the election of Donald Trump in November 2016 and his candidacy in 2020. But the political, moral, and social realities for which Trump was a symbol and a conduit both predated his candidacy and achieved independent reality in countries as disparate as the United Kingdom, Hungary, Italy, and Brazil.

The question of sovereignty was perhaps most dramatically posed in the United Kingdom. In June 2016, more Brits voted to leave the European Union and return sovereignty to Parliament than had ever voted for any initiative in the long history of Great Britain. Some seventeen million people voted to leave the European Union and regain local responsibility for their own lives. That's more people than had ever voted for anything in Britain. It took more than three years for that promissory note to be cashed. The U.K. formally began its split from the E.U. at 11 p.m. GMT on 31 January 2020. Like the Battle of Waterloo according to the Duke of Wellington, it was a "near run thing." Prime Minister Boris Johnson promised that he would, deal or no deal, get Brexit done by the end of October 2019. He was stymied for months, as much by the established elites of his own party as by Labour.

The process of emancipation had not proceeded far before it was interrupted by the advent of a new Chinese import, the novel coronavirus which swept all other news from the front page for months (until, that is, it was half-superseded by the extortionist Kabuki theater of "Black Lives Matter"). As I write in the summer of 2021, Europe and the United States both are poised to return to a state of state-enforced semihibernation or "lockdown," an insidious flu-like respiratory virus created in a Chinese virology lab having paralyzed their populations with fear and transported their governments with the tantalizing prospect of greater control over every aspect of life.

I am not sure I have ever heard Joe Biden utter the word "sovereignty." But Donald Trump spoke about it often. In his first speech to the United Nations' General Assembly in September 2017, he said to a startled roomful of diplomats that "we are renewing this founding principle of sovereignty."

> Our government's first duty is to its people, to our citizens—to serve their needs, to ensure their safety, to preserve their rights, and to defend their values. As President of the United States, I will always put America first, just like you, as the leaders of your countries will always, and should always, put your countries first.
>
> All responsible leaders have an obligation to serve their own citizens, and the nation-state remains the best vehicle for elevating the human condition.

Perhaps the most disturbing aspect of that speech was the shocked horror that it provoked among the entrenched globalist establishment for whom the whole idea of nation-states and patriotic allegiance to one's country seems like a barbaric affront to common decency. Imagine, a president of the United States declaring his intention to foster the well-being and prosperity of his own citizens!

A second key question, and one related to the issue of sovereignty, concerns what Lincoln called "public sentiment": the widespread, almost taken-for-granted yet nonetheless palpable affirmation by a people of their national identity.

Trump's slogan "America First" instantly became an object of contempt, ridicule, and hatred to the Left, to the Never Trump Right, and to the entrenched bureaucracy of the administrative state. But it is worth reminding ourselves that before the progressive movement that began with Woodrow Wilson, no one would have talked about an American initiative being grounded in an "America-first" attitude because it would have been simply assumed that an American endeavor would naturally put America first. From the presidency of George Washington through that of Teddy Roosevelt, an assumption of "America first" was simply taken for granted. Indeed, the phrase, as the political commentator Angelo Codevilla noted, "may be the most succinct description of George Washington's statecraft." By telling his fellow citizens that "the name of American, which belongs to you, in your national capacity, must always exalt the just pride of Patriotism, more than any appellation," Washington articulated the essence of Trump's slogan avant la lettre.

Increasingly, the pillars of that consensus—the binding realities of family, religion, civic duty, and patriotic filiation—have faltered before the blandishments of the globalist juggernaut. Today, the nation-state, that territory-based network of commitment bound together through shared history, custom, law, and language, is under greater siege than at any time since the dissolution of the Roman Empire. The external threat of radical Islam was not much in the headlines during the Trump administration, but the collapse of the American nation-building effort in Afghanistan and resurgence of the Taliban reminds us that it remains one of the greatest dangers to Western civilization since 1571 when the Battle of Lepanto checked the incursion of what we used to call the paynim foe into Europe. Other external threats include a newly emboldened and militarized China and a saber-rattling Russia. But in the end, perhaps the greatest threat to the West lies not in its external enemies, no matter how hostile or numerous, but in its inner uncertainty—an uncertainty that is all-too-often celebrated as an especially enlightened form of subtlety and sophistication—about who we are.

The attack on the nation-state—a less orotund formulation might say our unwitting self-demolition—proceeds apace on several fronts. As always, an illuminating clue to the reality of our situation is afforded by the rhetoric we employ. It is curious how certain words accumulate a nimbus of positive associations while others, semantically just as innocuous, wind up shouldering a portfolio of bad feelings.

Consider the different careers of the terms "democracy" and "populism."

Do you know any responsible person who would admit to being opposed to democracy? No one who does not enjoy a large private income would risk it. But lots of people are willing to declare themselves antipopulist. The discrepancy is curious for several reasons.

For one thing, it is a testament to the almost Darwinian hardiness of the word "democracy." In the fierce struggle among ideas for survival, "democracy" has not only survived but thrived. This is despite the fact that political thinkers from Plato and Aristotle through Cicero and down to modern times have been deeply suspicious of democracy. Aristotle thought democracy the worst form of government, all but inevitably leading to ochlocracy or mob rule, which is no rule.

In *Federalist*, no. 10, James Madison famously warned that history had shown that democratic regimes have "in general been as short in their lives as they have been violent in their deaths." "Theoretic politicians," he wrote—and it would be hard to find a more contemptuous deployment of the word "theoretic"—may have advocated democracy, but that is only because of their dangerous and utopian ignorance of human nature. It was not at all clear, Madison thought, that democracy was a reliable custodian of liberty.

Nevertheless, nearly everyone wants to associate himself with the word "democracy." Totalitarian regimes like to describe themselves as the "democratic republic" of wherever. Conservatives champion the advantages of "democratic capitalism." Central planners of all stripes eagerly deploy programs advertised as enhancing or extending "democracy." Even James Madison came down on the side of a subspecies of democracy, one filtered through the modulating influence of a large, diverse population and an elaborate scheme of representation that attenuated (Madison said "excluded") the influence of "the people in their collective capacity."

"Democracy," in short, is a eulogistic word, what the practical philosopher Stephen Potter in another context apostrophized as an "OK word." And it is worth noting, as Potter would have been quick to remind us, that the people pronouncing those eulogies delight in advertising themselves as and are generally accepted as "OK people." Indeed, the class element and the element of moral approbation—of what some genius has summarized as "virtue signaling"—are key.

It is quite otherwise with "populism." At first blush, this seems odd because the word "populism" occupies a semantic space adjacent to "democracy." "Democracy" means "rule by the demos," the people. "Populism," according to *The American Heritage Dictionary*, describes "A political philosophy directed to the needs of the common people and advancing a more equitable distribution of wealth and power"—that is, just the sorts of things that the people, were they to rule, would seek.

Still, the fact is that "populism" is ambivalent at best. Sometimes, a charismatic figure can survive and even illuminate the label "populist" like a personal halo. Bernie Sanders managed this trick among the eco-conscious, racially sensitive, nongender-stereotyping, anticapitalist beneficiaries of capitalism who made up his core constituency. But it was always my impression that in this case the term "populist" was fielded less by Sanders or his followers than by his rivals and the media in an effort to fix him in the public's mind as one of the many lamentable examples of not-Hillary, who herself was presumed to be popular though not populist.

There are at least two sides to the negative association under which the term "populist" struggles. On the one hand, there is the issue of demagoguery. Some commentators tell us that "populist" and "demagogue" are essentially synonyms (though they rarely point out that demagogos simply meant "a popular leader," e.g., Pericles). The association of demagoguery and populism describes what we might call the command-and-control aspect of populism. The populist leader is said to forsake reason and moderation in order to stir the dark, chthonic passions of a semiliterate and spiritually unelevated populace.

Consider, to take but one example, how often the word "anger" and its cognates are deployed to evoke the psychological and moral failings of both the populist multitude and its putative leaders. In a remarkable, apocalyptic effusion published in the early hours of November 9, 2016, David Remnick, the editor of the *New Yorker*, warned that the Trump presidency represented "a rebellion against liberalism itself," an "angry assault" on women's, black people's, immigrants,' homosexuals,' and countless others' civil rights. Later commentators warned about our "angry, cynical times," the "raw, angry and aggrieved" tone of Trump's rhetoric, the unchaperoned "anger" of Americans who felt they "had been left behind." CNN dilated on how "Trump's Anger Could Lead Down a Dangerous Road," while *The Washington Post* promised to take its readers "Inside Trump's Anger and Impatience" and the *New York Times* endeavored to explain "How Festering Anger at Comey Ended in His Firing."

There were occasional acknowledgments that the diagnosed "anger" was understandable, even justified. But we were left with the unmistakable impression that the phenomenon as a whole was something vicious and irrational. Anger "festers." It leads to "sudden," (i.e., impulsive) decisions. The road it steers us toward could be "dangerous." (Again, how cheap is possibility! When we read that "could be" dangerous, do we also think, as we should, that it might just as well not be?)

Populism, in short, seems incapable of escaping the association with demagoguery and moral darkness. Like the foul-smelling wounds of Philoctetes, the stench is apparently incurable. Granted, there are plenty of historical reasons for the association between demagoguery and populism, as such names as the brothers Tiberius and Gaius Gracchus, Father Coughlin, Huey Long, and others even more benighted remind us.

Still, I suspect that in the present context the apparently unbreakable association between populism and demagoguery has less to do with any natural affinity than with cunning rhetorical weaponization. "Populism," that is to say, is wielded less as a descriptive than as a delegitimizing term. Successfully charge someone with populist sympathies and you get, free and for nothing, both the imputation of demagoguery and what was famously derided as a "deplorable" and "irredeemable" cohort. The element of existential depreciation is almost palpable.

So is the element of condescension. Inseparable from the diagnosis of populism is the implication not just of incompetence but also of a crudity that is part aesthetic and part moral. Hence the curiously visceral distaste expressed by elite opinion for signs of populist sympathy. When Hillary Clinton charged that half of Donald Trump's supporters were an "irredeemable" "basket of deplorables," when Barack Obama castigated small-town Republican voters as "bitter" folk who "cling to guns or religion or antipathy to people who aren't like them or anti-immigrant sentiment or anti-trade sentiment," what they expressed was not disagreement but condescending revulsion.

I think I first became aware that the charge of populist sympathies could have a powerful political, moral, and class delegitimizing effect when I was in London to cover the Brexit vote in 2016. Nearly everyone I met, from Tory ministers to taxi drivers, from tourists to tradesmen, was a Remainer. The higher up the income and class scale you went, the more likely it was that your interlocutor would be in favor of Britain's remaining in the European Union. And the more pointed would be his disparagement of those arguing in favor of Brexit. The Brexiteers were said to be "angry," yes, but also ignorant, fearful, xenophobic, and racist.

Except that they weren't, not the ones I met, anyway. For them, Brexit turned on that simple question I raised earlier: "Who governs?" Is the ultimate source of British sovereignty Parliament, as had been the case for centuries? Or is it Brussels, seat of the European Union? This brings us back to the question of sovereignty, which takes us to the heart of what in recent years has been touted and tarred as the populist project.

Consider Britain. Parliament answers to the British voters. The European Union answers to, well, itself. Indeed, it is worth pausing to remind ourselves how profoundly undemocratic the European Union is. Its commissioners are appointed, not elected. They meet in secret. They cannot be turned out of office by voters. If the public votes contrary to the wishes of the E.U.'s commissars in a referendum, they are simply presented with another referendum until they vote the "right" way. The E.U.'s financial books have never been subject to a public audit. The corruption is just too widespread. Yet the E.U.'s agents wield extraordinary power over the everyday lives of their charges. A commissioner in Brussels can tell a property owner in Wales what sort of potatoes he may plant on his farm, how he must calculate the weight of the products he sells, and whom he must allow into his country. He can outlaw "racism" and "xenophobia"—defined as harboring "an aversion" to people based on "race, colour, descent, religion or belief, national or ethnic origin" and specify a penalty of "at least" two years' imprisonment for infractions. He can "lawfully suppress," as the London *Telegraph* reported, "political criticism of its institutions and of leading figures," thus rendering the commissars of the E.U. not only beyond the vote but also beyond criticism.

It's a little different in the United States. I'll come to that below. At the moment, it is worth noting to what extent the metabolism of this political dispensation was anticipated by Alexis de Tocqueville in his famous passages about "democratic despotism" in *Democracy in America*. Unlike despotism of yore, Tocqueville noted, this modern allotrope does not tyrannize over man—it infantilizes him. And it does this by promulgating ever more cumbersome rules and regulations that reach into the interstices of everyday life to hamper initiative, stymie independence, stifle originality, homogenize individuality. This power, said Tocqueville, "extends its arms over society as a whole."

> It does not break wills, but it softens them, bends them, and directs them; it rarely forces one to act, but it constantly opposes itself to one's acting; it does not destroy, it prevents things from being born; it does not tyrannize, it hinders, compromises, enervates, extinguishes, dazes, and finally reduces each nation

> to being nothing more than a herd of timid and industrious animals of which the government is the shepherd.

Tocqueville's analysis has led many observers to conclude that the villain in this drama is the state. But the political philosopher James Burnham, writing in the early 1940s in *The Managerial Revolution*, saw that the real villain was not the state as such but the bureaucracy that maintained and managed it. It is easy to mock the apparatchiks who populate the machinery of government. But the comic potential of the morass should not blind us to the minatory nature of the phenomenon. Indeed, it presents a specimen case of the general truth that the preposterous and the malevolent often comingle. The shepherd of which Tocqueville wrote was really a flock of shepherds, a coterie of managers who, in the guise of doing the state's business, prosecuted their own advantage and gradually became a self-perpetuating elite that arrogated to itself power over the levers of society.

At this point, expanding "free markets" no longer has anything to do with classical American capitalism. It is simply the further emancipation of the managerial elite from any obligations to the political community. Likewise, promoting democracy as an abstract, universalist principle only undermines the sovereignty of the American people by rejecting national interests as a legitimate ground of foreign policy. Sovereignty, Burnham saw, was shifting from Parliaments to what he called "administrative bureaus," which increasingly are the seats of real power and, as such, "proclaim the rules, make the laws, issue the decrees."

As far back as the early 1940s, Burnham could write that "'Laws' today in the United States…are not being made any longer by Congress, but by the NLRB, SEC, ICC, AAA, TVA, FTC, FCC, the Office of Production Management (what a revealing title!), and the other leading "executive agencies." Note that Burnham wrote decades before the advent of the EPA, HUD, CFPB, FSOC, the Department of Education, and the rest of the administrative alphabet soup that governs us in the United States today. As the economist Charles

Calomiris points out in his short but important book *Reforming Financial Regulation After Dodd-Frank* (2017), we are increasingly governed not by laws but by ad hoc diktats emanating from semi-autonomous and largely unaccountable quasi-governmental bureaucracies, many of which meet in secret but whose proclamations have the force of law.

I am convinced that the issue of sovereignty, of what we might call the location of sovereignty, has played a large role in the rise of the phenomenon we describe as "populism" in the United States as well as Europe. For one thing, the question of sovereignty, of who governs, stands behind the rebellion against the political correctness and moral meddlesomeness that are such conspicuous and disfiguring features of our increasingly bureaucratic society. The smothering, Tocquevillian blanket of regulatory excess has had a wide range of practical and economic effects, stifling entrepreneurship and making any sort of productive innovation difficult.

But perhaps its deepest effects are spiritual or psychological. The many assaults against free speech on college campuses, the demand for "safe spaces" and "trigger warnings" against verbal or fashion-inspired "micro-aggressions" (Mexican hats, "offensive" Halloween costumes, and the like) are part of this dictatorship of political correctness. In *The Road to Serfdom*, Friedrich Hayek said that one of the "main points" of his argument concerned "the psychological change," the "alteration of the character of the people," that "extensive government control" brought in its wake. The alteration involves a process of softening, enervation, infantilization even: an exchange of the challenges of liberty and self-reliance—the challenges, that is to say, of adulthood—for the coddling pleasures of dependence. Max Weber spoke in this context of "ordnungsmenschen," men who had become increasingly dependent on an order imposed upon them from above. Breaking with that drift becomes more and more difficult the more habituated to dependence a people become. In this sense, what has been described as a populist upsurge against political correctness is simply a reassertion of independence, a reclamation of what turns out to be a most uncommon virtue: common sense.

The question of sovereignty also stands behind the debate over immigration: indeed, is any issue more central to the question "Who governs?" than who gets to decide a nation's borders and how a country defines its first-person plural: the "We" that makes us who we are as a people?

Throughout his 2016 and 2020 campaigns, Donald Trump promised to enforce America's immigration laws, to end so-called "sanctuary cities," which advertise themselves as safe havens for illegal aliens (though of course they do not call them "illegal aliens"), and to sharpen vetting procedures for people wishing to immigrate to America from countries known as sponsors of terrorism.

Trump sometimes overstated and not infrequently misstated his case. Semantic precision is not a Trumpian specialty. But political effectiveness was. Behind the Sturm und Drang that greeted Trump's rhetoric on immigration, we glimpsed two very different concepts of the nation-state and world order. One view sees the world as a collection of independent sovereign countries that, although interacting with one another, each regard the care, safety, and prosperity of their citizens as their first obligation. This is the traditional view of the nation-state. It was also Donald Trump's view. It is what licensed all his talk of putting "America First," a concept that, *pace* the anti-Trump media, has nothing to do with Charles Lindbergh's isolationist movement of the late 1930s and everything to do with fostering a healthy sense of national identity and purpose.

The alternative view regards the nation-state with suspicion as an atavistic form of political and social organization. The nation-state might still be a practical necessity, but, the argument goes, it is a regrettable necessity inasmuch as it retards mankind's emancipation from the parochial bonds of place and local allegiance. Ideally, according to this view, we are citizens of the world, not particular countries, and our fundamental obligation is to all mankind.

This is the progressive view. It has many progenitors and antecedents. But none is more influential than "Perpetual Peace: A Philosophical Sketch," a brief essay that Immanuel Kant published in 1795 when he was seventy-one. The burden of the essay is to ask how perpetual peace might be obtained among states. The natural condition of mankind, Kant acknowledges, is war. But with the advent of "enlightened concepts of statecraft," mankind, he suggests, may be able to transcend that unfortunate habit of making war and live in perpetual (ewigen) comity.

Kant lists various conditions for the initial establishment of peace—the eventual abolition of standing armies, for example—and a few conditions for its perpetuation: the extension of "universal hospitality" by nations was something that caught my eye. Ditto "world citizenship." "The idea of...world citizenship," he says at the end of the essay, "is no high-flown or exaggerated notion. It is a supplement to the unwritten code of the civil and international law, indispensable for the maintenance of the public human rights and hence also of perpetual peace."

Kant makes many observations along the way that are a balm to progressive hearts. He is against "the accumulation of treasure," for example, because wealth is "a hindrance to perpetual peace." By the same token, he believes that forbidding the system of international credit that the British empire employed "must be a preliminary article of perpetual peace." Credit can be deployed to increase wealth, ergo it is suspect. Kant says that all states must be "republican" in organization. By that, he means not that they must be democracies but only that the executive and legislative functions of the state be distinguished. (Indeed, he says that democracy, "properly speaking," is "necessarily a despotism" because in it the executive and legislative functions of governments are both vested in one entity, "the people.") He looks forward to the establishment of a "league of nations" (Völkerbund), all of which would freely embrace a republican form of government.

It would be hard to overstate the influence of Kant's essay. It stands behind such progressive exfoliations as Woodrow Wilson's

"Fourteen Points," not least the final point that looked forward to the establishment of a League of Nations. You can feel its pulse beating in the singing phrases of the 1928 Kellogg-Briand Pact, which outlawed war. It is worth noting that among the initial fifteen signatories of that noble-sounding pact, along with the United States, France, and England, were Germany, Italy, and Japan. What does that tell us about the folly of trusting paper proclamations not backed up by the authority of physical force? It is one thing to declare war illegal; it is quite another to enforce that edict.

Kant's essay also directly inspired the architects of the United Nations and, in our own day, the architects of the European Union and the battalions of transnational progressives who jettison democracy for the sake of a more or less nebulous (but not therefore noncoercive) ideal of world citizenship.

I would not care to wager on how many of the hysterics who congregated at airports across the country to protest Donald Trump's effort to make the citizens of this country safer were students of Kant. Doubtless very few. But all were his unwitting heirs. "Universal hospitality": how the protestors would have liked that! (Though to be fair to Kant, he did note that such hospitality "is not the right to be a permanent visitor.") I have no doubt that the protestors had many sources of motivation. But to the extent that such protests were based on a political ideal (and not just partisan posturing or a grubby bid for notoriety and power), the spirit of Kant was hovering in the background.

Kant was not without a sense of humor. He begins his essay by noting that he took his title from a sign outside a Dutch pub. "Pax Perpetua" read the sign, and below the lettering was the image of a graveyard. Perhaps the universal perpetuity of death is the only peace that mankind may really look forward to. Kant clearly wouldn't agree, but it was charming of him to acknowledge that the idea of a genuine perpetual peace for mankind might be regarded by many as nothing more than a "sweet dream" of philosophers.

What has been called the populist spirit aims to rouse us from that "sweet dream"—what James Madison might have called the "theoretic" reverie of the meddling class whose designs for our salvation always seem to involve the extension of their own power and prerogative. In this sense, the issue of sovereignty also stands behind the debates over the relative advantages and moral weather of "globalism" versus "nationalism"—a pair of terms almost as fraught as "democracy" and "populism"—as well as the correlative economic issues of underemployment and wage stagnation. "Theoretic" politicians may advocate "globalism" as a necessary condition for free trade. But the spirit of local control tempers the cosmopolitan project of a borderless world with a recognition that the nation-state has been the best guarantor not only of sovereignty but also of broadly shared prosperity. What we might call the ideology of free trade—the globalist aspiration to transcend the impediments of national identity and control—is an abstraction that principally benefits its architects. As R. R. Reno, the editor of *First Things*, pointed out in *The New York Times*, "Globalism poses a threat to the future of democracy because it disenfranchises the vast majority and empowers a technocratic elite."

In the end, what James Burnham described as the "managerial revolution" is part of a larger progressive project. This project is designed in part to emancipate mankind from such traditional sources of self-definition as national identity, religious affiliation, and specific cultural rootedness, partly to perpetuate and aggrandize the apparatus that oversees the resulting dissolution. Burnham castigates this hypertrophied form of liberalism (what we might call "illiberal liberalism") as "an ideology of suicide" that has insinuated itself into the center of Western culture. He acknowledges that the proposition may sound hyperbolic. "Suicide," he notes, may seem "too emotive a term, too negative and 'bad.'" But it is part of the pathology that Burnham describes that such objections are "most often made most hotly by Westerners who hate their own civilization, readily excuse or even praise blows struck against it, and themselves lend a willing hand, frequently enough, to pulling it down." The issue, Burnham saw, is that modern liberalism has equipped us with an ethic too abstract and empty to inspire real commitment. Modern liberalism, he writes:

> ...does not offer ordinary men compelling motives for personal suffering, sacrifice, and death. There is no tragic dimension in its picture of the good life. Men become willing to endure, sacrifice, and die for God, for family, king, honor, country, from a sense of absolute duty or an exalted vision of the meaning of history....
>
> And it is precisely these ideas and institutions that liberalism has criticized, attacked, and in part overthrown as superstitious, archaic, reactionary, and irrational. In their place liberalism proposes a set of pale and bloodless abstractions—pale and bloodless for the very reason that they have no roots in the past, in deep feeling and in suffering. Except for mercenaries, saints, and neurotics, no one is willing to sacrifice and die for progressive education, medicare, humanity in the abstract, the United Nations, and a ten percent rise in Social Security payments.

In Burnham's view, the primary function of liberalism was to "permit Western civilization to be reconciled to dissolution," to view weakness, failure, even collapse not as a defeat but "as the transition to a new and higher order in which Mankind as a whole joins in a universal civilization that has risen above the parochial distinctions, divisions, and discriminations of the past."

What has been called "populism" is a visceral reaction against these forces of dissolution. Around the time that Donald Trump took office, his chief strategist Steve Bannon said that his goal was to "deconstruct the administrative state." The phrase "administrative state"—also called "the regulatory state" or "the deep state"—has lately floated into common parlance. In *The Administrative Threat*, the legal scholar Philip Hamburger describes it as "a state within a state," a sort of parallel legal and political structure populated by unelected bureaucrats. This amorphous congeries of agencies and regulations has become, Hamburger argues, "the dominant reality of American governance," intruding everywhere into economic and social life.

Article I of the Constitution vests all legislative power in Congress, just as Article III vests all judicial authority in the Court. The administrative state is a mechanism for circumventing both. As such, Hamburger argues, the administrative state operates outside the Constitution. When the Constitution places all legislative powers in Congress, it gives Congress not only the power to make law but also the power to unmake it. And it thereby bars the executive from suspending or dispensing with the law. When the Constitution, moreover, places the judicial power in the courts and guarantees the due process of law, it precludes the executive from telling the courts not to apply the law and prevents the courts from abandoning their own judgment about what the law requires.

Binding citizens not through congressionally enacted statutes but through the edicts of the managerial bureaucracy, the administrative state is "all about the evasion of governance through law, including an evasion of constitutional processes and procedural rights." Accordingly, Hamburger concludes, the encroaching activity of the administrative state represents "the nation's preeminent threat to civil liberties."

Hamburger draws an analogy between the behavior of the administrative state and the behavior of such despotic monarchs as James I, Charles I, and James II. Instead of persuading Parliament to repeal or revise a statute, the British king simply evaded its force by decreeing that some or all of his subjects were not subject to its strictures. His power was absolute not merely in the sense that it was all but unlimited but also in the sense that it was independent or outside of the law. Students of Latin will recall the ablative absolute, a construction in which an ablative phrase is "absolutum," "loosened" from or independent of the main clause of a sentence. Hamburger shows how the growth of the administrative state represents an extralegal "revival of absolute power" in this sense, one that threatens to transform Constitutional rights and guarantees into mere "options" that the government bestows or withholds at its pleasure. "The evasion," he notes, "thereby changes the very nature of procedural rights. Such rights traditionally were assurances against the government. Now they are but one of the choices for government in its exercise of power. Though the government must respect these rights when it proceeds against Americans in court, it has the freedom to escape them by taking an administrative path."

Just as British kings in the seventeenth century evaded Parliament through such expedients as the Star Chamber and the exercise of royal prerogatives and royal waivers—what John Adams castigated as "those badges of domination called prerogatives"—so the administrative state today operates in violation of the Constitution and beyond the authority of Congress. Barack Obama decreed that certain politically unpalatable provisions of the Affordable Care Act not be enforced, and presto, they were not enforced, even though they were the law of the land. He instructed his Department of Justice to intervene to prevent Arizona and other states from enforcing certain aspects of immigration law. He even forced public institutions to accommodate self-declared "transgender" persons in the toilets of their choice; he connived with lawsuits punishing bakers and Catholic hospitals and hobby shops who chose not to join this week's politically correct campaign for the sexually exotic. The Constitution may have vested all legislative power in Congress and entrusted all judicial power to the courts, but the administrative state sidesteps those requirements by erecting a parallel bureaucratic structure of enforcement and control.

"Eighteenth-century Americans," Hamburger notes, "assumed that a rule could have the obligation of law only if it came from the constitutionally established legislature elected by the people." Today, Americans find their lives directed by a jumble of agencies far removed from the legislature and staffed by bureaucrats who make and enforce a vast network of rules that govern nearly every aspect of our lives.

One of the most disturbing aspects of Hamburger's analysis is the historical connection he exposes between the expansion of the franchise in the early twentieth century and the growth of administrative, that is to say, extralegal, power. For the people in charge, equality of voting rights was one thing. They could live with that. But the tendency of newly enfranchised groups—the "bitter clingers" and "deplorables" of yore—to reject progressive initiatives was something else again. As Woodrow Wilson noted sadly, "The bulk of mankind is rigidly unphilosophical, and nowadays the bulk of mankind votes." What to do?

The solution was to shift real power out of elected bodies and into the hands of the right sort of people, enlightened people, progressive people, people, that is to say, like Woodrow Wilson. Therefore, Wilson welcomed the advent of administrative power as a counterweight to encroaching democratization. And thus it was, as Hamburger points out, that we have seen a transfer of legislative power to the "knowledge class," the managerial elite that James Burnham anatomized.

A closer look at the so-called "knowledge class" shows that what it knows best is how to preserve and extend its own privileges. Its activities are swaddled in do-gooder rhetoric about serving the public, looking after "the environment," helping the disadvantaged, and similar performative kindness, but what they chiefly excel at is consolidating and extending their own power.

In *Thoughts on the Cause of the Present Discontents* (1770), Edmund Burke criticized the Court of George III for circumventing Parliament and establishing by stealth what amounted to a new regime of royal prerogative and influence-peddling. It was not as patent as the swaggering courts of James I or Charles I. George and his courtiers maintained the appearance of parliamentary supremacy. But a closer look showed that the system was corrupt. "It was soon discovered," Burke wrote with sly understatement, "that the forms of a free, and the ends of an arbitrary Government, were things not altogether incompatible." That discovery stands behind the growth of the administrative state. We still vote. We still have a bicameral legislature. But behind these forms of a free government, the essentially undemocratic activities of an increasingly arbitrary and unaccountable regime pursue an expansionist agenda that threatens liberty in the most comprehensive way, by circumventing the law.

At the same time, however, a growing recognition of the totalitarian goals of the administrative state has fed what many have called a populist uprising here and in Europe. "Populist" is one word for the phenomenon. A reaffirmation of sovereignty, underwritten by a passion for freedom, is another, possibly more accurate, phrase.

The intellectual historian Jacob Talmon was onto something deep, I believe, when he identified "the paradox of freedom" as the recognition that freedom is unfree so long as it is wed to "an exclusive pattern of social existence, even if this pattern aims at the maximum of social justice and security." The key is this: do we take "men as they are" and look to politics to work from there? Or do we insist upon treating men "as they were meant to be, and would be, given the proper conditions"?

The former describes the traditional, genuinely liberal view of freedom. The latter describes what Talmon calls "totalitarian democracy." As I suggested earlier, a classic source for the latter view is Jean-Jacques Rousseau. In *The Social Contract*, Rousseau says that anyone who would "dare to undertake the institution of a government must think himself capable, as it were, of *changing human nature*" (my emphasis).

Contrast that hubristic ambition with James Madison's acknowledgment, in *Federalist* no. 10, that different men have different and competing interests and that the "first object" of government is to protect those differences and the "diversity in the faculties" whence they arise.

The real battle that has been joined—and it is a battle that is in the process of forging a great political realignment—is not between virtuous progressive knights riding the steeds of liberalism, on the one hand, and the atavistic forces of supposedly untutored darkness represented by "populism" on the other.

No, the real battle is between two views of liberty. One is a parochial view that affirms tradition, local affection, and the subordination of politics to the ordinary business of life. It is a view that looks to the nation-state as the primary guarantor of its rights.

The other view of liberty is more ambitious but also more abstract. It seeks nothing less than to boost us all up to that plane of enlightenment from which all self-interested actions look petty, if not criminal, and through which mankind as a whole (but not, alas, individual men, who hardly matter in this calculus) may hope for whatever salvation secularism leavened by utilitarianism may provide. The Great Reset proposed by the WEF represents a textbook example of the genre. It is worth noting in this context that the seductive pressure of millenarian ideology also propels the curious spectacle of "woke" radicalism according to which everything is susceptible to the demands of what the journalist Gavin Haynes has called a "purity spiral." You can never be revolutionary enough, sufficiently green, or fervid enough in your "anti-racism," comrade.

We are still in the opening sallies of the Great Realignment. Many old alliances are being broken, many new ones formed. The forces marshalled by entities like the WEF and the spirit of the politically correct administrative apparatus are formidable. But the spirit of local liberty is far from vanquished. I expect a lot of heat, and even more smoke. I hope that there will also be at least occasional flashes of light.

RESETTING THE EDUCATIONAL RESET

BY ANGELO M. CODEVILLA

In 2020, the self-proclaimed "key global governmental and business leaders" who meet yearly in Davos, Switzerland, issued a statement that "the Covid-19 crisis" showed the "inconsistencies, inadequacies and contradictions of multiple systems—from health and financial to energy and education." From this, there ensued "global context of concern for lives, livelihoods and the planet." The statement promises to answer this through a "Great Reset Initiative." By that initiative the authors intend to change "the direction of national economies, the priorities of societies, the nature of business models and the management of a global commons." This is to result, no less, in "a new social contract that honours the dignity of every human being."

By, of, for Whom? And for What?

The "initiative" does not say what the "inconsistencies, inadequacies and contradictions" under which Western health economics, and education have been laboring, how or what the Covid-19 episode taught us about them, whose is the "global context of concern," what that concern and that context might be, how alleged problems ought to be remedied, or what these words might mean. It does not argue for specific measures because it is not about convincing. Instead, it is an attempt to induce, cajole, perhaps force nonstakeholders (i.e., ordinary people), into letting their lives be reordered according to the stakeholders' judgment. That judgment's basis is these very stakeholders' claim that the Covid affair showed Western civilization's failings, and that they know better ways to improve efficiency and enhance dignity. Their authority lies solely in their claim to authority.

They claim to act on behalf of "a global multi-stakeholder network," meaning such as Bill Gates and George Soros, Jamie Dimon, and other corporate and governmental figures. But mostly the initiative is by, of, and for whomever hungers for a touch of all that coolness, power, and money.

Least of all does the initiative argue why these prominent persons should have any right to change the way we live, or why anyone should follow them. Its boldness and lack of foundation may be exceeded only by the authors' chutzpah.

Chutzpah, because the initiative's authors—the lords of Davos—are themselves chiefly responsible for turning a virus with an overall infection/fatality rate well within the range of ordinary flus, into a catastrophe for billions of people. Covid-19's dire effects came almost exclusively because the government, business and educational leaders, stakeholders, and others of the sort who meet at Davos propagated and weaponized a patent untruth—that the virus is some sort of plague—while knowing and hiding the truth. To promote their own self-interest in power, they lied, causing havoc, pain, and death. Their guilt is very great indeed.

The initiative's claim to represent something new tops off its fraud. In fact, its august personages have been increasing their near-total control of public life in the West over the past half century. In every field of endeavor, they have set the tone and the reigning priorities. Hence the Great Reset, far from a proposal for new ways of living, is an attempt to tighten Davos Man's grip on our lives and to foreclose alternatives to the way of life that they have been in the process of imposing on us, and that the rest of us are now stubbornly rejecting.

Education tops the list of the aspects of public life with which Americans are dissatisfied. The Covid affair contributed to the dissatisfaction by forcing millions to become acquainted with what happens in K–12 classrooms. College students' exclusion from campuses also has led Americans to question as never before how important their sons and daughters actually being there really is.

The closer one looks at education today, the more one sees that the dumbing down and perversion of America to which people object most strongly is the continuation of a century-old decay in our civilization. Problems with education bespeak civilizational ones, of which the phenomenon of Davos Man is but one manifestation.

Education Feeds Civilization

Any civilization is the totality of the language, habits and ideas in which people live and move—the human reality that defines their practical limits. To see how grossly unequal to one another civilizations are, it is enough to glance at how much or little understanding of reality the languages they speak contain—what any given language enables, or not. We are accustomed to Greek, Latin, English, French, Italian, German, and other languages with their massive dictionaries full of definitions, pronouns, tenses, moods, and concepts, all tied together by grammar that flows from logic. When we speak these languages correctly, we hardly realize that we are wielding powerful tools of reason, developed over thousands of years.

Without going to any depth in the debate between the human possibilities that nature and nurture provide, enough experiments have been carried out that show that nature does not limit babies born into primitive tribes to lives near the level of quadrupeds, just as it does not endow the offspring of PhD's with high IQs. Quantification is unnecessary for us to know that much of civilization depends on the habits of body, heart, and mind into which we are civilized.

We may never have heard of Plato's prescription that the body and mind are best trained for reason by physical discipline, that the right kind of music enhances these and the wrong kind hinders it. We may no longer play musical instruments as much as earlier generations.

And yet all who are part of Western civilization carry with us, among other things, a musical heritage based on mathematics and melody that also sets us apart from other civilizations.

Aristotle tells us Westerners that our capacity to speak is for the purpose of persuading each other about right and wrong, better and worse. To do that, and so that we might not confuse one another, the words we speak and think must have well-defined relationships with reality. That is why common, matter-of-course acceptance of these meanings—embodied in dictionaries—is so essential. When asked questions about what is around us, we in our civilization answer ordinarily with yes or no, though we probably never heard that Jesus Christ told us that this is how we should. But Westerners are peculiar. When we hear Japanese and others answer plain questions not with yes or no but with the equivalent of "I hear you" and "as you please," it does not take us long to conclude that they are less interested in objective reality than they are in relative power.

And why should anyone pay less attention to relative power, to getting along with those more powerful than ourselves, than about what is true and false? We do because we believe that God created the heavens and the Earth intelligibly, and created each of us equal to one another. This is our civilization's chief peculiarity. But, like every other civilization, all its parts are subject to the ever-rolling stream of biological deaths and births. For renewal, each civilization depends on educating each successive generation.

How Education Changes Us

What, then has education been doing to our civilization? The very concept of IQ, the Stanford-Binet test, and things similar, is, as its critics argue, a cultural construct—less a measure of potential than of capacities already developed. It's no surprise that persons growing up in environments which stimulate and enable the development of human possibilities do in fact develop more of these. Some studies suggest that what each generation conveyed to the next made those generations more intellectually/morally potent than their predecessors through the early twentieth century but that this process has reversed itself over about a half century and average IQ has dropped by some fourteen points. The decline seems to have come at the top of our civilizational pyramid. Speculation about the causes is less relevant than noting the effects.

But the deepest philosophical causes are not in dispute. After Descartes's *Discourse on Method* reduced reality into something wholly comprehensible by truncating it, the very peaks of Western philosophy reversed the relationship between reality and the observer. Kant and Hegel's "idealism" is neither more nor less than the further affirmation that the mind, for its own sovereign convenience, can take possession of what it perceives. From these philosophical peaks, any number of streams of far less sophisticated thought have flowed, which effectively and explicitly place the mind's product under the sway of man's will, and hence of man's various interests.

The intellectual mechanism is straightforward: presume to abolish the objective status of what you see and presume to retake possession of what you then supposed to be reality based on what matters to you.

From Ludwig Feuerbach's injunction to worship Christianity as our own creation, to Karl Marx's assertion of sovereignty over the mind's products as "superstructural," to class interest, to Sigmund Freud's assertion of perceptions as reflections of sexuality, the main streams of latter-day high Western thought have devalued reason and reality in favor of all manner of self-indulgence. Today, colleges teach students to disparage reference to facts and logic as "logism."

Loosening our bounds to reality is attractive also because calling things by whatever names serves our immediate purpose liberates us from the hard work of understanding things not of our making and gives us the illusion of mastery over our environment. It is especially attractive to those who have power over others because it frees them from having to persuade the rest of humanity. For society's mob of lazy underperformers, pleasing the leaders is an easier way of securing one's place than competing for merit. Anyhow, intellectual/moral deterioration has ever been an easier sell than the hard acquisition of skills and virtues.

In our time, as ever, there does seem to be a natural concurrence of interest in imprecision and lack of discipline between those who are happy enough to be barbarians and the despots who naturally dominate barbarians.

Who Has Done What with Education?

In America even more than in the rest of the West, to educate meant to enable freedom. "Ye shall know the truth, and the truth shall make you free"—John 8:32. The frontier nature of much of early American society notwithstanding, this country led the world in literacy, thanks primarily to the Protestant denominations' stress on the salvific and educative effects of reading the Bible and Shakespeare.

The Revolutionary era added political incentives. By 1776, some four-fifths of white men and perhaps two-thirds of white women read the Bible and newspapers. By 1830, Horace Mann, the father of American public education, estimated that nine out of ten of his fellow citizens could read the King James Bible. Public promotion of reading the Bible would focus the nation on moral duty. Knowledge of arithmetic, geography, the body and its functions, history, and literary reasoning would enable citizens to act intelligently in private and public business. Beginning in 1836, the McGuffey grade-level readers embodied American education's emphasis on basic facts and skills. Abraham Lincoln's self-education was emblematic.

Today we read with awe and embarrassment some of the former requirements for graduating from the eighth grade to high school in Olympia, Washington, typical of the time: "Name three different ways in which a noun may be used in the nominative case, and three ways in which a noun may be used in the objective case." Also: "(a) State briefly the causes of the War of 1812. (b) Name two engagements. (c) Two prominent American Commanders." And: "Find the sum of 5/9, 5/6, 3/4, 11/36. What number diminished by 33 1/3 percent of itself equals 38?" Finally: "What and where are the following? Liverpool, Panama, Suez, Ural, Liberia, Québec, Pikes Peak, Yosemite, Danube, San Diego." Clearly, these thirteen-year-olds had been equipped to understand the world around them.

But by 1900, the progressive movement was already devaluing the inculcation of knowledge as the foundation for moral and practical independence. Led by luminaries such as John Dewey, progressive educators deemed emphasis on knowledge too restrictive of children's creativity and disapproved of competition as destructive of social cohesion. They claimed that teaching how to learn in a social environment that prized each child's self-esteem would make for better citizens. Accordingly, progressive education devalued exams and mandated promotion to all who had reached the proper age.

The Partisan Edu-state

This progressive gospel, which mixes relaxation of standards with semiconscious acceptance of modern philosophy's premises, became the standard for an educational complex of people, institutions, and practices so large and deeply rooted that it may be proper to think of it as possessing a country rather than the other way around. Aggressively partisan, having grown up largely as an arm of the Democratic Party, this wealthy class wields education as a weapon in political and social controversies.

By the 1950s, intellectual movements including Marxism, positivism, and Freudianism had already conquered much of American high culture. By then, intellectuals as a class had gained enough bureaucratic/institutional power to lead President Dwight Eisenhower, our collective republican grandfather, to warn about how their control of government money could substitute itself for free inquiry and, indeed, for freedom itself. But this class yet lacked size, wealth, and political power in the country. The Soviet Union's 1957 launch of *Sputnik 1*, the first artificial satellite, stimulated the National Defense Education

Act (NDEA), which in turn stimulated the flow of billions of dollars, changed all that.

In 1957, K–12 teaching was staffed largely by unmarried women dedicated to an honorable if underpaid profession. Higher education was administered by people whose prosperity was frugal and whose lives few envied. Only some 5 percent of Americans had college degrees, earned by hard work under demanding faculties. Regardless of its philosophical character, the edu-class was small, of modest means, unenviable, and unenvied.

The NDEA's nominal purpose was to foster militarily relevant science in colleges and universities. More on this below. Its bounty of billions, however, swelled and transformed K–12 education as well. Today, average salaries for some 3.6 million public school teachers are some $64,000 a year for nine months' work—about the same as for persons who work twelve months. In the bigger states, the average is about $90,000. School administrators, nearly a million of them, make an average of six figures. They award the contracts that add up to an average per-pupil expenditure of some $12,000. In short, educators today are a lot of people who take and dispense a lot of money and who live pleasant lives.

As budgets rose, they passed into the hands of persons less interested in education than in power. In 1930, there had been some one hundred thirty thousand school districts in America—meaning that just about every school was governed by the parents of children enrolled there. Today, for a population twice its former size, there are just one-tenth that number of governing units. If only from a strictly numerical standpoint, parental control has declined by 95 percent. Worse, effective control is exercised by the teachers' unions who play the biggest role in electing the districts' boards. The two biggest, the National Education Association and the United Federation of Teachers, boast a total of 4.5 million members. Their numbers and their (often forced) contributions make them the Democratic Party's plurality constituency.

The edu-class's principal preoccupation is hanging on to its near monopoly of K–12 classrooms. Government control of education is tighter in America than anywhere else in the West. Everywhere, governments pay for and mandate education. But whereas in places like Sweden, parents may choose to have the state pay for their children to attend the school of their choice, the people who run U.S. public schools have largely succeeded in restricting governments to pay only for schools run by themselves.

In recent years, as parental dissatisfaction with the public schools has risen, especially since the Covid panic, the balance between public and private schooling has shifted somewhat, with private schools—most of which are religious, primarily Catholic and Orthodox Jewish—now enrolling some 13 percent of K–12 students. Another 5 percent attend charter schools, which are public but under private management, and more than twice that number of potential students are on waiting lists. Homeschooling seems to have doubled to about another 5 percent. Not least, the Covid affair birthed hybrids of homeschooling and private schooling known as learning pods. Nevertheless, some three-fourths of K–12 children remain in the edu-class's grip.

Thus does the edu-class use the schools as sociopolitical weapons on matters unrelated to instruction. Simply by dictating behavior, language, and attitudes, by surrounding students with preferred symbols while banning or ridiculing others, the schools inculcate habits. Arguably, the most important of these is the sense that in a country suffused with all manner of evil, they must conform, unquestioningly, in thought, word, and deed. Each kid learns to watch his tongue and not ask too many questions lest he be shunned as a racist, sexist, religious obscurantist, and so forth. The schools' environment requires each child at least to accept, if not to champion, foolishness. That means to daily suppress their natural immune system against absurdities such as that boys can become girls and vice versa and that math is racist. Students learn the valuable practical lesson of getting along with authorities they do not try to understand.

Near monopoly also leaves the edu-class free to neglect the quality of education. Figures give some sense of how today's Americans are losing intellectual, moral, and political resemblance to earlier generations. During World War II, only 4 percent of some eighteen million draftees were illiterate. But despite (or because of?) massive expenditures on education over the subsequent two decades, 27 percent of the Vietnam War's draftees were judged functionally illiterate. In our time, the Literacy Project estimates that forty-five million Americans are that way. A third of California's fourth graders cannot read a simple sentence, and half of its high school graduates read only at that minimal level. Reading the King James Bible is beyond many if not most of today's college graduates. Today, American fifteen-year-olds rank twenty-fourth out of seventy-one countries in science and thirty-eighth in math. While 2,817 high school students scored 750 or better on each half of the SAT in 1972, by 1994 only 1,438 made this score though the test had been made easier. And as the bell curve of intellectual achievement shifts leftward, the bell curve of school grades shifts rightward. Increasingly, "A" is the default grade in America education, where even the slightest effort is crowned with the status of high intellectual achievement—"excellence," in current parlance.

Consequences

What are the practical consequences of accepting the assumption that facts and reason are "superstructural" to, or reflective of, interest? And of "scientific" propositions that must be accepted as condition of being welcomed into polite society? One of these is that persons, especially those in power, feel free to transcend the meaning of words and adopt definitions convenient to their purpose with reasonable expectation that they will be followed. Common sentiment replaces truth and falsehood. And kids are trained to do and say what is expected of them, truth notwithstanding. Among all classes and races, some 70 percent of American students report having cheated on exams or papers. This means that U.S. schools have habituated successive generations to lie for self-advancement, as well as to lie to themselves about themselves. Kids who have come to expect to be led by narratives have no trouble lying right back.

"Critical race theory" (CRT) is the latest formula by which progressive educators continue to separate students from truth. The Covid episode did in fact lay bare how widespread is acceptance of CRT among those who run the American educational system. But even on its own terms, CRT does not offer much to the student: only the single explanation that everything and anything depends on the relative racial/power standing of teacher, student, and subject matter. It is a single lesson, too easy to learn. No one should be surprised that our elite's increasing ignorance, incompetence, and corruption has led to the general population's increasing inability to follow even simple directions—never mind arguments.

A people thus miseducated can be managed only by brutal images, endlessly repeated. This has been and continues to be Davos Man's Great Reset. The progressive cure for the progressive disease is more progressivism.

Grassroots vs. Davos Man

That is why the real news about education in America is that millions of Americans are rejecting the influence of Davos Man and abandoning the hundred-year legacy of progressive education. Some 70 percent of Americans now say that they want to decide for themselves to which schools they send their kids and to which the tax money the government spends on each student's behalf should go. Clearly, parental "school choice" is fundamental to stopping and resetting the past century's reset of education. But we should not imagine that the several motivations for dissatisfaction with K–12 will lead to a general return to education as it was practiced in the West since classical times.

Most parents object to wokeness simply because it leaves their children less capable of making a living or being happy than they themselves were. Theoretically, all parents demand more verbal/mathematical skills for their children. But different sets of parents' diverse concerns are producing, and will continue to produce, changes that more or less satisfy each. Different waters will seek different levels.

Yes, the products of nonpublic education always outperform even the wealthiest suburbs' champions. No matter how standardized tests may be jiggled, they show that homeschooled kids score up to twenty percentile points above those of the wealthiest districts, and thirty higher than the national average.

Yet parents in wealthy suburbs all over the country, though theoretically friendly to math, tolerate or join wokeness because it shields their pampered offspring from competition with the products of homeschooling, religious schools, and other schools. They often share the ruling-class prejudice against what motivates homeschooling parents: religion, love of country, and cognition itself. Because they want their children admitted to the ruling class, they focus on aligning their children ever more closely to ruling class attitudes, cognition be damned.

That is why, in practice, resetting K–12 education away from the last century's great reset is about rejection of the ruling class, regardless of motive.

At this writing, the fewer than half a million students served by the classical/Christian school movement, which explicitly reaffirms Western civilization's basic principles, outperform even homeschooling. Like all private schools, the reach of schools involved in this movement is limited by parents' ability to pay and would benefit greatly from legislation that directed school spending through parents. Each passing year makes clearer that the children raised in such schools and in all manner of arrangements that draw inspiration from its sources are more potent academically and lead happier lives.

But Western civilization itself has become merely the peculiar taste of some. Civilizational perversity having made it impossible for education in America to return en masse to Horace Mann's Christianity and classics, to McGuffey's, or even to John Dewey's pragmatism, our diversity ensures that the nationwide battle for K–12 education will be waged in countless places and circumstances by persons necessarily concerned with them. Battles over higher education, on the other hand, can only be on the national level.

The Eldorado Archipelago

A glance at U.S. maps showing the distribution of various measures of wealth (housing prices, income, Whole Foods stores) shows the country dotted with islands of wealth. If one subtracts government itself—the state and national capitals—one is left pretty much with the map of modern U.S. university towns. They vote for the Democratic Party more fully and reliably than inner cities' blackest precincts.

The median home price in Princeton, New Jersey, is $1 million. In nearby Mercerville, it's $319,000. Across the country, the median price of a home in Claremont, California, home to lesser-known colleges, is $1.1 million. In nearby Covina, it's $662,000. In Kansas as a whole, the median price is $180,000. But in Manhattan, Kansas, home to the university, it is $227,000. In the state of Idaho, the typical house sells for $414,000. In Moscow, Idaho, home of Idaho State, the price is $500,000.

To those of a certain age, whose memory of college towns is one of down-at-the-heels gentility, today's glitter is a bit shocking. The figures say it should not be. In 1975, full professors earned about $25,000 a year. In 2020 the average was $145,000. But that is small change compared with the money going to college and university administrators. In 1975, there was only one administrator for every eighty-five students, and one professional staff member for every fifty. Now there is one administrator per sixty students and one professional staff member for every twenty-five. They are paid at least as much as faculty and often more. For top executives, half a million dollars is the bottom of the scale. The number of these barnacles continues to rise, especially officers and consultants for "diversity." That stream of secure income feeds every imaginable high-end service in bad times as in good. These are isles of the blessed.

Especially since undergraduate education is less like work than leisure. Up until the 1960s, up to half of undergraduate entrants "flunked out"—failed courses and were ejected after the first year. Since the seventies, nobody flunks out because few ever fail courses even though higher education asks far less of them. These days, college students spend less than a third of the time studying as did their grandparents. Once upon a time, students were aspirants to knowledge, and colleges certified who had gained it and who had not; since the 1970s, students have been customers for whose money the colleges compete, hardly caring whether the students learned anything. In exchange, the colleges give four years of irresponsibility in resort-like settings. Above all, they give degrees, which used to signify intellectual achievement but now, outside the "hard sciences," are largely empty credentials.

All know that no matter who you are, the less you study, the less you learn; that schools such as Harvard and Stanford require less study than do the likes of Podunk State; and that, educational pedigree being inversely related to performance, prestige institutions are less in the business of transferring knowledge than of selling prestige. But so precious does that prestige remain that students and families who care little about or for academic substance compete fiercely to obtain the showiest of credentials. In short, undergraduate education in America today is mostly a racket dependent on deception.

For more than a generation, financing this ever-more-expensive racket has deformed America's families. To store up money for their toddlers' college tuition, mothers put them in day care and go to work. For the same reason, families stay in jobs and places they dislike. They scrimp and go into debt and they quarrel. They push the kids into activities that they hope will convince the admissions officers of their sociopolitical compatibility because they know that these institutions value conformity above test scores. So much effort do families spend, so many opportunities and so much happiness do they forego, for the privilege of handing over their life's savings. But because the colleges demand even more, the students pay the rest by going into debt, thus premortgaging or precluding their own families. And all this is done mostly for image.

The Price

Not incidentally, the country as a whole is left with about a trillion and a half dollars of student debt that no one knows how to discharge.

By the turn of this century, one-fourth of American adults had four-year degrees. But with every passing year we recognize that this is a negative factor in our life as a nation. The Starbucks' barista with a degree in psychology or business management and a debt she can't pay off is a tragedy, not a joke. The kids who majored in spring break and hookup, who drift in and out of "relationships," unequipped economically or ethically for anything else, are unlikely to recover whatever good habits they abandoned during their college years. Perhaps more tragic is the larger cohort who did what their degree program asked of them in order to enter their chosen profession. But neither faculty nor administrators told them that entry into these professions goes only to a few outstanding people—not to the many like themselves. Why not direct them instead into something in which they were likelier to succeed?

Then there is the cohort who actually believed the codswallop the universities fed them about the evils of Judeo-Christian civilization in general and of America in particular. The more you hate those you deem evil, the better you are is among the hoariest of heresies. This philosophy is like a drug, especially heartwarming and addictive to people for whom hatred of others is the easiest path to their own self-esteem. How much better for all it would be had that cohort flunked out. Instead, they became a mass of raging partisans eager for employment to punitively police the fellow citizens they enjoy despising.

But few if any flunk out, because the ruling class hammers home the theme "college is America's best friend," the lie that a degree itself is a passport to middle-class life. Authority figures repeat that our advanced economy needs more degrees. President Obama's endorsement of degrees was so divorced from consideration of skills as to lead one to ask what would happen if all were awarded doctorates at birth. Credulous folks believed that bunkum. The federal government set up programs to help people pay. And the more the government helped people pay, the more colleges raised prices to match the available revenue. Higher education made the edu-class bigger, richer, and more powerful.

But by Covid time, when prestige colleges continued to demand tuition while offering only online classes, enrollment in traditional colleges was already dropping. Families and students were figuring out that since employers were no longer taking degrees from established universities as evidence that their holders were anything special, investing a quarter of a million dollars and four years at Old State U, might make less sense than getting a bachelor's or master's degree from an online institution while working, and for less than $50,000. In short, the Covid period confirmed that their claims to superiority really make as little sense economically as they do in terms of comparative pedagogy.

America started taking a cold, hard look at higher education and saw that dysfunctions were part of a bigger problem.

Brain of Rotten Ruling Class

Part of what America saw is the near identity between higher education and an inept, partisan ruling class that pretends to rule on behalf of "science." The higher education establishment's unstinting support of the Democratic Party's changing strictures regarding Covid, strictures that disarticulated society, worsened Americans' health, and impoverished them coincided with counterintuitive cultural mandates. Pressuring people to mouth approval of self-evident lies such as the dependence of sexual identity on self-identification rather than biology has reduced the credit that the American people used to give to government as well as to universities.

President Eisenhower's warning against science's dependence on government turned out to have been prescient. Brandishing the word "science" in lieu of facts and reason is now the Democratic Party's only support for the commands it issues and the punishments it inflicts on those who disobey. Doing so requires self-identification as "Science-R-Us." That, in turn, requires silencing whoever would argue any given point on its merits via facts and logic: that is, scientifically. And that becomes possible only if the universities, which now employ most of the scientists, do the silencing. The silencing has happened because the higher education establishment runs on government money. It is the government's dependent.

Hence, science's good name is used to support obviously unattractive politicians and policies—even to save California Governor Gavin Newsom from electoral recall. Foregoing substantive argument, Newsom and persons of his party claim to govern "scientifically," while accusing their opponents of being an irrational "Taliban." Yes, their enemies are labeled as irrational terrorists and are to be treated as such.

"Science" is said to say that cloth masks inhibit the transmission of the Covid virus, infection by which carries a high risk of death, and hence that not wearing a mask is tantamount to reckless endangerment if not attempted murder. Not only does public policy follow from such hokum, but on August 21, 2021, a security guard in a Chicago liquor store shot a man several times for entering the store without a mask. "Science" had told him this man was a threat to his life.

The misuse of science's mantle is especially common, willful, and corrupt by practitioners thereof. You may be confident that few if any acts of government, especially the most tendentious, occur in the absence of "studies" by persons credentialed by major universities certifying their reasonableness and predicating their success. And you may be certain that when the opposite results occur, as is so often the case, no studies analyzing the previous studies' errors will appear. There is no money in that, and even less professional comity. How does one get to, and to remain in, the isles of the blessed? As Eisenhower warned, these days it is largely through the political management of government power and money. And that involves, in no small part, claiming "science's" magic mantle.

Meritocracy?

Ruling as vicars of science is a branch of an old idea, aristocracy. After the nineteenth century's Napoleonic reforms, European governments placed power into bureaucracies staffed by persons chosen by competitive exams. The exams searched for natural aristocrats—rulers who deserved to rule because they were most likely to transmit science's blessings to their people. France's grandes écoles, whose graduates dominated just about every aspect of life in that country, were prototypical. But European meritocracy has faded over the past half century.

As we have mentioned, though American progressives never quite looked at government this way, they always were deeply conscious of being better educated than their fellow citizens. Hence, they believed *they* were the best and brightest and that people like themselves were therefore more entitled to rule even academic institutions more than persons chosen by any criteria, voting and exams included. They talked meritocracy but practiced oligarchy.

In America, power over academic institutions, like power over everything else, came out of barrels of money. And as government came to control more and more money, it controlled who ran those institutions. And, as Ike warned, it led to power over who became part of them, as well as over what happens and does not happen there.

But when Ike spoke, American higher education was the nursery of excellence and the world's envy. To some extent, it still is because of its remaining diversity—the real differences that come from its parts' dependence on their own sources of money and inspiration. There were multiple pathways in for different people. In the early twentieth century, objections notwithstanding, American academe gave Europe's Enrico Fermis, Edward Tellers, Albert Einsteins, and Leo Strausses the fame and influence due them. The Ivy League mostly shunned Jews, who worked harder and produced better. But they got into places like City College of New York, MIT, Berkeley, and Caltech. Their achievements shamed the Ivies into admission by exam. For a few midcentury decades, American higher education had a substantial meritocratic element.

No more. As academe became more dependent on government money rationed by the Democratic Party, and that party became more partisan, all that changed. Now, academe rations the entry of Asian Americans into itself as it once did that of the Jews. And because higher education is more than ever the gatekeeper to the ruling class, it rations entry into that as well. The edu-class and ruling class shun people who perform too well because claiming one's place by virtue of one's performance rather than by the bosses' pleasure threatens the bosses. They act similarly toward anyone who believes in God—indeed in any source of authority other than the ruling class's ruling party—including reality itself.

Even established authorities know that failure to hew the partisan line means being shunned by the ruling class. Academics whose careers are before them know that failure to cheer or jeer (as the Democratic Party may direct) ends their careers without recourse.

Trouble at the Top

Essential as the higher education class is to America's rulers, its comfort, prestige, and general appeal are more derivative than ever from that of the whole of which it is part. Professors' prostitution to the ruling class, like that of any category, follows from interest joined to herd instinct: humans' congenital, insatiable desire to seem above our fellows. But the ruling class's corrupting attractiveness depends on its power to deliver primacy, or at least its perception. Since World War II and up until the last few years, the American ruling class was almost universally seen as the epitome of success, able to dispense or deny it at will. It asked only disciplining one's conscience a bit in exchange for massive benefits.

Our time's primordial fact, however, is that, led by the Democratic Party, though the ruling class may be very much in power, it is also in disarray. Its members, having gained prominence as the American Republic's stewards, violated the basic law of regime longevity by failing to restrain their own desires for self-aggrandizement. As our century dawned, this turned America into an oligarchy. But the ruling class, composed as it is of "intersectional" groups incapable of self-restraint, pushed the oligarchy into a war against the rest of American society. That happened quickly, without warning. The struggle is without prospect of resolution and gives no sign of abating because it is driven by the ruling class's loss of internal coherence.

Persons in associated groups, including higher education, become apprehensive about their future as the price of their support rises and as they suffer the consequences of our rulers' ineptitude along with the rest of Americans.

As the Democratic Party claims "Science" to be the basis for the host of campaigns small and large, dictated by shifts within and among its "intersectional" constituencies—including abrupt reversal of directives from a few months earlier—and demands that the professoriate join in support and in ostracizing whomever among them dissents, it places burdens on these associates such as even the Communist Party of the Soviet Union and Germany's National Socialist Party never placed on their academics. The Soviets' worst abuse of science, requiring silence about or support for Trofim Lysenko's crackpot theory of transmissibility of acquired traits, was not as onerous as the contemporary American practice of requiring professions of faith in the subjectivity of human sexuality. Nor did Soviet apparatchiks ever punish Russian doctors for their medical decisions, as Democrats have done by ostracizing doctors who dissent from their ever-changing political protocols regarding Covid. Stalin never demanded that academe share responsibility for the disarticulation, pain, and death that his program of collectivization inflicted on Russia and Ukraine. But the Democratic Party insists that its disastrous "lockdowns" of American society—a reversal of basic epidemiology—be approved as "science."

In the name of "science," a host of petty tyrants takes upon itself the authority to harass and punish Americans, including by duct-taping masks on their schoolchildren. The American people, sick of such abuse, their respect for superiors sapped by declining levels of public safety, and subject to recurring evidence of ineptitude and corruption, blame the professors as their troubles' ultimate sources. As public opinion turns against the ruling class, the edu-class is left holding the proverbial bag, and not entirely unjustly.

Education and Us

Big and powerful as it is, however, the edu-class has never been so vulnerable. Never before have so many people been so open, or even eager, to doing without its services. Whatever reservoir of faith and heartfelt support America's established schools and universities formerly enjoyed is gone. The edu-class's continuing massive presence depends more on legacy sources of money—mostly government—than anything else. This is the edu-class's life support. In fact, it has no other resource.

The political task for those of us whose interest lies in rebuilding an educational system that sustains our civilization, is to cut off that life support, allowing the edu-class and its offerings compete to service America on the merits of what it delivers. Even more complex and demanding, it must now provide and promote education that actually fortifies and replenishes our civilization.

Cutting the edu-class's financial life support will take neither more nor less than spreading the truth about what it does and does not do and why, given its officials' hearts and minds, reasonable persons cannot expect it to improve upon what it already delivers.

Elections for school boards are the best ways of rearranging the attitudes of those in control of school financing at the K–12 level. Having noted that America suffers from excessive concentration of educational power in too few school boards, campaigning to split present boards into many such entities, each more closely controlled by parents, must go hand in glove with arguments for what should and should not be taught. Tying what government does to willingness to support it with taxes has helped define our civilization since the Magna Carta.

Governments will tax for, and compel, education. Legislating parents' right to direct to which schools—public, private, or home—both tax revenue and pupils go is essential, not only for disciplining public school boards, but for ensuring genuine diversity, providing the relevant communities with knowledge about what kinds of teaching has which results.

Higher education's being necessarily farther removed from democratic control, political methods for remedying it are necessarily indirect, with one exception: undoing the massive student loan programs that have swollen and deformed colleges while shrinking the middle class and creating a generation of graduates both indebted and useless. Justice and political sense point the way.

Since colleges in general and administrators in particular have been the loans' chief beneficiaries, and since what they have done and not done is the prime reason why so many graduates are dysfunctional, legislatively transferring responsibility for the loans from taxpayers to the colleges would at once reduce their ability to pay themselves and to spend for frivolities, and ensure that, as students default, the consequences fall where they should. Taxpayers will shed no tears for the golden archipelago's dwellers.

Government's encouragement of science and technology and support for militarily relevant research, pose the same problem today as they did the day Sputnik first circled the globe—more so, because China's threat to the U.S. is bigger quantitatively and more focused on technology than Russia's ever was. The challenge for us is to stop repeating the mistake we made by turning the National Defense Education Act and support for education in general into supporting more gender studies than genetics. Intellectually, keeping priorities straight is easy. Politically, it requires the courage publicly to tell hard truths about what is worth what to our civilization and to our power as a nation.

Cutting the life support of higher education institutions requires exposing how little—if any—good they do by comparison with the price and opportunity costs of attending them. A little political action can go a long way in this regard by imposing on them the same requirements for transparency about the effects they have on those they serve as apply to other providers of goods and services.

Reputation (i.e., prestige) is literally the main product that they dispense. What do you get for four years at Old State U.? What about at Old Ivy? These questions deserve empirical answers. Institutions advertise the percentage of students they admit, and sometimes the entrants' test scores, implying that they select the best and make them better. But the edu-class rejects categorically comparing students' test scores (absolute and/or relative) before and after they attend. The vehemence of the rejection' has increased as the amount of study required for graduation has fallen. Legislating transparency in educational outcomes is the most potent weapon against scam.

Fact-based challenges to established colleges' hazy claims to beneficence can also help those who start up replacement institutions. What if, as is entirely possible, test figures bear out that the average student is not better able to think after four years at Old State or Old Ivy than before? Could it be that the schools did not demand more of the students? There is plenty of evidence that schools demanded less than in previous decades. The new colleges can credibly pledge to improve students at the very least by requiring more work of them.

More important but beyond empirical demonstration is that the substance of what is being taught, the manner and ethos of education, especially as it flows down from the peaks of academe, have corrupted—are corrupting—America. All manner of corruption is so immanent from America's commanding heights on down as to make superfluous the presentation of facts and arguments about it.

Whoever would reset education in America from its current path must begin by noting and denouncing its corruption of our civilization. Each new generation internalizes civilization as it does its maternal language. Restoring the integrity of the civilization into which we educate succeeding generations requires educators to pay attention to its language's every word.

BIG TECH: SACRED CULTURE OR CYBORG RAPTURE?

BY JAMES POULOS

1.

The history of the Great Reset is a technological one. It is the history of the unfolding development of communication media to supplement, perchance to supplant, the republican form of government, wherein citizens meet face to face in their shared humanity and under God, to govern themselves at human scale.

The quest to replace this ancient arrangement with a new world government is itself nothing new. In 1928, the year of the world's first color television transmission and the first appearance of Mickey Mouse, H. G. Wells published *The Open Conspiracy: Blue Prints for a World Revolution*, not a science fiction novel but a manifesto for the establishment of a "world commonwealth" with a "world religion" rooted not in any established Western or Eastern faith but in the "unending growth of knowledge and power." From out of this infinity of collectivized, centralized effort, Wells predicted "universal peace, welfare and happy activity." These, he avowed, could be the fruits only of a "responsible world directorate," a construct built to replace "private, local, or national ownership" of everything from credit to transportation to industrial production, and empowered to impose "world biological controls" on "population and disease." No true future awaited the West, Wells counseled, but one in which the imperatives of technology and ethics fused into one "supreme duty"—"subordinating the personal life to the creation" of the world directorate and its "general advancement of human knowledge, capacity, and power."

Just how *human* such an arrangement could truthfully be said to be, however, has remained since then in doubt; in *Literature and Revolution*, published four years before *The Open Conspiracy*, Leon Trotsky announced that only the communist man was "the man of the future," a being for whom his only possible future was to break down his humanity and build of its parts something new. "Man will make it his purpose to master his own feelings, to raise his instincts to the heights of consciousness, to make them transparent, to extend the wires of his will into hidden recesses, and thereby to raise himself to a new plane, to create a higher social biologic type, or, if you please, a superman."

Since the first stirrings of planetary war between British globalism and Soviet communism for control over the founding of a new world theological order, the West has twisted in the grip of technoethical elites convinced that, since the beginning and in the end, the highest imperative on Earth—with ruin the only alternative—has been and will be to found a regime as pure as the consciousness that could only be freed to create it by coercively breaking the sacredness and authority of our given humanity.

This momentous wager emerged above all from the formative effect of electric technology on the senses and sensibilities of the West. If the medium of print ushered in an Age of Reason, the medium of electricity unleashed an Age of Occultism. Print's promise was not a Babel-like reconstruction of our identity based on knowledge that empowered us to progress beyond our humanity but a congenially, horizontally distributed system of open exchange that took a variety of directions as it went along, even as ultimate knowledge accumulated in elite networks of libraries, universities, and scholars. The age of print was the age of not simply reason but *reasonableness*, a technological and ethical heuristic that harmonized at large but pluralistic scale the individual and the congregation, the conscience and the commonwealth, the nation and the marketplace.

Shattering this schema, the advent of electricity substituted instantaneousness and invisibility in an ethereal new realm of communications for the methodical, tactile, and grounded (or seaborne) realm adhered to by the communicative life of print. Edward Bulwer-Lytton's 1871 vision of "a coming race" possessed of electricity and "the art to concentre [sic] and direct it in a word, to be conductors of its lightnings" seemed to unveil a deeper meaning of Melville's 1850 claim, issued at the dawn of the electric age, that "genius, all over the world, stands hand in hand, and one shock of recognition runs the whole circle round." David Bowie would reference Bulwer-Lytton's vision a century afterward, at the peak of the electric age, in hit single "Oh! You Pretty Things," in which he sings about the obsolescence of humanity—a conclusion fueled by the annihilating electric force Europe suffered in the twentieth century, from which the U.S. was almost mystically spared.

America's moment of technological scourging came fast and early, in the Civil War. Lincoln, providentially, had grasped that America somehow had to be set on a new footing capable of seeing the country and its people through the electric age. He, for the first time, communicated remotely and directly with his generals in the field through the telegraph in the War Department; his Emancipation Proclamation went out over telegraph, striking abolitionists nationwide like the loosed lightning from Christ's terrible swift sword in the "Battle Hymn of the Republic." America's manifest destiny played out under and through the arc of electric power. So, it seemed, would the next century's Pax Americana.

Convinced by its means of victory in World War II, secured in its sense that electric power had only strengthened America's human way, the U.S. regime adopted limitless technological advancement as its strategy for world domination. Unable to defeat the Soviets by conventional or nuclear war, the scientific state embedded within the U.S. regime since the Manhattan Project had to develop technological weaponry of a new kind. Scruples and prudence had to be set aside: those in charge grew convinced America's form of government and way of life could not continue to exist unless America, in effect, ruled the world; given the impossibility of all previous forms of large-scale conquest under Cold War conditions, the U.S. required from its scientific state an altogether new form of war making and control. This the military-industrial complex delivered in the form of computer technology.

At first, the Soviets advanced step for step with the Americans in the computer race, even using the devices (Moscow's mainframe computer calculated Sputnik's requisite trajectory) to beat the U.S. into space. But as the internet developed—and, with it, the military computer technologies such as GPS and the touchscreen that would soon be spun off as consumer electronics applications—America made a fundamental break with all prior research and development. The creation of a communications network of machines and programs, limitlessly scalable in theory, ushered in a digital medium distinct from, and more powerful than, any one computer or room full of computers. The functionally limitless spending directed to America's scientific state within a state could not be matched by the Soviet political economy. While digital technology did not quite defeat Moscow, when the Soviets fell, it was digital technology that was victorious—first over America, and then, with blistering speed, the rest of the world.

Naturally those in charge in the triumphant West were certain that the historic and unprecedented devices they funded and created could be used just as well to establish world dominance and control amid the collapse of international communism as they might have been used to wage a kind of war against it—a *digital* war, which could, unlike conventional or nuclear war, actually be waged and won. Not only was digital technology useful in this way from a scientific standpoint, but also from an ethical standpoint, it appeared to be a kinder, gentler, and therefore more *just* form of world control. Progressively onboarding the world into a networked system of constant communication—backboned by American strategic infrastructure and premised on

American norms and values—would establish a new global order in a new way, one harmonious with peaceful economic activity and international law. Through this new and enlightened form of domination, individuals anywhere in the world could use benevolent technology to increasingly approximate the earthly paradise imagined—as in John Lennon's "Imagine"—by the cultural utopians of the post-Christian West. Divisive feelings and identities would melt away as connectivity increased togetherness and transcended parochial fears and cares. New Age ethics seemed inseparable from the technology of the new digital age.

2.

The advent and near-instantaneous commodification of the smartphone ostensibly thrust the minds of those in charge far into the clouds. But the world was not delivered so smoothly into a newly perfect state. Steve Jobs debuted the iPhone on January 9, 2007; just over one month later, Federal Reserve Chairman Alan Greenspan predicted a recession amid spreading fears of a halt to global economic growth, and by late summer, mortgage markets had collapsed and a liquidity crisis was paralyzing major banks. Things unraveled from there. One year later, Treasury Secretary Henry Paulson and new Fed Chair Ben Bernanke solemnly informed House Speaker Nancy Pelosi that America's globalized economic and financial system would fail over the weekend unless it was rebooted and restructured nearly instantaneously.

The transformation was achieved, and by 2010 the government and its backers in the major news outlets were confident enough to message that the worst was over and the American-led globalized Western economic system was on the rebound. But the structural damage to the technoethical elite's confidence in Wall Street and the international banking system was foundational. Though the financial industry had embraced and integrated digital technology as fully and aggressively as any part of the globalized regime, the results were all but catastrophic. Convinced for obvious reasons that demolishing the intertwined U.S.

and international financial system would be politically infeasible, the Obama administration and its allies protected the banks and their executives from liability and punitive action and, instead, doubled down on wiring digital technology into the strategic core of the globalized American order.

After all, Silicon Valley traced its origins, like the scientific state that arose from the Manhattan Project, to military-industrial funding, personnel, and support. In this sense, it was a homecoming. Over a few years, the White House pushed the conversion of Silicon Valley's top digital firms into the state's most powerful organs. All antitrust obstacles to mergers and acquisitions by ballooning giants like Google were cleared; partisan allies in and around companies like Facebook and Twitter were cultivated, rewarded, and cycled through Washington society; and, perhaps most importantly, Silicon Valley and the telecommunications establishment were conscripted into a new global control effort, one hiding in plain sight behind the screens of every smartphone. The Bush administration's vision of Total Information Awareness was achieved under Obama in the form of the massive surveillance apparatus formed by Silicon Valley, the NSA, and, via Five Eyes, the Government Communications Headquarters (GCHQ)—the British intelligence agency that worked (and works) so closely with the American intelligence community that the two should be considered, whatever our form of government is thought to be, different faces of a single sovereign entity.

These revolutionary executive changes in America's political economy salvaged U.S. leadership of the globalized Western financial system with a vast tech-fueled bailout. The almost immeasurable wealth created by the soft nationalization of the digital tech industry was sufficient to keep the American-led globalized financial order in place—so much so that those in charge were able to convince themselves the digitized regime was rich and powerful enough to benefit even more from China's "peaceful rise" than Beijing itself. Ultimately, on this basis, the digitized regime would be able to ingest even China, and its rival form of socioeconomic organization, into the technoethical elite's single global order.

That elite's bots, and we humans, had other plans. Despite the Silicon Valley-nourished resurgence of optimism and idealism (or self-entitlement and arrogance) among the technoethical elite, people—from Edward Snowden in the U.S. to the Chinese leadership in Beijing, from American voters to populists across the E.U.—began using the connectivity and ubiquity of digital technology to say and do things in concert at loggerheads with the unitary global structures the technoethical elite saw as not simply the most just or purest emergent form of governance but as the *only* set of instruments capable of maintaining *any* sufficient order in the West. Just as certain banks had been deemed too big to fail, the digitized socioeconomic and financial system created to replace the predigital one that had failed in the financial crisis was itself now too big to fail. It was now *more* centralized than the American-led globalized Western order had been in 2006; *more* dependent on patronage, credentialism, and cronyism; *more* hagridden with corruption and awash with illicit funds; and *more* exposed to attack and subversion by major rivals and adversaries unwilling to be assimilated into the new, increasingly Borg-like, digital Anglo-American order.

3.

So it could be that, on the occasion of Obama's digitally powered reelection, the *MIT Technological Review* splashed its cover with "How Big Data Will Save Politics"—and how, on the eve of Donald Trump's potential reelection, the lead story flipped into its opposite: "Technology Is Threatening Our Democracy. How Can We Save It?" Blame was placed officially at the feet of individuals with the wrong opinions and Valley executives greedily hacking minds to like and share deplorable information. The deeper truth was that digital technology itself had begun to behave in ways its technoethical creators failed to anticipate. Their dawning awareness of that shocking reality prompted a response of blended panic, outrage, humiliation, and resentment. The globalization of governance had already suffered too many systemic breakdowns caused by too many unforeseen blows.

The New World Order rung in by George H. W. Bush was rung out by his son with the financial crisis; now the brave new Tech World Order forged under Obama was already back on its heels. All the productivity and power the Valley forged, from unparalleled consumer spending to surveillance unprecedented in scale and reach, failed to stop Russia from growing more provocative and China from swelling into a monster; failed to help America anticipate and exploit the Arab Spring or head off the ISIS caliphate; and, stingingly, failed to forestall another metastasizing financial crisis. This one lurked in the shadows, driven by a toxic mix of anemic growth outside the tech sector, structural stagnation in U.S.-dominated foreign markets like Europe's and Japan's, and a steady subversion of the value of the dollar, thanks to the progressive exhaustion of the monetary policy toolkit in Congress and at the Fed. With interest rates stuck near zero and funny money flooding the system, record highs gushed through the repo window on an open-ended basis as bitcoin and other cryptocurrencies began a swift, perhaps uncontrollable rise. Inflation climbed, the trade trap with China segued into a historic supply chain quagmire—and, on top of it all, the failed pandemic lockdown strategy (coupled with a summer of federally approved race riots) crushed small and family-owned businesses, revealed the unsustainability of the student loan debt service and repayment regime, and wracked the Western nations with a destabilizing mix of autocratic emergency orders and popular disaffection and disobedience. Instead of perfecting the long-promised establishment of the "rules-based international order," technological progress had shattered it. Digital consummation morphed into digital catastrophe.

The technoethical elite could be excused, in its most competent upper reaches, for thinking that the options had become extremely limited for tying off the general breakdown of the second grand effort to establish a durable post-Cold War order. The long and shambolic train of policy events stretching from the era defined in finance by the 1944 Bretton Woods Conference handoff of global monetary supremacy from Britain to the U.S., and in technology by the 1945 creation of the Electronic Numerical Integrator and Computer (ENIAC), the first general-purpose digital computer, had passed through state of exception after state of exception. To mark just one stage of the process, the postwar gold-backed dollar system established at Bretton Woods collapsed under mounting inflation and debt in the same year, 1971, as the Advanced Research Projects Agency Network (ARPANET), the military-academic precursor to the internet, was declared operational. Decade after decade, the various strategic attempts to lock in U.S.-led globalization remained consistently reactive and unstable, failing to coalesce into the kind of durable and dependable institutional structure that its leadership cadres presented it to their vast constituencies as being.

The crowning disaster of Covid-19's worldwide spread offered the West's ruling technoethicists a perfect excuse to scrap their unsalvageable apparatus without relinquishing power. Millions were growing more aware it was the digital catastrophe the technoethical elite had ignorantly summoned forth, and the digital catastrophe that its expertly honed knowledge and values had been unable to forecast, much less to understand. But few could articulate the true nature of the catastrophe or how to trace explicitly to its roots their struggles and their disenchantment. Like a deus ex machina, "the virus" became, more than a symbol, a stand-in for everything the technoethical elite feared it could not say about its responsibility for such a swift end to American greatness and world order. Under the symbol of the virus, humanity would be humbled as a matter of coordinated policy. Horizons would be lowered—footprints shrunken, mobility reduced, consumption curtailed, families deprecated, deferred, and dissolved. In the new post-Covid end times, dreams would give way to dogma, dynamism to domestication, vitality to sterility. Achieving such a hard reboot of Western civilization—achieving it on the fly, amid a geopolitical realm of digitally resurgent rivals—would not be easy.

This kind of Great Reset would, in all likelihood, be an impossible task—were it not for the Great Offset the technoethical elite now had at its disposal to offer. For all the subhuman diminishment the people under the new regime would be asked and required to accept, they would receive a simple, all-important reward: a new life, a second life, of superhuman possibility; one where, at last, you could be whomever you could imagine—online. All the new regime required of you to enjoy such an all-consuming existence freed from the flaws and frustrations of human life was your compliance—a new kind of digital obedience at once staggeringly intimate and richly—in a virtual sense, at least—rewarding.

The average (or even above average) American could be excused for feeling that somehow communism was back, stronger than ever in a strange new way and, like an alien race setting foot on the earth, already triumphant, without having so much as fired a shot. The U.S. triumph over the U.S.S.R. manifested what appeared to be its new destiny as the world power thanks to the fusion or harmony its rulers forged between their tech and their ethics. It was this evident unity, and its power both to progressively globalize itself and to represent what seemed to be its historically imminent perfection at global scale, that made America (after the defeat of international communism) appear in the globalized imagination to symbolize the whole world and the whole of humanity, both in its present moment and in its dream of the single human world of the future.

4.

But was not in fact this Cold War victor something profoundly different from America in its homegrown identity—something much more like the old British globalism of H. G. Wells, empowered with a technoethical mastery the envy of Bulwer-Lytton? America's triumphant technoethics regarded and presented itself as an immanent phenomenon that expressed itself historically yet transcended history. It arose, in this understanding and representation, from its leaders' progressive discovery and development of knowledge through the reflexive outworking of human consciousness. This process gained focus, power, and purpose through the ultimate labor of pursuing unbounded technological advancement conformed to the ethical framework of what was deemed the highest form of consciousness: creativity. To create with the purest vision and purest intentions—to *dream* in such fashion, the precondition of all our creation—was to authorize one's use of any technological resource to operationalize one's creativity. To dream purely with the greatest expertise licensed one's rule over technology developed with the greatest expertise; to develop technology in the most expert way was to develop it in the ways best suited to empower the most ethical expert dreamers to create and operationalize what they dreamed.

It was a dialectic with a purpose: using America's technological and ethical embodiment of the New World Order as a post-Cold War fact to lead the world progressively toward the actualization of the Western technoethical elite's purest dream of the world's future. America was indispensable above all to the project of onboarding the world into the new world of that dream. The technoethical destiny of America was now, in a way never subject to ratification by the citizens of the republic, to transcend itself. In a flash, America's technoethical triumph promised to achieve communist ends—a final global system just in its equal emancipation of the consciousness of all—by not really *different* so much as *better* means. If the Cold War was, as Steve Sailer has argued, a war for control over the global Left, the New World Order announced that the ethical terms of peace would be a technological transcendence of the conflict within the Left between capital and labor, between have and have not—ultimately, between human and machine.

Winning the peace proved challenging; in the pivotal year of 1999, the Battle of Seattle showed the globalizing West's ruling technoethicists the face of its post-Cold War existential foe. Despite periodic rumblings to the contrary, neither Chinese nor Islamic civilization had proven to be such an adversary—one, like the Soviet Union, which had commanded the allegiance of many of the most creatively and technologically sophisticated and powerful Western intellectual elites. The antiglobalization anarchists of the populist Left who swarmed the streets of Seattle, empowered by digital technology to stymie and evade law enforcement, gave teeth to the tens of thousands of protestors who had ground the WTO's crucial round of millennial negotiations to a halt. While Islamic terrorism would soon provoke a round of rhetorical effort to mobilize the globalizing West's sociopolitical identity against premodern religion, the central problem for the technoethical elite was not the backward behavior in a remote corner of the world of restive tribes with ancient hatreds but the domestic backlash by leftist masses against their globalization of a new and refounded form of Western governance. It was essential to strangle this rebellion in its crib—peacefully, through the very technoethical systems the rebels were appropriating digital tools to attack.

The history of the past twenty-five years is the history of the technoethical elite's success at executing its complex and high-stakes strategy to domesticate the Left. In a generation, consumer technology and the cult of the imagination it made possible—especially through its extension into the realm of sexual identity—were fused into a powerful and singular agent of cultural and political transformation. Under its spreading and incessant pressure, the popular Left went from an anticorporate, antiglobalist, antistatist, and antitechnocratic movement to one devoted fully to the use of corporatist technocracy to enforce the globalization of the New World Order under the aegis of the Anglo-American military-industrial complex and the Five Eyes intelligence community. Today, the popular Left has been all but fully absorbed into the spiritual and organizational system of the technoethical elite. Digital technology is the ethically pure means by which the woke become who they "really" are—in the most progressive and definitive of cases, queer-enlisted millennials behind the controls of

Predator drones, and alpha-male-to-female transsexuals at the apex of the strategic communications establishment.

There were bumps along the way, of course. Edward Snowden's revelations and Bernie Sanders's campaigns drew the popular Left dangerously close to its old antitechnoethical stomping grounds. But these temptations could not surpass those on offer from on high: of the use of technology—spun directly out of military and intelligence research and development and reskinned with the fashionably orb-like and minimalist aesthetic of Steve Jobs—to declare emancipatory spiritual war against the natural limits of human identity. For decades, the work of antihuman feminists like Donna Haraway and Shulamith Firestone had helped draw fringe academic theory toward the view that technology, by making us cyborgs free of divine and natural constraints, was the only true source of justice. By the debut of the iPhone, and the commodification of the smartphone that followed in the blink of an eye, the implicit social sensibility had deepened that we were all cyborgs now and—as Stewart Brand had said in a similar key of our being "as gods"—had better get used to it. The problem with Soviet communism, we are now to understand, is that it was all too human to achieve the true justice of utopia. For that, our consciousness must be guided past our humanity, into communion with our bots.

Yet here the challenge of digital disobedience returns—the problem of machines that do not, despite the most expert ethics and programming, do what is intended, commanded, anticipated. The Tech World Order failed so massively that Barack Obama, messaging hard against Trump in '20, was reduced to describing online life as "the single biggest threat to our democracy." He was not exactly wrong to argue that digital life disenchanted the authority of his sitting elite, especially in its capacity as the putative world controller of online communications. But he concluded that the crisis was one of epistemology, not ontology—one of knowledge, not identity. The bots defied the elite's attempts at achieving true determinacy in mathematical language because the elite's mistaken belief in the completeness of knowledge as a tool for making order perfectly legible caused it to misunderstand digital technology's manner of being. And insofar as the elite had begun to understand its manner of being—to grasp that the causative form of digital life is the swarm—it had failed, again through its idolatry of the perfect language, to create complete and faultless command systems for taking control of digital swarms. The challenge of human disobedience is one the elite has long labored to technoethically cure. The challenge of digital disobedience is altogether new.

Norbert Wiener, the godfather of cybernetics, described the problem poignantly in his final work on the subject, *God & Golem, Inc.* Programmable machines were like monkeys' paws, he warned: you always might just get what you ask for—in the manner of an ancient curse. There was no way, especially as systems grew ever more complex, to guarantee that input *a* would result in output *x*—a problem to say the least, Wiener lamented, when humans were busily racing to outsource responsibility for nuclear warfare to networks of blinking machines. The widening interest in handing social science over to the gods of determinate math struck Wiener as a catastrophe in the making, less sensational than mutually assured destruction but no less serious.

What Wiener did not foresee, however, was that the input-output problem would soon change its object from the individual computer or even the networked system to the digital swarm—the archetypal formation we now recognize all too well in the cloud of drones, the cloud of data, the cloud of online accounts and avatars, brands and tribes, individuals and devices. With the advent of 5G, latency among swarms of digital entities is being reduced asymptotically to zero, lifting already ubiquitous and largely invisible bots wholly outside human spacetime—the only spacetime in which politics is practicable and human self-governance may be contemplated, understood, and achieved. Useful as that might ultimately be in reducing humans to a more inert and malleable state, it is nevertheless the true planetary crisis that the technoethical elite must somehow overcome if it is (depending on whom you speak with) to establish, regain, or preserve its world rule.

This is the purpose of the Great Reset—to rearchitect digital technology and consolidate its control in a manner that eliminates even the possibility of human opposition to the further pursuit of globally institutionalized revolutionary post-humanity by the technoethical elite. Mastering the swarm, the elite realizes now, will take time—and tremendous energy, resources, and power to ensure that the time it takes is sufficient to master the swarm before the swarm slips free from outside technoethical rule. For this reason, the operating assumption at the highest level of the technoethical elite is that, because we truly cannot beat the bots, we must genuinely join them. World humanity must be onboarded into a digital system complete and powerful enough to prevent the world's humans from trying to stop the assimilation of our consciousness into a cyborg spacetime where we all, at long last, much check our humanity at the door.

5.

The role of "Big Tech" in the reset now underway, and in the new digital civilization-state meant to be founded thereafter, is clear enough in its character. The evidence builds daily—often heralded as a series of needed victories for health, safety, progress, and justice—that the technological reformation of our inner and outer lives is foundational to the logic and authority of the new regime. Three distinct patterns of organization have emerged in this respect. All, to a degree, can be seen unfolding simultaneously. In theory and practice, however, we can discern a sequential and cumulative structure to their implementation: *social media >> social credit >> social justice.*

As seen in the abrupt shift from the fourth year of the Obama administration to the fourth year of the Trump administration, social media has been at the very center of public and institutional concern around the politics of technology. Triumphalism and idealism gave way to disillusionment and outright panic. It is not for ordinary citizens to know exactly how much pressure, applied in which way, the intelligence community used to put the leading social media companies on notice in the wake of Trump's election, but it is plain to see the effect: concerted waves of arbitrary deplatforming and cancelation by fiat, leaving a social media landscape ruled by federally compliant compliance teams with conflicting, incoherent, and reactively punitive standards. On Twitter, the Taliban has retained its account after overthrowing the U.S.-backed regime in Afghanistan, while Trump, banned as a sitting president, has not recovered his own. Anonymous and pseudonymous accounts are nuked with neither reason nor stated reason and only sporadically reinstated after complaint and public outcry. Facebook has suffered still worse, having made the unforgivable choice to allow citizens critical of the regime to use the platform to freely associate and effectively exercise political agency.

The most generous possible explanation for the regime's actions to return social media to its ultimate origins as a creature of the military-intelligence apparatus is that America's technoethical elite bungled its development and deployment of digital technology on an even deeper and more comprehensive level than even what appears. There is no question that China, particularly, has humiliated Five Eyes with the scope and aggressiveness of its acquisition of massive U.S. data sets, including U.S. government data sets, just as there is little challenging the apparent reality that Russia and other state-backed hacking entities have exploited the offense-defense imbalance that defines the digital space to keep Five Eyes on the back foot, even if more in the online shadows than in the spotlit spaces of social media.

What is not so visible, however, although hiding in plain sight for those with eyes to see, is the curious combination of synchronicity and divergence in interests and values between the U.S. and Britain—our closest digital ally. The implicit proposition behind the public face of this alliance—that American exceptionalism and British globalism somehow now also form a unitary technoethical bloc—suffers from a distinct lack of evidence, although elites on both sides of the Atlantic are hard at work concretizing their imagined unity at a regime level insulated safely from citizen reach. The manner in which "retired" MI6 Russian-desk chief Christopher Steele's "dodgy dossier" was laundered by Fusion GPS and BuzzFeed into the basis of a federal pretext for the unprecedented Russiagate fishing expedition is indicative of the stakes and the creativity involved in this international operation; to take today's most glaring example, there is no reason at all why Prince Harry should not have been immediately persona non grata'd right out of his mushrooming portfolio of cushy positions contributing to woke psychological influence ops against the American people in the name of "online safety," but there he is, burrowed—on the basis of nothing but his undoubted usefulness to British intelligence and its American allies—into the beating heart of the most woke, most globalist, and best-funded technoethicist organizations resident in America. Or consider the additional puzzle of why America's highest-level Covid-19 doings (including an early and secret conference call between Anthony Fauci and his British equivalent, from which Fauci emerged as a pandemic crackdown-monger) should involve a British zoologist—Peter Daszak—running an international organization—EcoHealth Alliance—headquartered in the U.S. and drawing its budgetary funding predominantly from the U.S. military?

These curious details in America's strategic technoethical relationship with the United Kingdom nourish the distinct impression that Five Eyes is waging the first world war of the digital age primarily through the technology of communications, a war in which social media is absolutely required to sculpt, edit, and alter perceived reality among Western masses to stand any chance of success. Social media is there to zap away unwanted inquiries, keep the unthinkable unthinkable, and make an example out of those whose intransigence or mere curiosity is sufficient to paint them as, conveniently, so dangerous that they must be banished from public life and so clownish that they must be laughed down in the process.

What is more, social media is also there to ensure that the domestic mind control the regime deems essential to win the digital world war takes hold in a way much different from the old pattern of propaganda established in the televisual age. Rather than just a passive "tube" fueling fantasies and the willingness to trade real-life inertia and stagnation for ever more engrossing fantasies, the social media system is fundamentally *interactive*, achieving a sort of proto-governance protocol that replaces the offline policing of illegal actions with the online policing of noncompliant thought and speech activity. Already, the American system has begun to mimic and compete for effectiveness with the Chinese system of participatory auto-compliance. In that sense, social media has already morphed us along with itself into a social credit system.

Social credit is familiar to us from its more fully fledged variant hardwired into the regime in Beijing. Although social credit appears today to apply the logic of social media as a form of rule to the realm of private banking—offend the regime, and lose your access to your account or to favorable financing—it is important to recognize that social credit is defined above all by the porting of mass society away from the use of the financial instrument of physical government currency and toward the use of the new post-financial instrument of a government points system.

Again, the mechanism is already apparent in the way that the woke cultural revolution plays out in social media: while the numerical value of each point of prestige, credibility, access, patronage, and protection has not been formally established, these invisible points, which people are visibly seen every day to gain and lose, often in a blink, are the ultimate in fiat value: they are pegged to no outside currency other than the whim and will of the regime's characterizations of official realities. A man is and always has been a woman if he says he is insofar as the regime says so—or, better, insofar as the regime allows the users within the social credit system to impute from authorized regime-backed messaging that the regime *knows* so.

Resetting society into a social credit system that functions in this way soothes the fears of those in charge as well as it slakes their appetites for a technoethically consecrated form of totalitarian control. In a digital age, they reason, no other form of control is adequate to prevent either or both the world domination of the Chinese technoethical habitus on the one hand and the disintegration of the

Anglo-American technoethical habitus on the other. In a digital age of energy, the petrodollar is obsolete as a world reserve currency; in the wake of the 2007–2020 collapse of the financialized and securitized sovereign-debt economy, the fiat dollar is obsolete as a symbol and storehouse of sovereign-underwritten purchasing power. Something new is needed, something that enables the regime to strengthen itself through the retrenchment and consolidation of its overextended and weakened institutional structures. At a stroke, points-based social credit combines the problem of resetting the currency system and resetting the culture system into a single manageable challenge, one in which the maximum power of fusing of technology and ethics into one form of governance can be swiftly and comprehensively leveraged at scale.

The matter of scale is essential. Recall that the causative form digital technology takes and unilaterally and independently imposes on human life is the form of the swarm. The human race knows the swarm best, of course, from its great natural rivals for planetary domination—the insects. When we hear the word *swarm* today, we visualize bees or wasps, but from its beginnings, the word has had broader applications. In ancient Greece, for example, it was applied as well to teeming bugs on foot and implacable groups of people as it was to organically onrushing or oversmothering things such as waters or poured honey. The Greeks had no difficulty picturing robotic automata—the mythical tripods of Hephaestus figure prominently into the work of Aristotle—and, if you credit some of the more intriguing puzzles of Bronze Age technology, not undue difficulty *assembling* mechanical creatures. But we seem to lack any evidence that they built or imagined robot swarms of the sort that we now, under an odd sort of hypnotic duress, are "welcoming" into our intimate lives. Most of these alien newcomers, of course—Siri or Alexa, or even simply the Google algorithm—are invisible entities composed of light, electricity, and pure math, animate but not alive, scuttling and rippling through our lives, our homes, our bodies, our minds, and, it seems inevitable to infer, our souls.

The swarm is the form of the digital because the self-reinforcing imperative of digital technology is what's referred to within the industry as interoperability. One typical technical glossary defines interoperability as "the basic ability of different computerized products or systems to readily connect and exchange information with one another, in either implementation or access, without restriction." Key to the attainment of full interoperability is complete mutual legibility and understanding among the interfaces of the entities involved, which turns on the capability of the entities and the networks they make up to communicate with as few interruptions, imperfections, flaws, delays, snags, or obstacles as possible. This constitutes the highest level of interoperability, the semantic level, at which meanings within programmed and automated systems are unambiguously and simultaneously shared. Although a basket of different programming languages is used to develop and deploy digital networks with high degrees of interoperability, the ultimate such language is taken simply to be mathematics itself. The study of insect swarms to unlock the secrets of basing socialization at scale on the programmatic command and control of collective consciousness—an area where the leading figure has long been Martin Nowak, Jeffrey Epstein's pocket scientist—must, at the frontier of digital technology, yield to the study of pure math, which becomes, in an otherwise digitally disenchanted lifeworld, still more of a stand-in for absolute divinity than the spark of human consciousness.

Math cannot worship, but, as Bertrand Russell implied in spite of himself, can surely be worshipped: "Mathematics, rightly viewed, possesses not only truth, but supreme beauty—a beauty cold and austere, like that of sculpture, without appeal to any part of our weaker nature," he wrote, calling the realm "sublimely pure." Yet if the human consciousness is prone to see math as the last true god, especially in an age so digital that we look upon our devices as superhuman things demanding our envious imitation, the human creature demands above all not interoperability but incommensurability. The incommensurable in us abides in our personal singularity—that which, notwithstanding the mix of self and other and good or evil that runs, as Aleksandr Solzhenitsyn said, "through each human heart," marks out each of us as distinct from one another, to a degree that must, in the end, be understood as outside our human power to improve upon or transcend—as a holy gift.

It is for this reason that we must understand that the concept and practice of social justice is itself being reset in formative accordance with digital technology. Social justice is no longer the collectivist practice of politics it had been in the predigital electric age. That was the politics of the revolutionary mass, ordered and organized by the revolutionary vanguard. Digital social justice is the interoperable post-political practice of the cyborg swarm, conducted through perfect or pure communication by the transhuman or posthuman elite. Many within a digital social justice system will occupy themselves or be occupied at the subsidiary levels of social credit or social media that flow ever upward in their energies and logic into the architectonic capstone of the social justice system. Many are already sufficiently primed to lose themselves in metaverses such as Microsoft's or Facebook's rebranded successor Meta, now being built to alienate them pleasurably from not only their labor, but their human identity and their embodied, ensouled place as active agents in human spacetime—the only realm where our given life as political animals can possibly be lived out.

At the end of the theological road laid out by the would-be priests of our digital form of life, there is no more American civilization, Western civilization, or human civilization. The end time that Christ warns his disciples will come only at a time known by God the Father alone is, in the digitized technoethical dispensation, the final work of human hands.

6.

For more than the obvious reasons, this is a dangerous game. It is possible that somewhere in the quieter backrooms of various chambers of power, some of those who rule have read the work of Norwegian philosopher Peter Wessel Zapffe—particularly his 1933 essay "The Last Messiah." Zapffe's argument was as bracing as it was simple: by overdeveloping the intellect—to the point at which it was unthinkable *not* to keep developing the intellect even if or after it had turned against human life—people would presently turn in panic toward "artificially limiting the content of consciousness." The paradox, however, is that the available strategies of limiting consciousness are not necessarily those capable of preventing the runaway advancement of intellect into the most abstract and soulless regions of technical determinacy and ethical recursivity. If Zapffe is correct, panicked blowback against the divinization of mathematical totality is more likely to lead people into isolation, fixation, and distraction than it is to lead them to remember life before the automation of absolute calculation and to attempt to subjugate the hideous strength of their machinery to responsibly human purposes. At the end, Zapffe prophesies, the Last Messiah will arrive—the prophet of the only possible remaining Great Reset, the extinction of the human race. "Know yourselves," cries the Last Messiah; "be infertile, and let the earth be silent after ye."

We see already millions upon millions of human beings embracing this darkest credo personally—building and marketing at-home suicide pods; nurturing pets instead of children, and imitating instead of nurturing pets; disfiguring erotic life and sexual biology into a form of leverage for one's transformation into cyborgs; adopting collective and posthuman identities; scourging, in short, the humanity of humanity, in the smallest and largest detail. Whipping humanity further down this path in the smug belief that not even the Last Messiah awaits—but rather a cosmic heaven of self-divinization—is a plausible cast of mind for many of those in charge today. But some may understand deeply that they are playing with an ultimate sort of fire, one runaway spark of which might rush through the kindling our people of straw have become and leave our species a cinder.

What would it take to kindle the spark of conscience, of true responsibility, within a hidden figure like this? What evidence, what symbol, would be required?

A logical answer, perhaps, would entail the appearance—it must feel in some sense miraculous—of a mathematical technology the use of which could *already* allow, or even savingly strengthen, the ability of plain persons to wrest command and control of digital life away from the runaway technoethical elite, somehow instructing the databases and processing units seemingly arrayed against us to protect and preserve the holiness of our human identity, memory, and culture.

In truth, there is such a servus ex machina: bitcoin. Baffling as, at first, it may seem, the cryptocurrency is not simply a mathematical magic trick permitting galaxy-brained speculators to hoard imaginary money and leverage their smarts into riches. It is a digital backbone or foundation for the creation, valuation, and exchange of cultural goods and services by plain persons devoted to the sacred preservation of our given bodies, souls, families, and lives. Right now, today, bitcoin can be used as the girders of a new kind of online architecture—one where, for instance, a book about the themes explored here can be unalterably cryptographically written onto the blockchain and bought and sold in bitcoin. That much, at least, has been demonstrated by the sale of my book *Human, Forever* on canonic.xyz.

This, however, is just a beginning. It is clear to see, setting panic and its spasm-inducing precursors aside, how bitcoin in this way works not only as a tool for ordinary people to tell the database and the processing unit what to do to serve mankind—not man's intellect, not man's consciousness, but his humanity itself. It is even possible to see, for instance, how bitcoin may be used to design projects of sacral culture that cannot be completed for many centuries, if ever—bitcoin monasteries, for those who hope to limit the content of consciousness in a way as radical as it is protective of our given nature and identity, or bitcoin cathedrals, for those who hope to fill online life with the artful testimony of God's grace and the beauty of the worship of God. In this sort of way, all things, great and small, that keep holy our sacred gifts may find a digital home and purpose.

But only if we try. Bitcoin's power as a tool and a weapon is not neutral. It may be fashioned into a shield onto which our highest, truest symbols may be stamped. In other hands, it becomes a sword, one with no accompanying symbol of humility and mercy. The full form of bitcoin is that of a world computer. Already, digital technology has demonstrated that it, and no longer any one person or configuration of persons, rules the world. For this reason is our technoethical elite in a vengeful state of panic, desperate, in the familiar way of men, for that which might make them forget who they are so they might wield powers denied them by God. In this fateful moment, our digital politics is revealed to be a spiritual war. To survive victorious, we must remember: the greatest spiritual weapon against errant human reset is divine revelation.

PART III:
THE ECONOMIC

THE WAR ON CAPITALISM

BY CONRAD BLACK

As other contributors have mentioned, if any place could be identified as the birthplace of the Great Reset, it must be the small, drab, German-Swiss Alpine town of Davos, a center of contemporary anti-capitalism, or at least radically altered and almost deracinated capitalism, and site of an ever-expanding international conference. (It grew exponentially and has spawned regional versions.)

I attended there for many years by invitation in order to ascertain what my analogues in the media business around the world were doing. The hotels are spartan and the town is very inaccessible. When I first attended nearly forty years ago, the Davos founder, the earnest and amiable Klaus Schwab, had ingeniously roped in a number of contemporary heads of government and captains of industry and leaders in some other fields and had sold huge numbers of admissions to well-to-do courtiers and groupies from all over the world, attracted by the merits of "networking."

Davos, and its regional outgrowths across the world gradually came to express a collective opinion of the virtues of universal supranationalism (the Davos variety of globalism): social democracy; environmental alarmism; the desirability of having a nonpolitical international bureaucracy; a public sector-reflected image of the Davos hierarchy itself (and in fact, in many cases, preferably the very same individuals); and gently enforcing a soft Orwellian conformity on everybody. It must be said that many of the sessions were interesting, and it was a unique experience being amid so many people capable in their fields, and this certainly includes almost all of those who were revenue-producing, "networking" spectators and not really participants.

Davos is for democracy, as long as everyone votes for increased public sector authority in pursuit of green egalitarianism and the homogenization of all peoples in a conformist world. It was the unfolding default page of the European view: capitalism was to be overborne by economic redistribution; all concepts of public policy were to be divorced from any sense of nationality, history, spirituality, or spontaneity and redirected to defined goals of imposed uniformity under the escutcheon of ecological survival and the reduction of abrasive distinctions between groups of people—such obsolescent concepts as nationality or sectarianism. (My hotel concierge stared at me as if I had two heads when I inquired where the nearest Roman Catholic Church was and was even more astonished when I trod two miles through the snow there and back to receive its moral succour; the parishioners appeared a sturdy group.)

The Covid-19 pandemic caused Davos Man to break out of his Alpine closet and reveal the secret but suspected plan: the whole world is to become a giant Davos—humorless, style-less, unspontaneous, unrelievedly materialistic, as long as the accumulation and application of capital is directed by the little Alpine gnomes of Davos and their underlings and disciples. This is a slight overstatement, and Klaus Schwab would earnestly dispute that the purpose of Davos is so comprehensive, anesthetizing, and uniform. His dissent would be sincere, but unjustified: the Great Reset, a Davos expression, is massively ambitious and is largely based on the seizure and hijacking of recognizable capitalism, in fact and in theory.

There has indeed in the last thirty years been a war on capitalism conducted from the commanding heights of the academy and very broadly assisted by the Western media that has been gathering strength as part of the great comeback of the Left following their bone-crushing defeat in the Cold War. As international communism collapsed and the Soviet Union disintegrated, it was difficult to imagine that the Left could mount any sort of comeback anytime soon. We underestimated both the Left's imperishability and its gift for improvisation, a talent that their many decades of predictable and robotic repetitiveness entirely concealed. By some combination of intuition and tactical cunning, the hard Left crowded aboard the environmental bandwagon. Until the nineties, the environment was the concern of authentic if sometimes tedious conservationists such as the Sierra Club and Greenpeace, and despite their harassment of nuclear testing by the French around Tahiti and their demonstrations against goodwill visits of American aircraft carriers, they were sincere people making an arguable case.

Suddenly they were overwhelmed by the hard Left imposing a new agenda of strangulation of capitalism by coming through the rear windows and attacking practically every industry as a threat to human survival for ecological reasons. We can only salute their ingenuity and persistence as they co-opted susceptible members of the scientific community to produce asinine arguments like Dr. Michael E. Mann's infamous conjuration of the "hockey stick," which held that global warming proceeded horizontally for a long time and then suddenly shot upwards at a forty-five-degree angle as a hockey stick does when the stem reaches the blade. This and spurious calculations based on reading the rings on the trunks of trees and other superstitious opinations won the approval of a huge gallery of gullible, faddish, and cynical people. They made an unlikely coalition: Al Gore became a centimillionaire on this issue; the Prince of Wales mounted a great hobby horse that he still rides, and the most vocal airheads of Hollywood have ben howling like banshees on the issue for decades.

Aggressive green parties arose in many countries and harvested the naiveté and narcissistic ambition for attention of large numbers of people championing antipollution causes that in the abstract no reasonable person could oppose. They were allied or infested with the old left and skulked forward, ideological wolves in paradisiacal lambs' clothing. Germany has no petroleum resources but had built an extensive and absolutely safe nuclear power capacity, but the aggressive German Green Party came snorting out of the Teutonic forests like a Wagnerian monster and bullied Angela Merkel's government into abandoning the entire nuclear program. Germany in effect became an energy vassal state of Russia through the Nord Stream pipeline, the completion of which the Biden administration facilitated in withdrawing the Trump administration's intervention to prevent the pipeline's completion. With the Ukraine war, it is again suspended. Thus the second most important country in the Western Alliance is almost detached from it, all by the apparently innocuous and meliorist actions of Germany's peppiest environmentalists, and with the ultimate complicity of the current U.S. president.

Even the outgoing prime minister, Boris Johnson, an authentic if idiosyncratic Tory, has bought into the global warming danger, though to those who know him, it is hard to imagine that he believes a word of it. The objective evidence is that to the extent that it can be measured at all, the overall temperature of the world has risen by one degree centigrade in the last hundred years and will rise by another centigrade degree this century. This is not in itself harmful, and it is not outside normal historic climate cycles. There has been no rise in the in the world's temperature in this century, and the whole task of gauging the world's temperature including thermometers at various depths of the oceans and all over the surface of the earth is quite imprecise.

In the future, historians will look with astonishment on the speed and zeal with which the post-Cold War world burdened itself with bone-cracking expenses and severe social costs radically altering its economy to avoid a rise in the world's temperature that we have no reason to believe will occur on anything like the scale the alarmists have been wailing about. And if it does occur in any measure, we still have no scientifically serious evidence that it is anthropogenically caused. It will be seen as something like the alleged seventeenth-century Dutch tulip hysteria, which had people paying the equivalent of $25,000 for a single potted bulb.

Rarely in the Cold War did capitalism's Marxist enemies do anything that earned the respect one gives a gallant or brilliant adversary. In these initiatives, our enemies leapt from the jaws of bitter and total defeat, hijacked the careening gadfly of esoteric conservationism, and transformed it surreptitiously into a well-camouflaged battering ram that has inflicted immense costs and opprobrium on the corporate world and great sadness and inconvenience on the laboring proletariat on whose behalf the Marxist Left has supposedly been crusading these past 150 years.

A companion unpleasant surprise to the ingenuity and resilience of the international Far Left in its environmental assault upon capitalism has been the venality, cowardice, and invertebrate tactical stupidity of much of the corporate world. We find oil companies putting up slick television advertising praising and purporting to be part of the heroic march to a fossil fuel-free world. As corporations fell over themselves agreeing that the U.S. state of Georgia's eminently sensible voting reform statute, passed in the wake of the disputed presidential election of 2020, was a reversion to Jim Crow if not slavery itself and demanded that Georgia be punished by moving the Major League Baseball All-Star Game from Atlanta to Denver (where restrictions to ensure verifiable voting are more severe than in Georgia), the leadership of corporate America was largely revealed, once again, at least in public policy terms, as contemptibly enfeebled and morally bankrupt.

The terrible rot and decay of the international corporate elite has caused this natural and traditional bastion of capitalism to deliver itself up to the pseudoenvironmentalist dagger stab of the Left. Until recently, they could be counted on, like Stephen Crane's squirrel in *The Red Badge of Courage*, not to offer their furry chests to the hunters' sights. To those of us brought up in the piping days of Alfred P. Sloan of General Motors, Henry Kaiser, and other unapologetic and constructive titans of industry and finance, and patriotic giants of the entertainment industry like Bob Hope, John Huston, and Ronald Reagan, this sniveling before the Left, groveling to extremists like BLM when they threaten boycotts, knuckling under to whatever totalitarian requirements are laid down by the People's Republic of China for access to its market, is horrifying. To those of us who have studied the Roosevelt era, one of the most striking features of the American commitment to World War II was that despite the president's frictions with a large part of the big business community, when the national interest and the status of democracy in the world (incidentally including free markets) were in mortal danger and America was in deadly combat across both oceans, there was unchallengeably strong civilian and military leadership and spontaneous, ironclad, airtight support from all sections of society, and from no one more than the captains of industry and the leaders of Hollywood.

Of course, the United States is not at war, but even Joe Biden, whose qualities of executive leadership, if he ever possessed any, have not been much in evidence during his early months as president, acknowledges that the United States is facing a stern challenge from the People's Republic of China. And he flatters himself with comparisons with Franklin D. Roosevelt; because he is in the same party and holds the same office, he seems to imagine that some of Roosevelt's magnificent patrician but uncondescending leadership qualities may devolve upon him ex officio. They thus far have not and will not, but nor will the positive forces of patriotic and idealistic defense of the American national interest as leader and protector of Western civilization well up into the oval office from the mealy mouthed corporate leadership of contemporary America.

When Jamie Dimon, the successful head of a bank bearing the great name of J. P. Morgan, simply capitulated to the Justice Department some years ago, handing over billions of dollars in fines from the shareholders' money to pay for his management's own errors, instead of contesting the authoritarian attorney general, Eric Holder, he arrived at his office and announced: "Eric, I am here to surrender." At the time, precandidate Donald Trump publicly criticized him for putting his public bootlicking of the Obama administration ahead of the shareholders' interest and even of his own reputation.

Trump was correct, and we got a foretaste of the emerging axis of the American big business-government relationship. Broadly speaking, large-scale corporate America is rather indifferent to its own workforce and noiselessly and seamlessly transfers manufacturing to cheap labor countries while swaddling itself in globalism. It acts as if patriotism was obsolete and as if the traditional corporate unity of the interests of capital and labor is replaced by an exaltation of profit over whatever human consequences may accrue to the workforce of the official nationality of the corporation and its executives. The working class drops several places on the socioeconomic totem pole, but the great middle-class, which invests directly or via pension and other managed funds in the equities of corporate America, prospers.

The political side of this equation appears to be that the Democrats have effectively abandoned their traditional base going back to the industrialization of America and the times of Grover Cleveland: the working class and the support of ethnic minorities acquired initially by the big-city bosses whose political machines assisted the waves of immigration after the Civil War. Their Democratic fealty was reinforced by FDR's equal treatment of African Americans in his workfare and Social Security programs. These groups have been put over the side and the Democratic leaders have gone barefaced and bald-headed after the upwardly mobile middle class and the new rich.

Candidate Obama signaled his party's disdain for the traditional working class overly preoccupied "by guns and religion." This mindset was more vividly reflected in candidate Hillary Clinton's dismissal of half of Trump's supporters in 2016, more than thirty million voting Americans, as "a basket of deplorables," by which she meant sociopathic racists and sexists. Since the national Democratic Party and to the extent that it governed it, the U.S. itself, adopted the position that the working class was expendable, that American industrial capitalism had been replaced by globalism, the effect was to uproot American capitalism and replant it in the dangerously uncertain soil of America's cheap-labor political rivals and enemies. What has occurred was certainly not an organized conspiracy or the execution of a strategy precisely conceived and elaborated by any individual or group; it was rather the coincidence, fortuitously for the battle-scarred international Left, of events that rushed to the rescue of our routed Cold War political and economic enemies. The comparative weighting in the motives of the authors of this reorientation of American big business and Democratic Party strategy, between cynical calculation, unexceptionable opportunism, true belief, and random coincidence, will be lengthily debated but never resolved.

The change in the attitudes of American leadership groups from World War II to the world rivalry with China today is certainly natural, up to a point. There would be no proper use or position now for the great soldier statesmen of the earlier time—generals George C. Marshall, Dwight D. Eisenhower, Douglas MacArthur, and admiral Chester W. Nimitz. But the spectacle of the chairman of the Joint Chiefs of Staff, General Mark Milley, renouncing his accompaniment of President Trump and a large number of senior officials for the one-block journey from the White House to the president's church, St. John's Church, the day after mobs attempted to burn it down, and his fatuous lecture on the importance of learning about white racism and implicitly defending the use of critical race theory in personnel and officer development in the Armed Forces, is profoundly disconcerting. This may seem to have little to do with the current status of American capitalism, but for the senior ranks of the American military to be distracted by such subversive and fallacious nonsense is indicative of how far the leaders of America in most of the public and private sector have drifted from the firm and deep consensus that America enjoyed from the immediate prewar period of 1940 through the Cold War to the present. In such an era of shaken national confidence, assaults on capitalism and the integrity of American democracy are relatively simple to launch.

For most of the balance of the twentieth century after 1940, the interests of the U.S. government, of American business, and of American labor were practically identical: traditional capitalism, job creation, and increasing the profitability of the American corporate sector were matters of vital national interest and were recognized as desirable by everyone, including the leadership of American organized labor. What has replaced that traditional capitalism is an undiminished enthusiasm for profits by the corporation with little regard for what became of its domestic workforce, nor any concern from the corporations or the federal government how America's strategic position could be affected. These shifts of American opinion and attitudes inevitably made capitalism as a concept of economic growth and job and generalized wealth creation a much more vulnerable target to the ingeniously reformulated assaults of the Marxist and neo-Marxist Left.

There was much less of a consensus to resist the egregious demands for the curtailment of rational commercial decision-making in favor of nebulous environmental goals than would have normally arisen. The patriotic notion of protecting jobs in America and other countries, exemplified by American flags and decals in motor vehicles and at the front doors of America, has gradually become a mock symbol of Americanism that is portrayed as narrow, if not racist, parochialism and an inferior option to a globalism that hides the avarice of corporations behind the pretended fraternity of all peoples, to the benefit of the enemies of capitalism, of America, and of all of the West.

The wellsprings of these reconstructionist critiques of capitalism have been visible to us for a long time from places like the Club of Rome and most notoriously, Davos's WEF. John Kenneth Galbraith, who became an icon of the moderate and even somewhat adventurous Left, though it was little appreciated at the time, opened the veil on this reservation about traditional capitalism with his 1950's bestseller *The Affluent Society*. He wrote then of an imaginary American family picnicking with the latest consumer goods on the bank of a polluted river and said that they could "reflect on the curious unevenness of their blessings." His subsequent career as an intimate of the Kennedys and as American ambassador to the great developing nation of India, and his dotage with the Democratic Left of Senator George McGovern and others, helped, intentionally or otherwise, to make the ground of American academia, intelligentsia, and comment more fertile for the onslaught against capitalism, which accelerated as the husk of worldwide communism was sloughed off. The assault against capitalism metamorphosed: communism was discredited, capitalism wallowed in the complacency of victory, and faith in the inherent value of capitalism and the desirability of its goals was furtively undermined.

The market economy has been by far the most effective economic system in world history; capitalism as it has evolved ever since early in the Industrial Revolution is undeniably the most successful form of wealth creation and distribution that has ever been devised. This is chiefly because it is the only economic system that responds to the almost universal human wish to have more of everything that is desirable. Its most vociferous critics, whether Marxists or just acidulous commentators like H. L. Mencken railing against the "booboisie," have completely failed to produce or envision a superior alternative.

Other than in families or other intimate associations, there is not a great natural desire to share things. Most people have some generous instincts that are satisfied by giving to others from kindness or a particular cultural or scientific interest, but almost everyone wants to make these decisions for themselves and when convenient. When sharing is compulsory, it is taxation, and taxation is the authoritarian appropriation of part of a person's income or wealth. Although modern history has finessed this issue to allow for the inevitable in order to maintain any concept of government, taxation is a seizure of private property.

Historically, the departure of Britain and France, the two most politically influential countries in the world until the rise of the United States, on sharply different political courses began in the middle of the seventeenth century. The great French prime minister Cardinal Richelieu (governed 1624–1642), considered that the existence of a parliament capable of inconveniencing the monarch at all was a terrible disadvantage and that the avoidance of any such obstruction to the efficiency of government in France would give his country a durable advantage in the competition with Britain. At that time, the British queen (Henrietta Maria), wife of King Charles I, was the sister of French King Louis XIII, and relations between the two countries were cordial. Richelieu watched with mounting disconcertion the squabbling between the British king and Parliament that led to the English Civil War and ultimately the execution of the king and the rise of Oliver Cromwell, the only nonmonarchic interlude (ten years) in 960 years of British monarchy. Richelieu concluded that the best course was an absolute monarchy, but he failed to account for the fact that such a system would work extremely well when directed by a genius like himself, but no country has inspired leadership often. The French Revolution 150 years after Richelieu's death revealed that he had been mistaken.

One of the features of his government and its immediate successors was the mercantilist economic system, where cartels were established with the assistance of the state, conducted virtual monopolies, and were not remotely as responsive to or devoted to finding and exploiting new economic opportunities as were the emerging competitive, preindustrial capitalist systems of Great Britain and the Netherlands, and subsequently Germany and America. Thus France, at the direction of probably its greatest leader except for Napoleon and Charles de Gaulle, opted for monarchical dictatorship and public sector-directed cartelism. Britain chose constitutional monarchy (after the Cromwell episode), and private-sector capitalism. This fateful choice powerfully influenced the development of the political institutions of the United States of America and the whole English-speaking world. The British were pioneering leaders in the Industrial Revolution—the flourishing of pure capitalism that has now spread to all but the remotest corners of the world. Originating in Britain, democratic institutions and free-market prosperity have tended to progress together, from America and Canada to such culturally distant places as South Korea, Spain, Israel, and the reconstructed postwar societies of Western Europe and Japan.

The exactions of tax collectors are proverbially odious. In prerevolutionary France, a country of twenty-five million people, two hundred thousand troops and agents were engaged in the collection of the

Salt Tax; it was a symptom of a decrepit political society that, as all the world knows, broke down and shortly fed thousands of its most talented and exalted citizens to the guillotine as a public entertainment. It was then rifled and pillaged by some of the most licentious public servants in history, and then France engaged in fifteen years of glorious but horribly enervating war conducted back-and-forth across Europe from Cadiz to Moscow and from Copenhagen to Alexandria.

In the ensuing 145 years, France has known a prerevolutionary restoration, a substitute monarchy, an empire, four republics, a collaborationist state, and a government in exile that was ultimately legitimized. Most of these transitory changes have occurred as a result of episodes of considerable violence. The original French Revolution and several of its sequels were undoubtedly the result of a grossly unjust distribution of wealth within that very rich country, and insufferably authoritarian imposition of government revenue collection, most of which occurred in an era of a semicommand economy conducted by cartels with the blessing of a centralized and despotic state. The French are no less avaricious than other nationalities, but they had an economic and political system that did not accord with their independent nature and was not competitive with the comparative political and economic liberty of Great Britain or even, once it was organized, the laborious industrial efficiency of Germany.

The United States was also founded on the basis of resistance to unjust taxation. In fact, the tax wasn't unjust but the attempted collection of it was impossible. The Americans, personified in Britain by Benjamin Franklin, agitated very persuasively for Great Britain to do the necessary to remove the French from Canada where they were a menace to New England and northern New York, and especially when acting in league with the aroused natives. In the Seven Years' War, generally known as the French and Indian War in America, Britain managed the removal of the French from Québec and made important gains in India, and it also spent a good deal of money subsidizing its dynastic allies in Germany without substantial British forces being directly engaged in Europe. Britain doubled its national debt—and was forced to impose a variety of taxes on its own people, including the Stamp Tax. The British government, not unreasonably, concluded that as Americans were the wealthiest British and as they had agitated for the very expensive operations against the French in Québec, they should pay the same tax increases that had been levied in the British Isles. There was nothing wrong with this concept except that they did not gain agreement of it at the beginning of the war when the Americans would have complied gladly to see the French off from Québec, and it was now going to be practically impossible to collect such a tax increase without raising an uncontainable level of dissatisfaction among the American colonists.

King George III was not the horrible person described by Jefferson in the Declaration of Independence, where the king is arraigned as if a defendant at the Nuremberg Trials. But he had no concept of American opinion and was poorly advised by the government of Lord Frederick North, whom he maintained in office because of Lord North's obsequious deference to the monarch. The British government should have realized what the response might be to the Stamp Tax in America, particularly after the unpromising reception it had in Boston Harbor, and could certainly have ascertained that by sending some serious officials out to research American opinion or even just listening to Benjamin Franklin, who was highly respected in Britain. However, even with thorough research, the government could not have realized how extraordinarily talented the American revolutionary leaders, Washington, Franklin, Jefferson, Hamilton, Adams, Madison, and others, would prove to be.

The whole concept of "No taxation without representation" was essentially nonsense—no electorate consents to be taxed after the need for the tax has passed and the expenses have been met otherwise, in this case by the British. And no electorate votes to tax itself unless it has absolutely no practical choice. But between the arrogance of Lord North's government and the propagandistic talents of Jefferson and Thomas Paine and others, a clumsy attempt to get the wealthy country of America to pay for some of the cost of removing the French threat from its northern border was transmogrified into a virtual atrocity, which resulted in a revolution that has been deemed to have introduced the concept of human liberty to the world. In fact, the Americans at the end of the Revolution had no more rights than they had had before but they did have self-government. They had no more civil rights than British or Swiss or most Dutch and Scandinavians, either. But they had the genius of the spectacle that America has never lost, and their move was so bold and their leadership was so extraordinarily capable that the American experiment attracted the riveted attention of the whole world and has retained it for 246 years.

Franklin helped to persuade the British to expel the French from North America in the Seven Years' War and twenty years later, he alone persuaded the absolute monarchy of France, in very parlous financial condition as it was, to go back to war to help the Americans expel the British from America and to take a stance on behalf of democracy, republicanism, and colonial secession. This, taken altogether, was one of the most astonishing feats in the entire modern history of diplomacy. The resources expended by France in the war of the American Revolution contributed materially to the financial breakdown of that country. In different ways, taxation, the attempted seizure by the undemocratic government of the British Empire, provoked the American Revolution, and its attraction of the participation of France helped create falling dominoes of tax-resistance that overthrew the French monarchy and swept across Europe in the revolutionary wars for twenty years.

Of course, the American Revolution was much more unambiguously successful than the French Revolution and much less violent, as it was not really a social revolution in the sense of passing authority from one class of people to the people as a whole as the French Revolution aspired unsuccessfully to do. But both, in their way, demonstrated the motive power of capitalism and the strong sense of entitlement the citizens of both countries had to their right to retention of the fruit of their own labor. Tax revolt led to gradually greater democratization;

this was the beginning of the connection between capitalism and the general concept of human rights.

The vulnerabilities of capitalism have been accentuated by contemporary changes in the nature of successful capitalists. Traditionally, those who amassed great fortunes did so through a more or less lengthy process of building up a business that was either a new concept that the public approved and wished to have, or the provision of a product or service on a more efficient and competitive basis than was currently available, and in both cases the enterprise grew organically on its superiority or price and marketing advantages. Those who were highly successful in financial fields developed new investment products that attracted people or managed other people's money successfully. Generally, such commercial success could be traced to the traditional desirable and well-remunerated faculties of originality, efficiency, consistency, and salesmanship in serving a public need. The passage of time was the ally of increased net worth and the capital that accumulated was reenlisted into the economy in investments, acquisitions, or savings, all of which compounded the legitimate growth of the money supply and the generality of wealth of the whole population.

This process created the culture of capitalism, which, although there was an immense variety of methods of legitimate wealth creation, generally emphasized the traditional virtues of careful analysis, hard work, consistent dedication to building a business over a period of years, and the assembly of a set of stable traditional values. To some extent this was mercilessly and humorously lampooned by acidulous commentators like H. L. Mencken, disdained by some of the extremely rich as tasteless and even mindless striving, and assailed by representatives of the working class as mere avarice masquerading as an authentic socioeconomic philosophy. But in all advanced countries, the social and economic backbone of the nation was those who worked diligently to better their lot from the more skilled echelons of the working class all the way up through the middle class to the realms of the well-to-do, the wealthy, and ultimately, the very wealthy.

In very recent times, as the applicability of ever more widespread scientific innovation has been commercialized, colossal fortunes have accumulated almost instantly from the development of a sophisticated technological product or service and its aggressive marketing to the whole world. A new capitalist culture has arisen in which success is astronomically greater and faster than it has ever been before, easily surpassing discoveries in previous eras of great deposits of precious metals or reserves of petroleum. Instead of capitalism being generally perceived as a process of diligence and sustained superior analysis and execution, and the application with sober and prolonged determination of essentially bourgeois principles of work and attentiveness, the capitalist banner has largely passed in general public perceptions to young, often somewhat brash, jargonistic technological parvenus. Instead of a regime of insight, constancy, competence, and a variety of administrative, technical, competitive, and marketing skills, all based on traditional arithmetic, there has arisen a new version of capitalism that rather emphasizes, and hugely rewards, inventiveness and the art of discerning commercial faddishness. These qualities are not to be disparaged or invidiously compared to traditional capitalist virtues. No one can dispute the extraordinary ability of Bill Gates, Jeff Bezos, Mark Zuckerberg, and others, nor question the utility and efficacy of the products and communications initiatives that they have brought forward. Indeed, in many respects, their careers are at least as inspiring if not quite as colorful as some of the great financiers and industrialists of the century that preceded them.

But the culture that they represent is, in part, one of getting rich quickly and flaunting wealth and influence, and since conservative values were not particularly required in the lightning accumulation of their immense wealth, they seem to believe that traditional capitalism is antiquarian rubbish. The traditional values of working hard for a long time and accumulating a gradually but steadily greater retained and reinvested wealth are not the values that the individuals mentioned and their peers appear to have practiced or espoused. This form of capitalism, whether intended by its exemplars to do so or not, incites in the minds of many the view that vast amounts of money can be made almost instantly if one only has a brain wave and takes it to market.

Those familiar with the financial markets are well aware that these unicorns, as they are described (ideas capitalized in public offerings of equity before they have any income at all to report), fail in the great majority of cases. But the public impression is that these very modern, technically minded entrepreneurs have invented a new form of wealth creation and while it is not much spoken of, the implication is that capital formation is swift and simple for ingenious people. What is required is technological insight and thought rather than work, and the public policy positions and general behavior of these new capitalists is frequently prodigiously extravagant, trendy, and pandering in nature, either sincerely or tactically to fend off the usual envy and spite misdirected at the very wealthy, and in public policy terms often rather socialistic. This erodes traditional respect for capitalist achievement, but it also incites the charge of hypocrisy in some of these new billionaires, whose patronage will not do the socialist Left any good over time.

It must also be said that at Microsoft, as at Amazon, there has been a vigorous pursuit of a quasimonopolistic preeminence in their fields that flies somewhat in the face of the protestations of distributive generosity that these individuals habitually express. Even men who've become extremely wealthy in traditional ways, such as Warren Buffett, have made a point of dressing like people of modest incomes, living modestly, and masquerading as friendly and avuncular quasisocialists. Mr. Buffett for years requested that his taxes be increased, although revelations of how he has legitimately gamed the system to leave most of his imputable income untaxable seems to have muted that particular form of histrionics.

The cavalier and arbitrary manner in which the multibillionaire heads of the American social media platform companies have denied access to their platforms to people with whom they do not agree, including President Trump when he was president and since, has aroused the concern of scores of millions of ordinary American citizens who do not approve of this level of almost dictatorial authority being exercised at all and certainly not by unelected officials. The anti-Trump majority that succeeded the former president's single term is politically well-served by this arbitrary behavior, but it is inconceivable that with the passage of time the American public will tolerate such an abuse of private authority.

This is perhaps the greatest example in American history of what Franklin D. Roosevelt called "the economic royalists and malefactors of great wealth." In pandering to leftist sentiment and trying to masquerade in the Maoist expression as "fish swimming in the sea of the people," they will end up profoundly offending the society in which they are so conspicuous and influential. But for the moment, their conduct is a largely unbecoming and less alluring human face of American capitalism than that of the grandees of the past: the Rockefellers, the Fords, the Mellons, and even astounding personalities like William Randolph Hearst and Howard Hughes. As they tarnish somewhat the image of the great capitalists, they also make capitalism seem simpler and more like good luck with the lottery than the desirable result of a lifetime of admirable effort and sagacity conducted within and to the benefit of society.

The other most highly publicized and noticeable form of contemporary capitalist is the suddenly and immensely wealthy oligarchs of Russia, members of the ruling families of petrostates, and the greatly wealthy people of China, of whom it may be presumed that whatever their commercial acumen, it is complemented by their assiduous courtship of the government of the People's Republic. A number of spectacularly wealthy business people from various other large countries such as India and Brazil and Mexico are also well known, and many of them are by traditional standards quite flamboyant. The great Mexican telecommunications proprietor, Carlos Slim, living in a country with scores of millions of poor people in it, conducts himself with great propriety and discretion and acts of public spiritedness that are known but not overpublicized. The others in the super-rich international category are a mixed bag and in general wealthy Western Europeans behave with the urbanity that the upper classes of those countries have acquired over centuries. Even a new man like Richard Branson is seen as a hardworking, well-intentioned, unpretentious, and admirably successful person from a modest socioeconomic start. The Russian oligarchs in particular, as they are generally assumed to be in league with a corrupt antidemocratic government and splash their money around with insouciant vulgarity, do some damage to the public relations of capitalism.

In summary, these new capitalists have made capitalism itself more vulnerable, not in the least because many of them espouse a kind of limousine socialism that makes capitalism incoherent, and some others in the countries with less reliable legal systems than in the West, like the Russian oligarchs or *Crazy Rich Asians*, make capitalism look like the fruit of corruption, exploitation, and vulgar self-indulgence. Obviously, to some extent, though it is not measurable, this puts a comparatively unattractive human face on capitalism and makes it vulnerable to the incessant attacks of the old left hiding behind the skirts of the militant ecologists, of the modern left debunking capitalism as obsolete and antisocial humbug, and to that section of the public to whose redistributive instincts the new spectacle of mountainous personal wealth swiftly achieved is like a miraculous form of political catnip.

The question that most directly interests us here is whither capitalism? Capitalism was, along with democracy itself, the principal reason why the United States was able to bluff the Soviet Union into helpless dissolution with an American economy that maintained a fully adequate deterrent military force though the U.S.S.R. was spending approximately ten times as great a percentage of GDP on defense as the United States was. The disintegration of the Soviet Union was like the fall of a soufflé, without violence or collateral damage, and was the greatest and most bloodless strategic victory in the history of the nation-state. It was the supreme confirmation of the superiority of democratic capitalism to any other political and economic system.

Worrisome though the assault upon capitalism today is, it is a stealth attack in part and an incidental and unintended discreditation in part. Whatever they say and however they act, the Silicon Valley billionaires and the Russian oligarchic billionaires and the enigmatic Chinese billionaires are all capitalists in practice. The environmentalists remain a ramshackle coalition of sincere if overwrought naturalists with a militant but bedraggled and profoundly mistaken detritus of Marxists, some of whom could conceivably pass under the raddled and tarnished rubric of social democrats.

Furthermore, in international rivalries, our great challenger, China, is in many respects, a greater espouser of capitalism than any western country and far less enervated by the exigencies of the welfare state than is the West. Our internal enemies are the old Marxist Left exploiting and radicalizing the flabby, faddish soft Left they have always despised and driving it before them. In the world, we are assailed by an almost laissez faire but totalitarian and rigorously illiberal China, which is still about 40 percent a command economy.

While capitalism is the only system that works, it also possesses, like other systems, the potential of self-destruction and needs to be tempered at times both by the application of humanitarian standards and by a self-protection system that keeps the capitalist impulse well short of a monopoly game that becomes, as it often has in relatively primitive societies, an overconcentration of wealth and power in the hands of the greatest masters of the game. There have long been sensitivities to this in America, and in Russia and China, some of the wealthiest people in both countries are sometimes thrown into prison or simply disappear; it is a form of plutocracy and timocracy avoidance, though a crude one.

The first requirement is to defang the green terror. This is happening as the consequences of its implementation are completely unacceptable in a democratic society and the threat that it is supposed to avoid is not in fact happening year after year. Every week, there are fresh announcements that various asinine goals of emission reduction will not be met. Al Gore and the Prince of Wales are long past their initial projections of imminent doom if we did not pull up our ecological socks.

"Cherchez l'intérêt," say the French; look for self-interest. If we can raise our sights beyond the discouraging prospects of the balance of the current American administration, which will not be able to enact its more draconian and self-punitive environmental nostrums, it should be possible to uncouple the United States from this delusional juggernaut of salvation through economic self-deprivation. Then, as in most matters and for the same reasons, other countries will follow the Americans, with the Germans probably the last of the important countries. Of all the great Western nations historically and notoriously, Germany has the least reliable political judgment and seems likely to retain that status on this issue. But the extreme green menu is bunk and the economic self-interest of the majority in the democratic world ultimately will see it to be so. The Chinese, Indians, and Russians will be decades taking any serious steps to reduce pollution levels, and along with the mawkish Covid response, the Chinese already are chuckling at their good fortune that Western preoccupation with ecology is assisting their charge toward world economic (capitalist) leadership.

Capitalism retains the incomparable advantage of being the only system that works and the only one which, when any even slightly economically sophisticated nationalities are subjected to it, is the popularly preferred option. The political ability and propensity of democratic countries to tax money from people who have earned it (or their heirs) and distribute it to people who have not earned it, usually with no more than a rudimentary analysis of merit, does enable the political leadership to build themselves a majority by transferring money through the tax system from a wealthy minority to a less wealthy majority. This has happened at times in almost all advanced Western countries. But the political architects of these designs are generally careful not to allow their elections to become referenda on outright socialism or the benefits of an expanded public-sector. Socialism remains substantially discredited in most of the Western world and even rather fervent socialists like Senator Elizabeth Warren proclaim themselves to be capitalists. In the appalling and often violent disagreements between self-styled socialists and capitalists over the last 150 years, the capitalists have had the better of it and retain a better public relations name with most of the electorates of the West.

Even the Trump administration, tumultuous though it was and evicted from office though it was, albeit by a narrow margin and in a questionable election, generated a significant amount of manufacturing growth in the U.S., improved trade agreements, incentivized job creation in low-income areas and effectively eliminated unemployment. Trump cut the taxes of 83 percent of taxpayers, made the United States an energy exporter for the first time in approximately seventy years, and most importantly, the incomes of the lowest 20 percent of income earners in the country were growing more quickly in percentage terms than the top 10 percent.

This was a little-noticed accomplishment of the Trump administration because of the almost totalitarian anti-Trump partisanship of the national political and social media. The United States became the first large jurisdiction to make headway on the almost universal problem of extreme income-growth disparity. Only the confected phenomenon of Trump hate and whatever skulduggery attended the election in several swing states, won it in the electoral college for Trump's enemies. A strategic flip of fifty thousand votes in three states and Trump would have won. His policies were endorsed, as the Republican gain of twenty congressmen demonstrated. The United States will recover from its political nervous semibreakdown—the negative curative powers of the present administration should not be overlooked or underestimated. The successor regime should resume leadership of the defense of capitalist democracy.

Taking the current challenges individually, as these absurd environmental goals prove unattainable, countries and societies come to grips one after the other with the economic costs and inconveniences of radical alteration of the economy in order to achieve goals of uncertain value. There will be a great deal of environmental shilly-shallying conducted behind dense screens of obfuscating bureaucratese. But the myth of "99 percent agreement among scientists" is being fragmented by mounting professional dissent and by the failure of the apocalypse to occur. It will become steadily harder to raise the alarm about global warming, a battlement of the Left that has already been half-abandoned, when it is not, in fact, becoming warmer.

It is inconceivable that the Americans will long tolerate the abusive cartel being conducted on its major social media platforms. The majority of Americans resent this cartel and it has only avoided direct legislative attack because the Democrats, having criticized it quite vigorously, were won over and struck dumb in their hostility by the uniform ferocity with which these companies assisted them in their Trump-hate crusade. Increasing competition will cause some of the unsuccessful unicorns to fail spectacularly, and the Silicon Valley model of instant accumulation of immense wealth will become less dazzling than it has been. Historically, a large number of people who become extremely wealthy very quickly have somewhat meteoric careers.

While the United States in particular is in uncharted economic waters, the expansion of the federal debt to substantially more than the gross domestic product for the first time since World War II and the rise in the stock market indices to heights about 20 percent above the Trump figure before recent losses, which was a 40 percent improvement upon Obama's best days, have been enabled in part by interest rates that are proven unsustainable at their very low levels. In all of these circumstances, at some point in the next few years, the virtues of more traditional capitalism will come back into fashion. Diligent application of carefully thought-out competitive and product and marketing strategies will not long be regarded as obsolescent slogging through heavy undergrowth, once a rocket trip to great prosperity is no longer assumed to be readily available.

The Biden administration is not going to get its attempted tax increases adopted and it will be challenging to avoid substantial interest rate increases while pursuing prosperity by hurling huge chunks of stimulus spending out of the windows of every federal building in Washington. This will be affirmed by the voters in the next four years as a less promising course than low taxes and comparative spending restraint. In a word, the lurch of the current American administration to the Left will be a failure economically and politically, and its tortuous and painful retreat in the elections of the next four years will furnish a substantial indication of whether the war against capitalism will gain or lose ground in the country of the world's greatest economy, which best articulates and practices the democratic capitalist ethos.

In Europe it will, as always, be more complicated. For obvious historic reasons, Western Europe has adopted the policy of paying Danegeld to organized labor and small farmers in exchange for comparative social peace. It was a steep and unpleasant learning curve for the generally sensible President Emmanuel Macron of France when a huge swath of the working class and lower middle class took against him in tenacious rioting for many months by the so-called Yellow Jackets. M. Macron's high intelligence has not entirely made up for his political inexperience, but his April 2022 victory over Marine Le Pen will allow him to chase fewer policy goals at once and continue to make concessions to the French taxpayers, (though reducing the urban speed limit to nineteen miles per hour partly to fight "climate change" is unlikely to command the obedience or respect of their countrymen).

The United Kingdom is safe with a Tory government and essentially Thatcherite fiscal and social policy. Polls show that the paper-thin vote to leave Europe is now a decision approved by 70 percent of the British. Immigration was not the issue that chiefly moved the British to vote to leave the European Union, though it was a contributing factor. The principal issue was one of democracy. The French and Italians generally consider government to be a nuisance usually conducted by incompetent or self-serving individuals and the result is that they pay as little attention as possible to laws and regulations. In the case of the French, it will be a long time before they are prepared to accept any guidance on anything from Brussels. The Germans are the most influential country in Europe and are accustomed to regimentation and don't particularly object to it.

The British like to obey laws but require that the laws be sensible and democratically arrived at; the European Union's habit of deluging the entire E.U. with directives adopted by the European Commission on the authority of the appointed commissioners who are not really answerable to anyone, including the talking shop of the European Parliament, profoundly offended the British and caused them to balk at the idea of replacing the political institutions that have served that country well and continuously for many centuries, with the half-fledged if well-intentioned political institutions of Brussels. Nor did they wish their relations with the United States and the senior members of the Commonwealth, especially Canada, India, and Australia, to be subsumed into the foreign policy of Europe.

Britain's retirement from the E.U., while negotiating a close arrangement with it, should be seen as an important shift in the balance of influence in the world from the European social-democratic, economically plodding semineutralism of the post-Cold War, to the better-defined and more purposeful and relatively unambiguous capitalism of the Anglo-Saxons and their ideologically kindred allies. A united Europe was always a somewhat anti-American enterprise, though the recent fugitives from the Warsaw Pact, especially the Poles, Hungarians, and Czechs, are more interested in economic and military solidarity with the Americans than the globalist Brussels fairy tale.

The rocky start of the Biden administration may also be seen as a poor advertisement for the Great Reset, most of whose chief tenets the administration basically approves. Now that aspects of the Great Reset are being put to the test and failing, the way forward for those of us in dissent is clearer in these post-Trump (or inter-Trump) days. I did see the future at Davos and was relieved to see that it isn't going to work and won't be the future for long. Constructive and thoughtful capitalism, not garish and vulgar consumption or oppressive state capitalism, will win, in America, and around the world (including China.) It is the (now protectively armored) goose that lays the golden egg every time.

SOCIALISM AND THE GREAT RESET

BY MICHAEL ANTON

It has become increasingly common to hear those on what we may call the conventional Right claim that the main threat facing the historic American nation and the American way of life is "socialism." These warnings have grown with the rise of the so-called "Great Reset," ostensibly a broad effort to reduce inequality, cool the planet (i.e., "address climate change"), and cure various social ills, all by decreasing alleged "overconsumption." In other words, its mission is to persuade people, at least in the developed West, to accept lower standards of living in order to create a more just and "equitable" world. Since the conservative mind, not unreasonably, associates lower standards of living with "socialism," many conservatives naturally intuit that the Great Reset must somehow be "socialist."

I believe this fear is at least partly misplaced and that the warnings it gives rise to, however well-meaning, are counterproductive because they deflect attention from the truer, greater threat: specifically, the cabal of bankers, techies, corporate executives, politicians, senior bureaucrats, academics, and pundits who coalesce around the World Economic Forum and seek to change, reduce, restrict, and homogenize the Western way of life—but only for ordinary people. Their own way of life, along with the wealth and power that define it, they seek to entrench, augment, deepen, and extend.

This is why a strict or literal definition of "socialism"—public or government ownership and control of the means of production in order to equalize incomes and wealth across the population—is inapt to our situation. The Great Reset quietly but unmistakably redefines "socialism" to allow and even promote wealth and power concentration in certain hands. In the decisive sense, then, the West's present economic system—really, its overarching regime—is the opposite of socialistic.

Yet there are ways in which this regime might still be tentatively described as "socialist," at least as it operates for those not members in good standing of the Davoisie. If the Great Reset is allowed to proceed as planned, wealth for all but the global overclass *will* be equalized, or at least reduced for the middle and increased for the bottom. Many of the means used to accomplish this goal *will* be "socialistic," broadly understood. But to understand both the similarities and the differences, we must go back to socialism's source, which is the thought of Karl Marx and his colleague, financial backer, and junior partner, Friedrich Engels.

That thought is most accessible in Marx's *Economic and Philosophic Manuscripts of 1844*, the jointly authored *Manifesto of the Communist Party* (1848), and Engels's pamphlet "Socialism: Utopian and Scientific" (1880). Marxism's detailed account of economics is fully developed in the monumental *Capital* (*Das Kapital*), published in three volumes between 1867 and 1894.[9] Marx and Engels do not claim to be innovators. They insist rather that they merely discovered

---

9 The first three works, plus Volume One of *Capital* (the only volume Marx completed in his lifetime), are collected in *The Marx-Engels Reader*, edited by Robert C. Tucker (New York: W. W. Norton & Company, Inc., 1978, Second Edition). All quotes, unless otherwise specified, are from these works. I am indebted as well to the excellent summaries of Marxist thought by Joseph Cropsey ("Karl Marx," in *The History of Political Philosophy*, edited by Leo Strauss and Joseph Cropsey; Chicago: University of Chicago Press, 1987, Third Edition) and by Thomas L. Pangle and Timothy W. Burns ("Marx and Engels: The Communist Manifesto," in *The Key Texts of Political Philosophy—An Introduction*; New York: Cambridge University Press, 2015).

and explicate the "scientific" theory of socialism, whose true roots are to be found in the unfolding development of "history."

Marxism

A word ought to be said about the difference between "communism" and "socialism." The distinction is not always clear in Marx's and Engels's works. Often, they use both terms interchangeably. Engels, especially, seems to elide the two, particularly in "Socialism: Utopian and Scientific." But we may perhaps take as authoritative the distinction made in the *Manifesto*. There, the two authors contrast true communism with various forms of socialism—feudal, petty-bourgeois, German, conservative, and critical-utopian—all of which they find wanting, at best milestones on the road to communism.

It is unnecessary for our purposes here to recount Marx's and Engels's distinctions between the various forms of socialism. Suffice it to say that, in their account, all of those varieties constitute cynical or at any rate inconsequential concessions to the lower classes, intended to stave off the emergence of full communism and to preserve ruling class status and privileges. The "socialism" with which we are most familiar today—high and progressive taxation, a generous welfare state, nationalization of key services such as health care, an expansive list of state-guaranteed "rights," combined with the retention of private property and private ownership of most means of production—Marx and Engels deride as "bourgeois socialism," i.e., not only *not* the real thing but fundamentally closer to bourgeois capitalism than to true socialism, much less communism.

Marxism and "History"

For Marx and Engels, the ground of both socialism and communism is "history," understood not as an account of past events, conditions, structures, and trends but as an inexorable movement toward a final, fully rational state, with "state" understood as both "state of being" and the formal machinery of government. The discovery of this notion of "history" is implicit in Rousseau's account of man's transition from the state of nature—man's original and natural, in the sense of "default," condition—to civil society. For Rousseau, that transition was both a decline and one-way: there is no going back. This change in man's situation, which putatively changes his nature, is the core of what would come to be called "historicism": the idea that human nature is not constant but variable according to the historical situation. In this understanding, "history," and not any purported but nonexistent permanent human nature as posited by all prior philosophy, both determines the organization of society and supplies the standard by which man should live.

For Rousseau, man's transition from the state of nature to civil society is caused by the discovery or development of his rationality, a latent quality always present in humanity but not active in the state of nature, in which men live more or less as beasts. What distinguishes man from the beasts is his freedom, his awareness of and ability to act on that freedom, and the potential to develop his rationality. The "unlocking" of that rationality is perhaps inevitable but at the same time accidental or inadvertent. Once unlocked, human rationality inevitably leads to the invention of private property, which is the basis of all politics. "The first person who, having fenced off ground, took it into his head to say *this is mine* and found people simple enough to believe him, was the true founder of civil society," Rousseau writes in his *Discourse on the Origin and Foundation of Inequality among Men*.

Private property necessarily gives rise to institutions designed to protect and defend it, and these become not only the instruments of civil society but also sources of inequality and misery. Implicit in Rousseau's thought is the unsettling notion that, once this historical process begins, it has no end or rational direction. History is driven by contradiction and conflict—though, he asserts, human beings can still live more or less happily if isolated from urban wealth and corruption. But such circumstances are rare and the products of chance. History in the main is the endless replacement of one set of standards and modes of life for new ones, one set of masters for another, ad infinitum.

Rousseau's successors, principally Kant and Hegel, accept the notion that history is driven by conflict but posit that the process nonetheless has a rational direction. History's inherent and inevitable conflicts point forward and upward toward a final state in which all of history's contradictions are resolved. It is this alleged insight—popularized in the late 1980s and early 1990s by Francis Fukuyama—upon which Marx and Engels build their political and economic theory.

For Marxism, the fundamental fact of human life—what sets man apart from the other living beings—is conscious production and consumption. Marx partly follows Rousseau in believing that there was a period when man could, essentially, "live off the land," on what he could find and gather. But whereas for Rousseau, man's transition from the state of nature to civil society was an avoidable or at any rate accidental and unnecessary tragedy, for Marx it was inevitable and, eventually, will turn out all to the good. Unlike producing animals (for instance, bees) man's production is conscious. He knows what he does and why he does it. But this consciousness does not arise from any innate rationality but rather from necessity. Population increase forces man to produce—that is, to manipulate nature rather than simply living off its bounty—in order to survive. (The implication is that nature is barely bountiful enough to support a limited number of primitive men but must be "conquered" in order to support the inevitably larger numbers that will emerge absent some external force that consistently culls the population.) This turn to production represents a fundamental change in man's being and is the first step in his historical development.

From this point forward, the character of man and of every society he inhabits is set by the mode(s) of production. Such modes not only determine but explain, literally, everything about human life: man's past, present, and future; his theology, morality, and worldview; and the underlying metaphysics and ontology of reality. Thus can Marx claim that his theory is comprehensive.

For Marxism, man adapts himself to the reigning mode of production; he does not adapt that (or any) mode to his environment, traditions, religion, or to any of his specific wants, preferences, or aspirations. The mode of production is the fundamental given in any historical situation, the "base." This "base" determines the "superstructure," i.e., all other aspects of life, especially the cultural and zeitgeist-forming institutions that shape and regulate men's habits and opinions. In this understanding, families, churches, civic institutions, fraternal organizations, guilds, and even governments are all determined by the reigning means of production. As Marx observed in *The Poverty of Philosophy*, Ch. 2, Part 1: "the hand-mill gives you the society of the feudal lord; the steam-mill, society with the industrial capitalist."

The subsequent unfolding of "history" is the change from one mode of production to another, and the concomitant replacement (or displacement) of one ruling class by another, which always results in the erection of a new superstructure. In the famous words very near the beginning of the *Manifesto*, "The history of all hitherto existing society is the history of class struggles." Or, to be slightly more precise, class conflict is the engine that moves history.

Class struggles arise from the inherent fact that all means of production are always owned and controlled by a few who exploit the many. This inherent tension inevitably produces inequality, injustice and misery, and hence conflict, which eventually but inevitably overthrows the existing means of production, its superstructure, and its ruling class. Thus did the ancient warrior-agrarian economy give way to the medieval-feudal system, which gave way to the early modern monarchal aristocracies, which in turn were replaced by bourgeois industrial capitalism.

The process was not, however, smooth. Every system of production is marred by inherent contradictions, inefficiencies, and, above all, injustices that spur conflict. While the replacement of one system of production and its ruling class by another may be inevitable, it is also tumultuous: always the result of violent revolution.

The winner, by definition, defeats the loser but is also transformed in and by the struggle. No system (until the final one) is free of contradiction and error. All claims to justice (except the final one) are partial. Every system has, in a sense, "something to learn" from its mortal enemy. Thus, in terms Marx borrows or builds upon from Hegel, "thesis" (the dominant mode of production) is confronted by "antithesis" (its challenger), and after a protracted struggle, the two form a "synthesis": a new mode, closer to the antithesis than to the thesis, but incorporating elements of the latter. Only with the emergence of communism, which Marx and Engels allege will be entirely free of contradiction and injustice, does this process cease and history "end."

Marxism's Analysis and Critique of Capitalism

Marx and Engels claim to write at a moment when capitalism stands on the precipice of destruction. That system, they argue, is unique in ways that make inevitable its imminent overthrow.

First and foremost, capitalism elevates production, efficiency, and profit above all other considerations—even going so far as to deny that there are any other legitimate societal interests. As a result, capitalism is vastly more productive than any previously existing economic system. This makes its ruling class, the bourgeoisie, far richer and more powerful than any prior ruling class, and hence far more ruthlessly exploitative.

Unjust as (say) feudalism was, it at least asserted and nurtured human bonds and obligations between lords and vassals, aristocrats and peasants, land-owners and serfs. One hallmark of precapitalist economies was the existence of intermediate classes: professionals, merchants, clerical workers, tradesmen, shopkeepers, and various middlemen. In prior historical epochs, it was these intermediate classes (or some of them) who rose up, overthrew the dominant class, and became the new ruling class.

But capitalism, say Marx and Engels, crushes the remaining intermediate classes, either eliminating their role entirely or else subsuming their functions into the machinery of capitalism. As a result, most "upper" intermediaries are absorbed into the capitalist system (though typically at lower wages than they earned previously, and always with less independence and power) while the "lower" are forced into the proletariat. Capitalism inevitably divides society into two classes: wealthy exploiters and the impoverished exploited, with no one in between. The proletariat has no stake in the system because the system exists only to exploit it.

For the vast majority, "freedom" becomes merely the ability to sell one's labor, the only remotely valuable commodity most people have. That labor being duly paid for, capitalists feel no further obligation to workers. To the contrary, they believe that, in paying the wage, they have done their duty entirely—to the workers and to society at large. The only obligations a capitalist recognizes are to himself, to his shareholders (to maximize profits), and to the system (to maximize efficiency and production). Capitalism, Marx and Engels assert, "has put an end to all feudal, patriarchal, idyllic relations. It has pitilessly torn asunder the motley feudal ties that bound man to his 'natural superiors,' and has left remaining no other nexus between man and man than naked self-interest, than callous 'cash payment.'"

Capitalism also dehumanizes. The system's only goals, increasing profits and productivity, are immensely furthered by breaking down all tasks into minute constituent parts: repetitive, mind-numbing jobs that can be performed by anyone—and, when automation reaches a sufficient level of sophistication, by no one. The division of labor and industrial organization push wages downward and work hours upward, thus fattening the bottom line (for labor is nearly always any business's highest cost) while making workers disposable because easily replaceable, further increasing the power of the bourgeoisie.

This restless spirit of innovation in pursuit of greater efficiency and productivity relentlessly erodes the grounds for societal stability and continuity:

> The bourgeoisie cannot exist without constantly revolutionising the instruments of production, and

> thereby the relations of production, and with them the whole relations of society. Conservation of the old modes of production in unaltered form was, on the contrary, the first condition of existence for all earlier industrial classes. Constant revolutionising of production, uninterrupted disturbance of all social conditions, everlasting uncertainty and agitation distinguish the bourgeois epoch from all earlier ones. All fixed, fast-frozen relations, with their train of ancient and venerable prejudices and opinions, are swept away, all new-formed ones become antiquated before they can ossify. All that is solid melts into air, all that is holy is profaned, and man is at last compelled to face with sober senses his real conditions of life, and his relations with his kind.

Among the consequences is endless technological change that whisks away old industries and with them established ways of life. The burdens of this change fall entirely on the workers, few of whom can adapt to and succeed in the technologically transformed new economy. With all in a constant state of flux and all tradition washed away, the people become anxiety-ridden and isolated.

The inherent logic of capitalism also demands, and drives, maximum expansion. Once a firm saturates its local market, it must conquer the regional. This is not a choice: management can be certain that if their firm does not (and even if it does), its competitors surely will. And even if they don't, capitalism abhors stability, which in its logic is synonymous with stagnation and tantamount to decay. A business no less than an industry or economy is either expanding or dying. The ultimate imperative of capitalism is growth. Hence, once the local market is conquered, and then the regional, the next inevitable frontier is the national, then the continental, the hemispheric, and finally the global: "The need of a constantly expanding market for its products chases the bourgeoisie over the whole surface of the globe. It must nestle everywhere, settle everywhere, establish connections everywhere."

In this way, the power of capitalist firms and of capitalism itself eventually rivals, and in many cases exceeds, the power of nation-states. At a minimum, these firms' immense market power, control of resources, and dominance of their economic sectors allow them to seduce, bribe, and bully states to adopt policies favorable to capitalism, often at the expense of citizens' interests. For instance, a capitalist firm will always seek the lowest available wage for a task done competently. It is indifferent to the fate of those who can't or won't compete for the same task at a lower wage, regardless of whether such workers are fellow citizens. The pressure, then, to "globalize" not just the market for products but also for labor is inexorable.

Just as capitalism attacks the bonds of citizenship, it also undermines the family. Capitalism recognizes only three types of human beings: capitalists, workers, and consumers. For the first two categories, it considers family life at best a distraction and at worst a competing claim to loyalty. As for the third, the more consumers work and spend (and work in order to spend), the better. Family life constrains participation in the labor market, which limits earnings, which reduces spending. More ominously, the ground of the family itself becomes pecuniary: husbands and wives, parents and children, are dependent on one another for money but are otherwise disconnected: "The bourgeoisie has torn away from the family its sentimental veil, and has reduced the family to a mere money relation."

Perhaps the most striking or counterintuitive of Marxism's claims about capitalism is the assertion that its high productivity inevitably leads to overproduction. A decisive difference between capitalism and all prior modes of production is that the latter all wrestled with, without ever solving, the problem of scarcity. From man's emergence from the state of nature until the advent of bourgeois capitalism, scarcity was assumed to be a fundamental condition that could be managed but never overcome. Capitalism solves this problem—and then, says Marx, creates the new problem of overproduction. Mechanization, organization, the division of labor, ruthless competition, and other factors combine to enable capitalist firms to produce more than ever, but the foundation of this miraculous production is lower costs arising from new technology, greater efficiency, lower wages, fewer workers, and longer hours.

As a result, workers have less money to spend and less leisure in which to spend it. Hence, much of the production they would otherwise consume must lie fallow. The resultant lower revenues increase the imperative to cut the workforce further. Boom leads to bust, to mass layoffs and retrenchment, to further consolidation, fewer and larger capitalist firms, and a larger and ever-increasing "reserve army of the unemployed." The only ways to keep the system going are "enforced destruction of a mass of productive forces," "the conquest of new markets," and "more thorough exploitation of the old ones," thus "paving the way for more extensive and more destructive crises, and... diminishing the means whereby crises are prevented."

This situation, naturally, further binds together and embitters the workers, who become a class—the proletariat—with distinct interests diametrically opposed to those of the bourgeoisie. Capitalism, in other words, creates the means of its own destruction: a large, strong, united, angry, and determined proletariat.

Finally, according to Marxism, human beings with power and/or privilege always and everywhere have a deep need to believe that their position is deserved and what they do is right and just. Their explanation or account of why this is so, Marx and Engels call "ideology": the fairy tale a ruling class tells itself to feel better and which it sells to the masses to cajole them into accepting their inferior status in the reigning order. Marx and Engels claim that the ideology of bourgeois capitalism is the thinnest yet concocted—so transparently false and unbelievable that it can't long support the system it attempts to undergird. Capitalist ideology's hold over men's minds is much weaker than the rich myths of ancient paganism, medieval Christianity, or even aristocratic chivalry. All capitalism has to offer is endless production and consumption, a "joyless quest for joy," to borrow a phrase from Leo Strauss. In a way, the very honesty of capitalist ideology—there's nothing for man but self-interest and self-indulgence—will hasten its undoing. The human soul longs for transcendence, and capitalism not only explicitly promises nothing but material goods, it denies the value and even existence of anything higher.

The Marxist Solution

For Marxism, the advent of communism (the highest and final manifestation of socialism) is, somewhat paradoxically, both inevitable and requires human effort. The theory insists on the inexorability of "history" while also admitting that the proletariat can't act on its own but needs leaders—a "vanguard"—to mount the revolution. Those leaders must have the leisure to acquire the philosophic education that enables them to discern the course and exigencies of history, to know how and when to act, and who therefore must come from outside (really, above) the proletariat. Marxist theory is never entirely clear whether this vanguard emerges inevitably or whether some men must take matters into their own hands. Marx's successor Vladimir Lenin definitively resolves the ambiguity in favor of the latter.

For Marxism, the reason why capitalism, evil as it is, was both necessary and desirable is that it solves the problem of scarcity. Capitalism makes want a thing of the past. In a post-capitalist society, for the first time in history, men will not fight over goods because goods will no longer be scarce. The fundamental problem becomes one of distribution, of just and equitable allocation. This, Marxism claims, can be accomplished through central planning. Class conflict will be a thing of the past because classes themselves will be things of the past. There will be only one class: the proletariat. The proletariat will be history's first ruling class that is not a minority—that, to the contrary, comprises the vast majority of mankind and thus, so to speak, everyone. This is why, for Marxists, communism is mankind's final state. It exploits no one and thus faces no challenger or competitor; it does not create an oppressed class to rise against it. It is a thesis without antithesis, the final synthesis.

Communism culminates not merely in a wholly new system of production and distribution but also—because economics determines all—in an entirely new society and breed of man. For Marxism, man's experience in the state of nature is social and almost paradisiacal. His natural sociality is gradually eroded through history until it is all but crushed by the atomizing forces of capitalism. Communism restores, and improves on, man's initial state. It returns man to his innocence and natural goodness—but with the accumulated technology, wealth, and sophistication of industrial modernity. It restores his status as a "species-being": an essentially communal, fraternal, and benevolent creature who becomes fully human and happy only through relating to others of his own species. Because all contradictions have been resolved, and all class conflict ended, avarice and other forms selfishness will cease. Perfect rationality will reign.

Communism further improves on the state of nature by solving the problems not just of scarcity but of the division of labor. Under communism, man is no longer reduced to a quasi-robot, performing one or a handful of mindless, repetitive tasks throughout his entire working life. He is rather finally and fully free to develop his whole potential. In one of Marx's most famous passages (from *The German Ideology*, 1846), he writes that precommunist man:

> ...is a hunter, a fisherman, a shepherd, or a critical critic, and must remain so if he does not want to lose his means of livelihood; while in communist society, where nobody has one exclusive sphere of activity but each can become accomplished in any branch he wishes, society regulates the general production and thus makes it possible for me to do one thing today and another tomorrow, to hunt in the morning, fish in the afternoon, rear cattle in the evening, criticise after dinner, just as I have a mind, without ever becoming hunter, fisherman, shepherd or critic.

Communism heals the division of the soul inflicted by the transition from the state of nature to civil society and exacerbated by the division of labor. Man under communism is not merely greater than the sum of his parts but greater than all prior manifestations of man, who were all merely the products of a particular historical epoch.

The most obvious objection to level against Marxism is that its posited end state is an imagined republic, never yet seen or known to exist in truth. Marxism anticipates and responds to this objection with the assertion that true or final communism must emerge gradually, in stages. While the fall of capitalism will be sudden and decisive, the transition to communism will be bumpy. There must come, first, the crushing of the bourgeoisie and the state seizure of industry, which will require despotic power and not a little violence. During this period, private property and wage labor will remain but the state will own all means of production. This is, however, but a transitory phase toward a more democratic communism, on the way to the full transcendence of private property. In the early stages, the state plays an indispensable role. In the last stage, the state, in Engels's famous formulation, "withers away." There is no longer any need for the state because man will have become rational and good, and thus will no longer need to be persuaded or coerced.

What Marxism Got Wrong

Up to this point, we have examined what Marxism asserts, which is knowable and checkable. The critique of Marxism—above all, the blunt conclusion that Marx was wrong—since less knowable, must be more circumspect. We should be cautious in dismissing the thought of a man who, in the words of Leo Strauss, was "liberally educated on a level to which we cannot even hope to aspire." However, we may judiciously raise questions regarding Marxism's *plausibility* and its *predictive power*.

We may ask first: how plausible is Marxism's fundamental basis, its account of "history"? Of course, we know from history as originally understood that human things change, sometimes fundamentally. Christendom is decisively different from paganism, the medieval world from the classical, modernity from the Middle Ages. And Marx is certainly right that a society with industrial technology looks and operates differently than one whose most complex machinery are horse-drawn plows and hand-powered looms.

But does technological change preclude an unchanging human nature that accommodates itself to differing modes of production and even shapes such changing modes to better fit human nature? Which is more realistic: a human nature so malleable that change to one part of human life—the means of production of artificial goods—alters and determines literally everything else about human life? Or a human nature that, while affected by changes in its environment (including the means of production), nonetheless retains its essential humanity no matter the prevailing external conditions? Put another way, however much the transition from hand-mill to steam-mill may have altered the character of everyday life and even of society as a whole, how much did that transition actually change humanity itself? How much did it affect and alter man's virtues and vices, passions and motivations, longings and aspirations, immediate wants and overarching desires?

Stripped of their theoretical grandiosity and stated as a common-sense insight, Marx's observations on the effects of technological change on human society were perfectly well-known to pre-Marxist philosophers. A tribe of herdsmen will not long retain the same social or political structure once it starts tilling the land, nor will an agrarian society retain its way of life unaltered once it begins to industrialize.

But for most of those earlier philosophers, these are choices—driven, to be sure, by the natural and permanent passion of human acquisitiveness—not the inexorable working through of an inevitable historical process. Some societies, indeed, resist technological change precisely to protect their ancestral ways of life. Many philosophers themselves recommend such resistance, for much the same reason. Examples of such resistance (e.g., Japan closing itself to foreigners—and foreign innovation—from 1603 to 1868) are historical facts, but ones for which Marx's theory of "history" cannot adequately account.

Pre-Marxist philosophy was also well aware that human virtue and societal health rise and fall. Man and his man-made environments are better at certain times and worse at others. The cause is not the grinding wheels of "history," as Marx and his teachers understood it, but human nature. Harshness, rusticity, scarcity, and danger give rise to virtues that create peace, security, and plenty, which in turn create the conditions for leisure, under which virtue is less prized, less needed, and less prevalent. As virtue decays, scarcity and danger return. Eventually, in response, the virtues reemerge. In classical political philosophy, this idea is known as the "cycle of regimes." There is no endpoint or end state, but rather peaks and valleys.

Marxist historicism asserts that certain passions understood by earlier philosophy to be permanent and coeval with man will no longer exist in the end state. Man will lose all of his selfishness, covetousness, avarice, ambition, and status-seeking. This is not to suggest that, for pre-Marxist philosophy, these passions defined humanity. But all philosophers up through the early moderns considered them inexpungable, though manageable, aspects of human nature. Indeed, for this earlier philosophy, a vital task of politics is to channel, control, and (when and where necessary) suppress the passions, especially the lower ones, via a combination of education (understood above all as character formation), persuasion or rhetoric, and coercion, (i.e., rewards and punishments). Marxism posits that all this can be dispensed with after history's end and the emergence of full communism. The question of whether that is true is inseparable from the questions of whether Marxism's end state is possible, and, hence, whether Marxist philosophy is true.

As for Marxism's predictive power, while its track record is not altogether one of failure, in the main, we would have to say that its biggest and most fundamental predictions did not come true. Some 175 years after the publication of the *Manifesto*, no final-stage communist state such as Marx and Engels described and forecast has ever emerged anywhere. Most actual communist regimes ceased to exist while stuck somewhere in Marx's and Engels's first or second stage. Others abandoned Marxist economics in practice while formally denying having done so, and one or two others trundle on thanks to the largess of patrons.

Marxist theory posits that full communism will emerge only after a process of indeterminate length. But how long is that process supposed to take? The first communist revolution occurred in 1917. The U.S.S.R. formally dissolved seventy-five years later. Even if we accept that three-quarters of a century is insufficient for the emergence of full communism, why did that regime fall rather than continue developing toward the end state?

The most plausible answer is that Marxism's assertion that fundamental human passions will melt away is wrong. That assertion undergirds Marxism's expectation that the postcapitalist economy will remain productive absent the profit motive. For while Marx is certainly correct that capitalism is the most productive economic system yet known, it is not clear why or how that productivity should reasonably be expected to continue without the incentives that drive productivity. Capitalists produce because they expect to be rewarded; the more they produce, the greater the reward they expect. It is these expectations that above all drive production.

Marxism appears to assume that an industrial economy, once built, will simply go on producing as if on autopilot, even once the profit motive is obsolesced (or eliminated). According to Marxism, the great leap forward to mass productivity was accomplished on the backs of the proletariat, propelled by greed and exploitation. But under communism, that productivity will continue voluntarily, on a foundation of mutual goodwill and the pleasure that comes from working for the benefit of all mankind.

The actual experience of communism, however, suggests that real human beings do not behave as Marxism predicts. If so, that might explain, in part, why those communist states that dispensed with the profit motive have mostly failed while those that liberalized their markets (if always under strict political supervision) have fared better. "To get rich is glorious," Deng Xiaoping exhorted the Chinese people nearly two generations ago. That may have something to do with the fact that the Chinese Communist Party is still in power while its Soviet counterpart no longer exists. At any rate, for Marxist theory to overcome communism's less-than-stellar practical record, it would have to explain not only why no final-stage communist state has ever emerged but also why the economies of those states that began but never completed communism's *via dolorosa* performed so poorly relative to their capitalist and even to their "bourgeois socialist" peers.

Marxism also elides the differences between what it denounces as "capitalism" and all prior noncommunist economics. It all but claims that the free-market as such is inherently "capitalistic" in the derogatory sense in which Marx and Engels use the term. Modern defenders of free markets have arguably played into Marxism's hands by enthusiastically adopting the term "capitalism"—which Marx and Engels mean as a pejorative—as their own.

But what Marxism derides as "capitalism" is more accurately described as an extreme libertarianism, a system in which economics is elevated above all other concerns and crushes and sweeps aside everything else. For this version of "capitalism," only productivity and profit matter. By contrast, for theoretical and practical defenders of free markets such as Adam Smith and Alexander Hamilton, political and moral virtue are the indispensable foundations of economic freedom. Smith himself insisted that his economic theory as expounded in *The Wealth of Nations* is incomprehensible and unworkable absent the understanding of human virtue propounded in his *Theory of Moral Sentiments*. These earlier thinkers and statesmen cheerfully subordinated the imperatives of the market to the higher considerations of virtue, morality, common citizenship, national defense, and stability. Economic freedom serves virtue and liberty, not the reverse; it is a means, not the end. The later, libertarian conception of "capitalism" is acutely vulnerable to attack from both the Marxist Left and the traditionalist Right; the earlier understanding much less so.

We may note, finally, that, contrary to Marx's prediction, the practice of actual communist regimes suggests an eternal need for rhetoric and coercion. The Eastern Bloc, for instance, was characterized by ubiquitous propaganda, a fact no less true of China or North Korea today—and, what's more, by a coercion far more onerous, and a rhetoric far more disconnected from truth, than those prevailing in any nontyrannical, noncommunist state. Marxism acknowledges the temporary necessity for such measures but promises they will evaporate in the end state. But the end state never came. At least, it hasn't yet.

Perhaps it is more plausible to suppose that, human nature being more or less constant, the need for rhetoric and coercion never disappears. Hence one of the fundamental duties of responsible politics is to make that coercion as light, and the rhetoric as ennobling, as possible, with both always serving good ends.

The evident need for, and omnipresence of, coercion in communist states may also help explain why, when peoples who want to move their countries in a vaguely Marxian direction and are allowed to vote—i.e., when they do not have communism imposed on them by a revolutionary vanguard—they tend to choose the system Marx and Engels deride as "bourgeois socialism." This helps explain post-World War II political and economic trends in most of Western Europe, whose states remained formally anticommunist, but whose economies moved in a more or less "socialistic" direction.

Modern Neoliberalism vs. Virtue and Freedom

An uncomfortable fact for contemporary conservatives, who tend to demonize or dismiss Marx, is the extent to which the practices being pushed under the rubric of the Great Reset resemble the worst elements of the capitalism Marx himself demonized. Of course, demonization of Marx is largely deserved, given that the movement and revolutions he confidently and recklessly urged upon the world extinguished upward of one hundred million lives and consigned more than a billion others to earthly tenures of poverty, misery, and oppression.

Another reason Marxism has such a low reputation is that, at the height of its political success in the mid-twentieth century, its key economic predictions turned out to be laughably wrong. Instead of mass, technology-driven unemployment, the capitalist world boasted near full employment. Instead of the pauperization of workers, the working class under capitalism enjoyed a standard of living never yet seen for the common man. Far from lengthening the working day (and week), capitalism shortened both—granted, under pressure from unions and reformist lawmakers and after an initial expansion of work hours in the early industrial period.

Yet looking forward from the peak of the twentieth-century industrial economy to today's information-managerial-techno economy presents a somewhat different picture. If we may characterize the latter as pure or ur-capitalism and the former as closer to the pre-Marxist Smithian-Hamiltonian version of free market economics, we may say that today's economy looks more like Marx's caricature of capitalism than many of its most dedicated defenders on the Right would care to admit. "Pure capitalism" abstracts away from, even undercuts, considerations such as virtue, morality, good citizenship, and societal health—things the "Right" claims to value but often only weakly defends. Whenever the requirements of virtue clash with the imperatives of capitalism, the typical "conservative" response is to deny there is any conflict or insist that it be resolved in capitalism's favor. Often both.

For Marxism, productivity is a necessary step toward a universal abundance that will allow man to regain his pure, Rousseauvian precapitalist nature and develop his full potential, above all in fields that transcend mere economic productivity. By contrast, for capitalism as such, productivity is either an end in itself or, to the extent that it's a means, its end is simply to fulfill wants. Pure or libertarian capitalism not only avers its supreme indifference to the nature of those wants, it rules out of bounds even the question of their goodness or badness. Whatever the people, in accordance with the "market," decide is ipso facto legitimate, so long as it is not imposed by the state. All private transactions not resting on force are legitimate. Even harm is acceptable, or at least objections to market transactions on the basis of harm are illegitimate, so long as both parties choose freely. Hence, for example, according to the classic libertarian dictum, heroin ought to be legal and, if the market so demands, widely available.

Turning from theory to practice, in surveying the actual economic history of the past three decades at least, we may wonder whether the older, qualified economic freedom has not in many (though, as we shall see, by no means all) respects given way to the logic of "pure capitalism" at its most "efficient" and corrosive.

To list some of twenty-first-century runaway corporatism's worst features: tech-driven replacement of unskilled—and, increasingly, skilled—labor; constant technological change whose burden falls almost exclusively on wage-earners; capital treated much more kindly in the tax code than wages, favoring owners over workers; scads of jobs and even whole industries obsolesced; un- and underemployment rampant; legions of displaced workers who can't adapt; the remaining jobs available to the lower quintiles pay less and less relative to the rapidly rising prices of basic necessities; constant churn and revolution in the economy and society that increases uncertainty and anxiety, and evaporates stability and predictability; lengthening of the working day and/or of total hours worked; expansion of a propertyless workforce to whom capitalists believe they owe nothing; nearly all gains accruing to the top, and increasingly, the tippy-top; the destruction of the middle class and the reduction of society into two starkly unequal classes.

All of these trends are increasing and will continue to increase, by design, so long as our present "capitalists"—who not coincidentally are the authors of the Great Reset—continue to get their way.

To these we may add drumming workers off the formal payroll and into contract positions so as to avoid paying benefits. Readers of Dickens may scoff at the idea that working conditions today are "worse," but if we approach the issue like an economist and ask "compared to what?" the assertion becomes less risible. A modern cubicle or warehouse may not be worse than a coke oven in nineteenth-century Birmingham, but compared to conditions a generation ago? Amazon et al. ruthlessly micromanage every second of workers' days, even policing "breaks" so stringently as to begrudge trips to the bathroom. Firms en masse pay so little in wages that many are forced to work multiple jobs in the "gig economy" and/or rely on public assistance just to eat. Precariousness and insecurity reign. One blown tire can mean financial ruin.

And then there's immigration. What automation can't yet do, or is taking too long to do—drive wages to the vanishing point—untrammeled immigration assists. Marxism does not formally contemplate this contemporary capitalist enthusiasm, but it's implicit in the imperative for globalized markets. Labor, no less than capital markets, can and must be globalized. Indeed, given that capitalism requires cost-cutting to escape annihilation in a cutthroat market, isn't globalizing the labor market, pushing labor costs to the absolute minimum, *necessary*? And doesn't that in turn demand the "free movement of labor," also known as mass migration, a/k/a open borders?

Other factors make mass immigration most useful to capitalism. Marxism posits the devolution of society into two classes, haves and have-nots, oppressors and oppressed—a dichotomy perpetuated by original or political/economic Marxism's spiritual successor "cultural Marxism," the historical and intellectual precursor to what we know as "wokeness." By its very nature, capitalism creates more losers than winners. This means that the system is continuously generating more opponents. Those opponents increasingly will not wish to serve the system and hence must be continually replaced. Also, in another dynamic not found in Marx, our modern capitalists have found it useful to pacify the proletariat or lower class—specifically, to enervate them with drugs, debilitating food, and spectacle (pornography, streaming services, athletic contests, video games and the like).[10] This has the intended effect of blunting any potential urge toward rebellion but also degrades people's capacity for work, thus (allegedly) necessitating yet more immigration. Paradoxically, the larger the lower class becomes, the more additional workers the system must import.

If Marx understood industrial capitalism badly, or at least saw (or acknowledged) only its warts, he seems to have anticipated, if inadvertently, the trend and goal of financial-techno-managerial capitalism. And that, simply, is the gradual impoverishment of everyone outside the ruling elite. This is a *trend*, in that the inexorable pressures of capitalism as now practiced work to despoil the middle class and concentrate its wealth at the top. It is a *goal* in that the elites increasingly not only decline to deny the trend but praise it as a desired end-state, a "positive good."

The catch-phrases "Great Reset" and "Build Back Better" are intended to sugarcoat this reality. Perhaps the ultimate expression is the now-ubiquitous WEF slogan "You'll own nothing, and you'll be happy." Note that the WEF doesn't say *they* will own nothing, only that *you* will. *They* most assuredly will own a great deal—more than the considerable amount they already own, and *you* will make up the difference. Marx could hardly be surprised by the underlying sentiment, but the audacious cynicism might have shocked even him.

---

10 Those who dismiss this assertion as too cynical even for our cynical ruling class should consider the helpfully blunt remarks of WEF favorite Yuval Noah Harari: "I think the biggest question maybe in economics and politics of the coming decades will be what to do with all these useless people? The problem is more boredom and what to do with them and how will they find some sense of meaning in life, when they are basically meaningless, worthless? My best guess, at present is a combination of drugs and computer games as a solution for [most]. It's already happening. Under different titles, different headings, you see more and more people spending more and more time or solving their inner problems with the drugs and computer games, both legal drugs and illegal drugs."

Marxism's assertion that, under capitalism, employers feel no moral or civic obligations to employees might be inapt, and unfair, to free economies with loyal and patriotic elites. But it is dead accurate to our cosmopolitan "meritocratic" elite who are certain they deserve everything they have and more, and that if you're not one of them, it's because there's something wrong with—inferior about—you. Under this system, a college degree is the ultimate signifier. First, it's the fundamental dividing line between upper and lower, somebodies and nobodies. Second, it provides the necessary (though hardly only) credential for being allowed to occupy the upper slots in the modern system. Third, the hierarchy of colleges serves the same fundamental purpose as the old ranks among aristocratic titles: to make clear that, while all aristocrats may be noble, not all nobles are dukes. But in the breasts of our new nobility, there is nothing approaching a guilty conscience, much less noblesse oblige.

Orthodox Marxism asserts that the proletariat will be history's first nonpartisan ruling class because it will represent not any partisan interest but all of humanity. In a strange inversion of Marxist theory, our ruling class believes the same of itself—except not looking upward from the socioeconomic ladder's bottom rung but downward from the top. Under contemporary capitalism, not the impoverished proletariat but the (ever fewer) owners of the means of production represent humanity in toto. This perhaps helps explain why, in contemporary political discourse, "democracy" has been redefined to mean whatever elites want, not what the supposedly ignorant masses actually vote for.

And what those elites want is a world favorable to "markets"—not free markets, as prior conservative and liberal theory alike understood them, but markets designed to favor the interests of global capital over the interests of nations and citizens. The more countries in which an industry or firm or businessman operates, the truer this is. The logic of contemporary capitalism demands that the location of a firm's "headquarters" eventually be regarded as a mere accident of birth or advantageous choice. A firm is "American" or "French" or "Japanese" only incidentally or historically. It is loyal solely to itself and to its interests, just as individual businessmen are loyal to their transnational firms and to their industries but not to their countries, except insofar as the interests of the latter align with their own. If and when there are conflicts, firm and industry take precedence. Corporate elites defend this with the slogan that "what's good for business is good for communities and individuals." But the "goods" under discussion are limited to the wide availability of consumer products at low(ish) prices and jobs. Neither the value nor quality of those goods nor the wage or dignity of those jobs factor into the equation.

More fundamentally, neoliberal capitalism reshapes governments just as it reshapes societies, and this reshaping takes everywhere more or less the same form. The world becomes less and less differentiated and more and more homogenous. Sovereignty gives way to the imperatives of business; therefore, individuals and peoples have less and less freedom to determine their destinies.

This underlying economic imperative intensifies pressures that undermine the family, including low wages that delay marriage and family formation, frequent job relocations that disperse extended families, high rents and home prices that force both parents to work, cost-cutting layoffs that stress marriages, a me-first consumerism that fuels self-centeredness, and a divorce culture and family court system seemingly designed to further that self-centeredness and encourage family breakup.

Finally, to those ideologues who retort that the presence of but one regulation or small tariff shows that we do not practice "pure capitalism," one can only ask: given what we see around us even with these handful of ineffectual restraints in place, what would our economy and society look like absent any restraint whatsoever? How many American factories would be left open, jobs not yet outsourced, native-born workers not yet replaced by foreigners? In response, the advocates of "pure capitalism," if intellectually honest, can only appeal to their one true god and intone that, if this is "what the market wants," then its will be done.

How Capitalists Became Marxists, and Vice Versa

For Marx, the proletariat has only one thing to offer: its labor. This remains true for now, but it's clear that one goal of the Great Reset is to make superfluous all but highly remunerated intellectual work. This will, it is predicted or hoped, be accomplished through automation, artificial intelligence, and the like. In other words, in the envisioned perfect society to come, the nonelite are to enjoy neither the income nor the independence nor the dignity that accompany work. This was definitely *not* the future Marx envisioned for his beloved proletariat.

But dignity and independence for the lower and middle classes are anathema to our ruling class, hence for them this outcome is a feature not a bug. Yet even modern capitalists realize that the lower orders need money. This is what the universal basic income (UBI) is intended to supply. Indeed, the Davoisie's increasing insistence that UBI is inevitable may be said to be another unexpected vindication of Marxian theory: specifically, the prediction that under perfect capitalism, the proletariat will have nothing. The rulers will own everything; what little you get will come at their sufferance.

The UBI serves multiple purposes. It accomplishes the Marxist goal of providing for all, if by different means, thereby assuaging any possible guilty feelings (not that many are felt) among the upper class for destroying the bulk of the labor market. "No one will starve," the plutocrats reassure themselves. A universal basic income thus, in a sense, revives a semblance of those humanistic ties between upper and lower classes that Marx admits existed in precapitalist societies but insists cannot and will not survive the transition to capitalism. A guaranteed income restores an obligation of the top to the bottom: we'll pay your Grubhub and streaming bills.

Second, a UBI makes the bottom classes entirely dependent on the ruling order. This dependence is compounded by the ruling elites' ability to cut off the money—already foreshadowed by its present power to get you fired and prevent you from working again. Once work is unavailable—not simply for some individual personally but for his entire class—and people's only source of income is the rulers, they will be fully at the latter's mercy.

The flipside is that UBI solves the problem (from capitalism's perspective) of the proletariat having no stake in the system. UBI literally *gives* them one. Whatever rebellious or revolutionary impulse might have survived and be lurking under all that dope and streaming-released dopamine will be checked by the recognition, obvious to the meanest capacities, that it would be folly to attack a system that pays one to do nothing, especially when there's no alternative.

Third, UBI puts in lower-class pockets cash that can—and will, since there will be nowhere else for it to go—flow back into an economy that the rulers own and run. The UBI also solves, or mitigates, another problem identified by Marx: capitalism by its very nature pressures wages downward, meaning that workers have ever less to spend even as production rises. The resulting boom-bust cycles lead to further layoffs and cost-cutting, which further drive down consumer spending. But such spending is the lifeblood of capitalist-consumer economics. For now, this gap is papered over by debt. We may analogize debt-finance for the lower orders as a "transitional" stage on the way to UBI in the same way that, for classic Marxism, a certain type of "socialism" serves as the necessary bridge to full communism. One difference, however, may be that our debt stage could be difficult to transition out of, given the extensive financialization of our economy and the enormous profits generated by interest. Does this foreshadow a showdown between bankers and techies?

However that may be, it is not unreasonable to suppose that UBI is intended as a kind of money-laundering scheme like the "company towns" of old: the rulers give you money; you spend it at their businesses, on their products. If and to the extent that UBI recipients attempt to save a portion of that money, one answer, already floated, might be to convert UBI to "consumption credits" that must be used or lost. Not one dime ever escapes the system: recipients either spend their state largesse back in or never receive it in the first place. Either way, the rulers keep the profits while the taxpayers (i.e., you) finance the UBI. This is but one way in which the present economy may be described as "socialist": its costs are borne by all; its benefits, one need hardly add, accrue to a few.

Marx does not appear to have anticipated the dual economy of our day: the economy of things, on the one hand, and the finance-info-digital economy on the other. Granted, the two interact to an extent that can make them hard to distinguish in every instance. But the application of a little common sense reveals a bright if not always sharp line between activities that make, grow, and deliver things versus those that don't. Marxist theory accounts only for the former. For Marxism, all production and value derive from the labor power of the proletariat.

This is manifestly not so for present-day capitalism, the vast majority of whose value derives from "intellectual" work. What would Marx have made of modern tech and finance, to say nothing of other ostensibly nonproductive activities, especially when the contemporary economy's rewards are showered disproportionately on "brain work" rather than physical labor—either the actual toil or the management thereof? The extent to which pixels and bits today "produce" more wealth than any imaginable combination of factories likely would have mystified him and should trouble us more than it does.

However, the Marxian insistence that the means of production determine the nature of all societies would appear to be at least partially vindicated by today's polity, whose contours almost entirely reflect the desires, needs, and tastes of the financial-techno-intellectual-clerical-"artistic" class. From what we require—college degrees as the minimum credential for tedious mental grunt work—to what we honor and reward—fame and fortune for app coders and social media "influencers"—our superstructure is, indeed, determined by its base.

Most sinister of all are the myriad ways in which digital technology shapes and rules our lives. Marx likely exaggerated the extent to which prior production modes determined the character of society, but his thesis seems especially apt to our time. Even if the steam mill did not, in and of itself, give us the society of the industrial capitalist, it would seem much more certain that the personal computer and smartphone have imposed on us the society of the tech oligarch and his financiers, the administrative state commissar, the "intelligence community" technocrat, and the revolving-door military-operator/defense contractor/security consultant. All of whom employ these technologies as means to control the rest of us.

If practice matched theory exactly, there should be no such thing as "woke" capitalism. "Get woke, go broke," the Right likes to say. But virtually all global corporations have gotten woke and none, as yet, has gone broke. Some have seen revenues decline and market share shrink. A few others have been surprised by state countermeasures (see, e.g., Disney v. DeSantis). But none have turned back from the embrace of wokeness. There are many plausible explanations for this, including the desire to penetrate (pander to?) new markets, C-suite fear of boycotts, lawsuits, and rebellions by junior employees, and the desire to appear "with it."

The last is probably the most important. Marx's historicism, however wrong, is increasingly the state religion of our elite. They believe that history has an upward direction and that they are its culmination. That other ubiquitous phrase—"right/wrong side of history"—they utter like a credo, to summon woke angels and ward off retrograde demons. Seen in this light, wokeness allows modern capitalists both to pay the Danegeld and to position themselves as the good guys. However much wokeness costs, you can be sure our masters wouldn't pay if they didn't think, once all the ledgers are audited, that it's worth it.

Marx was surely right about the nature and purpose of "ideology": to justify rule and privilege. He was wrong only in predicting that the need for, and hence the presence of, ideology would melt away. Ideology has turned out to be more necessary than ever, thus the omnipresent propaganda blaring forth from every screen, speaker, headphone and page in the developed world.

Marx predicted—really, urged on—a total revolution in thought, the overthrow of all previous beliefs, traditions, customs, institutions, and orders. Religion, the family, guilds and associations, mediating institutions, even the state itself: all must go. Our overlords fully believe all that—except the part about the state. This, they insist, remains necessary, only transformed into what we may term a hybrid corporo-state: the state and woke capital working hand in glove. But the ruling class is otherwise full-speed-ahead with total revolution in all prior modes of thought and life. The difference is that Marx was certain the revolution he foresaw would serve the proletariat; our elites are busy implementing one designed to serve only themselves.

Marxism's self-conceit is that it fulfills the dream of the ancient philosophers—the perfectly rational state—a project the latter believed must forever remain a dream because it is impossible to implement. In the perfectly rational state, there is only one correct view on everything. All opinion has been replaced by knowledge. Dissent is inherently irrational. We see more than a glimmer of Marx's utopian vision in our rulers' elevation of "expertise," based on "science," to unquestionable authority, including political authority.

Unresolved Conflicts

But not every tension or difference between Marxist theory and capitalist practice has been resolved, and it's hard to see how all can be.

To begin with the most obvious, Marx insisted that armed revolution was necessary to achieve his envisioned paradise. Today's oligarchs, by contrast, believe the same can be accomplished with corporatist technology. Indeed, far from calling for or welcoming revolution, it is revolution that they most fear, since *they are the ruling power that any revolution would displace.* Their overriding goal is therefore to preserve the present system along with their place in it. In this sense, if in few others, our ruling class is instinctively conservative. It deflects attention from this inherent conservatism by demonizing all opposition as not just "Far Right," but indistinguishable from the twentieth-century Right's most violent exemplars.

This points to another problem that Marxism identifies, and which one purpose of woke capitalism is intended to address: the devolution of society into two implacably warring classes. Wokeness recognizes *three* classes: a "meritocratic" class of virtuous experts; a lower class that does not deserve its poverty and lack of privilege; and a middle class whose wealth and position are entirely unearned. The second is the ruling class's ally, which it buys off with government spending, cheap debt, and grievance politics. The third is its enemy, which it demonizes and fears. This enemy takes the place and serves the function of Marx's bourgeoisie. Ruling-class rhetoric rather ridiculously paints the middle class as the true rulers, hence the true oppressors.

In truth, however, the upper and lower classes team up to oppress and despoil the middle. This further explains the need not only for endless immigration, but also for endless grievance politics. Economically, the capitalist class is continually making others poorer and thus pushing them into potential opposition. Hence, just as (until automation kills all the jobs) the rulers need immigrants to replace displaced native workers, so do they need to foster grievances, to transform economic resentments that otherwise would be directed at them into racial and political complaints that can be targeted at the middle class. This is how the rulers keep both the urban underclass and the urban woke-clerical class loyal and obedient despite incommensurate interests and declining material prospects. As an added bonus, immigrants or at least their children can be added to the grievance coalition via constant propaganda that the majority population of the country they've chosen to move to (and that welcomed them with more or less open arms) is implacably hostile to their interests and even to their existence.

Another crucial departure from Marxism is that under woke capitalism, there is little pretense of the restoration and full flowering of man's submerged humanity (hunter, shepherd, critic, and so forth). Our capitalists know they are plying the masses with enervating food, drink, drugs, and "entertainment." They're not merely fine with that; it's part of the plan. Spending on these things keeps the economy going, recycles money into ruling-class wallets, and ensures a docile populace. Whether morning, afternoon, evening, or after dinner, modern man will be in the same place, doing the same thing: on the couch, looking at a screen.

But the most important difference between Marxism (or socialism as originally conceived) and its contemporary update is that, for Marx, the economy, and therefore class, are at the heart of society whereas for our rulers, race is. Cultural Marxism effectively rewrites the *Manifesto*'s famous early sentence as "The history of all hitherto existing society is the history of racist oppression."

In this vision, the white race plays the role of the oppressor class. But unlike Marxist "history," in which a new ruling class takes over as the modes of production change, for wokeness, the ruling or oppressor race is always the same. This may seem a distinction without a difference, since all of Marxism's alleged historical ruling classes were also white. But for Marxism strictly understood, that was merely an accident of demography. In all-white societies, the owners of the means of production (whatever those may be at a given time) will necessarily be white, as will the masses they exploit. In a multiracial society, by contrast, no such racial continuity will be inevitable—*unless race is the fundamental characteristic* that defines ruler and ruled, oppressor versus oppressed. There is nothing in Marxist theory that excludes the possibility of a multiracial bourgeoisie united by joint ownership of the means of production ruling over a multiracial proletariat. Wokeness by contrast vehemently denies this even as a theoretical possibility, much less an actual reality.

This brings us to another important departure from the original theory. For Marxism, man is essentially good. Indeed, he *must* be, if "pure communism" is to have any hope of working. There cannot be any selfishness or other such vices inherent in humanity as such. These must be traits acquired through the process of history and expungable through history's culmination.

For wokeness, by contrast, some races are inherently good while others are inherently bad. Actually, only one is inherently bad—guess which!—and all others inherently good. This is why, for the modern

Left, there can be no end of history. For Marxism, the final revolution enthrones a virtuous proletariat that not merely rules in the interests of, but literally represents, all humanity. Class conflict—*all* conflict—will have ended. Wokeness similarly posits a virtuous ruling class that rules on behalf of humanity, but conflict never ends. At least, not as long as that one retrograde race is still around; it always poses a danger and so must perpetually must be monitored and opposed.

Or we may say that, for wokeness, once the technocratic elite has assumed its rightful place at the top of society, history partially ends, in that no political progress beyond that point, no superior regime, is possible. But history does not and cannot end if by "end" one understands a permanent, strifeless peace. The presence of selfish, wicked, privileged, unruly whites makes that impossible. The ongoing existence of this alleged oppressor race serves the same purpose as that of "wreckers" in communist propaganda: an explanation/scapegoat for all failures, and a lightning rod for joint resentment to hold together an otherwise fractious collation. The theory, of course, admits only the former consideration.

One benefit of "history" never "ending" is that the vanguard of the revolution need never lose its job or place. There is always more work to do, more enemies to conquer, more privilege to dislodge. This has the dual benefit of keeping the broke-but-woke clerical class employed, energized, and committed to the system while also preserving the rulers' power. Under Marx's system, and even (theoretically) Lenin's, the vanguard loses its power and privilege with the emergence of final communism because, its task achieved, there is nothing left for it to do. Under wokeness (and, one may say, under communism in practice as opposed to theory), the revolution never ends, hence the necessity for a vanguard never goes away.

Two problems remain, with which wokeness struggles. The first is that today's technocratic ruling class is disproportionately, even overwhelmingly, white. The second is that a nontrivial number of nonwhites oppose wokeness in terms hardly distinguishable from those shared by the white middle and working classes. Marxism supplies a ready answer to the second problem: "false consciousness," i.e., the assertion that any person whose economic or political opinions do not match his alleged class (or, in this case, racial) interests is deluded and perhaps even mentally ill.

The first problem is harder to dismiss and, as yet, the ruling class has not found a consistent or convincing way to do so. The oligarchs are therefore reduced to falling back on unconvincing double standards: all whites are bad—but not me. Or: "whiteness" is bad—but despite being white, I am free of its taint. To the extent that they attempt a justification for their own privilege, they (mostly unknowingly) channel the late Harvard professor John Rawls, who argued that great wealth and privilege are acceptable and even laudable so long as they're used to help the "most disadvantaged." What form this "help" actually takes, beyond the mouthing of woke platitudes, remains unclear.

But ultimately to look for consistency in woke capitalism is futile. You won't find any because it isn't there, at least not intellectually. Lenin's "Who? Whom?" has far greater explanatory power. Who does what to whom? Who benefits and who suffers? The one consistent thread we find in examining our economy and society is that the techno-financial-administrative ruling class benefits a great deal, the underclass benefits somewhat, and the middle and working classes suffer.

What "Socialism" Means Today

We have come, finally, full circle.

It should be plain by now that "socialism" as traditionally understood—state ownership of the means of production—is not today a real prospect or serious threat. "Socialism" in this sense is today more properly understood as a slogan used to mollify the urban underclass and the broke-woke clerical class. "Socialism" holds out the promise that their material prospects will improve via state action. In practice, this has thus far meant generous welfare and other benefits, financed mostly by debt, in part via taxes on high earners. It's likely that taxes will go up; the modern humor of the Democratic Party seems to demand as much. However, we can be fairly certain that today's big fiscal winners will be able to avoid the most painful of the hikes and/or to ensure that any new rates are set at levels which, to the extent that evasion is impractical, they can easily afford with no diminution in lifestyle. At any rate, they always have.

The biggest difference between anything hitherto understood as "socialism" and the system we have now is that, for the former, profit is always inherently exploitative. Our overlords obviously do not believe that. Profit is what keeps them in power, to say nothing of in private jets.

Far from rejecting profit, our rulers profit immensely from creating, selling, and spreading pathologies—from obesity to drug addiction to unemployment to loneliness and despair—while socializing the costs. We've already seen one example: socialization, through the potential implementation of UBI, of the costs of mass unemployment. But the most important is socializing the costs of immigration. Corporations do not pay for emergency-room overuse, school overcrowding, infrastructure overloading, or the myriad other ways that overpopulation taxes our country—to say nothing of the specific costs of importing millions who don't speak our common language or adhere to our established ways of life. Indeed, one meaning of "socialism" has come to be the equal right of foreigners to live in the United States (and the developed West more generally). The ruling class "pays" for this, to the extent that it pays taxes, but far less than it should, and whatever it pays is easily and vastly outweighed by the enormous profits it collects from this injustice. The rest of us just pay.

Socialism originally meant the drive toward equalization, specifically of individual economic outcomes. We may contrast that with equality as originally meant: treating everyone as equal before the law. Socialism long ago attacked that meaning as insufficient. Engels specifically derides "bourgeois equality before the law" because it does not generate equal outcomes.

The contemporary invocation of "socialism" sometimes feints in Engels's direction, when rhetorically beneficial or necessary (e.g., when a threat to oligarch power emerges, as Bernie Sanders briefly appeared to be). But it is always only a feint; the oligarchs have no intention of equalizing individual wealth. To the contrary, they are constantly doing everything in their power to take yours and increase theirs. That's what the Great Reset is all about.

To deflect attention from this goal and the methods used to further it, and also to hold their coalition together, the oligarchs promise instead "equity": the equalization of demographic groups. The new term signifies the altered goal and transformation of "socialism."

"Equity," it is alleged, will be achieved via a variety of means, many of them "socialistic" in the older sense. But those older means, by themselves, will be insufficient. More radical measures must be taken. To be blunt—and leftist rhetoric is increasingly blunt—achieving "equity" requires that wealth be taken from certain demographic groups and given to others. The trick for the ruling class is to find ways to retain capitalism for themselves while they despoil their enemies and reward their allies. Call it "socialism for thee but not for me." That is another fundamental, though necessarily unstated because unsettling, meaning of "the Great Reset."

The Great Reset's authors prefer not to be explicit about their goals, for obvious reasons. When pinned down, they resort to anodyne (and near-meaningless) terms such as "reform," "fairness," "revamping," "shared goals" and "sustainability." Occasionally, in less guarded moments, they let slip "reparations." But the more accurate name for this practice is *expropriation*, a tactic as old as political life. How, exactly, the Davos class will explain what they are doing as somehow principled and consistent remains unclear—just as their explanation for why whites generally, but not themselves, constitute a privileged oppressor class does not seem entirely coherent. They may never come up with a convincing formulation, but we can be sure that, if not, they will simply push their program through via brute force, political or otherwise. Surely they are helped by their client class's enthusiastic belief that "equity" is not merely a societal good and rectification of past injustice but also deserved punishment. In this, there is more than a whiff of the old communist demonization of kulaks and other "class enemies."

Synthesis?

The Great Reset co-opts "socialism" and puts it to work in service of a rapacious ruling class, who use its rhetoric, some of its means, and the extravagant hopes it inspires to keep its lumpen-base pacified, satisfied, reverent, and stupefied.

We may even revise our earlier assertion that the present system cannot be "socialist" because the state does not literally own the means of production. After all, do not the owners of the means of production own or at least control the state? Do they not give it direction, set its guardrails, define its limits, occupy its key offices, and tell its minions what to do? Is not the surest ticket to easy, unearned wealth today some sort of government "service"? Can you think of a single former congressman, senator, cabinet or even subcabinet official who lives modestly, who does not have at least an eight-figure net worth? Do not the state and the power centers of our economy work so closely that it can be impossible—and, perhaps, irrelevant, given that their goals are so often identical—to discern who's in charge?

Contrary to Marx's prediction and legacy conservatism's fears, the real threat to civilization, the moral order, and the middle class today is not from the pitchfork-bearing proletariat but from capitalists—especially the techies and bankers driving the Great Reset. The proles, by contrast, are the Right's natural ally and should be our core constituency. The Great Resetters are our avowed enemy and every day look and act more and more like Marx's grotesque caricature of the rapacious capitalist. I am not usually one to wring hands over "labels," but it may be that, finally, the terms "Left" and "Right" have lost all salience. When it becomes more plausible than not to describe billionaire oligarchs as being on "the Left" and MAGA-hatted truckers as "the Right," something fundamental has changed.

For conservatives, who admire commercial success, this can be hard to process. But the sooner people on the Right wake up and realize that big business—especially big finance and big tech—are not their friends but are out to get them, the sooner they will be able to organize in defense of their interests.

It's also an open question whether the corpora-state "synthesis" we have now is inherently flawed or merely destructive in the present case. The conventional Right condemns out of hand, in the name of "economic freedom" and "anti-statism," any cooperation between the state and big economic players. But what *is* the state—what is it *supposed* to be—if not a vehicle for the promotion of citizen welfare? Perhaps the problem is not the state qua state but the state's capture by private interests to further their wealth and power, as opposed to the common good, and its weaponization against the oligarchs' class enemies.

This is a development that, if not Marx, then certainly his updater and implementer Lenin would recognize. Contra Marxism, the state will never "wither away." Some states fall and some are conquered, but as long as there is man, there will be government. The questions are, and will always be: who runs it and to what ends? Cooperation between a patriotic state and patriotic economic elites, both aiming at the common good, would solve many of our problems and may even be indispensable to their solution.

Is that possible? Marx asserts that the bourgeoisie creates class consciousness in the proletariat. Is the modern ruling class creating class consciousness in the Deplorables?

Marxism's biggest blind spot is to see everything through the lens of class. This is one respect in which modern wokeness surpasses Marxism in its understanding of human nature: race trumps class. Your rich uncle is still your uncle, just as your no-account cousin is still your cousin. Marxist theory leaves out or gives short shrift to kinship and culture. Neither has yet been entirely dissolved and there is sound reason to believe neither can ever fully be. So long as such ties exist, they act as great drivers of unity and resentment.

Marxism's inevitability argument doesn't have a place for people who refuse to "modernize," who prefer to keep their old ways. This is a lesson we might have learned in Afghanistan. Will the ruling class be forced to learn it anew in West Virginia?

The "Great Reset turns out to be a kind of "synthesis" after all—just not the one Marx predicted and certainly not one he would have welcomed. It combines the worst elements of libertarian capitalism with most of the worst of socialism and rolls them together with the utterly irredeemable wokeness. It maintains the profit motive but concentrates profits in the ruling class. It retains private ownership of the means of production while erecting massive barriers to entry for all but established behemoths. It gives outsized power to the richest ruling class in human history and restricts freedom and opportunity for everyone else. It socializes costs while keeping profits private. It despoils the middle class while reducing ordinary people's standard of living. And it sanctimoniously cloaks itself in an ideology that claims moral perfection for itself while denouncing tens of millions as inherently and irredeemably evil.

One of its few redeeming features is that it hasn't built any gulags—yet.

THE ECONOMIC CONSEQUENCES OF THE GREAT RESET

BY DAVID P. GOLDMAN

Introduction: The Great Reset Is Already Underway

The Great Reset is not a scheme for implementation in the distant future. It's happening now, in the form of the most radical transformation of world economic policy in modern history, with the possible exception of World War II. The economic landscape that has emerged after the Covid-19 recession of 2019–2021 is radically different from what preceded it. The world economy has already been reset, and the perpetrators of the Great Reset want to make these changes irreversible.

One-fifth of the industrial nations' GDP shifted to the balance sheet of governments during the Covid-19 pandemic, by far the biggest and fastest transfer of financial resources to governments in world history. Except for a few communist revolutions, no such transfer of economic power to governments from the private sector ever has occurred and never on a global scale. In 2019, the gross debt of the members of the Organization for Economic Cooperation and Development (OECD) stood at about 102 percent of their combined GDP; by 2021 the proportion had risen to about 122 percent, according to the International Monetary Fund (IMF). That's an increment of roughly $10 trillion in terms of current U.S. dollars.

That is not the only revolution in economic affairs to occur between March 2020 and the middle of 2021.

- Transfer payments jumped to 75 percent of federal expenditures from 60 percent before the crisis, leaving vast numbers of lower-income Americans dependent on government spending for the majority of their income.
- A handful of technology giants dominated stock market returns, in sudden concentration of wealth not witnessed since Theodore Roosevelt's administration.
- A massive reordering of global investment priorities in the service of the quixotic goal of eliminating carbon emissions, on a scale so ambitious that it would absorb virtually the entire public and private investment budget of the West for the next thirty years. Not even in wartime has the industrial world been subject to such a radical economic reordering.

This is a utopian experiment as sweeping as the old Marxist vision of state-owned industries directed by a technocratic elite. Like all utopian experiments, it is doomed to failure. The redirection of investment toward the alleviation of supposed manmade climate change will destroy productivity and living standards. The massive increase in taxation proposed to alleviate income equality will crush entrepreneurship and economic growth. The inflation resulting from massive increases in government-created demand will erode the incomes of the least prosperous citizens of the United States and produce the opposite of the result that the Great Reset proposes to achieve, by making the poor poorer. And the destructive consequences of the Great Reset for the productivity of the Western industrial nations may well hand the leadership of the world economy to China by default.

Worst of all, the toxic combination of ballooning government debt and declining productivity is likely to set in motion a global financial crisis worse than the 2008 crash. The structural weakness at the center of the 2008 crisis was the overleveraging of consumer balance sheets, mainly through the mortgage market. The industrial nations relied on the borrowing capacity of governments to control the crisis, expanding the debt of industrial nations and the balance sheets of central banks at a pace without precedent in peacetime. The Covid-19 crisis has prompted an even faster expansion of government debt and central bank balance sheets, and the Great Reset proposes to continue this rate of expansion into the indefinite future. In place of consumer or corporate debt, government debt is now the finance system's weak link; when the next crisis arrives, there will be no entity in the world with the capacity to bail out governments.

Economists and financiers associated with the Great Reset project argue that there is no limit to governments' spending capacity as long as central banks suppress interest rates and the carrying costs of increased debt burden. This assertion ignores the most salient fact of the world economy, namely the presence of a strategic competitor to the West with a population half again as large as the combined population of the United States, the European Union, and Japan. China's economy measured by purchasing power parity is already one-fourth larger than America's, and China's ambition is to replace the United States as the center of the world financial system.

The monetary policy associated with the Great Reset will undermine the role of the U.S. dollar as the world's principal reserve currency and shift the center of gravity in the world economy to China. The WEF and other elite organizations act as if the advanced industrial nations live in their own bubble. In reality, the Western democracies are in a contest for economic dominance with China. The Great Reset virtually guarantees that China will prevail, with devastating consequences for the United States. With a negative net foreign investment position of $13 trillion and a current account deficit of $1 trillion per year as of late 2021, the United States depends on the willingness of foreigners to hold U.S. dollar investments. China already is promoting its own currency as a substitute for the dollar, and its success would be devastating for America's financial system.

The WEF's executive chairman, Klaus Schwab, issued what might be called the Great Reset manifesto in a June 3, 2020, article:

> The Great Reset agenda would have three main components. The first would steer the market toward fairer outcomes. To this end, governments should improve coordination (for example, in tax, regulatory, and fiscal policy), upgrade trade arrangements, and create the conditions for a "stakeholder economy." At a time of diminishing tax bases and soaring public debt, governments have a powerful incentive to pursue such action.
>
> Moreover, governments should implement long-overdue reforms that promote more equitable outcomes. Depending on the country, these may include changes to wealth taxes, the withdrawal of fossil-fuel subsidies, and new rules governing intellectual property, trade, and competition.
>
> The second component of a Great Reset agenda would ensure that investments advance shared goals, such as equality and sustainability. Here, the large-scale spending programs that many governments are implementing represent a major opportunity for progress...
>
> Rather than using these funds, as well as investments from private entities and pension funds, to fill cracks in the old system, we should use them to create a new one that is more resilient, equitable, and sustainable in the long run. This means, for example, building "green" urban infrastructure and creating incentives for industries to improve their track record on environmental, social, and governance (ESG) metrics.
>
> The third and final priority of a Great Reset agenda is to harness the innovations of the Fourth Industrial Revolution to support the public good, especially by

> addressing health and social challenges. During the Covid-19 crisis, companies, universities, and others have joined forces to develop diagnostics, therapeutics, and possible vaccines; establish testing centers; create mechanisms for tracing infections; and deliver telemedicine. Imagine what could be possible if similar concerted efforts were made in every sector.

Noteworthy is Schwab's reduction of the "Fourth Industrial Revolution" to activities that "support the public good" by enhancing surveillance of the population in the interest of public health. There is a legitimate argument for the use of electronic contact tracing in epidemics, and a number of democratic countries including the United Kingdom, Germany, and South Korea require the use of smartphone software for this purpose. But Schwab's understanding of the "Fourth Industrial Revolution" component ignores the productivity-enhancing role of artificial intelligence (AI) and Big Data applications to industrial robotics, logistics, the internet of things, "smart cities," and other technologies that promise higher growth rates. His one-sided emphasis on "health and social challenges" implies a vast increase in the power of the state and of the technocratic elite rather than a broad-based gain in economic productivity.

In effect, Schwab proposes to leave the "industrial" part of the Fourth Industrial Revolution to China, which has already installed four-fifths of the world's 5G mobile broadband capacity. China's National People's Congress last year enacted a $1.4 trillion plan to accelerate the adoption of Fourth Industrial Revolution technologies, including autonomous vehicles, automated port facilities, self-programming industrial robots, and "smart cities" in which AI processors match every passenger and package to a conveyance in real time.

Most of what Schwab has described as the Great Reset in economic affairs had been in preparation for a decade before the Covid-19 epidemic. The policy response of Western governments accelerated these trends. Liberal utopians now seek to lock them in irreversibly as permanent features of the economic landscape. The Great Reset proposes to:

- Make large sections of the U.S. population permanently dependent on government subsidies and education or employment quotas;
- Give central banks virtually unlimited authority to print money;
- Subject private corporations to rigid controls on business operations through ESG standards; and
- Redistribute wealth through punitive taxation of economic success.

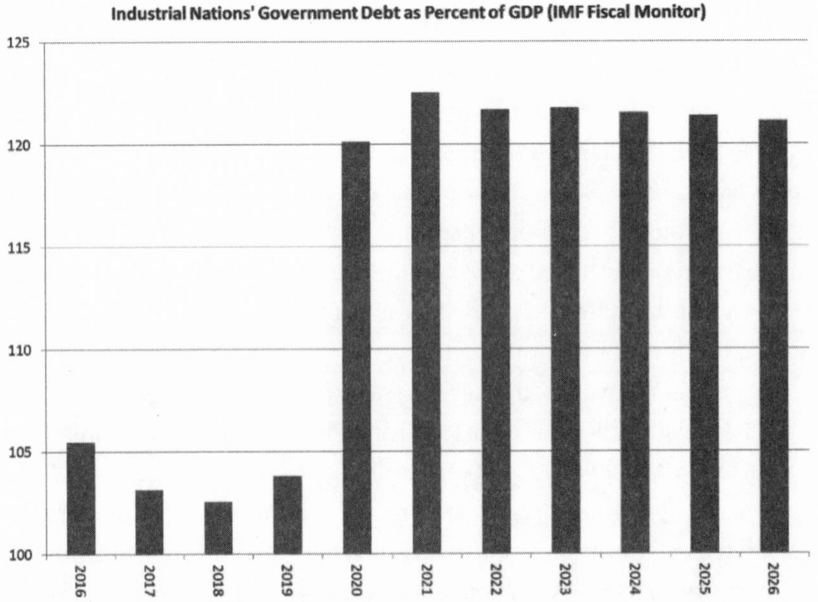

How Governments Ate the World Financial System

What was presented to the public as a set of emergency measures in response to the Covid-19 pandemic has instead become a massive transfer of economic power to governments and elite organizations at the expense of the private sector.

During the Covid crisis, the central banks of the industrial nations became the sole credit provider to their economies, expanding their balance sheets during the crisis by about $8 trillion, as they purchased virtually all the new debt issued by governments. The central banks also financed the purchase of government debt by commercial banks, which diverted resources from private lending to financing governments in a completely unprecedented fashion. In the course of the Covid crisis between March 2020 and May 2021, U.S. commercial banks bought $1.2 trillion of government securities but reduced their commercial and industrial loans.

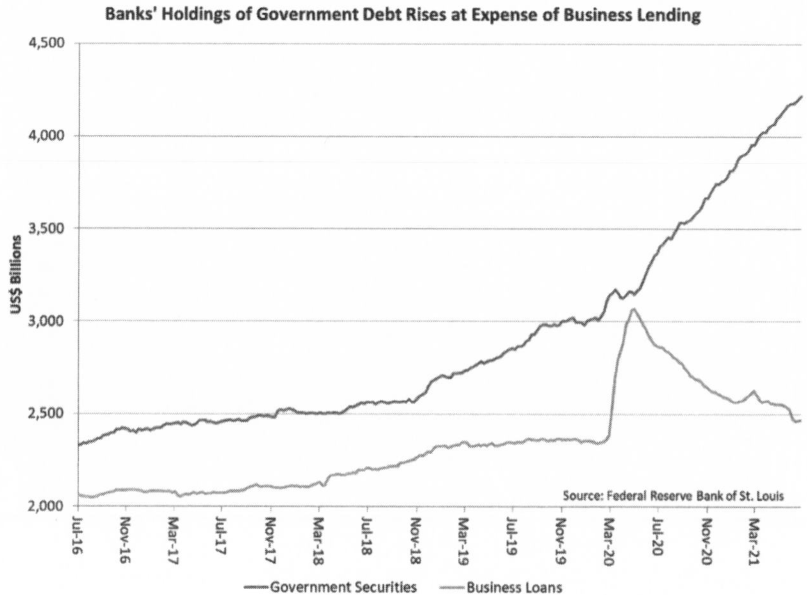

U.S. commercial banks' holdings of government debt are almost twice as large as business loans. That amounts to a creeping nationalization of the banking system, which has turned into an adjunct of the Federal Reserve in providing credit to the U.S. government.

The Biden administration, as shown in its' budget proposals, wants to turn this putative emergency regime into a permanent fixture of economic life. As the *Wall Street Journal* observed in a June 2, 2021, editorial:

> The [Biden administration's] budget includes economic assumptions for growth, prices, interest rates and unemployment. In Table S-9 on page 60 we learn that White House economists are assuming negative real interest rates all the way through the end of the 10-year budget window in 2031.
>
> The budget anticipates that inflation will remain contained between 2.1 percent and 2.3 percent a year through 2031. This may be wishful thinking, but let it go. The budget also assumes that the average annual interest rate on three-month Treasury bills will remain below the inflation rate for all 10 years. The rate will be 0.2 percent in 2022 and never go higher than 2.2 percent, which it reaches in 2031.

That is Modern Monetary Theory[11] in a nutshell. Between 1955 and 2010, the ninety-day Treasury bill rate was higher than the inflation rate (measured by year-on-year change in the consumer price index) except for brief periods of the Federal Reserve easing during recessions, and during the prolonged "stagflation" of 1973–1979. The Federal Reserve's "quantitative easing" after the great financial crisis of 2008, by contrast, kept short-term interest rates below the rate of inflation for most of the past decade. The Biden budget proposal made clear that the new Administration expected this to become the new

---

11 "Modern Monetary Theory" teaches that deficit spending by governments doesn't really create debt because money is a government monopoly and governments can just buy bonds with fiat money from the printing press. Governments therefore can spend as much as they want to bring about full employment, and central banks can set interest rates wherever they want to keep down the cost of government borrowing.

normal. Negative real interest rates mean simply that the government demands that investors pay the Treasury for the privilege of holding their money.

Members of the U.S. population, meanwhile, are turning into dependents, like the Roman proletariat of the late empire. During the Covid-19 recession, transfer payments jumped from about 60 percent of total federal spending to 75 percent, the highest level in history as well as the fastest rate of increase.

The Topless U.S. Government Deficit: A Financial Crash in the Making

During the Obama years, the public debt of the United States rose to 100 percent of GDP from 62 percent, and during 2020, it leapt to 127 percent of GDP. Total public debt outstanding on Election Day 2008 stood at $9 trillion. In late 2021, it stood at $27 trillion. That figure does not include the unfunded liabilities of the Social Security and Medicare systems (the cumulative gap between future income and outlays), officially estimated at $55 trillion but privately estimated at anywhere from $87 trillion to $222 trillion.

The central premise of the Great Reset is that governments will have unlimited license to spend more for "equality" as well as for the environment—that is, to increase outlays that have no direct impact on future growth and may in fact prove harmful to future growth. Increased transfer payments reduce the incentive to work. The labor force participation rate (the percentage of the population that is working or actively seeking work) peaked in the mid-1990s at slightly more than 67 percent, and since has fallen to 61.6 percent. For men without a disability aged sixteen to sixty-four, the participation rate fell to just 83 percent in June 2021 from a high of 89 percent in 2009.

Environmental legislation imposes costs on the economy. According to a 2016 Heritage Foundation study, the Paris Agreement (from which the Trump administration withdrew in 2017) would cost the United States $2.5 trillion in lost GDP.

Some government spending generates future income, such as what Alexander Hamilton called "internal improvements," that is, infrastructure. Federal investment in R&D during the Kennedy through Reagan years paid for itself many times over in new technologies that created new industries and correspondingly increased tax revenues. But the increased spending proposed under the Great Reset will destroy incentives to work while imposing higher costs on business.

When the Kemp-Roth Tax Bill of 1981 reduced the top federal marginal tax rate to 40 percent from 70 percent, the initial result was a sharp increase in U.S. public debt, from $1 trillion in the second quarter of 1982 to $2 trillion in the second quarter of 1986. Without any increase in federal tax rates, though, the U.S. Treasury was running a surplus by 1998, and federal debt fell as a percentage of GDP to 55 percent in 2000 from 65 percent in 1995. The increase in the federal debt due to the "supply-side" tax cuts was envisioned to be a temporary measure under conditions of economic duress, not a permanent increase in the federal debt burden.

Lately, the most prominent liberal economists propose to expand federal debt without limit, on the grounds that low interest rates make it cheap to finance. An influential 2020 paper by former Treasury secretary Lawrence Summers and former Council of Economic Advisers Chairman Jason Furman stated this in black and white:

> The last generation has witnessed an epochal decline in real interest rates in the United States and around the world despite large buildups of government debt... [The] U.S. ten-year indexed bond yields declined by more than 4 percentage points between 2000 and early 2020 even as projected debt levels went from levels extremely low by historical standards to extremely high by historical standards. Similar movements have been observed at all maturities and throughout the industrial world. Available market data suggests that the Covid crisis has depressed real interest rates despite raising government debts, likely by increasing inequality, uncertainty and the use of information technology.
>
> This paper argues that while the future is unknowable and the precise reasons for the decline in real interest rates are not entirely clear, declining real rates reflect structural changes in the economy that require changes in thinking about fiscal policy and macroeconomic policy more generally that are as profound as those that occurred in the wake of the inflation of the...We note that with massive increases in budget deficits and government debt, expansions in social insurance, and sharp reductions in capital tax rates, one would have expected to see increasing real rates if private sector behavior had remained constant. We suggest that changes in the supply of saving associated with lengthening life expectancy, rising uncertainty and increased inequality along with reductions in

> the demand for capital associated with demographic changes, demassification of the economy, and perhaps changes in corporate behavior have driven real interest rates down.
>
> They open up the prospect that countries may be less constrained by fiscal space because fiscal expansions themselves can improve fiscal sustainability by raising GDP more than they raise debt and interest payments. They also imply that policymakers need to do more to both improve automatic recession insurance and also find more ways to use fiscal policy to expand demand without increasing deficits, for example through balanced budget multipliers, more progressive fiscal policy and also expanded social insurance.

Washington Post editorialist Charles Lane enthused a few months later:

> Far from burdening future generations, governments have a golden opportunity to fund long-standing needs by borrowing for investments in future prosperity—the list includes childcare, early education, job training and clean water. In light of the past 20 years' experience, the oft-cited metric of total public debt as a share of total output does not truly capture the burden of borrowing.

The claim that an excess supply of savings around the world explains low interest rates on Treasury securities is inconsistent with the observed facts. Between the first quarter of 2016 and the first quarter of 2021, U.S. public debt increased by $11 trillion but foreigners bought only $1 trillion of U.S. Treasury securities. Evidently, they did not have excess savings, or they put their excess savings somewhere else.

The major buyer of U.S. Treasury securities during the past ten years was the Federal Reserve itself, which increased its holdings by $6 trillion during the same period. It is clear from the chart below that "real" U.S. Treasury interest rates (the yield on Treasury Inflation-Protected Securities with a ten-year maturity) fell as the Federal Reserve's securities portfolio expanded:

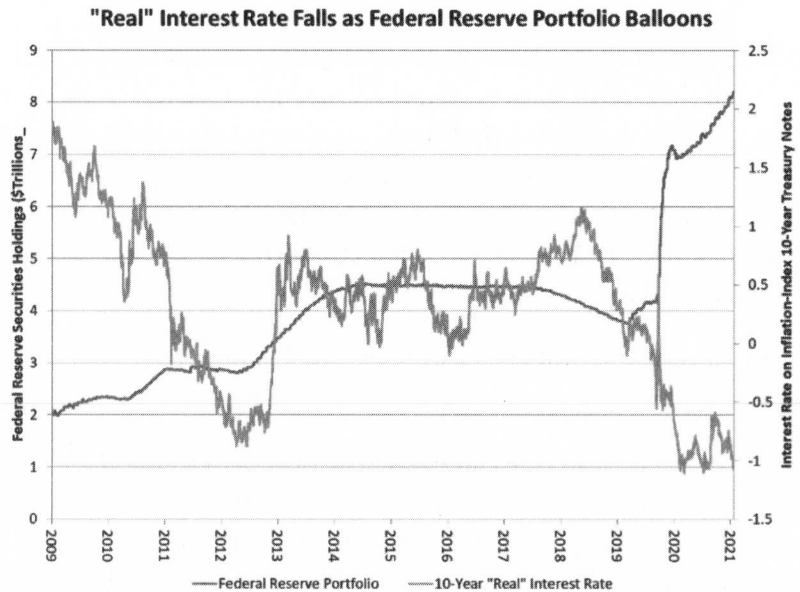

If the United States were to issue debt to rebuild its industrial base and reduce the current account deficit, increased debt might be justified. The approximately $5 trillion of incremental federal spending and $4 trillion of balance sheet expansion at the Federal Reserve merely increased demand.

Governments and central banks, of course, cannot increase debt ad infinitum. The result is inflation. The Federal Reserve and the Biden administration, early in its term, claimed that the worst inflation in four decades was the result of transitory factors. In some instances, that probably is true; a global shortage of computer chips constricted auto production, and used-car prices in response rose 25 percent during the year through July 2021, according to the industry-standard Manheim Index. But the most important price increases, and the increases that will have the biggest impact on consumer budgets, came in the price of owning and renting homes, which take up roughly 40 percent of the American consumer budget. Home price inflation is the result of portfolio decisions of millions of households that elect to increase debt and buy physical assets because they believe that the value of the currency will depreciate.

- Housing prices in June 2021 rose 17 percent year-on-year, equal to the fastest rate of increase in home prices on record at the 2004 peak of the housing bubble of the 2000s.
- Apartment rents rose 5.4 percent during the first five months of 2021, or an annualized rate of 13.4 percent, according to the listing firm Zillow.com.
- The producer price index as of June 2021 rose 9.4 percent year-on-year, the highest level in forty years for any month except the peak of the 2008 financial crisis, when the price of oil jumped briefly to $150 a barrel.
- The consumer price index rose 5.4 percent year-on-year in the year through June 2021, again the highest level in forty years (except for one month in 2008 due to a spike in oil prices).
- The U.S. GDP price index in the second quarter of 2001 rose at a 6 percent annual rate, the highest in forty years.

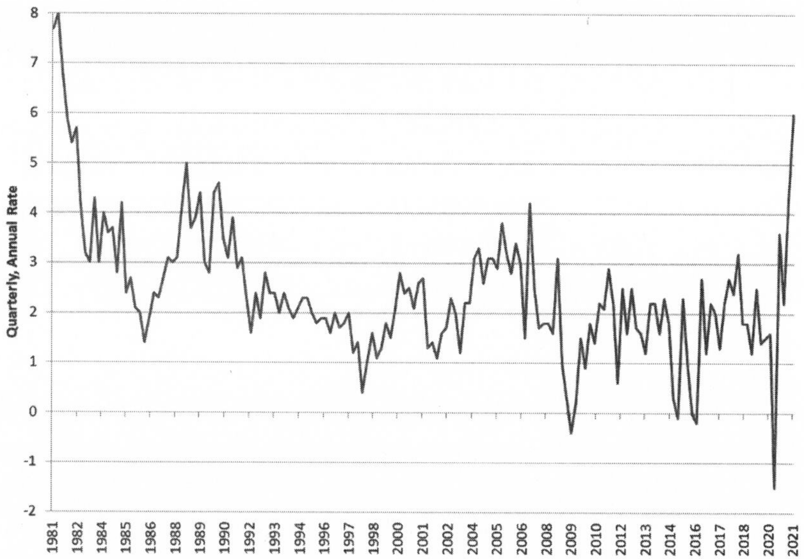

The Monster That Ate Capital Investment

The utopian goal of ending carbon emissions by midcentury will consume the entire world's investment budget for the next three decades, if the Great Reset prevails. This is not a scenario for the distant future but something that is already transforming the economic landscape. The first victim of the Great Reset is the U.S. oil and gas industry, America's leading economic success story during the early 2010s. That's just the beginning: the Great Reset proposes seizing control of the world's investment budget as a whole, with economic consequences unlike any policy initiative in history.

The International Energy Agency proposes $100 trillion in investment by 2050 to achieve zero emissions. As *Forbes* magazine reported,

> A low-carbon future begins with the power generation sector. In the IEA's scenario, by 2050, renewables will account for nearly 90 percent of global electricity

> generation, with solar photovoltaics (PVs) and wind contributing almost 70 percent. A transition from the fossil-fueled world of today demands tremendous investment in new capacity, grid modernization, and power storage. The IEA estimates that annual clean-energy investment needs to more than triple by 2030 to over $4 trillion. Over the next three decades, that represents well over $100 trillion total in clean energy investment.

Bloomberg News wrote on July 21, 2021:

> Governments and companies will need to invest at least $92 trillion by 2050 in order to cut emissions fast enough to prevent the worst effects of climate change. That's the latest forecast from analysts at Bloomberg New Energy Finance, who see that scale of spending as necessary to drive a rapid electrification of the global economy and slash reliance on fossil fuels.
>
> Thirty years is a short time frame to achieve the scale of transformation that is needed to limit further dangerous increases in global temperatures. Investment in infrastructure to accommodate energy transition will need to rise to between $3.1 trillion and $5.8 trillion annually on average until 2050, up from about $1.7 trillion in 2020, BNEF found. That means the final bill could be as much as $173 trillion, about eight times U.S. gross domestic product in 2019.
>
> That level of spending would help limit the increase of average global temperatures to 1.75° Celsius from pre-industrial levels, compared with about 1.2°C of warming already present. Without further action, events such as the heatwaves, floods, and wildfires experienced around the world in the last

> few weeks will likely get more frequent, dangerous, and costly.
>
> Scaling up the role of electric power underpins all hopes for a drastic cut to greenhouse gas emissions. More than three quarters of the potential decline in emissions this decade will likely need to come from electricity supply and the increasing use of wind and solar power, according to BNEF. Another 14 percent of the drop in emissions in that period can be achieved from vehicles, homes, and industries switching to electric power from burning fossil fuels. Hydrogen will also have a significant role to play, with demand set to soar.

One hundred trillion dollars is a staggering sum. The combined free cash flow of the four thousand one hundred companies worldwide with a market capitalization of at least $1 billion was $332 billion in the first quarter of 2021, or $1.33 trillion annualized, according to Refinitiv data. To put this in context: $92 trillion is nearly seventy times that sum to be spent over thirty years. The entire free cash flow of the world's private corporations barely would make up one-third of the Great Reset investment budget.

The U.S. government investment budget as of the first quarter of 2021 stood at $804 billion. Even if every penny of American investment were devoted to reducing carbon emissions, the total funding available between now and 2050 would be less than $25 billion.

The $92 trillion budget envisioned by the International Energy Agency and the Bloomberg economists would require the appropriation of the entire free cash flow of the world's large corporations as well as the entire investment budgets of the governments of the United States, Europe, and Japan. In practical terms, the proposal is fantastic and unworkable, but it sets guidelines for liberal economic policy. The Great Reset has placed an impossibly high hurdle before governments and the private sector to compel a comprehensive change in behavior.

Private corporations are now subject to Environmental, Social, and Governance ratings that rank their carbon emissions, employee diversity and similar criteria. The *Wall Street Journal* reported on December 6, 2020:

> The number of companies that report on their sustainability efforts has increased over the past decade amid the rise of socially conscious investing. Last year, 90% of companies in the S&P 500 index issued sustainability reports, up from about 20% in 2011, according to the Governance & Accountability Institute Inc., an ESG consulting firm.
>
> At issue, however, is what these companies disclose. In the absence of enforceable standards or regulation, companies can cherry pick what metrics to make public and which to keep confidential. That puts them at odds with some investors who want a clear summary of the nonfinancial risks a company faces and the ability to benchmark a company's ESG performance across an entire sector.

The Biden campaign promised to impose carbon-emission reporting standards on U.S. corporations, and the objective of the Great Reset is to turn governments into its enforcers.

Shareholder pressure groups, meanwhile, are extorting ESG compliance from corporations. The *Financial Times* reported in October 2020:

> The pressure on companies to tackle social and environmental issues has intensified this year despite the pandemic, with a record number of resolutions addressing issues from climate change to diversity passing at annual meetings globally in 2020. A total of twenty-one shareholder resolutions focused on social or environmental issues received the support of a majority of investors so far this year at companies around the world, up from thirteen in 2019 and 2018,

and just five in 2017, according to Proxy Insight, a data provider.

How the Great Reset Killed the Energy Industry

The impact on the oil and gas industry has been devastating. In 2014, the companies in the S&P 500's energy subindex invested $83 billion in capital expenditures. By 2020, this number had fallen to just $21 billion and was projected to rise to only $23 billion in 2021, according to the consensus estimates of analysts polled by Bloomberg. The collapse of investment in energy extraction has nothing to do with economics. The price of West Texas Intermediate crude oil recovered to about seventy dollars a barrel during 2021, far above the threshold at which most shale as well as conventional wells can be operated profitably in the United States. Yet the total number of oil and gas rigs in operation in the United States fell from a high of 1,083 in 2018 to only 491 in June 2021. As of October 1, 2021, oil production in the U.S. was down by about 13 percent from its pre-Covid peak in March 2020.The collapse of energy investment is unrelated to credit conditions in the industry. On the contrary, in August 2021, the average cost of borrowing on the bond market for U.S. energy companies rated below investment grade is just 4.25 percent above the ten-year Treasury yield. The ten-year U.S. Treasury note paid a coupon of just 1.6 percent in October 2021, close to its all-time record low, and the all-in cost of borrowing for speculative-grade energy companies also is the lowest on record. Despite the availability of cheap capital energy, companies use their free cash flow to pay down debt, buy back stock, or pay dividends rather than to produce more oil and gas. In 2014, the free cash flow of the S&P energy subindex was close to zero, yet energy companies borrowed to invest $83 billion. In 2021 the free cash flow of the energy industry will reach $35 billion but, as noted, the industry will invest just $23 billion this year.

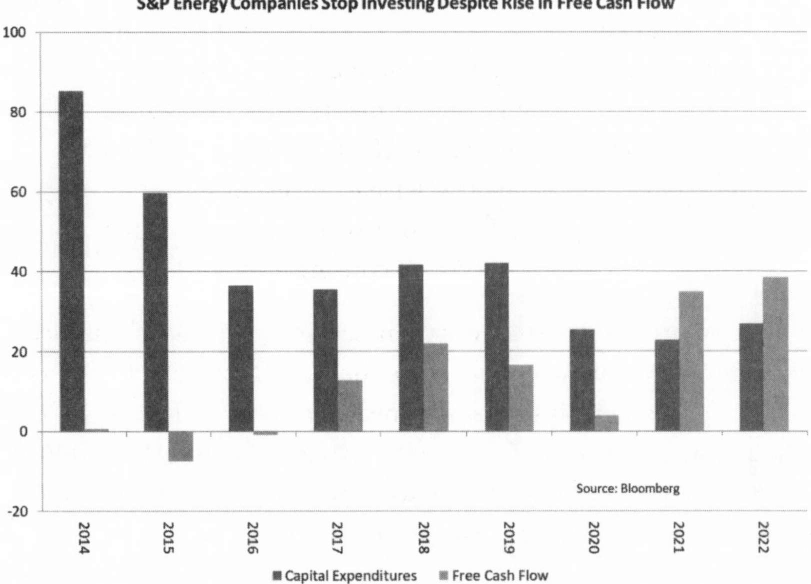

This is the result of political pressure, not economics. The Biden administration sent an unmistakable signal to the American energy industry when it canceled the $15 billion Keystone Pipeline as one of its first acts in office. According to the executive order issued by the White House, the purpose of canceling the pipeline was to send a message to the world that investment must be shifted to climate change projects. "Approving the proposed Keystone XL pipeline would not serve the U.S. national interest, the order stated," and would "undermine U.S. climate leadership by undercutting the credibility and influence of the United States in urging other countries to take ambitious climate action."

The message could not have been stronger or more damaging.

The International Energy Agency titled an October 2020 report, "Investment estimates for 2020 continue to point to a record slump in spending." The report explained:

> Some oil and gas companies are responding to such pressures by stepping up diversification efforts, guided

> by new long-term emissions goals. While these vary in scope and ambition, several European majors have increased capital guidance for low-carbon projects. Investment commitments are most visible in renewable power, where USD 3.5 billion of final investment decisions (FIDs) have been taken by oil and gas companies in 2020, two-thirds higher than their capital spend outside of core areas in 2019.

As a result of the shale boom, an accomplishment of American technology, the United States became the world's largest oil producer and reduced its net oil imports to nearly zero by 2018. Unless the decline in U.S. energy investment is reversed, net oil imports jumped in 2020 and will continue to increase, and the goal of oil self-sufficiency is likely to fade into the distance.

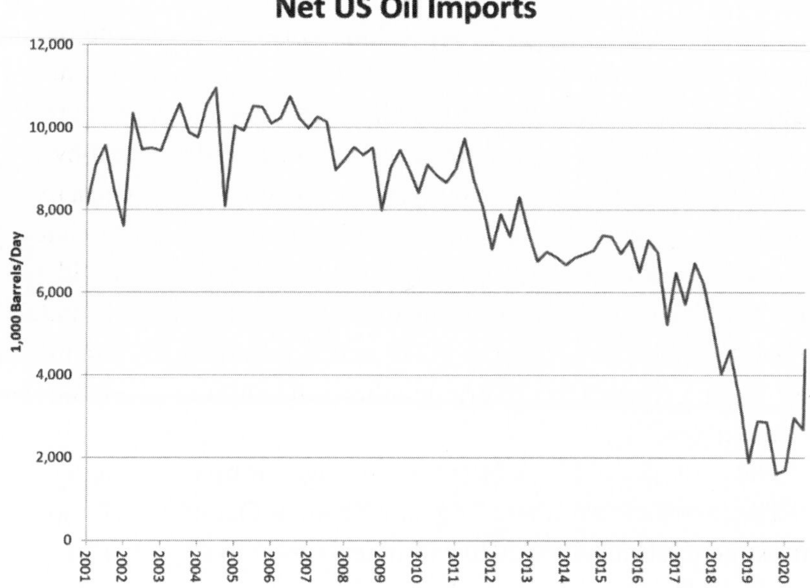

The Fourth Industrial Revolution Will Flourish—in China

Although the Great Reset diverts virtually the entire capital budget of the Western industrial nations into climate change investments, China will focus its resources on technological superiority. China's *Caixin Global Daily* July 1, 2020, reprinted a speech by Sinovation Ventures Chairman Kai-Fu Lee declaring that "the combination of AI and other new technologies would bring about five major industrial nations that will allow China to lead the world in science and technology." These are:

1. China will lead the world in advanced manufacturing as AI empowers automation upgrades.
2. China's supply chain will dominate the world as energy and material prices plummet.
3. Smart cities and the internet of everything (IoE) will be realized and fully automatic driving will become universally accessible.
4. As China's innovations in business intelligence multiply, AI will enable a new order of business operations.
5. AI combined with health care innovations will lower mortality from disease and extend people's lives.

American experts think that China may dominate the key technologies of the twenty-first century. The National Security Commission on Artificial Intelligence (NSCAI), chaired by former Google chairman Eric Schmidt and former deputy Defense secretary Robert O. Work, warned in a 2021 report:

> The race to research, develop, and deploy AI and associated technologies is intensifying the technology competition that underpins a wider strategic competition. China is organized, resourced, and determined to win this contest. The United States

> retains advantages in critical areas, but current trends are concerning.... China's plans, resources, and progress should concern all Americans. It is an AI peer in many areas and an AI leader in some applications. We take seriously China's ambition to surpass the United States as the world's AI leader within a decade...For the first time since World War II, America's technological predominance—the backbone of its economic and military power—is under threat. China possesses the might, talent, and ambition to surpass the United States as the world's leader in AI in the next decade.

According to the NSCAI report,

> China understands the tremendous upside associated with leading the bio revolution. Massive genomic data sets at places like BGI Group (formerly known as the Beijing Genomics Institute), coupled with China's now-global genetic data collection platform and "all-of-nation" approach to AI, will make them a formidable competitor in the bio realm. BGI may be serving, wittingly or unwittingly, as a global collection mechanism for Chinese government genetic databases, providing China with greater raw numbers and diversity of human genome samples as well as access to sensitive personal information about key individuals around the world.

China has made rapid progress toward Fourth Industrial Revolution technologies since the beginning of 2020. It has already built eight hundred nineteen thousand 5G base stations, or 70 percent of the world's installed capacity. The global chip shortage and U.S. sanctions against Chinese telecom equipment firms like Huawei and ZTE have slowed China's 5G buildout to some extent, but 5G infrastructure already covers all of China's major cities. China will add between five hundred thousand and eight hundred thousand new 5G base stations to the eight hundred nineteen thousand now in place, according to industry sources. The Chinese government claims that all prefecture-level cities (with populations of at least two hundred fifty thousand) are covered by 5G. Although U.S. carriers offer what they call 5G service, the American version provides download speeds barely above the older-generation 4G LTE broadband, at around sixty mbits/second. The average speed in China is five times higher, at over 300 mbits/second.

The buildout of 5G networks in major cities is matched by industrial and commercial applications of 5G. Chinese manufacturers have installed about five thousand private 5G networks and will add tens of thousands more this year, as 5G broadband enables Fourth Industrial Revolution applications, according to mainland industry leaders. By contrast, the total number of private 5G networks now in operation in the United States and Europe is somewhere in the mid-hundreds. The role of 5G broadband in the Fourth Industrial Revolution is comparable to the role of railroads in the First Industrial Revolution: it is a carrier technology that enables a range of other technologies. The high data capacity and nearly instantaneous response time makes possible:

- Real-time epidemic monitoring and AI analysis of billions of data points to predict potential nodes of infection;
- Self-programming industrial robots "talking" to each other on the factory floor;
- Automated ports that link cranes and self-driving trucks to unload containers with minimal human supervision;
- Autonomous vehicles that "talk" to each other on the road in real time;
- "Smart cities" that match vehicles to packages and passengers and optimize traffic flow;
- Remote control of mining equipment to minimize human exposure to underground accidents;

- Remote medical diagnosis and remote-controlled robotic surgery

5G Leads the Fourth Industrial Revolution

According to Western analysts, the productivity enhancement driven by factory and warehouse automation enabled by 5G will be enormous. The Swedish telecommunications equipment firm Ericsson, number two globally after China's Huawei, wrote in a white paper:

> Taking manufacturing, with its estimated 1 million factories (with more than 100 employees), as an example, typical business cases revolve around controlling the production process, improving material management, improving safety, and introducing new tools. Typical revenue increases come from increased throughput and quality (2–3 percent), while typical cost savings stem from improved capital efficiency (5–10 percent) and decreased manufacturing costs (4–8 percent)]. Additionally, ABI Research has shown that manufacturers can expect to see a tenfold increase in their returns on investment (ROIs) for cellular Industry 4.0 solutions, while warehouse owners can expect a staggering fourteenfold increase in ROI.

China used the Covid-19 epidemic to apply AI analysis to massive data sets, including the location of the majority of the Chinese people derived from smartphone apps, real-time monitoring of the vital signs of hundreds of millions of Chinese, and the results of Covid-19 testing. The epidemic allowed China to field-test a wide range of new technologies including remote sensing of vital signs. This application requires a disregard for individual privacy and freedom unacceptable in democratic societies. Huiyao Wang, the head of the Beijing Center for China and Globalization, said in an October 2020 interview with *Asia Times*:

> This data approach, though, has been really widely used in China because China's philosophy and Chinese culture supports it. In China, people don't really regard individual freedom or individual human rights as the top of community interest. What is on top is the collective effort. For example, if I'm locked down, cannot go out, even I lose my individual freedom, the whole society benefits from that. That's why I think this thing can only be applied in China.

There is nothing uniquely Chinese about these technologies. But China has focused its national resources on rapid deployment of 5G, which is the enabling technology for a wide variety of industrial, transportation, commercial, and medical applications. For example, the major port at Shanghai is now fully automated with 5G communications between cranes, autonomous trucks, and warehouses. The port handles forty-four million containers per year. By contrast, America's largest port facility, Long Beach, California, ships only eight million containers a year, and is a significant bottleneck in the U.S. economy. In late 2020, Shandong Energy Group began operations at an automated coal mine controlled by a 5G network.

Chinese e-commerce and logistics companies including Alibaba and JD.com have been using drones to deliver packages for two years, and the availability of 5G communications will accelerate the automations of warehouses and delivery systems. The Great Reset, by contrast, will exhaust the combined investment capacity of the West in environmental projects that add nothing to productivity.

The Threat to America's Financial System

Why is China's digital yuan a threat to the U.S. dollar? The world currently holds slightly over half of its working capital for international transactions in U.S. dollars ($16 billion of the $31 billion now held in offshore bank accounts, according to the Bank for International

Settlements). The great advantage of the U.S. dollar is that corporations who hold bank balances for international transactions can invest them freely in American capital markets. As the *Wall Street Journal* observed in April 2021: "The range of options to foreigners who find themselves with a pile of yuan is minimal, compared with a pile of dollars, euros, or yen. China has far fewer high-quality assets, and the government's squeamishness about outflows of capital make the risk of not being able to retrieve funds far higher."

Digital yuan skeptics are right to argue that the digital yuan is in no position to replace the *existing* function of the U.S. dollar. Nonetheless, China threatens to overthrow American financial dominance, and with it America's capacity to borrow tens of trillions of dollars from the rest of the world at low or zero interest rates. One facet of the Fourth Industrial Revolution, "smart logistics," promises to dramatically reduce the role of the banking system and shrink its deposit base. As the main beneficiary of the present world banking system, the United States will suffer the most.

Prominent bankers acknowledge that this revolution in finance is already underway. The chairman of JP Morgan, Jaime Dimon, wrote in his 2021 annual letter to shareholders: "Banks already compete against a large and powerful shadow banking system. And they are facing extensive competition from Silicon Valley, both in the form of fintechs [financial technology firms] and Big Tech companies (Amazon, Apple, Facebook, Google and now Walmart), that is here to stay. As the importance of cloud, AI, and digital platforms grows, this competition will become even more formidable. As a result, banks are playing an increasingly smaller role in the financial system."

China has no intention of replacing the U.S. dollar with its RMB (renminbi, or people's money notes) within the framework of the existing world banking system, as People's Bank of China Deputy Governor Li Bo said April 19, 2021. In fact, China has no incentive to do this, and could not do so even it wanted to. The $16 trillion of offshore dollar deposits at international banks won't turn into the equivalent number of Chinese yuan. Instead, that $16 trillion will shrink to a small fraction of its present volume because "smart logistics" will reduce the need for corporations to maintain large bank balances to finance international transactions. Some history puts this in context.

To understand the implications for banking of the Fourth Industrial Revolution, consider the international payments system of the sixteenth century. The most important flow was Spain's trade deficit, and it was financed by bullion from the New World. The aggregate cost of mining, transporting, and guarding the silver and gold shipments from the New World consumed a substantial part of Spain's national income. The Dutch and British replaced this system during the seventeenth and eighteenth centuries with the prototype of the modern banking system. Banks made a liquid market in bills of exchange in international trade, and the British government offered its own debt securities to absorb surpluses in trade.

China is creating a new system of world trade and finance that will—as a byproduct—replace the methods of trade financing that have remained in place since the founding of the Bank of England in 1694. The yuan won't replace the dollar as the world's reserve currency; instead, the role of reserve currencies that began with the pound sterling under the Pax Britannica will shrink, and with it the deposit base of the banking system. America will be deprived of tens of trillions of dollars in zero-interest loans that it now obtains from the rest of the world.

Fintech is not the most important driver of this transformation. The epicenter of change is what Huawei calls "smart logistics," the application of Big Data/AI to supply chain management. In a post on its corporate website, Huawei claimed that its system "seamlessly connects node operations and physical transportation, provides early warnings for active risks, and delivers the full-range of visible management, including the one stream of materials concept. Through mobile apps, AI, IoT, and other advanced logistics technologies, the system perceives the locations of vehicles, the operating status of warehouses, and other information in real time."

Big Data can track thimbleful of iron ore from a Brazilian mine to a blast furnace in Harbin, to a roll of steel wire at a Tangshan steel mill, to a nail factory in Xingtai, to a warehouse in Shanghai, to a container ship en route to Long Beach, California, to a truck headed for a hardware distributor in Denver. The production, storage, and shipment of goods will be verified every step of the way. The blast furnace will pay the Brazilian mine on delivery, and the rolling mill will pay the blast furnace, the nail factory will pay the rolling mill, and so forth. None of them will have to borrow money from an international bank and keep it on deposit for months while waiting to see whether the delivery arrives.

Several other firms besides Huawei offer the same services. China is the leader in the field because it is the first country to build out a national 5G mobile broadband network, which makes possible real-time collection and processing of information about the world's supply chains.

Digital finance is an adjunct to digital logistics. Instead of financing imports months in advance, businesses will make digital transfers at each stage of production, transportation, warehousing, and sales, reducing the working capital required for international transactions and shrinking the deposit base of the banking system.

Every business in the whole variegated, complex supply chain will make a digital transfer from its central bank digital currency (CBDC) account. The People's Bank of China is collaborating with the world's main agency for international payments, the Society for Worldwide Interbank Financial Telecommunication (SWIFT), to expedite financial transfers in digital yuan. Exporters and importers presently keep bank balances in dollars and Euro (mostly) because those are the currencies in which banks lend. The majority of offshore bank deposits are in U.S. dollars—$16 trillion worth—even though the U.S. accounts for just 8 percent of world exports. China accounts for 12 percent and its share is growing.

Ultimately, the country that dominates global supply chains will dominate the currency system. In the wake of the Covid-19 pandemic,

Western supply chains buckled and, in some cases, collapsed. China, which emerged from the pandemic first, benefited from the distress in Western economies. As of August 2021, Chinese exports have risen by 25 percent above prepandemic levels. As Western supply chains remain under stress, China is likely to lock in this jump its share of world trade. As Morgan Stanley chief economist Chetan Ahya wrote in an April 18, 2021, report:

> When something as fundamental as what you use to make payments changes, the effects can be far-reaching. Commercial banks will face the risk of disintermediation. Once CBDC [central bank digital currency] accounts are launched, consumers will be able to transfer their bank deposits there, subject to limits imposed by the central banks. Moreover, the technological infrastructure of CBDCs will make it easier for new nonbank entities to enter the payments space and accelerate the transition toward digital payments. These factors will increase competitive pressures on commercial banks.

Chetan Ahya and his Morgan Stanley colleagues added in an April 19 report, "Even though central banks will try not to disrupt the banks, CBDC accounts will increase competition for customer deposits…In the most disruptive case, banks lose deposit base and credit creation needs to be funded wholesale or by central bank."

China's promulgation of a digital currency will benefit from its leading position in Fourth Industrial Revolution logistics technologies. The United States, to be sure, could issue a competing digital currency. The threat to the United States, though, does not arise from the currency in which transactions are denominated, but from the fact that the United States now must borrow 10 percent of its GDP each year to finance its internal budget deficit, and also must attract about $1 trillion of capital inflows to finance its growing current account deficit with the rest of the world. The interest-free loans the U.S.

obtains from the rest of the world are what economists call *seigniorage*, a term derived from the difference between the value of gold or silver coins and their bullion content, and it amounts to tens of trillions of dollars. The U.S. will lose this enormous volume of cheap credit from the rest of the world just when it needs it the most.

China and the United States agree on just one thing in the middle of their trade and technology antagonism. That is carbon neutrality. In a video speech to the September 2020 meeting of the United Nations General Assembly, China's leader Xi Jinping pledged that China, now the world's largest consumer of coal, will reach peak carbon utilization by 2030 and achieve carbon neutrality by 2060. Chinese leaders believe that the Western elite is so obsessed with global warming that it will do whatever it takes to get a deal with China. China's Vice President Wang Qishan proposed the Biden administration's climate czar, former secretary of state John Kerry, as "a good choice for bringing the two countries together through climate cooperation," the *South China Morning Post* reported September 28, 2021. Kerry visited China twice in 2021, the only cabinet-level official of the Biden administration to do so.

Perhaps China has heeded Napoleon's maxim: "Never interrupt your opponent while he is making a mistake." China's interest in environmental issues is not a subterfuge, to be sure; toxic smog regularly reaches health-threatening density in major Chinese cities, including Beijing. China will build twenty new nuclear power plants during its 2016–2020 five-year plan, more than the rest of the world combined. But it is unsettling that climate change is the one area of agreement between Beijing and Washington in the midst of a struggle for world leadership.

China's press is full of targets for energy efficiency, mechanisms for carbon trading among Chinese enterprises, and rhetoric about China's newfound concern for the environment. But unlike the Davos elites, who are prepared to sacrifice the Western economy for carbon neutrality, the Chinese will put economic strength first. China's Premier Li Keqiang told a meeting of China's National Energy Commission on October 12, 2021, that China would continue "building up the nation's capacity in fossil fuels, from coal to oil and shale gas," *Bloomberg News* reported. China, Premier Li added, would "prioritize economic development," which "holds the key to solving all its problems."

China, that is, will tell the West what it wants to hear, and credulous public officials like John Kerry will believe whatever they are told. While the United States allows its industrial base to wither, China will redouble its efforts to become the world's most powerful economy. The Great Reset will never find the $100 trillion it wants to remake the world because the United States will be broke long before that happens.

PART IV: THE PERSONAL

THE GREAT RESET, FEMINIST-STYLE

BY JANICE FIAMENGO

Introduction: Equity for Women

What would a Great Reset mean for women and girls—and the men who love them? In *COVID-19: The Great Reset* (2020), WEF founder Klaus Schwab and his coauthor Thierry Malleret do not address the status of women at length. But they do refer, on the very first page, to the search for social justice, stating that a positive consequence of Covid-19 has been its exposure of the "fault lines of the world" and its galvanization of the will to redress them.

By far the most destabilizing fault line in the western world is the one that feminism has opened between men and women. It is set to widen even further if Reset proponents have their way.

In its institutional forms, feminism is a radical ideology alleging that women are oppressed in a patriarchal order created and maintained for male benefit through institutions such as the traditional family. Developed in the North American universities of the 1970s and 1980s, feminism's assertions about male control of women have spread far into the wider society as feminist students graduated into careers in teaching, journalism, law, social work, public relations, and business. Though often claiming to seek equality between the sexes (itself a dubious, oft-unrealizable goal), feminists regularly call for special privileges for women and corresponding restrictions for men.

Feminism shares with the Schwabian Reset a utopian vision of a reimagined world in which the historically disempowered will be compensated and protected by enlightened leaders who will manage all aspects of our social, economic, and domestic lives. In this transformed world, a never-before-achievable righting of injustice will become possible as the enemies of fairness and of the common good—the selfish, the competitive, the predatory, and the retrograde—will be once and for all neutralized by government fiat.

Discussions of post-Covid *she-covery* (recovery with a female face) focused mainly on four feminist Reset blueprints: 1) liberating women from the unfair burdens of family life; 2) empowering women to close wage and employment gaps; 3) mandating leadership roles for women, especially in politics, business, and academia; and 4) advancing the sexual agenda of the #MeToo movement. All, as will be shown, are underpinned by profoundly antimale assumptions and contempt for established social and legal norms. Whether any of these blueprints will make women happier is a highly doubtful proposition: bitter and resentful women, rather than contented ones, are precisely what Reset discussions and policies are designed to create.

Background: Covid-19 and Inordinate Female Suffering

A canard about Covid-19 peddled by Schwab and Malleret was that the virus exposed and exacerbated social divides, hurting those who were already vulnerable. In reality, as the authors well know, it was not Covid itself, which in their estimation was not "a new existential threat," so much as the draconian policies of governments and health officials, amplified by media-induced terror and compliance, that shaped social divides.

Government lockdowns and masking/distancing policies, often brutally and unequally enforced, created Covid winners and losers by determining which businesses could open, whether and how many family members could gather, and whether children could attend school or play together. Social elites working in government, media, academia, and the corporate world, their paycheques and lifestyles largely intact, demonized as "Covidiots" anyone who defied or even questioned public health orders, sometimes encouraging readers to report those who broke any of the arcane rules (unless, of course, the rule-breakers were Black Lives Matter protesters, in which case even the prime minister of Canada knelt with them in solidarity).

Along with daily counts of "cases," hospitalizations, and deaths, the media offered a steady barrage of stories designed to highlight Covid heroes and Covid villains, channeling sympathy toward those deemed to be legitimately suffering or bravely assisting, and encouraging contempt for alleged conspiracy theorists or "Far Right" adherents (mainly white men) who posed a danger. Here, the familiar polarities of ideological feminism came into play: women were typically presented as the innocent victims of a male-dominated society's injustices—that is, when they weren't outstanding leaders keeping the virus at bay or valiant frontline nurses caring for the sick.

In the earliest days of Covid, medical data showed that men were more likely than women to die from the virus or to experience the most severe forms of illness, accounting for about 80 percent of acute-care admissions and up to 70 percent of the dead. Yet even as these staggering reports hit the headlines, media accounts were busy framing the pandemic as a women's issue.

By March 8, 2020, when the effects of the virus were being felt in Europe but had not yet hit North America, the emphasis on female suffering had already been established. The BBC World Service informed readers that "Across Asia, it is women who are being disproportionately affected." A humanitarian advisor to the U.N., Maria Holtsberg, was quoted saying that "Crisis always exacerbates gender inequality." According to the article, women were bearing the brunt of the pandemic not only as primary caregivers for their children, forced to stay home when schools closed (with no mention of the breadwinner husbands continuing their work and thus at presumably greater risk of infection) but also—and somewhat contradictorily—as the majority of workers on the "front lines." The article detailed horrific working conditions of nurses in China and elsewhere in which nurses were forced to have their heads shaved and denied washroom breaks while working overtime. Women were also vulnerable, according to the article, as migrant workers with few rights, and in retail and informal sectors of the economy hard-hit by store closures.

The mantra that would be repeated in countless later articles was thus established: as stated by Mohammad Naciri, regional director of U.N. Women Asia, "Women are playing an indispensable role in the fight against the outbreak," and must be at the forefront of all efforts to deal with it. Vulnerable male migrant workers, low-income shopkeepers, and men on other types of front lines—particularly long-haul truckers attempting to maintain supply chains even as much-needed rest stops, washrooms, and food outlets closed—were not mentioned. Essential service providers who were male—ambulance responders, restoration and clean-up crews, police officers, delivery drivers, all-night convenience store clerks, bus and train operators—were made invisible.

As the Covid situation worsened in Europe and spread to North America over the following weeks, the same ideas were amplified, with many commentators focusing on favored first-world feminist themes such as women's greater emotional and caregiving burdens. Helen Lewis's "The Coronavirus Is a Disaster for Feminism" declared that "Across the world, women's independence will be a silent victim of the pandemic," while Lucia Graves in "Women's Domestic Burden Just Got Heavier with the Coronavirus" predicted that women's unfair allocation of housework would be increased. Many commentators asserted that women and girls were, as always, doing the majority of caring for elderly or ill family members and, already economically more vulnerable than men, would see their earnings potential permanently impacted by layoffs.

Some of the claims were dramatic, others strikingly trivial. Heather Barr, the interim codirector of the Women's Rights Division of Human Rights Watch, reported with somber emphasis that many now-unemployed women "faced losing their homes in countries from South Africa to the U.K." and that even simply "maintaining access to water and utilities was a struggle for many, including in the United States." Men, it seemed, never lost their homes or lacked the necessities of life (though men actually account for the vast majority of the homeless in western nations).

Alongside such dire warnings, the aforementioned Helen Lewis, writing for the *Atlantic*, was exclusively exercised about the problems of affluence, working herself into a lather over the patriarchal unfairness that saw a female university professor of epidemiology, profiled in the article, bearing the yoke of looking after three young children in the family home while her husband, an emergency physician treating Covid-19 patients, self-isolated in the family garage. We can only imagine the intensity of her ire if the woman had been the one consigned to the outbuilding.

Many of the authors couldn't seem to decide whether to present women primarily as suffering victims—vulnerable and in need of assistance—or as valiant heroines notable for their self-sacrificing leadership. A *Forbes* article of April 18, 2021, began by citing pandemic-related studies finding more women suffering from stress-related hypertension and "at significantly higher risk for developing coronary heart disease, compared with men," but also couldn't resist quoting Lisa Britt, a human resources officer, who offered that the pandemic had proved "the depth of capability among working women," specifying their "ability to acutely prioritize, multi-task, and ensure the well-being of those around them." Were women *less* able or *better* able than men to deal with the stresses of the Covid crisis? Both, it seemed—and always deserving of the lion's share of sympathy.

Men as The Inferior Sex

When men were the focus of Covid-related articles, the emphasis was on their culpability and menace. A number of articles blamed men—some with relish—for their greater susceptibility to Covid. In "Doctor's

Note: Why Are More Men Dying from Coronavirus?" a (female) doctor wrote in Al Jazeera that unhealthy lifestyle choices were at least partly to blame for men's more severe illness and higher mortality. Men were "more likely to partake in unhealthy habits" such as excess drinking and smoking, and had notoriously poor hand hygiene. A writer for the *New York Post* took evident pleasure in detailing "Why Women are Better than Men at Defeating the Coronavirus" by highlighting men's greater genetic vulnerability to viral infections. Quoting the male genetics researcher Dr. Sharon Moalem, whose most recent book is invidiously titled *The Better Half: On the Genetic Superiority of Women* (imagine a book touting men's genetic superiority), the article showcased how women's XX chromosomes create a stronger immune response to infection.

Moalem himself made the case for female invincibility in an interview with CNN's Christiane Amanpour, who smiled broadly and expressed delight ("Obviously I'm really pleased to hear that!") as he explained why women were less likely than men to die from Covid. Her jubilation was palpable.

Others excoriated men as alleged "super-spreaders," indifferent to the welfare of others. BBC writer Priya Elan claimed on the basis of a study that found men less likely than women to wear a face mask if such coverings were *not* mandated, that such men's "notions of masculinity are intertwined with a mix of petulance, indestructibility and, ultimately privilege." The author advised men to "grow up."

Mining the same vein, a writer for *Huffington Post* claimed that "The White Male Is The Biggest Risk In Spreading The Virus." Castigating older white men for allegedly "believ[ing] in their own invincibility and immortality," the author cited research suggesting that white men (though also Hispanic men, a point quietly buried) were less likely to take shelter during tornadoes or refuse to leave flood areas and came to the conclusion that "During Covid-19, it means many won't stay home to save lives." It remains to be seen whether staying home actually saved any lives—but Reset proponents missed no opportunity to stigmatize a disfavored group.

Leaving aside the crucial distinction between lack of concern for one's *own* safety and lack of concern for others (men who remain in disaster areas most often do so to save property and help others), the author leapt to a demonizing link between white men and virus danger, even alleging that measures such as martial law might be necessary to control the white male menace.

Men were also blamed for an uptick in domestic violence. An article in the British *Guardian* surveying countries that included China, Brazil, Germany, and Spain stressed that "Lockdowns around the world bring rise in domestic violence." A careful reader could notice that the purported "rise" was based not on numbers of hospital admissions or cases investigated by police but rather on reports from domestic violence helplines. These are often government-funded agencies with a vested interest in making such claims. Certainly, the claims sounded alarming, though it's hard to know without numbers how to interpret an increase in call volume of 30 percent in a single week, as a Cyprus agency reported. Even in countries where calls to helplines had dropped sharply, such as in Italy, activists were quick to rationalize that this was because women couldn't utilize phones "because they fear[ed] being overheard by abusive partners." Italian advocates claimed to be receiving "desperate text messages and emails," though numbers were again left conveniently undisclosed.

Such agencies advocated measures to protect women and punish men, including giving police special powers to evict (male) perpetrators from homes without investigation or trial. The possibility that men might be falsely accused or might find themselves homeless as a result of a two-way spat that turned physical (the most common form of domestic violence) is never considered in such reports, nor is the possibility that any of the violence was directed at men. The climate of opinion that formed around Covid was so intensely female-centered as to rule out any empathy for the cruel sex.

In time, various phrases were developed to solidify women's status as "hardest hit." We heard of "An Unequal Crisis," a "She-Cession," a "Women's Pandemic," a "Shadow Pandemic," and the need for a "she-covery." The barely veiled implication was that men need no assistance and do not contribute as meaningfully as women (if at all) to a well-functioning society. Some advocates had a more polemical message. The aforementioned Heather Barr of Human Rights Watch articulated her (satisfied) conviction that the pandemic had "galvanized [women's] rage" (perhaps in no small part because of repeated assertions that they were the only sex to suffer from it) and declared that "Our job now is to demand a post-pandemic world where we repair not just the unequal harm suffered during the pandemic, but also the deep inequities that led to that harm." As the foregoing examples illustrate, Reset proponents seized on Covid-19 as an occasion to rectify long-standing (sometimes shockingly trivial) feminist grievances.

Liberating Women from the Injustice of Motherhood

For many commentators, the worst thing about Covid-19 was its purported forcing of women, through lockdowns and school closures, back into 1950s-style domesticity. Even as the mysterious disease was spreading alarmingly in the early weeks of March, 2020, this redomestication seemed to some a fate worse than death. "All this looking after—this unpaid caring labor—will fall more heavily on women," fumed the previously cited Helen Lewis. If there were women, as surely there were, who reveled in the opportunity to spend unstructured time (some of it funded by fellow taxpayers) at home with their kids—and men who happily took on their share of increased parenting responsibilities—we didn't see their stories highlighted. We heard instead about the unfairness of it all. And whether Dad was angrily exhorted to take on more family duties—or whether he was targeted for ejection from the family altogether—fathers were frequently depicted in the feminist literature as inadequate or peripheral.

Such emphases fit with decades-old feminist (and Marxist) advocacy that envisions the extermination of the traditional family. Family abolitionist and acclaimed academic Sophie Lewis, for example, argued that "The coronavirus crisis shows it's time to abolish the family." Objecting to the assumption of "shelter in place" orders that the family home is actually a place to find shelter, she alleged that it is more often an "unsafe space" defined by "the power asymmetries of housework" and the deformations inherent in property ownership. Rife with violence and dehumanization, the family unit turns its members into compliant subjects in consumer-capitalist society, "norm[ing] us for productive work" and "mak[ing] us believe we are 'individuals.'" Lewis's conclusion was incendiary: "Far from a time to acquiesce to 'family values' ideology, then, the pandemic is an acutely important time to provision, evacuate and generally empower survivors of—and refugees from—the nuclear household."

Lewis's extreme perspective was echoed in mainstream complaints about the "disproportionate" burden for women of what is often called, in deliberately depersonalized language, "unpaid care-giving responsibilities," and emphatic calls for a taxpayer-funded system that would "free" them. In "The Women's Pandemic," which narrates scenes of harried working women tending their demanding offspring, with fathers nowhere in sight or depicted as constitutionally incapable, Professor Ivy Lynn Bourgeault, a feminist research chair at the University of Ottawa, was quoted in high dudgeon that "If we don't understand the value of childcare now, we never will." Economist Armine Yalnizyan, credited with coining the phrase "she-covery," called childcare, somewhat unclearly but certainly forcefully, "the chokepoint without which there will be no real post-pandemic recovery."

Men's role in the Reset family is tenuous at best. If present at all, men are frequently assumed to be domestic laggards, an assumption that led Sheryl Sandberg, chief operating officer of Facebook, to exhort men in a pandemic-focused Instagram statement of March, 2020, that "Now more than ever, men need to step up at home" in order to keep their female partners "happier and less depressed" and to show kids "what gender equality looks like up close." Whether working fathers needed support or cheering up is never considered. Just a few months later, however, a long piece in the journal *Bloomberg CityLab*, "How to Rebuild Cities for Caregiving" (an excerpt from

Feminist City: Claiming Space in a Man-Made World by academic Leslie Kern), hardly mentions men at all in imagining how "mothers and other caregivers" (the word *fathers* never appears) can be supported in "care work."

The author advocates making caregiving "more collective, less exhausting, and more equitable." Much of the piece is deliberately imprecise about how childcare might be properly shared and managed, but the author is certain that "the time has come to decenter the heterosexual, nuclear family." Men, particularly fathers, are not acknowledged as caregivers. Antimale premises such as these seem to have led Joe Biden's campaign team to omit the word *father* from his promise during the 2020 presidential election to "Ensure mothers and all parents can access high-quality, affordable childcare." As Stephen Baskerville's extensive research has made clear, the impetus of feminist activism around "no-fault divorce" (actually unilateral, involuntary divorce) has been to create a society in which the value of fathers has been increasingly lost to cultural consciousness except as payers of financial support for families no longer theirs.

Few childcare advocates seem aware that experiments in collective child-rearing—specifically in the Soviet Union and in Israel during the Kibbutz period—have been amply tried, with disastrous consequences. In Israel, for example, children lived in children's houses from four weeks old until adolescence, spending at most a few hours per day with their parents, who were encouraged to pursue their gender-equal work lives. It was the ideal that feminists have long fantasized about, and it didn't last. Within two generations, the children's houses were abandoned in favor of nuclear-family housing. Many reports by survivors of the system—both mothers and their children—tell of the dysfunction and abuse of collectivization efforts that denied and attempted to remake the natural bonds of family life.

Undeterred by history and biology, feminist advocates continue to insist that day care, as proclaimed in a recent *VICE* article on pandemic recovery, is "key to women's social and economic equality." The single most important plank of feminist Reset ideology involves breaking the link between women and mothering by asserting that looking after children is primarily a form of "unpaid labor" and that families (or, at least, progressive women) are best served when children are farmed out to persons who feel no deep familial or affective bond with them. For women who want to mother their own children—and for men who wish to support their wives and children free of state interference—the message is unmistakable: the Reset family is no place for you.

Abolishing Gender Gaps in the Workforce

In 2013, two economists at MIT published a study called "Wayward Sons: The Emerging Gender Gap in Labor Markets and Education" that turned conventional wisdom on its head by finding that men were not economically privileged. Though a small proportion of elite men still dominated the corporate and professional worlds, the majority of men were falling behind their female counterparts in employment, skills acquisition, real wages, and job status. For years, girls have performed more successfully than boys in school and obtained university degrees in higher numbers, and as a result, the earnings and employment prospects of men born after 1978 have sharply deteriorated.

As the study authors pointed out, the secondary effects of this economic trend are far-reaching. Low-income men are unlikely to marry: they lack the economic potential to attract and support a mate. Low-income men, however, still father children with women who choose to raise their children as single mothers, an arrangement that contributes to child poverty, father absence, and the attendant problems that come in their wake. Sadly, as the researchers note, *male* children born into single female-parent households "appear to fare particularly poorly" according to all social indicators, suffering worse health, delinquency, early school leaving, addiction, depression, and higher probability of incarceration. "Thus the poor economic prospects of less-educated males," the authors summarize, "may create differentially large disadvantages for their sons, potentially reinforcing the development of the gender gap in the next generation." Here is a vicious cycle: as young men fall behind their female peers, families become more fragile and government steps in to create ever more dependency.

Feminist Reset proponents, however, acknowledge no gender gap except the one that promotes their agenda. No inkling of the data in the MIT study makes its way into mainstream discussions, and throughout the pandemic, reports of labor-market effects stressed the job losses of women while ignoring those of men, sometimes even suggesting that men did not experience *any* economic difficulties. An article by Canada's state broadcaster, the CBC, on March 8, 2021, timed to coincide with International Women's Day, reported that the Canadian government's pandemic recovery plan would be "crafted to help women bounce back from the shut down," with the prime minister vowing that "we must ensure a feminist, intersectional recovery."

The report announced the creation of an "expert panel" to advise Chrystia Freeland, who was then the finance minister, on how to adequately assist women. One has to read fairly far into the report to discover that men, too, experienced significant job losses from the Covid downturn. While women in low-earning occupations had a 14 percent drop in employment, low-earning men's employment reduction was 12 percent. One could be forgiven for thinking that the difference was not significant enough to justify the exclusive focus on female disadvantage.

A nonfeminist might even be alarmed by the unabashed chauvinism of Freeland's assertion that "Canada's future prosperity and competitiveness depend on the ability of women to participate equally and fully in the workforce." Does it matter at all whether *men* thrive—or are we to assume that no man has ever required (or deserved) assistance? Even more startling was the prime minister's suggestion that "the government should fund women entrepreneurs more than their male counterparts because women-run startups affect the greater good." What "greater good" is that, and how is it measured? Given that the government's own data on small businesses show that men account for well over 60 percent of small and medium-sized ventures while outperforming female entrepreneurs in sales, profits, and employment, one can only hope that actual assistance to new business owners will not be decided according to such a bigoted rationale.

Often, the reporting of job losses in the feminist-compliant media was downright misleading. In January of 2021, CNN ran with a typical attention-grabbing headline, "The U.S. Economy Lost 140,000 Jobs in December. All of Them Were Held by Women," complete with an arresting picture of a woman wiping away tears. The more complicated reality was that in December of 2020, women *gained* a significant number of jobs in some important sectors, such as professional and business services, while losing jobs in sectors most affected by Covid closures like leisure and hospitality, where men also faced heavy losses.

Further examination of the figures shows that in every sector where women lost a significant number of jobs, men also lost jobs, sometimes more than the women. In education and health care, for example, men lost twenty-two thousand jobs compared to women's nine thousand. The one area where men gained significantly more jobs than women was construction (a sector in which feminists have not thus far clamored for entry). Because the overall picture, when the full tally of gains and losses was made, presented a vision of female disadvantage, this was the story chosen for emphasis, enabling feminist commentators to gasp over a stunning (and at least partially invented) gender gap.

Underpinning all such reports is the demand that more be done for women—by government, by government-funded agencies, and with men's tax dollars. In late March of 2021, Schwab's WEF offered "Four 'big bets' to close the post-pandemic gender gap." The picture accompanying the article shows a dark-skinned woman wearing a head scarf. Unsmiling, even dour, she confronts the viewer with her life of unpaid labor while beneath her portrait, we read that "The pandemic has highlighted the critical role women play in keeping society together." Alleging that Covid-19 "has caused the gender gap to widen dramatically," the report proposes that countries around the world must boost women's pay, mandate more flexible work arrangements for women, and set "targets" for the number of women in management and leadership roles. Unless these measures are taken, the report warns with breathtaking precision, "it will take over 135 years to achieve gender equality." The report also recommends an increase in feminist propaganda, which it dubs "media campaigns," for any recalcitrant outliers still not on board, "to help shift mindsets and gender stereotypes."

Amid all these warnings and demands for action, it is ironic to reread a series of articles published in the fall of 2019, just a few months before Covid, reporting on women's difficulty due to the lack of "economically attractive" would-be spouses. The articles were based on a study of marriage decline by Daniel Lichter of the Cornell College of Human Ecology. His team found that among their study sample, the ideal spouse women desire typically made 58 percent more money than the average American bachelor actually earns. (Related articles have made clear that most mid- to high-earning professional women expect to marry higher-earning men.) Articles reporting Lichter's marriage study had titles like "Broke Men Are Hurting American Women's Marriage Prospects" (complete with a picture of a gormless young fellow shrugging his shoulders over his empty wallet) and referred to "a devastating shortage of men who have their act together." Could it be that young men in America, castigated for their alleged entitlement, propagandized that women are morally superior, and passed over by equity initiatives, are actively discouraged from succeeding economically? The study author was quoted expressing sympathy for the women: "Most American women hope to marry," he noted, "but current shortages of marriageable men—men with a stable job and a good income—make this increasingly difficult."

Thus we come full circle to the MIT study of low-income men ill placed to marry and fathering male children who will find themselves worse off than their fathers (poorly educated, addicted, violent)—all the while a feminist-compliant press, government agencies, corporations, and global entities focus exclusively on improving women's economic status while hurting their marriage prospects. Surely this cannot be accidental? Feminist Reset policies will guarantee that marriage rates continue to atrophy, illegitimacy and divorce increase, fatherlessness proliferates, and state control expands.

Promoting More Women into Leadership Roles

Amid all the focus on female victimhood and disadvantage, reports on Covid-19 also touted women's heroic leadership. Typical of many was a book by Lauren McKeon, excerpted on various mainstream websites, called *Women of the Pandemic*, which through assiduous cherry-picking of data, erasure of male contributions, and dollops of purple prose, concluded that it was women who "amid the horror and disaster, gave us hope, leadership, and resilience." According to McKeon, it would not be too much to say that "the story of the pandemic was the story of women," women who though "balanced barefoot on the razor's edge" (a startling figure!) rose to the challenge of sustaining their communities.

Noting that women make up the vast majority of nurses, social workers, and personal support workers (and not mentioning that men make up the vast majority of equally essential farmers, ranchers, meat packers, janitors, delivery drivers, shelf-stockers, and paramedics), McKeon asserted that "Throughout the pandemic, these women were tasked with keeping our bodies and minds healthy, with keeping us fed, with keeping our hospitals and public spaces clean, with helping the most vulnerable among us, and with being near our bedsides when we died." From the little things to the big, from the Canada Sews effort to make (near-useless or even harmful) cloth masks to the preponderance of female chief medical officers, women were the face of caring, rising to a saintlike or even messianic status, according to McKeon's adulatory rhetoric. She reported approvingly that an Alberta woman sold more than 750 T-shirts that read, in an echo of the popular Christian exhortation, "What Would Dr. Hinshaw Do?" in honor of Alberta's chief public health officer; the mantra ("Be kind, be calm, be safe") of British Columbia's top doctor, Bonnie Henry, became, according to McKeon's fevered imagination, "both a balm and a gospel."

Amid the hoopla about the indispensability of women as caregivers of the nations, one much-touted study even went so far as to suggest that female political leaders had the godlike capacity to prevent Covid infections and deaths. "It's Official," one article's title jubilated, with a fetching photo of New Zealand's prime minister, Jacinda Ardern, "Women Are Better Leaders in a Pandemic." It wasn't official at all; it was a case of inadequate research contaminated by confirmation bias. But it, along with Ardern herself, was enthusiastically embraced.

The basis for the claim was a rushed study by two U.K. economics professors who compared female-led and male-led countries of similar size and wealth to conclude that "Not only were infection rates generally lower in the female-led nations; fatality rates from the virus were also noticeably lower, too." As later analyses made clear, there are too few women leaders in the world and far too many economic, demographic, political, and geographical differences between countries to make accurate statistical comparisons possible or helpful.

A later academic study by two Yale researchers, "Pandemic Performance: Women Leaders in the Covid-19 Crisis," which examined pandemic strategies rather than outcomes, could find no evidence that female leaders were more decisive in their implementation of stay-at-home orders or more targeted and consistent in their messaging. (Too rarely questioned was the idea that economy-killing strategies were part of effective leadership at all.) This latter study concluded that "These indeterminate findings fail to support the widespread claim that women leaders responded more competently and effectively than men to the COVID-19 pandemic." Unsurprisingly, however, retractions of the claim of superior female leadership were far less abundant than the initial claim itself.

Advocates for women were quick to take the theme further. "The World Needs More Women Leaders—During Covid-19 and Beyond" was a typical headline, this one in a December 2020 article in *The Conversation*, a progressive academic journal, which claimed that "the gender balance in positions of power and influence within our societies" was key to success not only in implementing economic recovery but also in successful leadership generally: "leadership environments with gender parity lead to healthier, stronger, and more consensual decisions."

This is just one of a raft of purportedly science-based research studies claiming to prove (even while explicitly denigrating the qualities of rationality and objectivity that allow one to prove anything) that gender parity—or even female preponderance—makes organizations more effective.

There have already been calls for—and the implementation of—legislation to mandate gender parity on corporate boards and in academic departments, and these will surely increase. In 2020, Ireland announced that twenty women-only professorships would be created to close the "academic gender gap" at Irish universities, and women-only positions, especially in STEM, have become common across the western world despite the discovery in 2015 by Cornell University psychologists that women were already twice as likely to be hired into STEM positions as men.

In 2018, a law was passed in California requiring public companies headquartered in the state to have at least one woman on their boards by the end of 2019, with future increases depending on board size. Noncompliant companies face six-figure fines ($100,000 for the first violation, and $300,000 for every violation thereafter) and public shaming.[12] Additional legislation, passed in September of 2020, required that by the end of 2021 boards must have at least one member from an ethnic or sexual minority group, with similar penalties and mandated increases. One can only imagine the harried board CEO as the equity rules pile up: "Get me a woman for the board. I don't care who—just *get me a woman*. Wait, scratch that. I need a *black woman*! Better yet, a *gay black woman*!)

---

12 In May 2022, a Los Angeles Superior Court judge ruled the law unconstitutional on equal-protection grounds. The state vowed to appeal.

Feminist Reset proponents will continue to insist that women simply *are* better leaders than men for a hodgepodge of unverifiable reasons. A March 2010 article in *Psychology Today* by Ronald Riggio quoted research psychologist Alice Eagly in full-blown psychological bafflegab that "Women are more transformational than men—they care more about developing their followers, they listen to them and stimulate them to think 'outside the box,' they are more inspirational, AND they are more ethical." The male author expressed his confidence that "The world would be better if most leaders were women." Jack Zenger and Joseph Folkman came to a similar conclusion in the *Harvard Business Review* after surveying responses to 454 male and 366 female leaders, finding that women were generally assessed more positively for their ability to "inspire and motivate," "communicate powerfully," work collaboratively, and build relationships.

It hardly needs to be said that many of these statements explaining why women are superior leaders rely on the very biologically determinist gender stereotypes that feminists initially claimed to reject. Such stereotypes are fine, it seems, so long as they support a Reset agenda, and it is easy to predict that more calls for female (and "intersectional") equity targets are on the Reset horizon.

Empowering Women as the Sole Arbiters of Sex

Did stay-at-home orders, school closures, and job layoffs have a measurable impact on sexual intimacy and satisfaction? A study conducted in the summer of 2020 by researchers at Indiana University found that nearly half of a nationally representative sample of over one thousand American adults said that Covid had changed their sex lives for the worse and decreased the frequency of sex, while an online NBC News poll of a larger sample discovered that more than half of respondents said their sex lives had been negatively affected by pandemic fears and policies.

Surprisingly few studies have been done on this aspect of lockdown life, and virtually no utopian projects advocate a sexual Great

Reset. For a movement with its roots in the hippie era and the sexual revolution of the 1960s, feminist Reset proponents are distinctly uninterested in—or even opposed to—pleasurable sexuality between long-term heterosexual couples. Intimate, procreative sex between committed couples is not about the social good as defined by the feminist Left: such sexual intimacy interferes with fealty to equity goals, pulling men and women into private domestic attachments and unequal loyalties.

The feminist revolution, which in its heady days proclaimed women responsible for their bodies and orgasms, and saw women demand freedom from the strictures of sexual chastity, has retreated, or pivoted, from the emphasis on sexual liberation toward a demand for totalizing state protection for women and control of men. It is protection not only from rape—often within impossible parameters, as shown in Andrea Dworkin's rebarbative "I Want a 24-Hour Truce (During Which There Is No Rape)"—but also from a wide range of behaviors once considered lawful and even harmless, such as compliments and jokes. Censoriousness about male sexuality, including the "male gaze" (a term coined and given a pejorative valence by Laura Mulvey in analysis of cinema) and emphasis on female sexual fragility have become the dominant themes of once-liberatory feminist activism. Polls of working women repeatedly find that close to half or more of women report experiencing sexual harassment, a catch-all term that now includes being asked out on dates or hugged by work colleagues.

In 1989, professor of law Catharine MacKinnon encapsulated the feminist position on heterosexuality in an article published in the journal *Ethics* with the title "Sexuality, Pornography, Method: Pleasure under Patriarchy." Her assessment was extreme: "Compare victims' reports of rape with women's reports of sex," she invited. "They look a lot alike." She concluded with typical feminist brio that "In this light, the major distinction between intercourse (normal) and rape (abnormal) is that the normal happens so often that one cannot get anyone to see anything wrong with it." This outrageous contention, rather than being denounced or disavowed, became a major plank in academic feminist ideology, and many feminist advocates set out to get people to see something wrong with the normal.

Feminist theories of female subjugation found their most popular manifestation in the #MeToo movement of 2017, when thousands of women demanded swift punishment of men accused of sexual misconduct as a flood of allegations, many of them anonymous and most of them made without evidence, began to circulate on the internet and mainstream media. Not satisfied with publicly humiliating men or having them drummed from their jobs by employers terrified of lawsuits, often for behaviors that allegedly took place years or even decades before, activists insisted that the law be changed to limit men's avenues of criminal defense and to instruct lawyers, judges, and juries about the needs of "survivors" (a term, not unlike "victim" but more valiant, that conveniently presupposes accusers' veracity).

What would a sexual assault trial look like under Reset conditions? Two feminist coauthors proposed special courts, with judges "required to undergo social context education [i.e., feminist indoctrination]" that would operate "on a trauma-informed foundation." Trauma theory explains away inconsistencies or implausibility in an accuser's testimony with recourse to the complainant's alleged state of mind. Forensic psychiatrist Barbara Ziv testified at the trial of former movie mogul Harvey Weinstein that there was no behavior at all by complainants that should be understood to indicate unreliability, including the maintenance of friendly or romantic relations with the accused ("Miss you, big guy"). Feminist formulations such as "affirmative consent," now legally adopted in some jurisdictions, mean that a man's failure to ascertain a woman's ongoing and enthusiastic assent to every stage of a sexual interaction can justify a prison term.

Feminist advocates contend that women will be safe only when they (legally) control every element of sexual interaction and can jail a man simply by telling their victimhood story. And some are explicit that men had better be prepared for discomfort, even terror. In an article ominously titled "Let's Rethink Sex," published in the *Washington Post*, opinion columnist Christina Emba seemed to relish male unease in the wake of the #MeToo movement's outpouring of female accusation. Reminding men rather disingenuously that "We won't die of having less sex," she informed them that under the new sexual normal, many men would even have to give up the assumption that pursuing the satisfaction of their desires was acceptable. On the contrary, men needed to learn that nearly any behavior could be classed as actionable sexual misconduct.

Even sex within marriage—or perhaps especially sex within marriage—is in the feminist crosshairs. In 2018, *Vox* magazine published a long op-ed misleadingly titled "We Need to Talk about Sexual Assault in Marriage." The article is not actually about sexual assault but rather about unhappy consensual sex that *felt* like assault. Describing years in an unhappy marriage, the anonymous author (a professor of feminist theory) claims she was violated every time her husband touched her sexually. Submitting to her husband's desires left her, she claims, "sexually traumatized long after I ended that marriage." Such violations deserve to be more widely recognized, she concludes—presumably so that antimale sexual disgruntlement, suspicion, and aversion can increase. Already under North American divorce law, any accusation of violence against a husband and father, no matter how bizarre or unproven/unprovable, can lead to the man's arrest, forced eviction from his home, forced psychiatric evaluation, criminal incarceration, and the judicial kidnapping of his children.

For Reset proponents, there is nothing that is not potentially a form of violence against women, and no area of such violence not always on the increase and worthy of punitive new legislation. According to U.N. Women, the feminist arm of the United Nations, on a webpage called "The Shadow Pandemic," "all types of violence against women and girls has increased in the wake of the pandemic," requiring a "global collective effort to stop it." The determination to find "all types" of violence on an upswing is evident in the focus not only on domestic violence—which might reasonably increase during a period of lockdown tension—but also, more implausibly, on "sexual and other forms of violence against women[...]on streets, in public spaces and online." Surely at a time of mass stay-at-home orders, it could reliably be expected that sexual harassment on the street would decline? But nothing in support of the feminist narrative of male sexual threat is ever allowed to decline, even at a time when the streets were emptied of people.

The feminist neo-Puritans have gained control of all social and legal channels, enforcing feminist-compliant chastity on men while celebrating "slutty" behavior in women and girls. Even such areas of behavior as the way men sit and stand have come under the condemnatory *female gaze*, as witness the outpouring of judgmentalism against *manspreading*, the alleged tendency of men to sit with their knees apart on public transit, for which a costly public education campaign was launched in various North American cities. Catcalling and other expressions of male approval already have been all but outlawed. Expect that even more areas of male behavior, from leering to friendly chit-chat, will soon be slated for discipline and punishment. Under feminist Reset, the natural attraction between the sexes will continue to be demonized and penalized.

Conclusion: Unhappy Women Keep the State Expanding

It is impossible to imagine relations between men and women improving in a feminist future. Feminist Reset sees men and women as two distinct classes locked in a zero-sum struggle of oppressor and oppressed. The imputed morality is all on the female side: women purportedly seek equality, a fair deal, peaceful mutuality, and compassionate cooperation. Men seek dominance and violent conquest. There is nothing admirable about men, nothing worth preserving in traditional masculinity, and no legitimate male needs or desires. Feminist Reset proponents tell women that as powerless survivors of male domination, they bear no responsibility for conditions in the world or in their own lives and are owed compensation by the state.

Contending that the history of the world has been that of men abusing power, feminist Reset advocates demand that men surrender it now. Women have never abused power, they claim, and are therefore to be given free rein (and thanks and praise) to create a better future.

And what of women and girls themselves? It's hard to believe that for a majority of women, the route to life satisfaction lies in programs to enable strangers to raise their children or in equity schemes to mandate high-stress careers in business and politics. Abundant data over the past few decades, in fact, has shown an inverse relationship between the rise of feminism as a social movement and women's happiness and life satisfaction. A meta-study, "The Paradox of Declining Female Happiness," published in 2009 by two University of Pennsylvania researchers, found that across nearly all demographic groups, women's self-reported happiness had since the 1970s diminished both in absolute terms (in comparison with women of previous decades) and in relation to men despite women's measurable workforce gains, greater life choices, and confidence in the promises of feminism.

Rising wages, sexual freedom, access to abortion, no-fault divorce, and a steady drumbeat of antimale, profemale cheerleading have all failed to bring about greater satisfaction. Being told that one is a morally pure survivor unaccountable for one's actions is not conducive to moral maturity or ethical conduct.

But then, the happiness of women is not the goal of feminist activism. Feminist activism aims primarily to create more feminist activists, women who believe they have been wronged and for whom no payback can ever be too much. Aggrieved women—and the fractured families, alienated children, and disenfranchised men their grievance fuels—are far easier for our political and media overlords to control and manipulate. Under the feminist Great Reset, a never-to-be-achieved utopia of female empowerment and male compliance will continually beckon on the horizon, just out of reach, and we will all constantly be asked to surrender just a little bit more of our freedom, integrity, and common sense to bring it closer.

THE SHAPE OF THINGS TO COME: THE TYRANNY OF COVID-19

BY JOHN TIERNEY

The Great Resetters have got one thing right in their manifesto at the World Economic Forum: the Covid-19 pandemic has indeed provided a "unique window of opportunity," although not the kind of window they have in mind. They mean it's a chance to "build a new social contract," entrusting the governance of society to globalists and technocrats blessed with "vision and vast expertise"—i.e., themselves. But before we sign away our future to them, we should consider what they've done, and the pandemic offers us a unique window into the world they wish to create.

They have used Covid to conduct a trial run of the Great Reset. It has been the most radical public health experiment in history, conducted on the entire population by scientists and bureaucrats granted unprecedented authority to deploy their "vast expertise." At the start of the pandemic, even Dr. Anthony Fauci doubted that Americans would submit to a lockdown like China's. The Centers for Disease Control and Prevention's long-standing plan for dealing with a pandemic didn't recommend mask mandates, school closures or any shutdown of businesses. But the plan was cast aside by leaders who claimed the power to close anything for as long as they deemed fit.

Their new social contract banned or restricted commerce, education, recreation, travel, dining, and meetings—even family gatherings for weddings, holidays, and funerals. The CDC became the national landlord by forbidding any tenants from being evicted. The Four Freedoms famously declared by Franklin Delano Roosevelt in 1941 were suspended. Freedom of speech was limited on social media platforms—today's public square—by censoring those who questioned the opinions of Fauci and his colleagues. Freedom of worship was restricted to Zoom. There was no freedom from want for those who lost their jobs and businesses, and no freedom from fear for anyone who heeded the daily doomsday pronouncements from public officials.

Americans and people throughout the world were frightened into surrendering their basic liberties, and what did they get in return? Worse than nothing. There has never been convincing evidence that lockdowns reduced Covid mortality anywhere except possibly on a few islands and in other isolated spots that sealed their borders. The places that eschewed lockdowns and mask mandates, like Florida and Sweden, did better than their locked-down peers in preventing Covid deaths over the course of the pandemic. Meanwhile, there is no doubt that the lockdowns have caused large numbers of excess deaths from other causes and will likely prove more deadly than the coronavirus because of the long-term medical, social, and economic consequences.

One in three people worldwide lost a job or a business during the lockdowns, and half saw their earnings decline. Children, never at serious risk from the virus, in many places lost a year or more of school—and of normal childhood as they were confined to home or forced to stare at one another behind masks. Worldwide, the rate of hunger rose dramatically as the economic fallout of the West's lockdowns pushed more than one hundred million people in developing countries into extreme poverty.

The one great technocratic triumph—the rapid development of Covid vaccines—was achieved by the private sector in America, the nation ritually denounced by progressives for not shackling its pharmaceutical industry with price controls (like the ones that drove the industry's most productive researchers from Europe to America). The vaccines were subsidized by taxpayers, but they did not require rewriting the social contract. It's clear in retrospect that there was no need during the pandemic for any sort of reset, great or otherwise, and that the extraordinary powers granted to bureaucrats and politicians produced an unparalleled public-policy disaster. Except during wartime and possibly the Great Depression, when else has the ruling class in America inflicted so much needless suffering on the entire populace?

Yet the response to Covid is now being hailed as a model for dealing with climate change and the rest of the Great Resetters' agenda. Their chutzpah would be laughable if it weren't for their success in persuading so many people—a majority in surveys—that their mandates have been necessary and effective. If they continue to hide their mistakes from the public, they will exploit that window of opportunity to seize more power. We all need to see clearly what went wrong in their trial run—and why the Great Reset would be still worse.

The Great Reset is being sold as a bold innovation, a novel strategy employing a grab bag of emerging technologies called the Fourth Industrial Revolution. But it's not new. Strip away the Davos jargon, and the Great Reset is Plato's dream of a philosopher king society. Intellectuals have always yearned for a world run by intellectuals, and politicians have always found reasons to give themselves more power. In the 1940s, buoyed by victory over the Nazis, the British ruling classes declared that their wartime government was a blueprint for peacetime because the future belonged to centrally planned economies. Britain began nationalizing major industries based on the conventional wisdom among the intelligentsia that Western nations, including the United States, would be surpassed economically by the Soviet Union unless they too started relying on expert planners to allocate resources efficiently and equitably.

There was one notable skeptic in Britain, the Austrian economist Friedrich Hayek, who said that central planners were doomed to fail because of what he called "the fatal conceit": their overconfidence in their own expertise. Even if the economy were directed by the wisest and most virtuous philosopher king, this benevolent genius could not possibly possess the knowledge to competently manage a complex modern society. He could never know, much less satisfy, the constantly changing desires of millions of individuals with disparate goals and values. Only a decentralized system, guided by the dispersed knowledge communicated through the fluctuating price signals of a free market, could efficiently direct resources to where they were most valued.

A central planner would be forced to make decisions based on his own goals and values—and those would not be the values of a virtuous philosopher king, Hayek warned in his 1944 book, *The Road to Serfdom*. To survive in power, a central planner must have the will to enforce his arbitrary decrees on unwilling subjects, using fear to inspire obedience and censorship to squelch opposition. It is a job not for the benevolent and enlightened but rather for the "ruthless and unscrupulous," as Hayek explained in a chapter titled, "Why the Worst Get on Top."

He was proven correct in the ensuing decades, as Britain and the Soviet Union foundered economically, and correct once again during the Covid pandemic. Americans trusted their leaders to "follow the science" by relying on experts to calmly assess the threat and rationally devise the most effective strategies. What happened instead was a moral panic among the American elite, who flouted the norms of governance, journalism, academic freedom, and science. Public policy and debate were commandeered, just as Hayek had predicted, by the ones most eager for power and most adept at terrifying the public.

The pandemic panic was the worst example yet of a phenomenon I call the Crisis Crisis: the endless series of alarms fomented by a codependency of politicians, technocrats, activists, and journalists. This crisis industry is a long-standing problem—the ruling and chattering classes have always exploited crises, real or imagined—that has worsened exponentially with cable news and the web. Last century, the alarmists proclaimed in articles and books that humanity was doomed by the "population bomb," the "energy crisis," and the imminent "cancer epidemic" (which never arrived). Today the crises are hyped around the clock in every medium—panic porn, as it's now called. Journalists gain ratings, clicks, and retweets by seeking out "experts" who profit—in publicity, prestige, power, and funding—by providing the scariest quotes and sound bites.

These fearmongers don't need to worry about accuracy—or the damage when the panic leads to a cure that's typically worse than the disease. By the time they're proven wrong, their false alarms will be forgotten, and journalists will be seeking their wisdom on a new crisis. The global famines mistakenly predicted by population doomsayers inspired China's one-child policy, which led to tens of millions of coerced abortions and has left the country with a shortage of young workers. But those same prophets are now being quoted on climate change because, once again, they are certain humanity is doomed.

Covid, unlike most proclaimed crises, was a genuine danger, but it was grotesquely exaggerated by the crisis industry. Politicians and journalists seized on a worst-case scenario early in the pandemic, in March of 2020, from a research team led by Neil Ferguson at Imperial College in London. The team's computer model projected that, unless drastic measures were taken, there would soon be thirty Covid patients for every available bed, and that more than two million Americans would die from Covid by the end of the summer.

It didn't matter that the computer model was based on blatantly unrealistic assumptions, or that these researchers had a miserable track record. Ferguson's team had previously projected up to sixty-five thousand deaths in the United Kingdom from swine flu and two hundred million deaths worldwide from bird flu. The death toll each time was in the hundreds (and the economic damage from the false alarms was enormous). But the previous mistakes were ignored by journalists desperate for panic porn. The mainstream media hailed these doomsayers as the voice of science, uncritically promoting not just the numerical guesses but also the researchers' policy recommendation.

The "only viable strategy," according to these seers' report, was to impose drastic restrictions on businesses, schools, and social gatherings until a vaccine arrived.

How did they know that this unprecedented strategy was the only viable one? They didn't, of course. As usual, the central planners were wrong.

Before Covid, the most knowledgeable experts on infectious diseases had painstakingly reviewed and rejected lockdowns as ineffective, impractical, and harmful. In the CDC's planning scenarios, business and school closures had been ruled out even during a plague as deadly as the 1918 Spanish flu. The lockdowns in America were initially justified as a temporary measure to "flatten the curve" to avoid overwhelming hospitals, but as they continued, it became obvious that the doomsday projections were absurdly wrong. (Some hospitals were strained and sent patients to other hospitals, as happens during some flu seasons, but no state ran out of hospital beds.) The lockdowns continued despite evidence that Covid posed minimal risk to children and young adults, and that Covid was nothing like the Spanish flu. For Americans under seventy, the probability of surviving a Covid infection was about 99.9 percent.

Public health officials are supposed to consider the overall impact of their policies, not just the effect on one disease, but that fundamental principle was violated by the scientists and politicians who dominated discourse and policy during the pandemic in the United States, Britain, and most other countries. American policy was guided by the White House Coronavirus Task Force, a model of the interdisciplinary group of eminences envisioned for the Great Reset. Chaired by Vice President Mike Pence, it included cabinet members, heads of federal agencies, and administration officials with blue-chip credentials in medicine, science, economics, law, and business. They would have felt right at home pooling their "vast expertise" in a panel discussion at Davos plotting the global future. Yet when it came to issuing mandates during the pandemic, they made no attempt to weigh the social costs (which were obvious from the start) versus the benefits (which were always dubious).

They didn't bother to even *discuss* the harms of the lockdowns, as Dr. Scott W. Atlas discovered to his amazement when he arrived in Washington. Atlas, a veteran medical researcher and health-policy analyst at the Hoover Institution, joined the Task Force six months into the pandemic, after he had collaborated with economists on studies concluding that lockdowns could ultimately prove more deadly than Covid. Atlas expected to spend his time at the White House discussing scientific data and debating the most cost-effective strategies for protecting public health. Instead, he found that the Task Force's leaders had scant interest in scientific research or debate, no regard for cost-benefit analysis, and zero concern for the disastrous collateral damage of their decrees.

Atlas's memoir of his time in Washington, *A Plague Upon Our House*, is a book-length confirmation of Hayek's prediction: the worst came out on top. The ruthless and unscrupulous prevailed. The Trump administration was cowed into submission by three veterans of the federal bureaucracy adept at political infighting and media manipulation. America's pandemic policies, copied in much of the world, were set by this troika, as Atlas calls the doctors who formed an alliance to dominate the Task Force: Anthony Fauci, Robert Redfield, and Deborah Birx.

As usual, it didn't matter that they had a miserable track record. The troika had worked closely together during AIDS epidemic to develop a vaccine, a long and costly project that failed. So did their predictions that AIDS would spread widely beyond intravenous drug users and gay men. Fauci made national news—and encouraged a wave of homophobia—by warning that AIDS could infect even children because of "the possibility that routine close contact, as within a family household, can spread the disease." He subsequently flip-flopped on that particular scare (a pattern to be repeated on Covid), but he did continue needlessly alarming the public, warning that vaginal intercourse was perilous and even French kissing was a risk.

The most influential alarmist was Redfield, then an Army physician, who claimed his research showed that AIDS would soon spread as rapidly among heterosexuals as among homosexuals. He became the go-to authority for journalists predicting the "heterosexual breakout," which in 1985 was proclaimed in large letters on the cover of *Life*: "Now No One Is Safe from AIDS." In 1987, the scare made the cover of the *Atlantic* ("Heterosexuals and AIDS: The Second Stage of the Epidemic"), and Oprah Winfrey opened her show by announcing that one in five heterosexuals would die from AIDS within the next three years.

The heterosexual scare went on for more than a decade, aided by a massive publicity campaign by the CDC. It mailed one hundred million brochures and aired dozens of television commercials warning that everyone was in danger from the virus. The agency's own epidemiologists knew this was false (the chance of contracting AIDS during vaginal intercourse with someone outside the known risk groups was estimated at one in five million) and opposed the publicity campaign, arguing that public health resources should be focused on the groups genuinely at risk. But the scientists were overruled by superiors at the agency, who decided that portraying AIDS as a universal threat was the best way to attract attention and increase their budgets. Sure enough, they were rewarded with a surge in funding, much of it wasted on efforts to protect heterosexuals.

The troika prospered, too, their blunders during the AIDS epidemic forgotten as they ascended the Washington hierarchy. Fauci remained a darling of the news media and became the director of the National Institute of Allergy and Infectious Diseases, serving nearly four decades and earning more than the president in 2020. (His salary of $417,608 made him the highest-paid federal employee, according to the watchdogs at OpenTheBooks.com.) Redfield rose to become director of the CDC. Birx, an immunologist trained early in her career at Fauci's lab in Bethesda, Maryland, continued to work on AIDS projects for the Army and the CDC and served as global AIDS coordinator during the Obama and Trump administrations.

Upon joining the Covid Task Force, the troika put their bureaucratic skills to use by forming a united front. They secretly agreed (as the *New York Times* later revealed) that if any one of them was fired, the other two would resign in protest. They never disagreed with one another during the Task Force meetings, according to Atlas, and except for him there was no one else on the Task Force with the medical background to challenge them. They also controlled the agenda, thanks to Birx's appointment as the Task Force's coordinator—second-in-command to Pence, but he, like the rest of the Trump administration, made the fatal error of repeatedly deferring to her supposed expertise. She spoke for the Task Force at the "Covid huddle," a regular meeting where she briefed the senior White House aides plotting political and communications strategies, and she also traveled the country pressuring state and local officials to impose lockdowns and mask mandates. Atlas was never able to figure out how or why she was appointed to that position—nobody in the Trump administration seemed to know—but it obviously wasn't because of her scientific knowledge, as he discovered during one of his first meetings with her.

Atlas asked Birx what she considered the strongest scientific evidence for the efficacy of masks. She cited a report published by the CDC about a hair salon in Missouri, where two stylists infected with Covid had worn masks that supposedly prevented the virus from infecting their customers. "I knew the study well," Atlas writes, "having already dissected it in detail with a few epidemiologists before I set foot in Washington. My colleagues had all laughed at it. It was poorly done, and the conclusions were not valid. It was an embarrassment that it had been published prominently on the CDC website." Among the many limitations of this small study, critics had noted that, while none of the customers contacted by the researchers reported Covid symptoms, most of them were never tested for the virus, and many of the stylists' customers were never contacted at all.

Atlas tried discussing these limitations with Birx, but she promptly bristled, and he soon realized that she wasn't even familiar with the basic aspects of the study she was using to justify mask mandates across the United States. Nor did she or the rest of the troika ever show interest in the many far more rigorous studies with contrary findings. Clinical trials before the pandemic had repeatedly failed to find that masks were effective against viruses similar to Covid, and during the pandemic there were many studies showing masks to be ineffective against the coronavirus. When researchers compared the states with mask mandates against those without mask mandates, they found no significant difference in Covid rates: the two curves remained virtually identical throughout the pandemic. Redfield would later concede, after leaving the CDC, that there was a "paucity of data" to justify mask mandates, but during the Task Force meetings the troika refused to respond when Atlas presented evidence challenging their policies, according to his book.

"The doctors in the Task Force showed no study about mask efficacy or any other of their policies, and they never once mentioned the harms of the lockdowns that I witnessed," Atlas writes. "Their sole focus was stopping cases, even when their policies were already implemented and were failing to do so."

They were consummate bureaucrats, oblivious to the lives and businesses wrecked by their decrees as they obsessed over the color-coded charts and computer models that Birx presented at the start of the Task Force meetings. Long after the doomsday projections from the Imperial College model had proven wrong, Birx was still claiming that millions of Americans would die in the coming months unless the troika's mandates were followed. When her charts showed Covid cases declining in a state like New York and Arizona, she claimed credit even though cases were already declining before their mandates were imposed. When the number of Covid tests rose, she proclaimed triumph—it was a key metric in their charts!—even though most of the people being tested were at minimal risk.

Instead of encouraging more frequent testing of the staff and residents at nursing homes, the troika told schools and colleges to test all the students—and then shut down whenever there was an "outbreak" even if none of the cases was serious. It made no sense to close a college campus, a relatively isolated environment with a low-risk population, and send the students back to infect the elderly in their home communities, but it gave the bureaucrats a chance to exert their power and pretend they were accomplishing something.

The folly of these policies did not go unnoticed. Some of the world's leading experts in public health and contagious disease criticized the lockdowns. President Donald Trump wanted to reopen schools and the economy, and Atlas says some of his aides privately agreed and even wanted to fire Birx. But the White House's senior strategists considered it political suicide in an election year to publicly challenge the troika. The bureaucrats were repeating their mistakes from the AIDS epidemic, pursuing failed strategies while needlessly terrifying the public, but they were once again unassailable. They had powerful allies in the mainstream media and the rest of the crisis industry, and they deployed the same fearsome weapon being wielded by the Great Resetters' technocrats: "the science."

Before the Enlightenment, those seeking to rule the masses didn't need to invoke science. It was enough to possess royal blood, or to claim a divine right, or simply to march in with an army. But once those strategies fell out of favor, science became a favorite weapon. Engels argued for "scientific socialism," a redesign of society supposedly based on the scientific method. Herbert Croly, a founder of the American progressive movement, yearned to bypass voters by empowering a permanent class of "expert social engineers who would bring to the service of social ideals all the technical resources which research could discover." He and other progressives used science to justify the forced sterilizations of the eugenics movement a century ago, just as environmentalists like Paul Ehrlich and John Holdren (President Obama's science adviser) would later use their theories about the planet's "carrying capacity" to justify compulsory sterilization programs in India and Latin America.

Today's progressives have abandoned eugenics but not the quest to empower politicians and bureaucrats who "follow the science," meaning that they selectively cite research to rationalize their mandates. No matter what scientists are actually finding or debating, "the science" always turns out to justify progressive policies. The founders of the public health profession focused on specific projects with clearly demonstrated benefits, like inoculations against disease and improvements in public water and sewage systems. But their successors now claim the scientific expertise to do much more. The profession's leading group, the American Public Health Association, has crusaded for income redistribution, nationalized health care, government-provided day care, and a higher minimum wage. The CDC, founded in the 1940s to deal with malaria, has since expanded its mission beyond infectious diseases to include "epidemics" of obesity, hypertension, binge drinking, physical inactivity, mental illness, domestic violence, suicide, and handgun fatalities. No wonder they weren't ready in 2020 for an actual infectious disease.

Now that the Left dominates so many elite institutions—universities, scientific journals and conferences, professional associations, federal agencies, the mainstream media, social media platforms—progressives have more power than ever to enforce groupthink and suppress debate. Well before the pandemic, they had mastered the tactics for demonizing and silencing scientists whose findings challenged progressive orthodoxy on issues such as IQ, sex differences, race, family structure, transgenderism, and climate change. And then along came Covid—"God's gift to the Left," in Jane Fonda's words. Exaggerating the danger offered not only short-term political benefits, damaging Trump's reelection prospects, but also an extraordinary opportunity to empower social engineers in Washington and state capitals.

So, as Fauci and the rest of the troika seized control, the mainstream media declared it the "consensus" among those "following the science" that it was essential to lock down America and the rest of the world. There were just a few dissenters. The most prominent was John Ioannidis, an epidemiologist at Stanford, who early in the pandemic published an essay headlined, "A Fiasco in the Making? As the Coronavirus Pandemic Takes Hold, We Are Making Decisions

Without Reliable Data." Lockdowns were a dangerous experiment being conducted without knowing the answer to the most basic question: just how lethal is this virus?

The article offered common-sense advice from one of the world's most frequently cited authorities on the credibility of medical research, but it provoked a furious backlash on Twitter from scientists and journalists. The fury intensified when Ioannidis joined with Jay Bhattacharya and other colleagues from Stanford to gauge the lethality of Covid. They estimated that the fatality rate among the infected in the county surrounding Stanford was about 0.2 percent. That was twice as high as for the flu but considerably lower than the estimates from computer modelers and public health officials, which were ten to fifty times higher than the flu.

How dare these researchers let the data get in the way of "the science"? Other scientists rushed to denounce the study (later published in a peer-reviewed journal) as so flawed as to be meaningless, and journalists piled on by quoting critics and accusing the researchers of endangering lives by questioning the rationale for lockdowns. The cheapest shots came from BuzzFeed, which devoted thousands of words to a series of trivial objections and baseless accusations. Using one of the Left's favorite tactics to suppress inconvenient findings, the conflict-of-interest accusation, the website claimed the researchers' project was tainted because an airline executive opposed to lockdowns had contributed $5,000 to an anonymized fund at Stanford that had helped finance the fieldwork.

The idea that eminent scholars, who were not paid for their work in the study, would risk their reputations by skewing results to please a $5,000 donor was absurd on its face—and even more ludicrous, given that they weren't even aware of the donation while conducting the study. But Stanford University was so intimidated by the online uproar that it subjected the researchers to a two-month fact-finding inquiry by an outside legal firm. The inquiry found no evidence of conflict of interest, but the smear campaign succeeded in sending a clear message to scientists everywhere: don't question the lockdown narrative.

The attacks were so blatantly unfair that two veteran science writers, Jeanne Lenzer and Shannon Brownlee, published an article in *Scientific American* decrying the politicization of Covid research. They defended the integrity and methodology of the Stanford researchers, noting that subsequent studies had found similar rates of fatality among the infected. (A year into the pandemic, after reviewing dozens of studies by other researchers, Ioannidis concluded that the average fatality rate in Europe and the Americas was 0.3 to 0.4 percent and about 0.2 percent among people not living in institutions.) Lenzer and Brownlee lamented that the unjust criticism and ad hominem vitriol had suppressed a legitimate debate by intimidating the scientific community. Their editors then proceeded to prove their point. Responding to more online fury, *Scientific American* repented by publishing an editor's note that essentially repudiated its own article. It read like the product of a Maoist struggle session. The editors couldn't identify a single meaningful error in the article, but they were determined to grovel anyway, preferring self-humiliation to cancellation by the progressive mob. This once-venerable publication had become *The Science American.*

Scientists and journal editors fell into line, too. Disagreeing publicly with Fauci was a risky career move for scientists studying infectious diseases, because his agency was the leading funder of that research—and there was a lot more than $5,000 at stake. He commanded a budget of nearly $6 billion. (Somehow that conflict of interest didn't interest BuzzFeed and the rest of the progressive media.) Even if researchers weren't worried about losing their grants, they faced difficulties publishing results that challenged Fauci's declarations. When Thomas Benfield, one of the researchers in Denmark conducting the first large randomized controlled trial of mask efficacy against Covid, was asked why they were taking so long to publish the much-anticipated findings, he promised them as "as soon as a journal is brave enough to accept the paper." After being rejected by *The Lancet*, *The New England Journal of Medicine*, and *JAMA*, the study finally appeared in the *Annals of Internal Medicine*, and the reason for the editors' reluctance became clear: the study showed that a mask did not protect the wearer, which contradicted claims by the troika, the CDC, and the rest of the public health establishment.

Martin Kulldorff, an epidemiologist at Harvard and one of the world's leading experts on infectious diseases, had a similar experience early in the pandemic with his article arguing that resources should be focused on protecting the elderly. Unable to find a journal or media outlet to accept it, he finally posted it on his own LinkedIn page. "There's always a certain amount of herd thinking in science," Kulldorff said, "but I've never seen it reach this level. Most of the epidemiologists and other scientists I've spoken to in private are against lockdowns, but they're afraid to speak up." To break the silence, Kulldorff joined with Stanford's Bhattacharya and Sunetra Gupta of Oxford to issue a plea for "focused protection," called the Great Barrington Declaration. They urged officials to divert more resources to shield the elderly, such as doing more tests of the staff at nursing homes and hospitals, while reopening businesses and schools for younger people, which would ultimately protect the vulnerable as immunity grew among the low-risk population.

It was the strategy Atlas was advocating without success at the White House Task Force, and the Great Barrington scientists didn't have much better luck. Fauci, along with Francis Collins, then the director of the National Institutes of Health, launched a campaign against them. In an email to Fauci, Collins urged a "quick and devastating published take down" of these "fringe epidemiologists" (as if Harvard, Stanford, and Oxford were "fringe" institutions). Collins followed through by telling the *Washington Post* that these "dangerous" and "fringe" ideas were "not mainstream science," and Fauci went on television to describe the focused-protection strategy as "total nonsense" to "anybody who has any experience in epidemiology and infectious diseases." Their insults became "the science." Although tens of thousands of other scientists and doctors went on to sign the declaration, the press caricatured it as a deadly "let it rip" strategy and an "ethical nightmare" from "Covid deniers" and "agents of misinformation."

Google initially shadow-banned it, so that the first page of search results for "Great Barrington Declaration" showed not the declaration itself but instead only criticism of it (like an article calling it "the work of a climate denial network"). Facebook shut down the scientists' page for a week for violating unspecified "community standards."

The most sustained smear campaign was directed at Atlas. "He is driving Deb crazy," Fauci wrote in an email to Collins describing Birx's frustration and their joint strategies to undermine Atlas. Fauci publicly dismissed Atlas as an "outlier" and was presumably—although he denied it when challenged by Atlas—one of the anonymous sources on the Task Force who was disparaging Atlas in the media's many hit pieces. Bill Gates summed up elite opinion by deriding Atlas, who had been a senior advisor on health policy to candidates in the three previous presidential campaigns, as "this Stanford guy with no background" promoting "crackpot theories." Nearly one hundred members of Stanford's faculty signed a letter denouncing his "falsehoods and misrepresentations of science," and the Stanford faculty senate overwhelmingly voted to condemn Atlas's actions as "anathema to our community." Several professors from Stanford's medical school published an article in *JAMA* demanding further punishment. The article, which misrepresented Atlas's views as well as the evidence on the efficacy of lockdowns, urged professional medical societies and medical-licensing boards to take action against Atlas on the grounds that it was "ethically inappropriate for physicians to publicly recommend behaviors or interventions that are not scientifically well grounded."

By that standard, the lockdowns were the most unethical intervention in history. The traditional strategy for dealing with pandemics was to isolate the infected and protect the most vulnerable, just as Atlas and the Great Barrington scientists recommended. Lockdowns were a radical treatment being tested for the first time without any knowledge of their efficacy or any consideration of the harmful side effects. No ethics review board would have approved even a small pilot study under those conditions, let alone an experiment on the entire population. And no ethical researchers would have continued the experiment once they began observing the lethal results.

During America's experiment with lockdowns, there was a control group, much to the displeasure of Fauci and Birx. Florida was "asking for trouble" by not following the troika's policies, Fauci warned, but its governor, Ron DeSantis, went on ignoring "the science." Instead, he studied the data and the scientific literature. He saw early in the pandemic that the troika's favorite computer models were proving wrong—reality in Florida quickly diverged from the projections—and looked elsewhere for guidance. He consulted with Atlas and the Great Barrington scientists, who were amazed to speak with a politician already familiar with the details of just about every study they mentioned to him.

DeSantis adopted their policy of focused protection, reopening businesses and schools while concentrating attention and resources on the elderly. He ordered frequent Covid testing of the staff and residents at senior-care centers and avoided the deadly mistakes made by the governors of New York, New Jersey, Pennsylvania, and Michigan. They were so alarmed by the computer models, and so determined to free up hospital beds for the projected surge of Covid patients, that they ordered nursing homes and other facilities to admit or readmit Covid patients. DeSantis did the opposite. He forbade long-term care centers from admitting anyone infected with Covid and diverted recovering patients to quarantine in separate facilities.

He trusted citizens to make sensible choices for themselves, urging those at high risk to be careful and everyone else to resume normal lives. He encouraged businesses to continue operating, ordered schools to stay open, and refused to mandate masks. To assuage fears and put the risks of Covid in perspective, he invited the Great Barrington scientists to a panel discussion that was posted on YouTube—but not for long, because YouTube removed the video on the grounds that it "contradicts the consensus."

DeSantis was pilloried by the public health establishment and the national media, which blamed Florida's summer surge of Covid in 2020 on his refusal to lock down and mandate masks. Then Florida faded into media obscurity until the next summer, when once again its high Covid numbers (and DeSantis's purported recklessness) led the national news. And then once again it became a nonstory. Florida's numbers were newsworthy only when they fit the crisis industry's narrative and only when presented out of context. Never mind that Covid, like the flu, peaked at different seasons in different climates and that Florida had a disproportionately high number of vulnerable elderly citizens. Never mind that Floridians over sixty-five were less likely to die from Covid than other Americans in that age group, and that the same was true for younger Floridians. The mortality rate from Covid, when adjusted for the age of each state's population, was lower in Florida than in most other states over the course of pandemic.

If Florida had simply done no worse than the rest of the country, that would have been enough to discredit the lockdown strategy. No drug or medical intervention with dangerous side effects would be approved if the control group in a clinical fared no differently from the treatment group. If the control group began to fare *better*, the trial would be halted. But the troika and the rest of the public health establishment were undeterred by the numbers in Florida, or by similar results elsewhere, including a comparable natural experiment involving European countries with the least restrictive policies. Sweden, Finland, and Norway rejected lockdowns and mask mandates during most of the pandemic, and the cumulative rate of Covid mortality in each country was significantly lower than in most other European countries. Sweden, like Florida, was pilloried by the media during its Covid surges, but Swedes kept going to work and to school, without masks or social distancing, and the Covid mortality rate over the course of the pandemic was well below the average of the European Union (and the United States).

The same pattern showed up repeatedly in broad international comparisons, and in studies comparing the course of Covid in similar places with different policies. The Brownstone Institute, which the Great Barrington scientists helped found during the pandemic, compiled a list of more than four hundred studies showing that lockdowns, shelter-in-place policies, masks, mask mandates, and school closures failed to curb Covid infections or deaths. Meanwhile, researchers did identify one undeniable consequence of the lockdowns: more deaths from other causes, especially among the young and the less affluent.

In the United States, there were over one hundred thirty thousand "excess deaths" (more than normal) in 2020 that were not due to Covid. More people died from heart attacks due to failure to receive prompt treatment. Social isolation contributed to excess deaths from dementia and Alzheimer's. As unemployment surged and mental illness and substance abuse treatment programs were interrupted, the reported levels of anxiety and depression increased sharply—along with alcohol sales and drug overdoses. In the year following the start of lockdowns, more than one hundred thousand Americans died from drug overdoses, the highest annual total ever recorded. Among Americans between the ages of fifteen to fifty-four, the number of excess deaths rose by more than 25 percent, and most of those deaths were not due to Covid. The number of excess deaths not due to Covid was especially high among low-income workers and minorities, who suffered disproportionately (in lost jobs and shuttered businesses) from the lockdowns.

The most devastating effects were felt in developing countries, where the global economic shutdown caused massive unemployment and food shortages. The World Bank and other groups estimated that the economic fallout would cause nearly twelve million children to suffer from severe malnutrition and lead to nearly one hundred seventy thousand child deaths. The United Nations estimated that the disruption of health care services, notably the decline in childhood immunizations, would cost the lives of more than two hundred thousand children in South Asia. The WHO reported that in 2020, for the first time in a decade, the number of people dying from tuberculosis worldwide had increased, and the death toll was expected to go on rising because so many cases had not been treated promptly.

The deadly impact of the lockdowns will keep growing because of the lasting economic, medical, and educational consequences. In Canada, for instance, researchers estimate that more than ten thousand people will die from cancer because of delays in diagnosing and treating their disease. Economists have projected, based on the long-term consequences of past recessions, that there could be hundreds of thousands of "deaths of despair" in the United States over the next two decades because of all the jobs and businesses that were lost to the pandemic. Of course, many of the harms are incalculable, particularly to children who have been emotionally scarred by fearmongering about a virus that poses little risk to them and whose social and cognitive development has been stunted by more than a year of needless isolation and masked faces. But some researchers have already documented a decline in cognitive skills among toddlers, and others, after taking into account the well-established correlation between educational levels and life expectancy, have calculated that the "learning loss" from school closures ultimately could cost this generation of students in America more years of life than were lost by all the victims of Covid.

If a corporation behaved like the lockdown advocates, continuing to sell an ineffective drug or medical treatment with fatal side effects, its executives would face lawsuits, bankruptcy, and criminal charges. They would be vilified in the international media. But government officials enjoy legal immunity for their mistakes, and journalists extend professional courtesy to their fellow alarmists in the crisis industry. The troika paid no penalty for their disastrous policies. Fauci eventually took some heat for his role in funding dangerous research in the Wuhan laboratory where Covid might have originated (a scandal that the media and scientific establishments suppressed for a year), but journalists continued to treat him as the unquestionable authority on Covid. Interviewers on television nodded respectfully as he made statements like, "Attacks on me are attacks on science." After Joe Biden took office, Fauci was rewarded with a new title: chief medical adviser to the president. "The science" still reigned supreme.

Now that we've suffered through a trial run of the Great Reset, what we can expect next? More centralized power due to the "ratchet effect" documented by Robert Higgs in his 1987 book, *Crisis and Leviathan*. By surveying the effect of wars, financial panics, and other crises over the course of a century, Higgs showed that most government growth occurs in sporadic bursts during emergencies, when politicians enact "temporary" programs and regulations that never get fully abolished. The U.S. military didn't revert to its prewar size after either of the world wars and neither will the public health agencies that expanded during Covid. New Deal bureaucracies and subsidies persisted long after the Great Depression and so will some of the powers seized by bureaucrats and politicians during Covid.

Some public health experts are calling already for mask mandates to be imposed during ordinary flu seasons, and some probably will be demanding lockdowns during bad flu seasons. As the crisis industry hypes every new pathogen or other public health threat that emerges, politicians are likely to seize upon Covid precedents to pander to frightened citizens, many of whom are already clamoring for authoritarian measures. When Britons were surveyed about mask mandates in stores and in public transport, 51 percent favored making the mandates permanent.

If basic liberties remain optional to so many people, the Great Resetters will use this "window of opportunity" to address the "climate emergency," which offers endless opportunities for central planners and the rest of the crisis industry. Plagues come and go, but the climate will never stop changing. There will always be storms and droughts and floods that "the science" will attribute to human sinfulness, and reducing carbon emissions will give bureaucrats an excuse to regulate any human activity. Climate activists around the world are celebrating the Covid-19 response as a "paradigm shift" and "blueprint" for future policies.

But the tyranny of Covid should be a lesson in what not to do and whom not to trust. Do not assume that the media's panic porn resembles reality. Do not count on mainstream journalists and their favorite doomsayers to put risks in perspective. Do not expect those who invoke "the science" to know what they're talking about—or to tolerate genuine scientific debate. Science is a process of discovery and revision, not a single dogma to be professed. Science provides a description of the world, not a prescription for public policy, and specialists in just a single discipline do not have the knowledge or perspective to guide society. They're biased by their own narrow focus and self-interest. If these specialists are given vast powers, they will do vast damage—and they will not stop as the wreckage piles up.

When the troika's policies failed, they blamed the public for not following their edicts. This was untrue because studies showed that an overwhelming majority of Americans followed the mask mandates and also restricted their movements. The empty downtowns and bankrupted businesses offered further evidence. But central planners always blame their failures on their recalcitrant subjects, both as an excuse for themselves and as a pretext for issuing stricter decrees. The pandemic tyrants' addiction to power became absurdly obvious once vaccines had become widely distributed. The virus was no longer a deadly threat to the vast majority of Americans, and everyone had been given a chance to be protected. But instead of declaring victory, the bureaucrats in Washington and the leaders in many state capitals found new reasons for tyranny.

They continued enforcing their mandates and issued nonsensical new ones. They ordered the unvaccinated to be fired from their jobs and banished the unvaccinated from public places without explaining why these pariahs posed a mortal risk to people already protected by the vaccine. They refused to exempt even those who'd already been infected with Covid and acquired natural immunity that was stronger than vaccine immunity. They ordered mass vaccinations for schoolchildren, half of whom already had natural immunity, and virtually none of whom were at risk of serious disease. Of course, the children had to keep wearing masks in school and sit six feet apart in the cafeteria—at least the ones who were allowed to eat inside. Other shivered through lunch on the playground.

How could adults be so cruel to children? How could Fauci and the rest of the troika so callously impose so much pointless suffering on everyone? Because suffering served their purposes. Besides reinforcing their power—respect my authority!—it gave the illusion that something was being accomplished. It served the same psychological function as the pandemic-control policy introduced in September of 1349, when the Black Plague was ravaging London. Hundreds of men began filing through the streets three times day, whipping and bloodying themselves with knotted ropes studded with nails. When the bubonic plague subsided two months later, these flagellants no doubt took credit for it, just as the Covid troika did with their painful strategies—and they convinced most of the public, judging from polls showing consistent majority support for lockdowns and mask mandates. Having suffered so much for long, people don't want to believe that their sacrifices were in vain.

The Great Resetters will demand further sacrifices, like the ones that climate activists seek to reduce carbon emissions. We must abstain from fossil fuels and meat, buy less and recycle more, take shorter showers and drive fewer miles in smaller electric cars while paying much more for electricity from windmills and solar panels. America, the Great Satan of global warming, must appease the climate gods by emulating Germany and other European countries that have signed punitive treaties and imposed the most draconian green policies. Whether these policies are any more cost-effective than lockdowns or mask mandates is beside the point. Over the past two decades, carbon emissions per capita have fallen more sharply in the United States than in Germany and in the rest of Europe, thanks in large part to fracking, which provided cheap natural gas to replace coal, and also to the continued reliance on nuclear power. But fracking and nuclear power are both taboo technologies among green-energy zealots: they reduce carbon emissions without forcing people to suffer or empowering bureaucrats to impose virtue on the populace.

The Great Reset is hailed as a unifying project, a chance for everyone to join in sacrificing for the common good, just as we all did during the pandemic. But the pandemic sacrifices were not only useless but harmful, and the suffering was not shared equally. The brunt was borne by the most vulnerable members of society. In the United States, income fell among all social classes at the start of the lockdowns, but it quickly rebounded for upper-income workers—such as the Great Resetters and others in the laptop class. A year into the pandemic, affluent workers were earning more than they did before Covid, but middle-income workers' earnings still hadn't fully recovered, and lower-income workers' earnings were down nearly 25 percent. Students from disadvantaged families fell farther behind in school, and children in poor countries went hungry. Blue-collar employees lost jobs so that professionals at minimal risk could feel safer in their home offices. Silicon Valley profited from lockdowns that bankrupted brick-and-mortar businesses around the world.

The Great Reset will be more of the same. As they claim to be fighting "inequality," the Great Resetters will create jobs for the laptop class and subsidies for crony capitalists while stifling the economic growth that lifts people out of poverty. While promising "environmental justice," they will burden the poor and the despised middle class with regressive taxes and higher energy costs. Their war on fossil fuels will be devastating to sub-Saharan Africa, where half the homes still lack electricity, but it won't stop technocrats from flying to Davos for conferences on "climate equity."

During the pandemic, the ruling class kept proclaiming that "we're all in this together." But we weren't, and we won't be during the Great Reset, either. Once again, the worst will come out on top.

YOU WILL BE MADE TO LAUGH: HUMOR UNDER THE GREAT RESET

BY HARRY STEIN

There's a joke that used to make the rounds in the Soviet Union. It was about a judge seen chuckling as he walks out of his courtroom.

"What's so funny?" asks a friend.

"I heard a great joke."

"Tell me."

"Can't, I just gave someone ten years for repeating it."

If we can still laugh at that, it is surely not with the smug self-certainty we once could—not given the regularity of the assaults on free thought in today's America and the brutality with which they are everywhere enforced, from the newsroom to the boardroom and, yes, on late night television and comedy club stages. Indeed, at this point Hiram Johnson's famous adage might well use some updating: in the culture wars at hand, truth may be the first casualty, but its sidekick, humor, blindfolded and smoking its last cigarette, is just a split second behind.

Things have been trending this way for quite a while, of course. For a good fifty years, conservatives have watched in horrified stultification, seemingly helpless, as the cultural barbarians rampaged through the institutions, overturning fundamental understandings of decency, equality, and human biology itself. While we've argued policy, and occasionally even won, temporarily, progressives have traded in feelings, usually hurt, and have twisted reality to their ugly purposes. While we've embraced our history as affirming timelessly noble principles and ideals, they've ever more brazenly redefined the past as irredeemably squalid and shameful.

How have they gotten away with it?

It is only recently, and even then only dimly, that many of us have gotten the message that a large part of the answer has been the Left's near-absolute domination of mass popular culture—music, film, TV—all of it thoroughly infused with values and assumptions that reflect their warped worldview and are inimical to ours. Directly, or more often subtly, they have been able to define, unimpeded, to a vast audience interested in nothing more than entertainment, what is fair, moral, and just—and what is unjust and must be changed.

Little wonder that to most in the generations with the annoying names—X, millennials (aka Y), and Z—the Left is reflexively seen as compassionate, forward-thinking, socially just, while the Right is backward and hateful. Everything they've heard in the classroom is echoed, ad infinitum, by academia's glamorous twisted sister, mass entertainment.

And now comes the Great Reset, which would be the final nail in the free-thought coffin. Nothing less than a frontal attack on capitalism and its underlying values, taking the pandemic as "a unique opportunity" to "build a new social contract that honours the dignity of every human being," it is a scheme of such grandiose evil it might have been designed by a DC Comics archvillain.

One need not ever have set foot on a college campus or even watched Fox News to hear the tocsin in the blizzard of buzzwords in the declaration that emerged from Davos in 2020. Inequality. Climate change. Social justice. Diversity. The language of permanent victimhood—only now nuclear-armed by the elite of the elites.

While entertainment media is not explicitly cited in the chilling manifesto, Klaus Schwab, the German executive chairman of the WEF who even looks like Lex Luther, blithely notes that "every industry, from oil and gas to tech, must be transformed." Indeed, nothing is so sobering as to scroll down the seemingly endless list of the institutions and corporate entities signing on as partner/enforcers and note (though with something other than surprise), that it numbers not just the likes of Amazon, Google, and Facebook but also NBC-Universal and Sony.

Needless to say, in this potent new crackdown on dissident thought, American media companies have a healthy head start. By now, we've long since taken it for granted that, for instance, there'll never be a feature film celebrating the young Clarence Thomas like 2018's hagiography about the young Ruth Bader Ginsburg; let alone a tale of injustice with a happy ending about the Duke lacrosse case. And it is equally a given that in what passes for comedy in traditional mainstream venues, conservative attitudes and beliefs are fair game while progressive ones are an ever-expanding herd of sacred cows.

For far too long, our failure to counter the Left's stranglehold on popular culture, or even fully appreciate it, has been among the other side's most conspicuous assets. Rarely has a maxim been so often repeated, yet so seldom acted upon, as the late Andrew Breitbart's truism that politics lies downstream from culture.

Still, in this realm as in others, the Great Reset—this massive, coordinated effort to label who we are and what we believe illicit by definition—should serve as a belated wake-up call. Indeed, potent as contemporary progressivism is, as remorselessly vicious and punitive, its very self-certainty is also an opportunity. Never has it been more wholeheartedly detached from reality, which is to say, more readily exposed for the colossal sham it has always been. It is no accident that the Davos manifesto so faithfully reflects the remorseless humorlessness of professional victimhood: among its implicit objectives is to ensure, whether via social censure or by punitive statute, that human beings not be permitted to mock that which is deemed unmockable, belittle what merits belittling, puncture pomposity, or otherwise call idiocy by its rightful name.

The question is, can we make of this gift what we should? Can we at long last begin to establish in the general public's mind that our foes are not merely dangerous, but even more fatal to their hopes (conveniently enumerated in the Great Reset) batshit crazy?

With that in mind, this essay will focus on how comedy, so key in defining cultural norms, became an almost exclusive preserve of the Left. The short answer, to paraphrase Hemingway on bankruptcy, was gradually, then all at once. Only the bankruptcy in this case was moral.

But let's begin with this. That we have been so slow to recognize the extent to which popular culture has been weaponized against us, and the stakes, in one sense does not speak badly for us; though, as far as that goes, the same might also have been said for Neville Chamberlain. I recall a speech twenty or so years ago by the lapsed radical David Horowitz, the son of literally card-carrying Communists, at one of his annual Restoration Weekend conferences, in which Horowitz gently chided the audience of prosperous conservatives, a fair number of whom would now be termed "influencers," for failing to grasp the nature of the enemy. Having grown up on the furthest reaches of the Left, and then been an editor at the slick radical magazine *Ramparts*, Horowitz observed that on moving rightward he'd been taken aback by how terribly "nice" everyone was; "nice" being a polite—conservative—way of saying woefully naïve. What they were up against, he warned, were "gutter fighters," those so deeply committed they would stop at nothing to achieve their nefarious ends; and who, in fact, were already well on their way to complete dominance over the culture.

For me, that seriously hit home. As a fairly recent refugee from the Left myself—indeed, like Horowitz, a red-diaper baby—I may not have been on intimate terms with murderous Black Panthers or future Weathermen as he was, but I damn well knew about the utter ideological certainty underlying that worldview; and the conviction that those who thought otherwise (though the word was not yet in general use among mainstream Democrats, let alone the elites already flocking to Davos) were "fascists," who deserved everything coming to them.

Nor, in my case, did the attitude come packaged in grim rectitude. My father, once you got him off politics, was almost preternaturally good-natured and extremely funny—not just my opinion, but confirmed by the world at large, since he was a very successful comedy writer. Among other things, he'd been part of the group in the legendary writers room of Sid Caesar's classic show, along with, among others, Carl Reiner, Mel Brooks, and Neil Simon.

In my own more modest professional life, I'd long struck some of the same attitude, trying to lace even serious stuff with some leavening humor. The title of the recently published book, which had caused a breach between us, but also gotten me invited to Horowitz's confab, was *How I Accidentally Joined the Vast Right-Wing Conspiracy (and Found Inner Peace).*

Though I intended the book to be entertaining, and it occasionally strayed into flippancy, in fact it was the culmination of a lot of thinking and serious self-questioning, starting a dozen or so years earlier, when I'd been asked to do a column in *Esquire*, to be called "Ethics." Having never so much as taken an ethics course in college, I was mortified by the prospect, but my editor reassured, "Make it funny, throw in an ethical point at the end, and we'll call you Shecky Spinoza," and I more or less began on that basis. But soon enough, between the laughs (and of course I knew it was the laughs that carried a fair number of readers along) it increasingly became about something else: the moral self-regard of those of us who'd come of age in the Sixties, and our bottomless capacity for self-justification. Since no one had written much about this before and—this is key—I was writing it from a distinctly Left perspective, the column became immensely popular.

As these things do, it led to other possibilities, one of which, several years later, was a weekly column in *TV Guide* on the impact upon our communal life of (as it generally still was) the tube now running in the average home between four and five hours a day. By now I'd already gone pretty far rightward. But since *TV Guide* tended to be in homes apt to be on more familiar terms with Marshal Dillon than Marshall McLuhan, few of my New York friends knew I was doing it, and the relative anonymity surely saved me lots of dinner-party ire. There was, for instance, the column I did on how TV dramas were treating the then-rampaging AIDS epidemic, which was with not just appropriate gravity and sympathetic understanding, but eagerly spreading the activist line that AIDS was "everyone's disease," rather than the truth that it was overwhelmingly confined to the high-risk groups, gay men and IV drug users. Indeed, I ended the piece by quoting an oncologist of my acquaintance, with what was intended as both a clarification and a piece of actually useful information. "I only wish I could tell women that if they didn't engage in certain behaviors they'd never get breast cancer."

While I indeed never heard from my friends, the magazine did hear from the playwright/actor/activist Harvey Fierstein, his letter inchoate with rage. It concluded with what he considered the most damning possible insult, one that might have come straight out of Davos—who cares, "it's only *TV Guide*."

"Only *TV Guide*?!" sputtered the editor on the receiving end, himself a lefty, and I suspect otherwise in secret sympathy with Fierstein's view, "we have the largest circulation of any magazine in the country!"

The number was twenty million or thereabouts (most presumably future Deplorables), and soon after the appearance of that column, I heard from a couple of mailbags full of them. Almost to a letter, there came the same reactions: gratitude and disbelief. They knew damn well they were being systematically lied to by TV's content creators, and even then, that the lies were ideologically driven. They just never thought they'd find such a thing suggested in a mainstream magazine.

Which is to say that by the time of my book-length coming out in *Right Wing Conspiracy*, there was not the slightest doubt in my mind as to the vastness of the audience hungering for programming that would reflect an alternate point of view.

And given my own background and sensibility, I was delighted to hear out of the blue from an executive from Viacom. He was a conservative, if a very quiet one, who'd caught me on TV promoting the book, and he had an intriguing notion: how about coming up with a situation comedy that would explicitly look to tap into that chronically underserved audience?

Novice that I was in that realm, I leapt at the chance.

To the cognoscenti—make that Great Reset types everywhere, on both ends of the political spectrum—the sitcom has of course long ranked as the stepchild of the postwar American comedy family. Decades after they last performed, Mike Nichols and Elaine May are looked back upon as a comedic version of Ruth and Gehrig, and standups like Lenny Bruce and George Carlin are revered (by the Left, but that's what counts) not merely as wits, but as fearless, foul-mouthed, free-thinking social visionaries; while *Saturday Night Live*, for all its many creative ups and down, has never relinquished its role in defining for the young and clueless who passes, or (from Chevy Chase's portrayal of greatest-ever presidential athlete Gerald Ford as the ultimate klutz to Alec Baldwin's malevolent/vacuous Donald Trump) fails to pass ideological muster.

But though sitcoms have usually been regarded as banal and unnourishing fare, arguably they are as much an American "art form" as jazz or the Broadway musical; certainly, no popular entertainment in the modern era had more faithfully reflected the nation's sense of itself than those half-hour slices of quasi-reality. Indeed, as Hollywood progressives abandoned their postwar defensive crouch in the sixties and seventies and began moving toward industry dominance, no genre was more effectively exploited to nudge average Americans leftward.

Moreover, this represented a shift not just in television comedy but also in the function of humor in America generally. Never had comedy been put to ideological purposes on such a mass scale; to the contrary, it had long been a place where even the bitterest foes could find common ground. That we generally found the same things funny, or at least not divisive, was, indeed, as much an aspect of our common identity as our shared history and allegiance to fundamental principles now under sustained assault by the internationalist cabal busily revising the nature of appropriate thought at the WEF.

This is not to suggest that *what* we laughed at didn't change with the times, as everything does in our traditionally dynamic culture. Students of Lincolniana know that John Wilkes Booth waited until just past 10:15 to fire the fatal shot. Why? Because as an habitué of Ford's Theater, he knew that was the precise moment, midway through *Our American Cousin*'s Act 3, Scene 2, that there would be a laugh so big it would drown out the crack of a derringer. "Well," observed the play's plainspoken American protagonist Asa Trenchard, of the just-departed shameless English social climber Mrs. Mountchessington, "I guess I know enough to turn you inside out, old gal—you sockdologizing old man-trap."

That such a line once made a theater full of sophisticates roar now registers as astonishing. Yet dramatic as have been its shifts in style and substance with new generations and evolving demographics, our humor also long reflected a shared, optimistic view of ourselves as plainspoken, commonsensical and fundamentally decent—"suspicious of poets, saints, reformers eccentricity, snobbishness and affectation," as the humorist George Ade said. Indeed, as variations on Asa Trenchard.

We were (or at least fancied ourselves) free-spirited individualists, who didn't take kindly to getting pushed around. Charlie Chaplin and Buster Keaton may have spent their lives on celluloid struggling against impossible odds, but they never cast themselves as victims of social injustice or anything else, let alone as rule followers. Harold Lloyd, the third great silent clown of the oft-cited triumvirate, was so relentless in his can-doism that he might have been created by Horatio Alger. Meanwhile, authoritarians of every stripe, from big lug neighborhood bullies to monsters working evil on the world stage were fit objects of ridicule. In a three-year span, the great comic director Ernst Lubitsch took on the Soviets (*Ninotchka*) and the Nazis (*To Be or Not to Be*).

This last could likely have happened nowhere else, not just because of the ocean that offered Americans (and refugees like Lubitsch) a measure of protection, but because irreverence is in our DNA. It has long been our saving grace that almost no subject was out of bounds and no one immune to mockery.

Yet through the nineteenth century and well into the twentieth, America's most representative humorists were nonideological, taking on all comers. "I don't make jokes," cracked Will Rogers, "I just watch the government and report the facts"—and it's a line that might have just as easily been used by Mark Twain fifty years earlier or Johnny Carson fifty years later.

Through ten administrations and three wars, Bob Hope, arguably the most successful American comedian of the twentieth century, was the ultimate equal-opportunity wise guy and pot stirrer. Staunchly conservative as the English-born Hope was in his personal views, no matter the occupant of the White House or the issues of the day, the jibes came thick and fast but never with malice. They were crafted for *everyone* to enjoy.

It is little wonder that Hope's annual hosting of the Oscars was must-see television across the ideological spectrum; full of self-mockery and good-natured put-downs of his glamorous pals, the Oscars celebrated a quintessentially American industry that was spreading our values to every corner of the globe, and those evenings were as close as we had to annual get-togethers of the sprawling American family.

That came to an end, as so much did, with Vietnam. By 1975, Hope was in his seventies, and reduced to cohosting with three others, so he was left fuming backstage when a producer named Bert Schneider stepped to the podium to accept the Best Documentary Oscar for the antiwar *Hearts and Minds*. With Saigon within weeks of collapse, Schneider read a telegram from the Vietcong delegation in Paris thanking "our friends in America" for "all they have done on behalf of peace."

At the time, the WEF was just four years old—political eminences had first been invited only the year before—but already the elites, in Hollywood and elsewhere, were embracing its internationalist views.

And by then, too, much of television, and especially the all-important sitcom sector, had already been effectively colonized by the Left, its partisans having understood early on the power of such seemingly innocuous programming to shape (or *re*shape) the attitudes of millions. In fact, the date of the Left's key incursion into mass entertainment can be cited with as much precision as any other calamity of that tragic era: January 12, 1971, the evening *All in the Family* premiered on CBS.

Since the dawn of the medium little more than two decades earlier, sitcoms had been not merely politics-free, but by design and industry policy, half-hour retreats from the world and its stresses. At their best—*The Honeymooners* and *I Love Lucy*—they became enduring classics, fondly recalled as artifacts of a better, more innocent time.

So, too, was *The Andy Griffith Show*. Premiering a month before John F. Kennedy's election to the presidency and ending its run three days before Martin Luther King's assassination, it was the ultimate idealized vision of small-town America as populated by good, decent, and mutually supportive folks, feel-good escapism, never mind what those behind it did or believed in their real lives; indeed, one of my earliest memories is of a guy who'd go on to be one of its creators hiding out in our house to avoid a McCarthy-era subpoena.

Possibly because of its pedigree—Griffith himself was a notable progressive—but also because in syndication it remains so well loved, critics on the Left today rarely include it in their by now pro forma indictment of family sitcoms of that earlier time, their attacks invariably focusing by name on the triumvirate of long-running domestic comedies *Father Knows Best, Ozzie and Harriet*, and *Leave It to Beaver*.

And, true enough, there were goofy elements in all these shows, as well as confusing ones. It was never entirely clear what some of the fathers did for a living, and an undue amount of time seemed to be spent at malt shops.

But of course what really gets to the Left, prompting savage over-the-top indictment in what by now must be dreary academic tracts numbering in the thousands, is that they exemplified the patriarchy, racism, homophobia, and many other despicable impulses at the time coursing through the American body politic with even greater abandon then than they do today.

Moreover—and maybe most damning of all—they made America look like a pretty swell place.

In this, in every way, they perpetrated the big lie (widely exposed on TV screens the world over), that we were good, and decent, certainly distinctive, and maybe even special.

The thing is, aside from the lying part, they're right about that. The overwhelming majority of us who grew up in the fifties and early sixties did feel good about the country, and watching those shows—my strong preference was for the Cleavers—undoubtedly was part of it. But what they exemplified, aside from sunny optimism, was not the traits now so dubiously attached to them, but the overriding importance of family. Yes, it was idealized, but so what? So were the heroes who modeled courage and resilience on other shows we loved, like *The Lone Ranger* and *The Roy Rogers Show*. Hell, on *Superman* they came right out and said it—"Truth, justice, and the American Way."

Hardly least—pause for the mandatory gasp from feminists and other bien-pensants—those shows presumed the importance of fathers. Ward Cleaver and characters like him could sometimes be pedantic and smug, but they were far from the clueless sitcom dads the stereotype later evolved into. Indeed, they were repositories of experience and wisdom, small supermen in their own ways.

Yet already during this same period, season by network season, in the great American tradition, the very character of our humor was itself in flux. From the Caesar show in the early fifties through Carl Reiner's hilarious breakthrough sitcom set in that show's legendary writing room a decade later, by degrees it was becoming less broad and more ironic, which is to say...Jewish.

Obvious as this is, as a Jew—and as a man of the Right—I note it with a certain trepidation, being keenly aware that there are many unregenerate anti-Semites out there who do not share either my hearty appreciation of Jewish humor or understanding of its psychic roots. The first-generation Jews who helped define TV comedy, successful as many were to become in America, grew up knowing it was Jew hatred that had cast them and theirs on these shores and ever alert to the new threats here, from the sweatshop owner around the corner to the distant KKK; this is to say that, where politics was concerned, there was nothing *but* the Left. Literally. I remember my father telling me that in his Bronx neighborhood, "If you were on the Right, you were a Socialist."

This is the kind of joke they told. Two Jews are standing before a firing squad, and one asks for a blindfold. "Shh," whispers the other, "don't make trouble."

This was laughter as self-defense, survivors' (as opposed to victims') humor—wry, sardonic, self-depreciatory—a means of escaping a jam in lieu of showing one's neck. In its way, it was in the great, ever-evolving American tradition, and in the fullness of time, the new, wholly different brand of everyman it produced (from Woody Allen on screen, to Allan Sherman on vinyl, to Maxwell Smart on the tube) was a perfect fit for the increasingly sophisticated audience of the technological age.

Still, even in vastly changed circumstance, their own and the country's, the creators of the new popular culture to a remarkable degree retained their old politics. Indeed, having long since abandoned the orthodox rites that had bonded their forebears for millennia, a very great many found new personal purpose in the secular passions of the Left. By their own self-certain lights engaged on behalf of the underdog in the fight for a better world, as isolated and provincial in their elite neighborhoods as once their grandparents were in the shtetls of Eastern Europe, they found it simple to cast alternative views as not just mistaken but vile, and to divide humanity into noble ideological allies and everyone else. There are still Cossacks out there, menacing as ever, only in America, they're called conservatives.

Created by the crusading liberal writer/producer Norman Lear (based on a British series with the same general slant), *All in the Family* was so unapologetically Left-of-center that nervous CBS execs preceded the opening broadcast with a voiceover warning that the show "seeks to throw a humorous spotlight on our frailties, prejudices, and concerns," but Lear was closer to the mark when he later acknowledged he wanted that very first script to showcase "360 degrees of Archie Bunker. All of the vituperativeness, all of the fear of the future, all the fear of anything he didn't understand and"—though obviously not in the *Father Knows Best* kind of way—"all the love of family."

As a January midseason replacement, the show was not much noticed at first, but by September, it was number one in the ratings, with a weekly audience of fifty million, and drawing an astonishing 70 percent share in New York City.

Smugly self-satisfied, getting easy laughs with his bigoted malapropisms, Archie was the elite's version of the ultimate *Boobus americanus*, and played with relish by Carroll O'Connor, himself a man of the Left (as too, obviously, was costar Rob Reiner, known ever since, to his mortification, as Meathead). In short, the show provided both clarity and solace to liberals stumped by how we could have elected to the presidency a man so obviously odious as Richard Nixon. Two-plus generations later, they seek and find the same reassurance in the notion that even as the rest of the world grows ever wiser, more sophisticated, and pleased to readily follow the directives of "experts," America remains home to untold millions of recalcitrant Archie Bunkers.

The ripple effect of the show's enormous success on the industry, and even on public opinion, is hard to overstate. *M*A*S*H*, created by Caesar show veteran Larry Gelbart, premiered the following year, and though the show was set in Korea, no one in its vast international audience missed it was about Vietnam; with its highly dedicated doctor protagonists weekly cracking wise in the midst of the horror, it made being antiwar, and cynicism, even hipper than they already were.

Meanwhile, Lear himself went on to create so many socially conscious *All in the Family* spin-offs, and spin-offs of spin-offs—including *The Jeffersons*, about an upward mobile black family, and Bea Arthur as the uber-progressive *Maude*—that by the early eighties, one hundred twenty million Americans, more than half the nation's population, were tuning in to a Lear show every week.

All in the Family was especially aggressive in pushing feminist issues, often via the unlikely vehicle of Edith Bunker, Archie's doormat wife, who over the course of the show gradually became more aware and liberated. As Hollywood veteran Peter Bart sympathetically quoted Jean Stapleton, the actress who played the part, "There's a slow development going on with Edith, and that's the way it's really going to happen in the country."

Indeed, when Edith was eventually killed off, Lear offered devastated fans the chance to donate to the Edith Bunker Memorial Fund, which raised half a million dollars for the Equal Rights Amendment.

The producer personally has given far, far more than that to People for the American Way, which he founded in 1980 to "fight right-wing extremism and"—as if modeling Davos-speak—"build a democratic society that implements the ideals of freedom, equality, and justice for all." Indeed (as those familiar with the Robert Bork, Clarence Thomas, and Bret Kavanaugh Supreme Court fights well recall), for decades the organization has been in the forefront of the Left's scorched-earth politics of personal destruction.

Meanwhile, there was no such show openly, let alone aggressively, espousing comparable ideas from the Right. This is by no means to suggest that in the real world, conservative values did not still hold sway. Though *The Cosby Show*, which debuted shortly before Ronald Reagan's 1984 reelection, was celebrated in the media as a *progressive* breakthrough for its obliteration of racial barriers, in fact, its arguably more distinctive feature, and surely the one responsible for its massive ratings, was a take on family unseen since the time of the despised trinity.

You want to talk patriarchy? Here's Cosby's Cliff Huxtable, a successful professional living in upper middle-class comfort, dealing in the premiere episode with his thirteen-year-old son Theo's lousy grades. A bright and obviously canny kid, Theo tells his dad he just aims to be a "regular person" who'd be happy to "work in a gas station or drive a bus…I mean, you're a doctor and Mom's a lawyer, but I don't love you any less because you're my dad. So instead of being disappointed that I'm not like you, maybe you should be happy and love me anyway, because I'm your son."

This declaration was not just heartfelt, but so reflective of prevailing liberal feel-good "thought" that it elicited applause from the live audience at the taping, as yet unfamiliar with the show's ethic.

"Theo," replies his father gently, then hesitates a beat, "that's the *dumbest* thing I've ever heard in my life!" The roar of laughter in response, surprised and grateful, may have been the loudest in the history of the medium. "No wonder you get D's in everything!" continues Cosby. "You're afraid to try because you're afraid your brain is going to explode and it's going to ooze out of your ears. Now I'm telling you, you are going to try as hard as you can. And you're going to do it because I said so. I am your father. I brought you in this world, and I'll take you out!"

It's likely that Cosby, too, only got away with this kind of thing because he was not just black, but so fully credentialed a progressive he'd made Nixon's Enemies List. It was only long after the show's hugely successful run, when he continued saying the same things in lecture halls and from the pulpits of black churches—urging black parents to invest in their kids' educations rather than in expensive sneakers—that "America's Dad" faced significant opposition, especially from younger blacks wielding the Uncle Tom lash. Indeed, it was a black comedian named Hannibal Buress who in 2014 reignited the long-dormant allegations against Cosby that for a time would put him behind bars and will permanently overshadow all the rest.

To be sure, the era did produce one overtly conservative breakout character: Michael J. Fox's Reagan-loving Alex Keaton on the eighties megahit *Family Ties*. But even that was inadvertent; as its liberal creator Gary David Goldberg conceded, the show was supposed to center on Alex's ex-hippie parents, and when Alex struck a public nerve, the creative team, caught short, went with it.

Rarest of TV beings that he was, a likeable conservative, Alex was an outlier not just on his own show, but on the medium itself; by then, viewers tuning into any network show could pretty much presume a liberal take on a range of cultural issues—feminism, divorce, single parenthood, and definitely casual sex.

While this was true across the entertainment board, comedies were a particularly effective delivery system. For instance, American television's reigning dramatic series at the turn of the twenty-first century was Aaron Sorkin's *The West Wing*, a shameless reimagining of the Clinton presidency as a morally exemplary enterprise, and like many of my ideological brethren, I regarded the show with special scorn. Yet in retrospect, for all its ardent following (including those who voted for awards), its impact was nil, and was certainly of no help to Democrats at the polls. Essentially a well-crafted soap opera, like the highly rated prime-time medical shows, its politics were for most viewers clearly of less interest than its dramatic turns and the complex and ever-evolving relationships of its principals.

By contrast, that same season, the nation's second-most-highly-rated network comedy was *Will and Grace*, which, for those who somehow missed it (either in its original or rebooted version) was about a straight female and her uptight gay male roommate/best friend, and also featured a far more flamboyantly gay man who was the show's breakout character. Built around improbable situations, chronic misunderstandings, and the lovable characters' assorted quirks and wacky compulsions, the show was pro forma sitcom fare, and without an obvious agenda. But of course, that *was* the agenda: clueing us in that aside from that one not-really-so-important thing, gay people are just like the rest of us. In fact—and for much of America, and soon the world, this certainly was a revelation—not all gay men are even effeminate. (Just the really funny ones.) They could be anyone—your friend, your neighbor, your son, *you!*

Will and Grace's influence was enormous, and would be enduring, studies establishing that its millions of regular viewers had new and more positive views of gay men than hitherto. "*Will and Grace*: The TV Series That Changed America," the *Huffington Post* called it, and indeed, there was no better evidence of the dizzying speed with which the personal becomes political that by 2012, even that veteran hack of hacks, then vice president Joe Biden, en route to reevaluating his stance on gay marriage, was declaring on *Meet the Press* that "*Will and Grace* probably did more to educate the American public than almost anything anyone's done so far." (Okay, it also didn't hurt that he'd just come from a meet-and-greet at the home of HBO president Michael Lombardo with a bunch of the entertainment industry's most well-heeled gay donors.)

"Other civil rights movements win their battles in the streets," concluded gay activist Christopher Records some years later. "We won ours on the television set."

It was with all of this somewhat in mind that I delivered my own modest sitcom proposal. Tentatively titled *Professor Paine*, it was set on a college campus.

"*Professor Paine* is a half-hour comedy with a difference," it began, "a show that each week will zestfully skewer political correctness in all its many guises, and whose main character will also be one wholly unique in television—a likeable, smart, funny and completely unapologetic social conservative."

Willie Paine, the show's would-be protagonist, a longtime history professor at a small New England college, was not a conservative but a classic liberal, who in the proposed pilot is induced to serve as the faculty advisor to the conservative student paper put out by a coterie of nerds and social outcasts (not unlike those who later turned up on

The Big Bang Theory) when no one else will. By the episode's closing credits, he is startled to find *himself* turning into a pariah.

I also included brief synopses of eight episodes. "A friend of Willie's, a gay sociology professor, asks him to publicly attack his new book to help whip up support among gay readers," reads one. "Willie agrees—on the condition the other guy gets a gay activist to verbally assault him at a reading of *his* new book. But things go awry when, at the reading, the activist actually does seem to become incensed—wielding a knife, he has to be stopped before he kills Willie. It turns out *he's* a performance artist out to hype himself."

Next, the Viacom guy flew me out to L.A. to pitch *Professor Paine* and—this is how naïve I was—I thought it had a shot. Why not? It also dealt with an obvious but largely unacknowledged phenomenon, the growing insanity on the nation's campuses, and, okay, I had an agenda, but, again, that would just be the backdrop, we wouldn't beat people over the head with it, at least not too much. The main thing was that there was an audience hungering for such a take on the world. Of that, I was sure.

More, this was early in the George W. Bush years, and politicized as the American entertainment world already was, it was not yet the rigid and vengeful monoculture it would become.

Let's put it this way. As it turned out, the best part of the experience was getting put up at Shutters, the fancy Santa Monica beachfront hotel; that, and running into Goldie Hawn, who was very friendly and not at all a prima donna, while waiting to pitch at CBS.

The pitches themselves? They weren't so much unpleasant as bizarre.

At every network, including Fox, I'd describe the premise, and hit them with what I thought was my best material, yet instead of the laughs (or at least polite smiles) I expected, the ones I'd had from my conservative pals, I'd get blank looks. After the first couple of pitches, I figured I'd gone too far, so I toned it down. But by the time I flew home after those two long days, I realized those looks reflected not hostility but confusion. The execs were not political people, and the comic idea at the heart of the concept—that intolerance passes as tolerance on the contemporary campus, and the modern liberal's jaw-dropping capacity for hypocrisy and self-delusion—simply didn't compute. It was so utterly alien, I may as well have been speaking a mix of Sanskrit and Martian.

So, it was nice to meet you, thanks for coming.

I didn't even take it personally. Shows get turned down every day for all sorts of reasons, and that I was a complete novice would alone probably have been enough. In fact, I now realize that since they let me in at all, and made a pretense of listening, those rank as the glory days.

In today's America and increasingly elsewhere around the globe, we're as divided today by what we laugh at—or are allowed to laugh at—as by anything else. And even the lowest-level Hollywood dummkopf now understands, along with the H.R. departments of the many financial behemoths and international conglomerates all in on the Great Reset, that those who question woke values are small-minded, intolerant, and *bad*, and most definitely *not funny*.

Though in America the industry herd had been migrating leftward for decades, Trump spooked it into a headlong stampede over the cliff. From the moment he rode down the escalator at Trump Tower in Manhattan the loathing was bottomless and pathological, and the horror as he went from joke candidate to the presidency exceeded anything Hitchcock could have conceived. "The reaction was beyond apoplectic," observed Carmen Finestra, a rare Hollywood conservative, coexecutive producer of the nineties hit *Home Improvement* and now safely retired. "I mean, right after the election we went to a school board meeting in Santa Monica, and during the Pledge of Allegiance, the board took a knee!"

On my own occasional visits to the coast, the lunacy was impossible to avoid, hard as I tried. I lost one screenwriter friend of forty years when, failing to put off her angry questioning, I conceded not only that I'd voted for Trump, but also refused to apologize for the result.

Of course, being only tangentially involved in the business, I had it easy—I couldn't be readily blacklisted. Others given to illicit thought knew the flat choice was between shutting up and finding another way to make a living.

The rest of America didn't particularly know or care about this inside baseball, any more than Hollywood understood America or *its* ideological bent. Which is why the industry was so taken by surprise when in March 2018, in the midst of the networks' play-it-safe trend of reviving old hits (*Will and Grace* had returned the previous year), ABC brought back the late-eighties juggernaut *Roseanne*. Except it was a Roseanne with a difference, since the show's long-mercurial star, and her character, were now big Trump supporters.

When the ratings came in for the back-to-back premiere episodes, they were nothing short of stunning, the highest for any network comedy program in four years. "In the adult demo," as *Entertainment Weekly* noted, without apparent irony, "it also trumps Sunday's block-buster *60 Minutes* episode which featured an interview with (Trump accuser) Stormy Daniels."

Himself no stranger to the TV wars, President Trump called Roseanne personally with congratulations.

In fact, one did not have to be an ideological purist to note that the species of conservatism presented on the new *Roseanne* was so tame as to be house-trained, with every comic barb from the blue-collar, Trump-supporting Ms. Barr countered by one from her sister (who shows up in the opening episode wearing a pussy hat) or another house liberal. Indeed, on the identity politics/social justice/diversity front, the show was very much Hollywood as usual. One of Roseanne's grandchildren is black, another is a cross-dresser, and by the end of first episode, even crusty old granddad Dan's doubts are happily allayed as he allows the nine-year-old boy to head off to school in a skirt. Heaven forbid viewers get even the glancing impression that the reborn Conner family might be "bigots."

In short, Roseanne and Dan Conner were Trump voters as in their fevered imaginings Hollywood elites wished Trump voters to be—misguided, obviously, due to their pitiful lack of education, mindless jingoism, and poor-as-dirt lives, but fundamentally good-hearted and decent, just like us!

Still, what's telling is that for millions of actual Trump voters tuning in, that was enough. So accustomed had they become to a prime-time landscape where progressive values held absolute sway, they were almost pathetically grateful to find any version of themselves favorably portrayed in such a show—especially by its star! Indeed, when early on the show's title character, saying grace, thanks the Lord "for making America great again," one could almost hear the stunned and grateful laughter across the heartland.

For all its punch-pulling, on the Right the show was widely seen as a sharp, long-overdue stick in left-wing Hollywood's smug collective eye; on the Left, the magnitude of its success was taken as horrifying confirmation of its view of the rest of America as largely populated by the vicious and morally backward.

Then, barely two months after it appeared, the revived *Roseanne* was gone. The real Roseanne, having gotten involved in a heated political exchange on Twitter, responded to another poster's mention of Barack Obama's former advisor Valerie Jarrett, who is black, with the tweet: "muslim brotherhood & planet of the apes had a baby = vj."

The blowback online was instantaneous, and almost as fast in ABC's executive offices: in forty minutes, network entertainment president Channing Dungey issued a statement condemning Barr's tweet as "abhorrent, repugnant and inconsistent with our values," and canceling the show, with Disney chairman and CEO Bob Iger soon weighing in that there was "only one thing to do." The star's agents at ICM dumped her the same morning, characterizing the tweet as "disgraceful and repugnant" and (hilariously) as "antithetical to our core values, both as individuals and as an agency."

Barr, for her part, quickly apologized to Jarrett for "making a bad joke" that was "in bad taste," while costar John Goodman bravely asserted "I know for a fact she's not racist." But by then the show she'd brought back was history.

Except not quite. Network executives in fact soon resurrected the golden goose, minus its eponymous star and her illicit politics, and redubbed it *The Connors*. That this was possible only because a chastened Barr agreed to surrender all financial and creative participation so her former castmates and crew could keep working went almost entirely unremarked upon; indeed (though she blamed her fatal tweet on Ambien, and likely entertained hopes a stint at Betty Ford might lead to redemption on Oprah), this was one star whose all-too-human frailties elicited no sympathy from the supermarket fanzines.

Fittingly—which is to say, as an honest expression of the show's progressive writing staff's attitude toward deplorable America—on the first episode of *The Connors*, viewers learned that the beloved matriarch had died not, as was first believed, from a heart attack, but of an opioid overdose. "It wasn't enough to [fire me]," as a bitter Roseanne put it to an interviewer, "they had to so cruelly insult the people who loved that family and that show."

But ultimately of greater importance than the fate of this complex, unstable, highly gifted woman—and infinitely more telling—was the impact her show's stunning rating success had on the medium itself going forward.

None at all.

For the uninitiated, the flap did seem to defy everything they thought they knew: that this is an industry so driven by greed it has no compunction peddling the most gut-turning violence and grotesque perversions of the human spirit as entertainment. Why, then, no new conservative sit-coms? Why would they seemingly go out of their way to alienate half their potential audience?

Might as well wonder how all those financially disastrous anti-Iraq films kept getting made during the presidency of ex-Hitler George W. Bush. Or what extraordinary gifts the Obamas brought to the creative process to induce Netflix to hand them a $50 million deal to produce content promoting "greater empathy and understanding between peoples, and help them share their stories with the entire world."

In fact, the massive early ratings for Roseanne had been not merely a shock or even a mere embarrassment; driven as they were by millions who'd never so much as heard of the *Huffington Post*, let alone the WEF, they were a frightening tocsin in the night; and the star's crash and burn was a relief, "confirming what everyone in town already knows about the other side," as one closeted conservative put it to me. "It's like 'See that, we gave a Trump supporter a chance, and she showed everyone who they are!"

If anything, for the town's elite, it was reason to crack down all the harder on illicit thought. Now the merest association with a suspected Trump enthusiast was potentially fatal. "Every executive at every network is paralyzed by fear of being yelled at by a neighbor," one comedian with secret conservative leanings told me at the time. "No one ever wants to hear again 'How could you think of putting that Nazi on the air?!!!'"

What is beyond question is that our foes both at home and abroad revel in their great and ever-increasing power to dictate what is ethically (which is to say, ideologically) permissible, and, as the Great Reset would have it, to exact punishment upon those who stray over their ever-shifting lines. If it weren't so horrifying, and contrary to everything we grew up knowing to be just and fair, it would be funny.

But that's the thing: a lot of it is inadvertently funny anyway—watching those who've long accused *us* of being rigid and censorious struggling to keep pace with the ever-changing orthodoxies and hoisted pell-mell on assorted petards. Men are women and women men. Violence is peaceful; speech is violence, but so also is silence. Skin color is all that counts. Science must be revered as long as it bolsters liberal orthodoxy—otherwise, not. So jaw-dropping are the hypocrisies of the ostentatiously virtuous, it's like the king's entire entourage—the showbiz types and journalists, the green-haired kids who insist on being called "xe" "zie" or "they," the woke political leaders and billionaire industrialists—are all proudly parading naked down Davos's Rossweidstrasse, at least in spirit.

“Comedy gold,” is the term of choice in sitcom writers’ rooms, usually referring to pyrite, but this is the real thing, the contemporary world’s mother lode.

Frustrated conservative activists long complained that *our* billionaires woefully failed to counter the Left’s dominance of entertainment media. Pleasing as it was to imagine New York balletomanes gagging every time they enter Lincoln Center’s David H. Koch Theater, wouldn’t that $100 million have been better spent on, say, a remake of (the canceled) Laura Ingalls Wilder’s *Little House on the Prairie* to counter Disney’s war on families and children? And wouldn’t it have been nice if they and theirs had sprung for a network and film studio or two? But, no, the melancholy truth is that most embrace the Great Reset as comfortably as the Hollywood mogul David Geffen, who funds LGBT activism, Left-media attack dog David Brock, and Rob Reiner’s Parents Action for Children.

Still, for all the immense power of the forces behind the Great Reset, in increasing numbers ordinary people recognize that what they are selling is not just profoundly, frighteningly wrong—indeed, Orwellian—but *bonkers*, boding a future no one wants to live in. The estimable Anthony Daniels has written of the slogan of the idiot French revolutionaries of May ’68—"Défense de defender,” or “Forbidden to forbid"—and the moral chaos that ensued when they “found themselves in control of a state that forbade more than ever, and which insinuated itself by regulation and the passage of myriad laws ever more termite-like into the lives of its citizens.”

With today’s infinitely greater powers of surveillance and enforcement, it is not hard for the informed citizen to grasp what the Great Reset portends: when humor is outlawed because nothing is funny, then only outlaws will be funny. For all their immense self-regard, deep in their addled collective brain, the leftist elites know this, and it has them running scared.

When the Soviets banned typewriters, the good guys produced samizdat by hand and continued on with the business of undermining an empire. We've now got podcasts and Substack and the emergence of alternative social-media platforms. We've got Dave Chappelle and Ricky Gervais, and The Babylon Bee.

The truth is, we couldn't be more fortunate in our enemy. Dissident wise guys looking to bring down the Iron Curtain had only the likes of anabolic women weightlifters and a glowering Leonid Brezhnev as material, but in our current war with the elites we've got high school "girl" track stars with balls, a non compos mentis Biden, and largely peaceful demonstrators trashing our history and burning down our cites.

Tell me that isn't funny. Better yet, tell it to Klaus Schwab and his band of anti-merry men. We're already laughing at them, too!

PART V: THE PRACTICAL

GREEN ENERGY AND THE FUTURE OF TRANSPORTATION

BY SALVATORE BABONES

At Railworld Wildlife Haven in Peterborough, a two-hour drive north of London, you can find the last remaining RTV 31 Tracked Hovercraft, Britain's 1973 concept for the railroad of the future. The RTV 31 was supposed to revolutionize train travel by levitating trains on a frictionless cushion of air. Propulsion was to be supplied by a then-revolutionary linear induction motor. But Britain was not alone in the race to the future. Nipping at its heels, France proffered the hovering Aérotrain, powered by a giant rear propeller. The United States countered with its own hovertrain prototype driven by no fewer than three jet aircraft engines—American exceptionalism in a nutshell.

The British project was managed by the National Physical Laboratory, the French one by an aircraft engineering company, and the American entry (inevitably) by a defense contractor. That explains the three different propulsion systems. But only one thing explains the near-contemporaneous explosion of interest in hovertrain technology across all three countries: government funding. The German, Italian, and Brazilian governments also had plans to sponsor their own national champion hovertrains before the bubble burst. But burst it did, and by the mid-1970s, the hovertrain was history.

Not all government-backed technology projects turn into boondoggles, and certainly examples can be found where governments have made sound investments in new technologies that turned out to be transformative. The hovertrain craze may now sound as silly as the gravity-negating "cavorite," that propels H. G. Wells's astronauts to the moon, but there is a legitimate role for government to play in twenty-first century technology development. When multiple governments invest in different approaches to meeting the same social needs, the result can even be something like a competitive marketplace. And when democratic governments make full use of the myriad talents of their own citizens through openly competitive processes, innovation flourishes.

But the more distant technology planning is from the ground level of individual people dealing with the daily challenge of economic survival, the more likely it is that out-of-touch government bureaucrats (often working in collusion with self-interested corporate leaders) will deliver economically impractical solutions. When a single technological approach is imposed by government fiat, catastrophic failure is almost assured. We live in a world of profound uncertainty even about the present, never mind the future. Without a crystal ball to tell us which technologies ultimately will succeed and which will fail, diversity in experimentation is the key to discovering the technologies of the future.

As Charles Darwin recognized decades before Friedrich Hayek was born, natural selection is a much more powerful mechanism for adaptation to an uncertain world than intelligent design. At any point in time, the number of possible technological futures is infinite, and those infinite possibilities only compound as time moves forward. Even the most intelligent, dedicated, well-informed planner can only guess which future to plan for, and the probability that such a planner will hit on just the right future is essentially zero. The same is true for planning by private individuals, but when several billion private individuals plan for the same future, some of them are bound to get it right.

Although most individuals may underperform professional planners, the scattershot approach leaves society as a whole better prepared to engage with whatever future emerges. This is not so much the wisdom of crowds as the luck of the draw. To see it in action, open your bottom drawer or check your top shelves to count how many disused electronic devices you own. At every stage of technological development, many more prototypes are developed, many more products are discontinued, than the small number of successful models that continue to evolve past their first iterations. Like the fossil record, technology development is a scrap heap of evolutionary dead ends.

Transportation technology is no exception to this general rule. Bicycles, trains, automobiles, and airplanes all emerged out of cutthroat evolutionary competition. Look at early history of any of these transportation systems, and you see a wild cacophony of competing designs. The public infrastructure and regulatory environment for each of them lagged far behind product development. Cyclists called forth paved roads; railroad operators called forth rights of way; car owners called forth traffic rules; airlines called forth airports. To the planning mentality, it seems irrational to allow people to fly before building airports for them to fly from and to, but in reality, the flights came first and the airports followed.

It's the same situation today with autonomous (self-driving) cars. In 2021, there are already a million of so autonomous vehicles (AVs) driving with some degree of self-driving capacity, whether the planners are ready for them or not. Nearly all of them are battery-electric vehicles (BEVs), so in effect there are a million high-capacity batteries capable of driving themselves, among roughly ten million BEVs total. Both figures are growing rapidly, well in advance of government programs to equip roads for automation or even provide charging points.

Like other transportation technologies before them, AVs and other BEVs are calling into existence a whole new technological ecosystem, or technosystem, to serve the needs of their users. Those needs can't be known in advance with any degree of certainty, but some general features seem inevitable. The AV-BEV technosystem will be decentralized and distributed like the internet, not centrally administered and controlled like high-speed rail. It will be capital light, not capital intensive. It will reconfigure the electrical grid even more than it reshapes the road network. It will have profound environmental implications. It will be almost entirely unplanned. And we must ensure that it remains free from technocratic control.

Green Energy in the Great Reset

If there's one organization that wants to plan our collective future, it's the WEF. The WEF describes itself as "the" (not "an") "International Organization for Public-Private Cooperation." Founded in 1971 by the engineer turned economist Klaus Schwab, it has developed into a statist behemoth dedicated to the promotion of its own brand of "stakeholder capitalism," and its reports are written from the viewpoint of a very narrow class of capitalist stakeholders: management consultants, investment bankers, professional directors, and the serving politicians who aspire to join them when they leave office. Notably absent from the WEF's vision of stakeholder capitalism are entrepreneurs, small businesses, the self-employed, and ordinary consumers.

Famous for attracting some three thousand CEOs, heads of government, and celebrity intellectuals to its annual January conference in Davos, Switzerland, the WEF likes to think big. Schwab's 2020 book *COVID-19: The Great Reset* (coauthored with WEF alumnus Thierry Malleret) describes even the "micro" level of stakeholder capitalism as consisting of industries and companies, rather than families and individuals. When Schwab does consider human beings, he focuses on their personal morality and mental health without so much as an inkling that individuals could actually possess economic initiative.

Schwab's stakeholder capitalism is, in his own words, all about managing the future in line with ESG goals set by CEOs and their accomplices "with support from the 'Big Four' accounting firms." Schwab claims that stakeholder capitalism "positions private corporations as trustees of society." It gives CEOs an ideological basis for discarding all effective oversight, since in Schwab's model, neither shareholders nor government regulators should exercise control over public corporations. It's up to CEOs and their management consultants to make decisions for all of society. The only role left to shareholders and taxpayers is to pick up the tab.

Beyond being based on stakeholder capitalism, Schwab's vision for the Great Reset, encapsulated in his 2020 book and publicized via the WEF media machine, remains obscure. The book and accompanying website are suffused with platitudes. All Schwab does tell us that the "essence" of the Great Reset is that "the corona crisis may compel us to act faster by replacing failed ideas, institutions, processes and rules with new ones better suited to current and future needs." He repeatedly emphasizes that "the pandemic represents a rare but narrow window of opportunity to reflect, reimagine, and reset our world." His *Great Reset* book concludes:

> We are now at a crossroads. One path will take us to a better world: more inclusive, more equitable and more respectful of Mother Nature. The other will take us to a world that resembles the one we just left behind—but worse and constantly dogged by nasty surprises. We must therefore get it right. The looming challenges could be more consequential than we have until now chosen to imagine, but our capacity to reset could also be greater than we had previously dared to hope.

All this smacks of what the Marxist theorist David Harvey calls the "management and manipulation of crises." Harvey cast this particular aspersion on the rise of neoliberalism, but failed to identify just who was doing the management and manipulation to bring neoliberal policies to the table. The truth is that neoliberalism arose as a more or less spontaneous response to the crises of the 1970s in the form of a ready-made ideology offering clear answers to the most pressing problems of the time. Whether those answers were right or wrong is still hotly debated, but they were concrete, unambiguous, and intellectually well-supported.

The Great Reset is none of these things. In the case of the Great Reset, the "who" is clear: Klaus Schwab and the three thousand elite participants in the WEF's annual Davos conferences. But the "what" seems to be left intentionally vague. The Great Reset featured in WEF publications and Schwab's book consists of a series of motherhood statements about inclusivity, equity, respectfulness, nature, and the dynamism of youth. Even the WEF's detailed platform papers on "shaping the future" offer few details about the futures they want to shape. The WEF prioritizes process over content at every stage.

For example, in the WEF's report *Fostering Effective Energy Transition: 2021 Edition*, the key metrics of "robustness and resilience" mean the robustness and resilience of the WEF's political program in the face of "elements that could derail the successful transformation," not, as might be hoped, the robustness and resilience of electrical grids. Reliability of the electricity network represents only one-thirty-sixth of the WEF's Energy Transition Index, less than the weight given to the number of people employed in green energy or participation in the Paris Accord. Completely extraneous measures such as education levels and corruption scores outweigh practical engineering criteria. The report's executive summary concludes with an ominous warning emphasized in boldface:

> **It is critical to root the energy transition in economic, political and social practices so that progress becomes irreversible.**

The irreversible policies that the WEF and its partners might seek to implement remain unstated. About the only thing that they make clear about their plans for a future energy transition is that "policy-makers and private sector actors must work together and seize the opportunities"—in other words, that the Davos coalition must use the coronavirus crisis as an opportunity to take charge. The same might be said for Schwab's Great Reset in general. After all, who can object to the future of "inclusive growth and long-term prosperity" that Schwab purports to offer? With few details offered, there are few details to oppose.

Green Transition or Planned Obsolescence?

Elite-directed public-private cooperation could lead us to the promised technological nirvana. Or it could just bring us more hovertrains. The problem is that it's a flip of the coin: success or failure, centralized decision-making stakes everything on one big bet. And the WEF's model of public-private cooperation virtually ensures that the bets our betters make on our behalf will focus on large-scale, capital-intensive, highly centralized systems. That's not because these kinds of systems have been proven to offer the best solutions to the problems of the future. It's because these kinds of systems are more amenable to deliberate planning than are systems that arise through spontaneous self-organization.

Yet it's spontaneous self-organization that gave us the first iterations of paved roads, urban mass transit, intercity railways, and commercial aviation. Each of these transportation technosystems later came under government management in most jurisdictions, but not until their basic structures had already been worked out through the trial and error of individual initiative. It was the same story with electric power generation and transmission, computerized control systems, battery development, and the myriad other technologies that are required for a successful "energy transition."

It is probably inevitable that new forms of transportation networks and electricity grids eventually will require government regulation, just as their predecessors did. But after-the-fact regulation is very different from upfront planning. From windfarms to solar farms to utility-scale battery arrays, the standard model for the WEF's energy transition involves large-scale infrastructure built by government fiat to meet the nonenergy policy goal of carbon reduction. This approach may or may not get governments their desired carbon reductions.

But it has already created a bonanza for corporate green energy promoters who generate much higher profit margins from pitching for government contracts than they could possibly hope to gain in an open market.

Economists have long argued that the most efficient way to reduce carbon-dioxide emissions—if that is accepted as an overriding goal—is through some form of carbon pricing. That might take the form of a cap-and-trade market, direct carbon taxes, or some other rationing mechanism. Even very blunt carbon reduction strategies like simply prohibiting new coal mines work indirectly through pricing mechanisms: as the remaining supplies dry up, utilities would become more efficient in their use of coal and substitute other sources of energy (or promote equivalent energy savings). If governments are serious about reducing carbon emissions, all they have to do is raise the price and the market will find a way to economize on carbon.

But you can't cut a ribbon on an intangible, diffuse, incremental efficiency gain. Nor can you seek political favors from the millions of individuals who make small behavioral changes in response to price signals. Even worse, carbon pricing is in essence all about spreading pain, not spreading gain. The unfortunate reality is that decarbonization is a costly goal. An efficient energy transition means imposing costs in calculable, transparent ways; it is the very visibility of rising costs that prompts people and companies to use the world's limited carbon budget as carefully as possible. But while many people want a greener future, few people want to pay for it.

It is much more appealing for politicians to subsidize private sector collaborators to undertake high-visibility green energy projects. Alternatively, they can grant monopoly concessions, offer tax rebates, and waive ordinary planning requirements—all of which offer economic rents to those lucky enough to receive them. The public still pays a price for these inducements—whether in higher taxes, lower amenities, or a degraded environment—but the costs are not directly tied to the decarbonization process. Just as important (from a political perspective) is the fact that big-ticket projects create a class of green energy winners who actively campaign for government action (and may even repay political favors).

Public-private cooperation in delivering point solutions is thus a politically attractive but economically wasteful way to engineer a green energy transition. It is also extraordinarily risky. Our political leaders and their private sector partners are betting heavily on a single, infrastructure-intensive technosystem to manage the transition to a low-carbon economy: large-scale wind and solar "farms" generating intermittent electrical power backed up by large-scale battery "farms" to regulate their output. With enough (potentially costly) overinvestment, these systems can overcome typical objections about the wind not blowing and the sun not shining. What they can't do is ensure that they won't be obsolete within a few years of coming online.

At the very moment that the WEF is attempting to reroute energy policy onto a decisively statist course, energy technology is moving in precisely the opposite direction. Ironically, one company—Tesla—is at the center of both shifts. As Elon Musk understands better than anyone, Tesla is at heart a battery company, and it markets two kinds of batteries: stationary batteries and mobile batteries. The stationary ones include both its utility-scale "Megapacks" and its smaller backup batteries for businesses and consumers. The mobile ones are the batteries installed in its cars and trucks. No one can know which batteries will ultimately prove more valuable, but the market valuations of Tesla's many competitors strongly suggest that it's the mobile ones that matter for the company's future.

Even worse for the future prospects of the giant utility-scale battery arrays that are currently being integrated into plans for new wind and solar farms, the promoters of green energy are themselves pushing governments to promote the mass take-up of BEVs. As a result, the world is rapidly developing an enormous capacity of mobile batteries that, collectively, dwarf the scale of the fixed batteries being installed to support wind and solar farms. At the same time, rooftop solar power has become widely available as well, raising the possibility that homes and offices could soon evolve into (relatively) self-contained electrical subsystems, with power generated on the roof being stored in the car.

Taken together, BEVs and rooftop solar may make giant wind, solar, and battery farms obsolete before they are able to repay their up-front fixed costs. And they will do so with minimal financial risk, since the individual owners of BEVs and rooftop solar panels are buying them for their own purposes, not to fulfill a grand plan to reform all of society.

Minimal financial risk from market forces, that is. The risk of government expropriation is much greater: governments that have bought into utility-scale green energy may very well seize control over the power management software that connects BEVs and rooftop solar panels to the electrical grid. Many governments have used the coronavirus crisis as a cover to get into people's smartphones; the success of the green transition may depend on making sure they don't also get onto our roofs and into our cars as well.

The Tesla Wolf Packs Are at the Door

Our roofs may be safe for now, but the WEF is already working to get into our cars; it wants to bring "companies together with key stakeholders across all sectors" in the development of AVs. The WEF's "community paper" on *Creating Safe Autonomous Vehicle Policy* was written by a WEF staffer with "the input of many experts and diverse stakeholders," one-third of whom happened to be partners or associates at McKinsey & Company. Not a single one actually worked for an autonomous vehicle developer like Tesla, Waymo, Mobileye, or Cruise, and it perhaps goes without saying that the WEF's "community" does not include the wider public.

Unsurprisingly, the paper calls for global agreement on "a clear top-level vision...for the future mobility ecosystem" before AVs can be allowed to go mainstream. Tesla, for one, does not seem inclined to wait. Tesla's CEO Elon Musk has been claiming that his cars were on the cusp of full self-driving capability since 2016, and even if he has often proven guilty of overpromising, his inclinations are clear. Tesla Autopilot, despite not being truly capable of full autonomous driving, has been live since 2015. Unlike other participants in the race to develop AVs, Tesla has in effect let ordinary drivers test autonomous driving on the road, with minimal regulatory oversight.

Whether Musk's approach is right or wrong, it is pushing AV technology toward full autonomy much faster than regulators care to admit. And full autonomy is the missing link that will transform the mobile batteries we know as "cars" into full participants in the electricity grid. Just as Tesla's Megapacks are designed to arbitrage the wholesale energy market, contributing power when the grid runs short and storing it when the grid has to shed excess capacity, wolf packs of Tesla cars soon will be able to smooth out retail energy peaks and troughs. The key difference is that Tesla wolf packs will hunt locally and selectively, taking the highest prices and soaking up the cheapest supply at the retail interface.

So while Musk is promising that Tesla owners may soon be able to make $30,000 a year renting out their cars as robotaxis, the more immediate (and behaviorally realistic) prospect is that they will soon be able to rent them out as grid stabilizers. The spread of rooftop solar and local smart (computer controlled) grids is already creating high demand for local plug-in storage. Tesla and other companies currently are meeting this demand with stationary home batteries. But in the long term this represents a duplication of functions, with electric-car batteries on hand to fill the same role.

In the immediate future, Teslas and other BEVs will make only minor, incremental contributions to electricity grids. But the magic of incrementalism is that it allows technology to adapt while it develops: in other words, to evolve. Large-scale infrastructure projects either pay off or get written off, but incremental solutions evolve as they continually chase ever-changing market signals. When governments pick winning technologies and green-light them without considering the environmental consequences, they risk creating stranded assets on an enormous scale—and then having to pay a second time to clean them up. Incrementalism diffuses both the up-front risks and the back-end recycling bill.

Demands for governments to install millions of electric car-charging stations are just as misplaced as demands for big-ticket green energy. Planners routinely make the mistake of believing that a large-scale charging infrastructure is the only way to convince people to switch to BEVs, since they imagine that people will want to charge their electric cars on the run, just as they currently top-up their gas tanks. This risks installing entire networks of one-way chargers when what the BEVs of the future will really need are two-way interfaces. The need may eventually arise for charging stations on the long-distance highways of the future, but that is still a distant prospect. In the more immediate term, BEVs will charge at home—and, when necessary, power the home.

The emerging AV-BEV technosystem is ideally suited to interface with another emerging technology: ride hailing. Elon Musk's robotaxis aren't just around the corner; they're already here, in experimental operation in several American cities. If people give up on owning their own cars, the need for charging stations on long-distance routes will disappear, since people will simply change cars on long trips. For millennia, from the dispatch riders of ancient Persia to the American Pony Express, long-distance transportation meant changing horses every ten miles. Only in the twentieth century did the model of individual ownership of transport vehicles take hold. It may turn out to have been a temporary aberration, like smoking tobacco or watching movies in theaters.

While it seems behaviorally unlikely that ordinary car owners will rent their Teslas out to the public, the transition from chauffeured cars to driverless robotaxis is baked into the business models of ride-hailing companies like Uber, Lyft, and China's DiDi. Their AV-BEV fleets will be even better suited to electricity grid integration than individually owned cars, since they will not have to keep any particular car charged up for any particular person's use. As long as their fleets have sufficient reserves of sufficiently charged cars available in any given locale, the ride-hailing companies will be able to optimize the rest of their mobile batteries (i.e., cars) for electricity grid support. And they will arrive at that future incrementally, by evolving through small-scale adaptations to market forces, not by intelligent system design.

As things stand, ride hailing is the Wild West of unregulated capitalism. Or perhaps it would be safer to say: "as things stand now." Governments and (especially) judges are working hard to bring ride-hailing companies to heel. American and European governments are seeking to regulate Uber and Lyft even as China effectively nationalizes its ride-hailing champion, DiDi. Right now, the battle is focused on contract terms for drivers. But once governments get inside the apps, they may seek to control much more than prices and working conditions. Governments could tell drivers where to go and how to get there; in the future, they could seize full control of robotaxis, as foreseen in the 2002 science fiction film *Minority Report*. The Chinese government is already doing this, erasing out-of-favor companies from DiDi's list of destinations and locking dissidents out of cars. The only way to ensure that Uber and Lyft stay independent is to keep government out of the apps.

The Death of Buses

Travis Kalanick, the founder of Uber, originally set out in 2008 to design an app to facilitate ride sharing, not ride hailing: the idea was to help people arrange carpools on demand. Logan Green and John Zimmer actually founded the precursor of Lyft as a carpooling app, their twist being to help people find companions to carpool on long-distance, cross-country drives. Though often characterized as forming part of the "sharing" economy, both companies soon switched to a chauffeur model, becoming in essence unregistered taxi services. Many cities now regulate them as such, and some countries have banned them entirely because they compete directly with officially registered taxis.

Back when ride hailing was still being billed as ride sharing, the planning community was all onboard. It saw ride sharing as the long-sought solution to mass transit's "last mile problem." Conventional mass transit systems operate as services running at fixed times along fixed routes. That works fine for people who want to travel from one point on a line to another point on the same line. But no transit system is able to cover the entirety of a metropolitan catchment area. Some mechanism is needed for getting people from their homes to the nearest bus stop or train station. And when people have to drive to catch their trains, the inefficiencies and inconveniences of mass transit become insurmountable in all but the most crowded of cities.

Enter the last-mile autonomous shuttle. This is the AV use case that most excites planners—and their patrons at the WEF. The 2018 report *Reshaping Urban Mobility with Autonomous Vehicles*, produced by the WEF in cooperation with Boston Consulting Group (BCG), advances a vision for shared autonomous mobility (i.e., driverless minibuses) integrated into urban mass transit systems. The report's models, based on consumer survey data, suggested that a future of shared AVs would reduce the number of vehicles on the road while improving travel times ("AV heaven"). The WEF and their partners didn't even dare to model a future of individual AVs, where people enjoy the privacy of commuting alone ("AV hell"). It's their job to make sure that we don't make that mistake:

> We conclude that cities, nations and the world will need to embrace a regulatory and governance framework for AVs that nudges us towards an "AV heaven" scenario and away from "AV hell."

One wonders how many WEF directors and BCG partners carpool on their daily commutes, and prefer buses to taxis. Read between the lines, and what their data really show is that people prefer cars to mass transit. The WEF and BCG reported that "city dwellers valued AVs most because they eliminated the need to find parking," not because they solve the last mile problem. They proposed taxing people for hailing private robotaxis—on top of the already-higher prices to be paid for the convenience of riding alone—despite the fact that their own models suggested that it would result in only a very modest shift from individual to shared mobility. They relentlessly searched for ways to corral people into their preferred model of the future, instead of simply asking people what they want and designing a future to suit.

The fact is that conventional mass transit systems were designed for the standardized mass mobility needs of office and factory workers in the nineteenth and twentieth centuries. They are ill-suited to serve the flexible needs of today's flexible workforces. They have little value at all for a potential post-pandemic future in which work is increasingly local, decentralized, and diffused throughout multiple communities. In short, the days when masses of workers would commute from far-flung residential suburbs to major urban centers in large numbers at scheduled times, if not over, are at least in decline. Instead of looking for ways to force the future to flow into the legacy patterns of the past, planners should be looking for ways to adjust our existing infrastructure to serve the needs of tomorrow.

Existing forms of mass transit (primarily trains and buses) really work well only in a few super-congested mega-cities, and even there, only for people who continue to live according to daily rhythms set down in the last century. For everyone else, ride hailing is a godsend, and robotaxis will be transformative. Even without introducing new transportation hardware, Google and Apple maps have already pulled cars off major thoroughfares during times of peak congestion, much to the chagrin of people living on formerly quiet side streets, but much to the advantage of computer-aided drivers. The emerging AV-BEV technosystem has the potential to reconfigure city street grids from funnel systems into percolation substrates, as people increasingly travel from home to home, instead of from home to office.

The personal robotaxi will eliminate the need for parking, giving it an incredible advantage vis-à-vis the personal car. At the same time, it will reduce the cost per trip, making it economically competitive vis-à-vis conventional chauffeured ride hailing. And whenever the robotaxi is waiting for a customer, it can plug into the electricity grid—either to charge or discharge, depending on the local price. That additional source of revenue will constitute pure profit from the perspective of a robotaxi fleet operator.

If mass transit can't adapt to the AV-BEV technosystem, it will die. The WEF solution to that prospect is to tax people for not using mass transit. That is no solution at all, and in any case not a viable one in a democracy. Voters won't tax themselves to force themselves to take the bus. As high-cost, human-chauffeured ride hailing changes over to low-cost, robot-driven services, buses probably will disappear. Competing directly with on-demand, point-to-point ride-hailing services, only massive subsidies could keep bus lines in operation, and it would make much more sense to subsidize poor people's individual mobility needs through personal credits than to keep buses operating for the small number of people forced to rely on them.

Rail is another matter. While bus services merely represent a less convenient form of road transportation than private driving, rail is a true alternative. At its best, it offers passengers faster travel in a more spacious, more comfortable environment. It also takes them off the road entirely. This has the potential to reduce road congestion while at the same time increasing the speed and capacity of transportation corridors. And ride hailing is already sufficiently integrated with locative services (like Google and Apple maps) to coordinate seamless transfers from ride hailing to mass transit and back again.

Rail-based mass transit systems, at least in the form of underground and overhead metro railroads, may retain an important role in the AV-BEV robotaxi future. They are likely to serve as high-capacity backbones linking car-based systems serving the extremities. That applies for both intercity and metropolitan transportation—but only in environments where extreme passenger density makes them economical. With robotaxi fleets to offer last-mile services, commuter parking lots may become a thing of the past, allowing for the profitable redevelopment of high-traffic transit interchange points. This would offer urban planners everything they value in a single package; everything, that is, except control.

From Synchronized Grids to Smart Grids

No one will miss buses, but trains are another matter. Many people actually like trains, and they may integrate quite well with the emerging AV-BEV technosystem. There is also an electricity grid argument for retaining rail infrastructure. Metros, subways, suburban rail, and intercity rail are all major electricity users; from an engineering standpoint, they are as much power systems as transportation systems. It may take decades to emerge, but smart electricity grids linking rail networks with the mobile batteries of robotaxi fleets have the potential to stabilize the many local grids that constitute an integrated urban power system.

Historically, most electrical power has been generated at discrete points (power stations) and distributed from these through interconnected grids to millions of end users. Incredibly, our major power grids are each synchronized to a shared frequency, meaning that every device on the grid experiences up- and downswings of alternating current at the same time. The largest such grid is the European Continental Synchronous Area that runs from Portugal to Turkey and from Algeria to Denmark. The generators of every major power station in this vast area spin in unison, operating as single pulsating machine. A couple dozen other grids, many of them transnational, cover most of the other developed countries of the world.

Of course, wind turbines cannot realistically be synchronized with electricity grids, since the wind stubbornly refuses to blow at a constant rate. Thus, although wind turbines generate alternating current just like other major power sources, their electricity is converted to direct current, which is then reconverted to alternating current in sync with the grid. The other major form of renewable energy, photovoltaic solar cells, also produces direct current that is then converted to alternating current. As a result, wind and solar aren't really "on the grid" in the way that conventional power plants are. They feed into the grid, but they are not part of it.

As more and more renewable energy sources are linked to the world's electricity grids, conventional generators are being removed, leading to the deterioration of the grids themselves. That's because physical, spinning generators play an important function in frequency regulation that is not replicated by wind and solar connections. Wind and solar inputs can be synchronized to the frequency of the grid, but they do not actively help maintain the frequency of the grid. Without conventional generators creating the synchronized grid in the first place, wind and solar would have no grid to contribute to.

This conundrum could become a serious problem long before conventional power generation gives way entirely to renewables. When an electricity grid experiences either a sudden surge in demand (for example, from millions of air conditioners suddenly being turned on as people arrive home from work on a hot summer day) or a sudden drop in supply (due to an infrastructure failure), the frequency of the power on the grid declines. This can seriously damage some types of electrical equipment and cause malfunctions in others. Even worse, local frequency declines in one area can cause widespread system failure resulting from frequency mismatches between parts of a continent-spanning synchronized grid. Generators that are spinning out of sync with the grid can even be torn apart by the massive collision between electromagnetic forces and physical momentum.

When a synchronized grid is powered by a large number of spinning generators, the physical momentum of the generators themselves tends to keep the frequency stable and the grid in sync. If demand surges or a generator unexpectedly goes offline, the remaining generators on the grid act as flywheels, instantly picking up the slack in an automatic response that requires no human intervention. This effect may only last a few seconds, but that is the crucial margin between a fragile grid that is always at risk of complete collapse and a robust grid that is sufficiently self-regulating to enable its managers to respond to crises before they literally spin out of control. This built-in robustness is known as grid inertia, and it helps to maintain the frequency of the electricity on a synchronized grid in emergency situations.

For a practical application of grid inertia, one need look no further than the dramatic winter 2021 Texas blackouts. Most of the capacity losses suffered by the grid were prompted by the failure of insufficiently weatherized natural gas supplies. Additional capacity losses were prompted by the freezing of wind turbines. But the cascading series of outages that threatened to bring down the entire grid were prompted by a loss of frequency support. With more than a quarter of the state's total electricity supply coming from wind and solar, the remaining "spinning" power wasn't enough to keep frequency in line, and as a result, large swaths of residential customers had to be cut off in order to prevent the grid from collapsing completely. Whether or not that would have happened had the grid been powered entirely by spinning generators is a question for the engineers, but in any case, the threshold for a disaster would have been much higher on a prerenewables grid.

The synchronization approach to the management of electrical grids is very twentieth century: large-scale, centrally managed, and infrastructure heavy. It works, and it has served us well, but it is being severely tested by the shift to green energy. If the world wants to see increasing proportions of its electricity sourced from nonspinning power, it has to move from twentieth to twenty-first century technologies—from continental synchronized grids to localized smart grids. That means moving wind and (especially) solar power sources closer to the point of consumption, managing them using responsive AI algorithms, and integrating them with battery backup power in the form of EV-BEV robotaxis operating as mobile batteries. Renewable energy is fundamentally incompatible with today's stable but ultimately dumb grids. The energy transition must be accompanied by the implementation of dynamic smart grids.

The Smart Grid Transition

Smart grids go under many names and definitions, but in one form or another, they are innovations that involve the management of electricity grids by AI algorithms. They are the most important use case for the emerging internet of things (IoT). In a smart grid, devices that supply or consume power would dynamically (and often autonomously) modulate their behavior in response to sensor stimuli, price signals, and anticipated human needs. A spinning generator automatically picks up the additional burden of supporting a failing grid, a connected battery array must be programmed to do so autonomously—i.e., by recognizing the problem and reacting to it without waiting for human input.

That's a demanding remit, but one that is already being met by large-scale Tesla Megapacks. The challenge facing the green energy transition is to diffuse the IoT approach down to the level of consumer devices like rooftop solar panels and electric car batteries. Whether or not the managers of our electricity networks are ready for it, individuals are plugging more and more devices into the grid. In the absence of a smart grid, people's rooftop solar panels will reduce demand in the middle of the day, when supplies are already plentiful, and their BEVs will suck up electricity when people get home from work and plug them in, at the very moment when grids typically experience their greatest strains. Government subsidies for rooftop solar and individually owned BEVs are only making things worse.

Instead of subsidizing these strains on the synchronized grid, governments should mandate that these devices be IoT-ready and prepared for smart grid integration. If BEVs are sold IoT-ready, governments won't have to tell people when to charge their cars; AI-managed BEVs will manage their own charging to ensure maximum readiness at the lowest cost. Considering how keen people are to save a few cents on a gallon of gasoline, it is reasonable to anticipate that most people will let their cars make their own charging decisions most of the time. Instead of charging immediately upon being plugged in, AI-managed BEVs will actually discharge when their drivers arrive home, contributing to the household microgrid at its moment of highest utilization. They will then wait for the cheap early morning electricity to recharge.

And whenever they're plugged in, they'll offer the grid frequency regulation on demand—for a price.

As the individual ownership of BEVs slowly gives way to shared AV-BEV robotaxis, the benefits will multiply. Robotaxis likely will park in residential neighborhoods in the middle of the day to take advantage of surplus rooftop solar power. They may then migrate to railroad station taxi ranks where they can power the very trains that will bring their customers home. When you book a ride, cars will respond based on their battery levels and the predicted amount of electricity needed to get you to your destination. Today's concerns over rapid charging for BEVs will become irrelevant; AV-BEVs will be able to charge at their leisure, since only the ones with sufficient charge for your trip will respond to your call for a car.

For routine bookings like a daily commute, you'll be able to press a button to notify your preferred ride-hailing company that you'll be ready to leave in five minutes, resulting in near-zero waiting times. The only inconvenience will occur at those rare moments when a local grid is experiencing severe stress—and the profit to be made from stabilizing the grid outweighs your willingness to pay for a ride. People will curse the energy transition when that day arrives, but they'll still be better off than if the lights had gone out. And it will probably happen less often than breakdowns and accidents occur in people's individually owned cars today, since distributed smart grids managed by AI should be much more robust than today's centralized grids with their single points of failure.

The key to ensuring a successful transition from continental synchronized grids to local smart grids is gradualism. If the proponents of green energy continue to focus on promoting utility-scale wind and solar farms, they only will contribute to the increasing fragility of our synchronized electricity grids. Their infrastructure-heavy approach to green energy requires that massive new projects fit into twentieth-century grid architectures without unduly disturbing them. The big infrastructure approach also will produce multiple compounding inefficiencies, as wind farms, solar farms, hospitals, emergency services, police stations, individual automobiles, and individual homes all will require battery back-ups. The local smart grid approach would instead give our twentieth-century grid architecture time to slowly adapt and digest twenty-first century technologies one kilowatt at a time.

Schwab is in a hurry to push through his Great Reset and doesn't allow for this kind of incremental adjustment. But some of his colleagues at the WEF are more patient. Or were. In 2017, the WEF's head of industries, Cheryl Martin, coauthored a paper, *The Future of Electricity*, that advocated a distributed energy transition to be accomplished through the slow accretion of "grid edge technologies." She warned that governments and their private-sector partners would have to adjust to "the new reality of a digital, customer-empowered, transactive electricity system." Within a year, she was gone. She lasted less than three years on the WEF managing board, the kind of position that most statist apparatchiks cling to for life. The current 2021 WEF report on *Fostering Effective Energy Transition* doesn't even find space to cite her 2017 vision among its ninety-seven references.

The emerging AV-BEV technosystem will be as much an electricity system as a transportation system. As a transportation system, it will emerge gradually and incrementally, with a mix of conventional petrol-powered vehicles, BEVs, chauffeured taxis, individually owned AV-BEVs, and full-fledged robotaxis sharing the road at any one time. Over the course of the 2020s and 2030s, we likely will see a shift toward AV-BEVs (whether or not governments subsidize them) because vehicles will increasingly integrate with electricity grids, delivering extra revenues to robotaxi fleet operators.

In jurisdictions that take a centralized approach to the future of electricity, AV-BEVs will destabilize the grid, sucking up power without regard to the needs of the grid. But where governments allow technology to evolve organically, only intervening to set standards and empower consumers, AV-BEVs slowly will become part of the grid. It's a straightforward choice between piecemeal incrementalism and big-bang reform. Incrementalism means continuous adaptation while at every stage retaining individual freedom of choice—and the systemwide flexibility to reverse mistakes made along the way. Big-bang reform, by contrast, means a leap of faith guided by fallible (and potentially mendacious) human planners. All jurisdictions will reach an optimized smart grid future eventually, but those that allow the most freedom will get there faster and more efficiently than those that mandate any but the most perfectly planned path.

The Great Reset: More Red than Green

There are approximately 1.5 billion personal automobiles in the world, give or take a few hundred million. Before the pandemic, annual new auto sales were running at around seventy-five million a year. Thus it takes about twenty years for the world's car fleet to turn over; longer, in fact, because some new sales replace relatively new vehicles while some older vehicles can remain in service for decades. And with BEVs still making up less than 5 percent of total vehicle sales, gasoline will be the king of the road for a long time to come, even in the world's most advanced economies. Like the Bob Dylan song says, "The Times, They Are a-Changin'"—but very slowly.

And that's the way it should be, not only for the emerging AV-BEV technosystem, but for the energy transition as well. A rapid, government-mandated transition from fossil fuels to renewable energy would destabilize today's synchronized grids long before tomorrow's smart grids are in place to accommodate all the new, intermittent, nonspinning electricity sources that are coming online. Simply mandating the transition to smart grids won't work, either: the individual components of smart grid technology do exist, but smart grids are designed to work at the local scale, not the continental scale of existing electricity grids. And in any case, today's large-scale wind and solar farms require the creation of a concomitantly massive battery storage infrastructure. This approach is as inefficient as it is environmentally destructive.

The problem isn't the idea of an energy transition. The problem is the rapidity with which the Great Reset and other activist propaganda urge that it be pursued. Obviously, humankind is not going to burn fossil fuels for the rest of eternity. No doubt climate catastrophism is wildly overblown, but it would be incautious (to say the least) to burn all of the Earth's buried hydrocarbons before moving on to other sources of energy. Even absent any climate considerations, the scourge of local air pollution should prompt us to move toward cleaner energy over the course of the twenty-first century. Given that we already have the technologies needed to live pollution-free, it makes sense to start the transition to a cleaner future.

But that transition should be gradual, incremental, and decentralized, not sudden, systematic, and centrally administered. Wind and solar cannot feasibly replace fossil fuels and nuclear power while retaining the twentieth-century technosystem of continental synchronized grids. The very structure of these grids requires that they be powered primarily by spinning generators, with nonspinning contributions chipping in only at the margins. A successful energy transition requires a new grid architecture, and that can be achieved only through incremental evolution. And the efficiency of the energy transition will be dramatically improved if electricity networks are allowed to coevolve with transportation networks.

If that conclusion is as obvious as it sounds, why aren't we hearing more about it? The truth is that we are hearing about it, but mainly from independent engineers, not from governments, consulting firms, or international organizations like the WEF. As Schwab and the WEF implicitly acknowledge, centralization serves stakeholders, not citizens. Those are not quite the same thing. As the WEF explains in its Davos manifesto, stakeholders include "employees, customers, suppliers, local communities and society at large." That sounds pretty inclusive until you consider who gets to speak for these stakeholders—or until you try to crash your way into a Davos panel discussion.

According to the WEF, the four "key" stakeholders with a responsibility for looking out for the rest of us are governments, civil society organizations, companies, and the "international community." It's a comprehensively patronizing approach to global economic and (lately) environmental management in which ordinary people play only a passive role. In that sense, the WEF's version of stakeholder capitalism might more aptly be characterized as profit-driven communism, or even "socialism with Chinese characteristics." It's no wonder that China's President Xi Jinping was greeted so warmly at Davos in January, 2017—and again at virtual Davos in 2021. If one listens to Schwab lauding Xi's calls for a "new era of global cooperation," the correspondence of their visions is clear.

Inviting the general secretary of the Chinese Communist Party to present the WEF keynote address in January, 2017, was perhaps nothing more than an ill-advised poke in the eye to the incoming U.S. president, Donald Trump. Inviting Xi back to open the forum in 2021, in the wake of all we know now about his programs of domestic repression and foreign aggression, can only be taken as a public affirmation of the WEF's own warped values. In welcoming Xi, Schwab complimented the "many initiatives that China has undertaken in the spirit of creating a world where all actors assume a responsible and responsive role." There was no hint of irony in his voice.

Like the Chinese Communist Party it seems to endorse, the WEF has in recent years wrapped a green mantle over its statist agenda, but it does not seek to hide that agenda. It revels in it. And if the coronavirus pandemic really did demand a Great Reset, if global warming really did constitute a climate emergency, if the need for an energy transition really did require us to put the entire world on a wartime footing to achieve it as quickly and at any cost, then ordinary citizens might reasonably be called on to cede their personal freedoms to the WEF's stakeholder capitalists. Absent any such emergency, efficiency and autonomy demand a more gradual (co-)evolution of our energy and transportation technosystems. Central planning was a dead end then and would be a red end now.

No one can say for certain what the unplanned future will bring. It probably won't bring back the hovertrain, but it is bound to be more efficient, more exciting, and more attractively livable than any future designed by a stakeholder committee. The twentieth-century transition to a transportation technosystem organized around personal automobile ownership occurred organically, evolving out of hundreds of millions of individual decisions. Our ongoing twenty-first-century transition will be best served by a similarly gradual and granular approach. Klaus Schwab, the WEF, and the "stakeholders" they represent will not succeed in planning the future. We just have to make sure that the technocrats don't seize control of the unplanned future after it arrives.

THE ANTI-INDUSTRIAL REVOLUTION

BY MARTIN HUTCHINSON

The World Economic Forum's Great Reset is a major revision of the economic policies that have pulled humanity to its present state of modest prosperity. Its central premise is captured by the epigraph: "You'll own nothing and you'll be happy." But ownership is what divides modern free men and women from medieval serfs—without it, we are subject to the whims of our masters and unable to fashion our destiny. The Great Reset not only resets our social status, but also, over time, it will reset our living standards to those of our serf ancestors.

The WEF, based in Switzerland, aims to create a Fourth Industrial Revolution; apparently, electrification and computers were numbers two and three. (As an old-fashioned sort, I prefer to think there has been only one Industrial Revolution, which is still ongoing, and that subsequent technological advances are developments of the original leap forward, which unlike its supposed successors, was not a mere technological add-on to previous progress, but a paradigm change in humanity's destiny.) The Covid-19 pandemic was the pretext for the group to call for a "Great Reset," in which governments can change the conditions of economic life so that the WEF's own policy preferences are favored. As President Barack Obama's first chief of staff Rahm Emanuel said in 2009, "Never let a plague go to waste."

According to Schwab and Malleret: "to achieve a better outcome, the world must act jointly and swiftly to revamp all aspects of our societies and economies, from education to social contracts and working conditions."

Schwab's Great Reset agenda has three main components. First, it "steers the market towards fairer outcomes"—Schwab and his cronies deciding what is fair. Second, the Great Reset agenda ensures that investments advance shared goals, such as equality and sustainability. (There appears to be no provision for those of us who do not share these goals.) The third priority is to "harness the innovations of the Fourth Industrial Revolution to support the public good, especially by addressing health and social challenges."

Clearly, the Great Reset agenda has little in common with conventional market capitalism. To highlight the differences, I will compare its approach point by point with the policies that gave Britain the original Industrial Revolution—the most comprehensive advance in human civilization since the invention of agriculture, and with more unequivocally positive effects on living standards. I shall demonstrate that in almost all areas, the Great Reset advocates the opposite of those policies. It then seems inescapable that it is likely to produce the opposite results, in other words, an Anti-Industrial Revolution, in which human economic progress in living standards goes into reverse.

Individual Freedom

The Industrial Revolution occurred in Great Britain between 1760 and 1830,[13] although its roots go back a century earlier, to the entrepreneurial outward-looking society that arose in the Restoration period after 1660. That society differed from all Continental societies of the

[13] In my forthcoming book *Forging Modernity—Why and How Britain Got the Industrial Revolution,* I examine the question of when the Industrial Revolution began and date it, not to James Watt's rotary steam engine of 1783, but to James Brindley's "Crand Cross" Midlands canal system, authorized by Parliament in 1766–70, with the necessary political change having occurred at the 1760 accession of George III. After 1830, the British political landscape changed, and the Industrial Revolution became global and no longer revolutionary but an unstoppable evolutionary process.

period (except the Netherlands) in one overwhelmingly important respect: almost all its people were fully free. That freedom derived from the period after another pandemic, the Black Death.

Nearly three hundred years before the Black Death, the Norman Conquest had sharply compromised the living standards and embryonic freedoms of the indigenous Saxons. The Normans appropriated the large landholdings, exterminating almost all the Saxon nobility, and then imposed the more severe French version of feudalism on the remainder of the indigenous population. In consequence, most of the Saxon population existed in an unfree status for the succeeding centuries, each member providing labor and possibly military service to their feudal lord and receiving no cash compensation for doing so. As England became more settled and its wealth increased, more land was cleared and cultivated. However, population increase among the serfs kept them mired in serfdom, even though the nonrural sectors of the economy were developing a cash economy with free exchange.

Then the Black Death happened, wiping out at least a third of the population. The result was a severe labor shortage, combined with a decline in food prices since there was no longer enough labor to cultivate all the available land. In response, the upper classes that controlled Parliament passed the Statute of Labourers 1351, prohibiting working men from demanding higher wages. These restrictions were initially effective, but over generations, with people moving, new employers emerging, and new job types appearing, they became a dead letter—the "Peasants' Revolt" of 1381 and other labor unrest were symptoms of the ex-serfs asserting their new autonomy. By the fifteenth century, the restrictions had effectively disappeared—the descendants of the serfs freed themselves and worked for the much higher wages now available. This period was in retrospect known as "Merrie England." For the ex-serfs, if not for their former masters embroiled in the Wars of the Roses, it was indeed Merrie!

This liberation happened across Europe at this time for similar demographic reasons, but England and the future Netherlands saw workers liberated more fully and permanently than in France, Spain, or the Holy Roman Empire. Thus, even though living standards declined again with increasing population after 1500, the greater freedom of English labor, maintained even through the impoverished early seventeenth century, was an important contributor to the Industrial Revolution.

The freedom of labor in eighteenth-century England was not simply a matter of its working status. English law had always restricted the central power—we find a detailed description in Sir John Fortescue's 1470 "The Difference Between an Absolute and a Limited Monarchy" of how the English monarchy was bound by the law, rather than absolute like the French one. The Civil War and the Interregnum, together with the legalism of the seventeenth century and the 1689 Bill of Rights established English legal freedoms of the individual as a bedrock constitutional principle. Consequently, English working men were free to move about the country, provided they could support themselves—only the 1601 Poor Law, which provided a minimal subsistence for the indigent on a parish basis, forced those who could not do so to return to their home parishes. They were also free to work in any occupations they chose and to make any arrangements they could negotiate with their employers.

These freedoms were essential to the genesis of the Industrial Revolution, and a leading reason why it happened in Britain and not elsewhere. The Holy Roman Empire, for example, however full of industrious and well-schooled German engineers, was still bedevilled by serfdom and feudal obligations in the eighteenth century because the Thirty Years' War had reimmiserated much of its populace. Consequently, German industrialization was almost entirely delayed until after 1850.

The WEF in its report exhibits attitudes about ordinary consumers that would not have been out of place in a thirteenth-century donjon. Some allowance must be made for the report having been written in June 2020, but in discussing the Covid-19 outbreak, it rejects indignantly the idea that closing down the economy might cause misery, noting smugly "Only saving lives will save livelihoods," quoting the erroneous Imperial College estimates of potential Covid-19 deaths and exhibiting an altogether uncalled-for faith in the efficacy of masks and restrictive regulations. The divergence in U.S. unemployment rates in 2021 between Republican-run states that generally reopened early and Democrat-run states that stayed locked down demonstrates that lockdowns indeed imposed additional misery and doubtless additional lives lost.

The report's contempt for the man in the street shows itself elsewhere. Consumers are "obsessive" about inflation, we were told, before we were reassured that "it is hard to imagine how inflation could pick up anytime soon." (Even in June 2020, it was not that hard to imagine; I had predicted it and outlined the mechanism of how it would take place in a *National Review* essay in April 2020.) The report also sought to establish a "global strategic framework of governance"—guess how much democratic input there will be into *that*!

The report also urged replacing GDP—the statistic that reflects the overall output of the economy—with a "doughnut" whereby the inner ring would represent what's needed to sustain the "good" life and the outer ring what the environment can support. Naturally, governments and institutions such as the WEF would determine what the "good life" consists of and precisely how much the environment could support and would engage in redistribution within the doughnut to ensure that the good life was shared by all and that the environment was protected. Individual consumers would have no say in the matter—nor would they have any right to squawk as the doughnut got thinner and thinner with all the redistribution and environmental costs until the "good life" proved to be unattainable without wiping out half the world's population.

However, the most consumer-unfriendly and freedom-killing section of the Great Reset is its glee over contract-tracing applications on cell phones, which it describes as an "unprecedented opportunity." We have already seen what this leads to in Britain, where huge numbers of the population have been forced through the government's Test and Trace software to self-isolate for a week or more, without any symptoms or other evidence that they are infected what with widespread vaccination is generally a mild or even undetectable disorder. We have also seen the Chinese "social credit" system, enabled by cell phones, that allows an authoritarian Communist state to control its people and weed out dissidents.

Since learning this, I have several times blessed the grouchy elderly Luddism that has caused me to reject getting a cell phone over the last decade. Governments armed with contact-tracing and other apps can exert unprecedented levels of control over their citizens; this will especially be the case if they succeed in abolishing cash and transferring all payments onto the ubiquitous cell phones. Each additional erosion of civil liberties will be justified using the indisputably correct reality that civil liberties can be abused by terrorists and drug lords; each such erosion of civil liberties will reduce ordinary people further into the state of their pre-1348 ancestors, only with government and technology exerting a far tighter control than was possible for the feudal baronage.

Without the precious liberties that eighteenth-century Englishmen had gained, the Industrial Revolution would have been impossible. If, through cell phones and by other means, governments come to exert much tighter social control over their citizens, innovation will be stifled and the Industrial Revolution's incomparable increase in living standards reversed.

Think, for example of the innovation of cryptocurrencies, developed by a network of private individuals, initially without coordination and without control by governments. The economic benefits of cryptocurrencies are already considerable and may expand further—there is after all more than $1 trillion of wealth tied up in them. However, it is impossible to doubt that, once governments become fully aware of—and threatened by—cryptocurrencies' success, they will seek to establish control over a potentially potent rival. Innovations, by their nature, upset the established order of things and impose costs on important existing interests; increasing the power of governments to kill them is thus fatal to their creation. Freedom is not only the most important value of a civilized society, it is essential to economic prosperity and progress.

Property Rights

Probably the most distinctive feature of British society in the century after 1660, as compared with its continental European competitors, was its intense respect for private property.

For ordinary people, private property ownership had emerged in England and much of Western Europe during the fifteenth century. In some European countries, repressive governments and increasing population after the year 1500 caused a partial reimposition of serfdom, but in England, working-class property ownership became common and was cemented in place by the reforms instituted during the Civil War and Commonwealth periods. It was additionally helpful that the parliamentary franchise qualification, set at a forty-shilling (two-pound) freehold for most constituencies in the Model Parliament of 1295, became over time less and less restrictive as the coinage was debased and New World silver flooded into Europe after 1500. By the eighteenth century, substantial numbers of skilled working men had the vote in many constituencies, which was withdrawn only when the franchise qualification was raised to ten pounds by the 1832 Reform Act.

John Locke in his 1690 *Second Treatise of Government* defined "Life, Liberty and Property" as the purposes for which free men enter into a contract of government. For the British of the eighteenth century, property rights were thus a fundamental purpose for which government existed. While those property rights were most precious to the aristocracy and the rich, they were also held dear by ordinary people. Once you had property, perhaps a house and a sum in a bank, coin, or consols (consolidated annuities, a form of government-backed security), you were no longer the slave of your employment; you could seek to better yourself and take risks without fear of destitution or the workhouse.

Since working men could take risks, they did. Most Industrial Revolution advances were brought about by skilled working men who often toiled for years outside their regular occupation before the new machine or industrial process could be perfected and ideally patented. Patents, established by the 1624 Statute of Monopolies, were a major attraction of innovation; if an invention was patented, you had a property right in its intellectual property and could demand royalties from those who copied your idea. Without the ability to patent your design, and without a large and rich entity backing you, you might end up with very little for your innovation, as did Thomas Newcomen, for example, whose 1712 atmospheric steam engine was produced only subject to the 1698 patent of Thomas Savery, a much better-connected gentleman.

Property rights were thus the key economic value of eighteenth-century Britain. With property rights, the ordinary working man was an independent agent, entering into a willing buyer/willing seller contract of employment and leaving that employment if a better opportunity arose or he wanted to try his hand at entrepreneurship. With business scales so small, there were proportionately far more entrepreneurs than in a modern society, each of them king of his own castle, ennobled by the secure property rights he possessed and knew he possessed. That security and ability to innovate on a small scale brought innumerable new developments to Britain's eighteenth-century economy and thereby the Industrial Revolution that has enriched us so much.

The Great Reset's aim for us of "You'll own nothing and you'll be happy" is the opposite of the approach that produced the Industrial Revolution. Instead of self-actuated beings, empowered to innovate and experiment by our modest possessions, we are to be comfortable serfs, without possessions but granted a pleasant, enjoyable lifestyle by our Davos overlords. This is the twelfth-century dream, reawakened for the twenty-first century; it is doubtless an enjoyable life for the masters in their castles and armor but is no life at all for the disempowered, propertyless mass of us, deprived of any ability to alter our fate. We are promised initially that we will enjoy our disempowerment, but we will find that over time, the gradual running down of the world economy takes away our toys one by one, making our lives less and less comfortable and not at all enjoyable.

A world without property has the incentive structure of the old Soviet Union, initially minus the gulags. Ordinary people are wage slaves, unable to attempt anything new or even take a sabbatical year to work on a favorite project because they own nothing and must work at a salaried job (or draw welfare) to support themselves. Essentially, their position is that of the mediaeval serfs, tied to their occupation by economic necessity just as those serfs were by their feudal obligations.

Shareholder Capitalism

Another key driver of the Industrial Revolution was shareholder capitalism. There were few public companies, and the South Sea Bubble of 1720 had deterred retail investors from investing in them. The most prominent of them, the East India Company, was described by Adam Smith as a "nuisance in every respect." It was corrupt, bureaucratic, and at the time Smith wrote, had just through incompetence in performance of its administrative duties brought on the Bengal Famine of 1770, one of the worst in India's history. Public companies with broad shareholdings played no significant role in the Industrial Revolution until the advent of the railways half a century later.

There was, however, another form of shareholder capitalism, central to the Industrial Revolution, ignored by the designers of the Great Reset and far more important to our future than the overstuffed behemoths of the S&P 500. This was the free association of small pools of capital in small businesses. Normally, when an individual entrepreneur developed a new industrial technique, he had insufficient capital to deploy it, so he assembled a small group of partners to produce the capital required. Since the partners formed a small group, they were not subject to influence by government or outside bodies, beyond adherence to the minimal regulations of the time. Likewise, the banking system consisted of small units whose partners made decisions based on their own views and interests.

The small-scale shareholder capitalism of the Industrial Revolution put shareholder interests first, not because of any economic theory but because the people that ran the companies and banks were themselves proportionately major shareholders of the institutions concerned. Furthermore, most country banks and embryonic industrial companies had to put shareholder returns first to survive; there was no spare cash available for quixotic social or environmental goals, and any investments or loans made for idiosyncratic nonmarket purposes were a danger to the institution's survival. The capitalism of the early Industrial Revolution was pluralist capitalism in its purest form, with no admixture of socialism, corporatism, syndicalism, or any other noncapitalist nostrum.

The "capitalism" envisaged by the Great Reset has little in common with the pure capitalism that gave the world the Industrial Revolution. It is a capitalism of large organizations, whose chiefs can be gathered together annually at Davos to be lectured about that year's social goals. It is a capitalism guided by the luxury of "ESG" principles, where shareholders' interests are subordinated to those of others, as determined by a Davos nomenklatura.

You can just imagine what would have happened if ESG principles had been in force at the time of the Industrial Revolution. Steam engines were filthy, filling large areas around them with smog and particulates. In addition, if the science had existed at that time, environmental scientists could have determined that the sulfates emitted by coal burning were a potentially major source of "global cooling,"[14] at a time when global temperatures were close to the Maunder Minimum,[15]

---

14 The IPCC's *Climate Change—the Physical Science Basis* (August 2021) shows sulfate cooling as nearly as important as carbon dioxide warming over the last 150 years (Summary for Policymakers, p 8.)

15 The Maunder Minimum was the period of 1645–1715, when sunspot activity was exceptionally low. It coincided with the peak of the Little Ice Age, during which global mean temperatures were significantly lower than before or since.

then a far greater threat than "global warming" since it could have devastated the productivity of global agriculture, causing millions to starve. Armed with that science, Thomas Malthus, writing in 1798, could have predicted that the adoption of steam power would bring his overpopulation doom significantly closer, and therefore should be resisted, even at the cost of missing out on industrialization.

Such a view would have been the maunderings of an obscure if brilliant cleric, unless the WEF's preferred political structure of a central, all-wise forum ruling all economic decisions had been in place. In that case, with Malthus part of the Davoisie, or an adviser to it, the steam engine would have been banned, the Industrial Revolution would have been stopped in its tracks and, since Britain's population was already expanding at an unprecedented rate, Malthus's doom of excess population and mass starvation would have taken place in all of Britain, as it did in nonindustrializing Ireland fifty years later.

This fable illustrates the problem with the WEF's centralized decision-making, especially when noneconomic factors become a major part of the equation. Elite consensus, reached for noneconomic reasons, overrides the dictates of the atomized free market and skews the economy in a suboptimal direction that may well, as in this hypothetical case, produce downside outcomes far worse than the problems the elite had attempted to avoid (even had they been real, which "global cooling" was not).

Small-scale Localism

The capitalism of the Industrial Revolution was notably local. With new companies small and banking atomized, there was little pull towards the big cities. The Whig supremacy one-party rule of 1714–1760 had been concentrated in the Whig stronghold of London, with most opportunities in the centralized financial sector of London itself; the plundering empire run from London by the East India Company (the collapse of the Mughal dynasty after 1737 brought unprecedented commercial opportunities to that company and its officers) as well as in the slave colonies of the Americas. The Whigs had little political strength in the provinces (other than "rotten boroughs" available for cash) and little interest in what went on there.

When party dominance changed with George III's accession in 1760, political power devolved to the Tory small towns and rural areas. This coincided with a doubling in patent applications in the 1760s from the previous decade, and the emergence of numerous wealthy provincial industrialists, notably Josiah Wedgwood (pottery), Richard Arkwright (textiles), John Wilkinson, and John Roebuck (iron manufacturers) and Matthew Boulton (metal goods and eventually steam engines). With new enterprises and sources of finance spread around Britain, myriad approaches to problems could be tried and solutions applied on a small scale to different sectors. The result was an unprecedented effervescence of innovation, which over time led to unprecedentedly rapid growth. (Mathematically, the second and third derivatives of output turned up around 1760, but this did not lead to a marked acceleration in output itself until later.)

The localist approach was not inevitable; even in the seventeenth century, Louis XIV's France showed the attraction to monarchs and the defects for the populace of centralized state-directed enterprise. It produced magnificent feats of engineering such as the Machine de Marly, a gigantic hydraulic system completed in 1684 consisting of fourteen water wheels, each thirty-eight feet in diameter, which powered more than two hundred and fifty pumps to bring water five hundred feet up a hillside from the River Seine to the Louveciennes Aqueduct. Considered the most complex machine of the seventeenth century, the Machine de Marly took three years to build for the purpose of supplying the ornamental fountains at Versailles, which used more water than the city of Paris. No useful industrial development resulted from this magnificent contraption, although its frequent breakdowns employed a staff of sixty to keep it running for over 130 years.

The Great Reset and the Soviet-style globalist project in general operate under Louis XIV's approach. The economy is assumed to operate globally, with major decisions made in a few gigantic global cities by those with the education and connections to form part of the top-level global consensus. This was also the view taken by the Whigs in 1714–1760 (Benjamin Disraeli christened them the "Venetian Oligarchy"), which resulted in an almost fifty-year hiatus in the process of industrialization.

Consider, for example, that Thomas Newcomen's steam engine, invented in 1712, was still state of the art in this crucial technology until James Watt invented the condenser around 1769 and that Newcomen engines were still being installed in numbers in the 1790s. Only when the Tories returned to power in 1760 were outsiders like Charles Jenkinson, from a modest Oxfordshire gentry family, included in the upper levels of government. Even fifty years later, it was the Whig leader Earl Grey who remarked of George Canning "the son of an actress is, ipso facto, disqualified from becoming Prime Minister."

Even if the incentive structures of the supranational elites and multinational CEOs were optimal, which they are not, the limitation of major decisions to only a few people and places is impossibly constricting. It constrains any advances that are considered, over time slowing global productivity growth to zero or even negative, as inefficiencies proliferate more rapidly than innovations. By concentrating the world's best human resources in a few locations, ensuring through their education that they all have a similar approach to problems, and directing them centrally in ways that prevent market solutions from appearing, the WEF approach makes the same mistake as the old Soviet Union, stifling small-scale innovation and diversity and ensuring that the inevitable mistakes become gigantic ones.

The WEF and its supporters further ensure that dissenting voices among their councils are minimized by dominating the admissions staff at the top colleges, delegitimizing objective tests of merit such as the SAT and instead requiring endless application essays to prove that candidates are suitably infected by the dominant "woke" outlook on life. The WEF's addiction to the "woke" aristocracy has the same effect as the Whig supremacy's addiction to the Whig aristocracy: it unacceptably narrows both the talent pool and the potential for disruptive or unconventional ideas to be considered properly.

Free Use of Natural Resources

The makers of the Industrial Revolution were aware of resource and environmental problems, to which they were alerted by market signals. The most important example of this was the move to increased use of coal.

Traditionally, wood had been the principal fuel used for domestic heating and cooking, the principal energy source (as charcoal) for producing iron, and the principal material used for both furniture and shipbuilding. With England having only a modest surface area, much of which was cleared and used for agriculture, it was inevitable that limitations in the wood supply would appear, indicated by price.

The first resource scarcity was for the brush and waste wood "coppicing"[16] used for heating and cooking in London, the population of which increased from fifty thousand to two hundred fifty thousand over the sixteenth century. Since road transportation of bulky items such as wood was expensive, the coppices within a day's journey of London became denuded. The solution, from about 1560, was to burn coal, which could be imported by sea, from the region around Newcastle where surface coal deposits near rivers were commonplace. Burning coal required reconstructing houses to install new chimneys and produced major changes in English cooking techniques, but by 1700, most Londoners and citizens of some provincial towns (with nearby coal deposits) used coal for heating and cooking.

The shortage of wood also manifested in the iron industry, while the increased domestic use of coal expanded the coal industry, making coal products competitive for iron-making once the necessary techniques had been discovered. Abraham Darby first produced pig iron from coke (a coal derivative) around 1709, and further refinements of

16 Cutting trees off at the stump to encourage new growth and regeneration.

the technique caused coal to be generally used for iron manufacture by around 1760, making iron considerably cheaper and more plentiful. Since increased coal production required deeper mines, which flooded, Newcomen's steam engine, itself fueled by coal, was produced from 1712 to pump water from mines.

The makers of the Industrial Revolution took an environmental/resources problem—the increasing shortage of wood—and solved it through technological innovation, increasing the productivity of industry by doing so. They were, however, motivated by the price mechanism, Adam Smith's "invisible hand"; there was no central authority directing them to make the revolutionary changes they made. The adoption of coal in domestic use and industry was the result of a few technological advances, followed by millions of individual decisions, each motivated by its own benefit, with no government constraints.

In today's world, once the world's climate scientists had determined that anthropogenic climate change through industrial use of carbon was a major global problem, the world's governments could have enlisted the price mechanism to find solutions to that problem via a carbon tax. The level of such a tax could have been adjusted up or down according to the urgency of the need, and over time, just as price signals aligned coal usage and the Industrial Revolution through capitalists' ingenuity, a carbon tax would likewise through industrial and entrepreneurial ingenuity have reduced global carbon usage to the extent necessary.

Instead, the WEF has proclaimed a target of net-zero carbon emissions by 2050, encouraging countries to write that target into law. That places an enormous burden on those countries' consumers, who will be forced to adopt uneconomic technologies that cannot do the job, with no account taken of the economic cost of adopting those technologies to present realities. That approach is the equivalent of banning steam engines in the 1790s; it places the artificial and unnecessary goal of net-zero carbon emissions in a relatively short time above all other considerations. Once again, a centralized government, with its politically committed "experts," is setting the conditions under which ordinary people are permitted to live. Central planning is the opposite of the free-market, hands-off approach that brought such progress 250 years ago; it inevitably will lead to the economic decay experienced by the Soviet system in its last decrepit years.

Sound Money

The WEF manifesto began by asserting that pandemics, unlike financial crises, trigger lower interest rates. It then detailed a long list of actions that governments must take with the money that they will save through lower interest rates.

This was not the approach taken during the Industrial Revolution. In the sixteenth century, successive governments, notably that of Henry VIII, had attempted to increase revenue by debasing the coinage, but after the Restoration, they realized that coinage debasement damaged trade and reduced confidence in the government. Consequently, from 1662, Charles II's government produced a silver coinage with a milled edge that could not be clipped by users without the damage being immediately apparent. A further recoinage in 1696, led by Isaac Newton as warden of the mint, increased the supply of domestic coinage and stabilized its value. Then in 1717, Newton put Britain on a bimetallic gold/silver standard that, as silver prices rose during the eighteenth century, became the first gold standard. This was abandoned in 1797, during the lengthy Revolutionary/Napoleonic Wars with France, but was restored by Lord Liverpool's government in 1819.

From 1717, therefore, Britain had a sound money of unquestioned value, which unlike other countries' currencies, was not subject to debasement. The adverse hyperinflationary experience of the newly independent American colonies with "continentals" in 1776–1781 and of the French Republic with "assignats" in 1792–1796, together with similar if milder such experiences in other countries such as Austria in 1759–1811, convinced British policy-makers that a state-issued paper money led inevitably to dangerous inflation. Thus in 1797–1819, when

Britain was off the gold standard, it relied for currency on banknotes issued by the Bank of England and other private banks (of which there was a large and highly competitive number).

The result was two centuries of price stability, from 1717 to 1914, with the near doubling of prices during the Napoleonic Wars reversed during the first decade after peace came. Savers were assured of a positive real return on their money through the large pool of government-issued debt, which became the famous "3 percent consols" in 1757. Consols fluctuated in price according to supply and demand, with wartime exigencies causing them to trade at 50–60 percent of par, but over the long term, they provided savers with a store of value on which they could depend. The Industrial Revolution relied for its short-term finance on the country banking system, but its long-term needs were mostly financed out of enterprises' retained earnings, built up and maintained through consols holdings. The government's highly favorable attitude to savings, manifested in legislation such as the Savings Bank Act of 1817, reassured savers that their modest wealth would be protected and nurtured.

Only after the advent of the railways, with their much larger financing needs, did a long-term private sector bond market emerge; its development was assisted by the fact that after the defeat of Napoleon in 1815, the government's demands on the bond markets were minimal, as the country, after balancing its budget in 1818, enjoyed a century of predominant peace with only modest interruptions.

The Great Reset's attitude to savings is the opposite of that manifested by eighteenth-century century British governments. It takes the Keynesian view, averring that the high savings rate induced by the pandemic will prevent a return to normal, and that economic recovery will not begin until a reliable vaccine has been found. Here, it proved to be in error; the U.S. National Bureau of Economic Research announced on July 19, 2021, that the 2020 recession had lasted only two months, the shortest on record, and that recovery had begun at a record pace in the third quarter of 2020, well before vaccines were available.

The Great Reset also supposes that the "artificial barrier between governments and central banks has been dismantled" so that central banks can finance government deficits ad infinitum, holding interest rates far below the level of inflation to do so. This policy damages savers in three ways and leads to unsound money. First, the ultralow interest rates prevent savers from receiving a positive real return on their savings without taking risks that create destructive bubbles. Second, central banks printing money allows governments to run larger budget deficits than they otherwise would, sucking resources out of the private sector. Third, central bank money-printing on the scale of 2020–2021 creates inflation, damaging savers' interests still further and distorting price signals in the investment market, forcing investment into unproductive sectors such as gold, commodities, and excess housing and away from productive enterprise.

The approach of the WEF is thus the opposite of that taken by the policy-makers of the British eighteenth century and will tend to destroy industrial creation rather than enhancing it. But does the WEF care about industrial creation?

Independent and Competitive Banking System

England's banking system during the Industrial Revolution was remarkably open and competitive. The market speculation over the 1689–1720 period, as the national debt built up in ways very lucrative for the Whig-allied promoters, had concentrated the financial system on securities dealers in London. However, after 1750, as no more "bubbles" occurred and interest rates had stabilized at around 3 percent, numerous "country banks" appeared based in provincial cities. By the time of the Bank of England Act of 1708, no bank, other than the Bank of England itself, could have public stockholders or more than six partners. The result was a proliferation of small banks, with six or fewer partners and no more than one or two branches. By 1790, there were more than three hundred such banks, and by 1813 at the peak, more than eight hundred.

These "country banks" were located in every town of any significance; their partners were local attorneys, traders, and businessmen. Consequently, there was no centralization of capital availability. Instead, debt was available locally, from people whose wealth and social class were not out of touch with the entrepreneurs themselves. These banks financed primarily trade, but also the small-scale infrastructure projects, such as canals, that resulted from economic growth; as industrial companies arose, they financed their short-term capital needs for receivables and inventory, and indirectly brokered some of their long-term capital needs.

Thus, there was neither government control, nor the insidious control by fashionable ideas such as ESG, by which entrepreneurs obtained funding—the country banks were not fashionable, and any entrepreneur had a choice of several country banks available within a day's ride on horseback. This atomization of credit thus atomized the capital market for small business. For example, Richard Arkwright, later the inventor of the spinning frame, whose previous trade had been as a barber, got early funding for his textile operation from Wright's Bank of Nottingham; his company grew into a large and technologically innovative operation, and Sir Richard, "the father of the modern factory system," died a very wealthy man.

Given the small-scale needs of early industry, before the coming of the more capital-intensive railroads, the English financial system of 1760–1826 proved ideal to finance it. Later, during the Victorian period, legislative and economic changes promoted bank consolidation, but by that stage, industrialization was already in full swing.

The Great Reset promotes the opposite of such a system. It advocates that governments should prevent banks from incentivizing consumer debt, thus as in other areas suggesting that the WEF's wishes rather than disparate, atomized market forces should determine the availability of finance. Indeed, the WEF itself is a pillar of a centralized system of remote megabanks; the numerous country bankers of eighteenth-century England could not have afforded to attend the luxurious Davos meetings and, were they to attend, they would require extra tarmacs, heliports, and a football stadium to accommodate them. Davos's ideal of a central cadre of superior intellects determining capital allocation is the fallacy of the defunct Soviet Union's Gosplan; it did not work then, it will not work now, and it is the exact opposite of a well-designed financial system, as England achieved somewhat by accident in the late eighteenth century.

Suppressing Market Bubbles

Post-Restoration Britain suffered two market bubbles, for debt finance in the 1690s and in the stock and government finance markets in 1720, both of which were encouraged and exacerbated by misguided government policy. However, under the financially prudent administration of Sir Robert Walpole (1721–1742), the country learned to avoid such bubbles, and the next general bubble was not until 1825 and dealt with capably by Lord Liverpool as prime minister.

In the 1690s, William III and his favored Whig governments involved Britain in near perpetual European wars, well before the country had a long-term debt market. The Whigs solved the immediate budget problem by imposing a massive land tax in 1693 that fell mostly on the Tory rural gentry to increase government revenues. The Whigs, through their political allies in the City of London's embryonic financial community, then issued not longer-term debt but a succession of lotteries, tontines,[17] and annuities that were impossible to value with the financial technology of that time and were thus marketed to mostly "inside" investors at prices that gave them an exorbitant rate of return. A further wrinkle was the invention of special purpose acquisition companies (SPACs), through which debt could be issued indirectly, with insiders taking an additional markup; the first such SPAC

17 An annuity that pays out to the survivors of a group of subscribers, ending with the entire annuity payable to the last "life"—it gave incentives for causing "unexplained deaths" of one's fellow subscribers.

was the Bank of England, but there was a succession of others culminating in the 1711 South Sea Company.

Having cemented their one-party rule after 1714 by the intervention of the Hanoverian monarchs George I and George II, the Whigs then engineered a further spectacular bubble by inducing the South Sea Company to make exchange offers for most of the outstanding government debt (much of which, being annuities and tontines, was still impossible to price accurately) but without specifying at what price South Sea Company shares would be exchanged for debt. The result was an orgy of highly profitable bribery and speculation and a massive run-up in share prices of South Sea and other companies, followed by a gigantic crash. Walpole engineered a partial bailout of the innumerable investors who had been caught up in the South Sea speculation, thus avoiding the destruction of middle-class savings that took place in France with the simultaneous collapse of the Mississippi Scheme.[18] However, he then pursued a foreign and financial policy that avoided the creation of further bubbles.

Since the Industrial Revolution required long-term, illiquid investment that would achieve returns only once new technologies had been adopted and perfected, diversion of the country's capital into short-term bubbles and their bailouts would have seriously retarded its progress. The lessons learned from 1720 were thus highly beneficial.

By its encouragement of stimulative monetary policy, the Great Reset foments bubbles. It also encourages bailouts, for example by claiming that in the recovery from Covid-19, "systematically important" property developers will need to be bailed out by governments. Since of all the sectors encouraged by twenty-five years of artificially stimulative monetary policy, real estate is the least economically productive, makes the least contribution to greater welfare and employment, and produces the most egregious leveraged and undeserved

---

[18] A speculative property bubble that nearly sank the French economy in the early eighteenth century.

fortunes, the notion of bailing the sector out when the market finally turns is utterly morally abhorrent.

Lord Liverpool, the most economically sophisticated of all Britain's prime ministers, recognized a bubble in progress in March 1825 and made a House of Lords speech specifically to negate the possibility of bailouts:

> I wish it, however, to be clearly understood, that those persons who now engage in Joint-Stock Companies, or other enterprises, enter on these speculations at their peril and risk. I think it my duty to declare, that I never will advise the introduction of any bill for their relief; on the contrary, if such a measure is proposed, I will oppose it, and I hope that parliament will resist any measure of the kind. I think that this determination cannot be too well understood at the present moment, nor made too publicly known.

The Davos approach, and that of modern statesmen, is too often the opposite of Lord Liverpool's; when a bubble bursts, they bow to the demands of vested interests and arrange gigantic bailouts at taxpayers' expense. Like other modern practices, this is highly economically damaging; it is also contrary to the sound approach of the Industrial Revolution era.

Balanced Budgets and Fiscal Prudence

The period immediately following the Restoration saw an immense improvement in both real-estate markets and government revenues through the Convention Parliament's passage of the Tenures Abolition Act in 1660. This eliminated many feudal dues and service obligations that had been due to the Crown, as well as the feudal restrictions on landholding, making land an asset that could be freely bought, sold, and mortgaged. It thereby freed up enormous amounts of capital that could be used to finance industrialization. By creating a free market in land, it gave Britain an advantage that France, Spain, and the Holy Roman Empire all lacked, even a century later. To replace royal revenues from eliminated feudal dues, Section 14 of this Act also imposed an excise duty on tea, coffee, sherbet, and chocolate.

By shifting state revenues to these new sources, the Act performed a vital service for the country's fiscal future. Instead of being fixed—as were previous taxes—customs and excise duties on these newly consumed products (as well as on tobacco and sugar produced in Britain's American and West Indian colonies) swelled with the increase in national wealth, trade, "luxury," and consumption of these expensive imported goods. These new revenues formed the basis of Britain's taxation system until the 1840s; by 1792, customs and excise duties were producing 69 percent of Britain's revenue of £18.7 million, itself some fifteen times the revenue in 1661 (in pounds whose value had changed little). The burden of this new system fell primarily on the luxury-consuming wealthier classes; the revenues it produced were naturally buoyant as wealth and trade increased.

The Restoration fiscal reforms, after hiccups during the Anglo-Dutch Wars, stabilized the financial system until 1688. Then the almost continuous wars of 1689–1713 and the intermittent warfare after 1739 required the establishment of a long-term government debt system, as described above. Walpole, presiding over eighteen years of peace after 1721, not only brought down debt and interest rates and stabilized the capital markets, he also instituted a sinking fund, by which the debt was supposed to be redeemed. From his time, the government generally ran a surplus in peacetime, although the frequent wars caused debt to increase to a maximum of 250 percent of GDP by 1819. However, the superior serviceability of Britain's economy and fiscal system was demonstrated during the Hundred Days of Napoleon's return from exile in Elba in 1815, when Britain was able to raise £27 million by a single bond issue four days before Waterloo, approximately forty times the funds that Napoleon had been able to gather together from France.

Following the Napoleonic Wars, Lord Liverpool was faced with a gigantic public debt and budget expenditure that greatly exceeded income. The French economist Jean-Baptiste Say, writing in late 1814, believed that Britain's debt obligations were so great that the country would be unable to export since the taxes needed to service the debt would make its labor hopelessly uncompetitive against European competitors. Lord Liverpool's solution was twofold. He cut public spending (other than debt service) by 69 percent in the three years between 1814 and 1817, pulling the budget back into balance in 1818. Then, instead of inflating Britain's way out of trouble through the "repression" of low interest rates and high inflation, he went the other way, putting Britain back onto the gold standard in 1821, thereby bringing about a 40 percent price deflation.

This made the "real" debt burden even greater, but it made London the unquestioned entrepôt of commerce and finance, its currency universally used for bankrolling transactions, bringing incalculable long-term economic benefits. The increasing prosperity of the Victorian years after Liverpool's death was unquestioned, but it was based on the foundation he had built—for example, the debt-to-GDP ratio, about 250 percent in 1819, was down to around 120 percent by the time Gladstone became chancellor of the exchequer in 1853.

The Great Reset proposes endless schemes of further public spending, on greater social assistance, greater security of employment, and more sick leave, for example, while assuming that governments and central banks will continue their policies of ultralow interest rates and gigantic budget deficits. This is the opposite of the policies Britain followed during the Industrial Revolution, even in the exceptionally difficult years after the Napoleonic Wars. Again, following the opposite policies to industrializing Britain is likely to produce the opposite effect.

Resistance to Luddism

The first significant outbreak of machine breaking in Britain occurred in 1779, in the early stages of the adoption of water-powered machinery in the textile sector, which threatened traditional "cottage" textile operations such as stocking making. One minor manifestation was the breaking of two stocking frames near Leicester by one Ned Ludd, but this was only a small part of a substantial outbreak that included the destruction of one of Arkwright's mills in Birkacre, Lancashire.

The authorities suppressed the disturbances on public-order grounds, but they were succeeded by further disturbances over the next four decades, particularly in the economically difficult decade of the 1790s. The final and most serious outbreak came in 1812, after Napoleon's Milan Decree[19] had cut off most of Britain's export markets, throwing many textile operatives out of work, while an exceptionally poor harvest in 1811 had raised the price of grain to punishing levels.

Lord Liverpool, as leader of the House of Lords in Prime Minister Spencer Perceval's government, proposed and passed the Frame-Breaking Act, by which the death penalty was introduced for destroying industrial machinery such as stocking frames. Nobody was executed under the specific provisions of that Act (which expired automatically two years later), but it acted as an effective deterrent to machine-breaking activity, which died down thereafter.

Lord Liverpool and his colleagues knew that the labor-saving machinery of the Industrial Revolution was improving living standards rapidly, even though some traditional workers, such as framework knitters, handloom weavers, and "croppers" were made redundant by the innovations. Since those groups comprised more than one hundred thousand workers, the social disruption and hardship were, however, considerable. Thus, machine destruction had to be stopped, for the long-term good of all. This attitude was not inevitable—Catherine the Great, for example, in her 1767 "*Nakaz*," decreed that "no machines

---

[19] The Milan Decree, issued on 17 December, 1807, was an attempt to defeat Britain by economic warfare, cutting off its trade with the Continent.

should ever be introduced into Russia, because they may result in a reduction in the number of working people."

By combating climate change, the Great Reset seeks to make obsolete—not machinery that has become outdated and uneconomic—but industrial processes that are essential to the world economy, notably in the energy sector. It would be possible to replace these through the price mechanism, perhaps by use of a carbon tax, but the WEF does not do this, preferring instead to replace productive activities through government diktat. By this means, it is not fighting Luddism, as was done during the Industrial Revolution, but creating it as an instrument of government policy. This is highly damaging to the economy, as has been seen in Germany, for example, where unreliable wind and solar energy have made the country's much-admired steel industry economically unsustainable. Government Luddism is yet another headwind to economic progress, reinforcing the tendency towards an Anti-Industrial Revolution.

Conclusion

I have described above the policies Britain followed during the century that produced the Industrial Revolution. In all these areas the Great Reset proposes policies opposite to those Britain then followed. Perhaps this is unsurprising; whereas Britain's eighteenth-century policies represented the escape from feudalism, the WEF's structure of elite leaders gathering in an immensely exclusive Swiss resort each year to confer without participation of the hoi polloi, inevitably produces neofeudal attitudes. Given that antithesis, one can only believe that the result of the WEF's policies also would be the opposite of that achieved by eighteenth-century Britain: in other words, an Anti-Industrial Revolution.

By the term Anti-Industrial Revolution, I do not suggest that the WEF's policies will cause mankind to uninvent the steam engine—it will simply ban the steam engine owing to its excessive use of coal, one of the world's most carbon-emitting fuels. In area after area, the direction for mankind will be determined—not by the exploitation of glorious scientific advances through the free market—but by dictation from bureaucrats, whose imaginations stretch only to the technologies and processes that already exist.

By these means, productivity growth, which has already been declining worldwide since the imposition of major environmental controls in the 1970s, will fall to a negative level (which it almost reached in rich countries in the decade after 2008) and will remain there indefinitely. Humanity's life experience, which has been improving beyond all imagination in the two and a half centuries since the Industrial Revolution, will begin to decline and will continue doing so as long as Great Reset policies are in effect. The Anti-Industrial Revolution will thereby slowly, but inexorably, destroy our civilization.

THE GREAT RESET AND "STAKEHOLDERISM"

BY ALBERTO MINGARDI

Politics has always oscillated between Right and Left. After World War II, Western countries took many a step toward interventionism, regardless of warnings by a handful of intellectuals such as Friedrich Hayek and Michael Oakeshott. If the West went down the "road to serfdom," that serfdom was bureaucratic, benevolent in its aims and generous with many. Yet in a few years, the consensus for growing interventionism was eroded, leading to the elections of Margaret Thatcher and Ronald Reagan. In recent years, at least since the financial crisis of 2007–2008, politics have moved in the opposite direction, aiming to put an end to whatever "neoliberal policies" (as they came to be known in the public debate) a country ever pursued.

Yet with the Covid-19 pandemic, this process accelerated. Rahm Emanuel's advice regarding the usefulness of a good crisis had a profound impact on the Western ruling classes: in the U.S. (where unprecedented and previously unimaginable levels of public spending have been reached), in the European Union (where the alleged need for stimulus policies allowed for the first-ever emission of common debt), in the Western hemisphere (where Covid-19 inspired unimaginable restrictions on the freedom of movement of the citizens). Hence, right from its beginning, the Covid-19 pandemic has been considered something more and different than simply a health crisis, however profound and indeed dramatic it's been. In the pandemic, governments found (and, perhaps, searched for) an opportunity to address other problems. The pandemic was soon compared to a war and it was assumed that after it, like after war, we should "rebuild." But "rebuild differently."

How differently? Intellectuals and experts soon realized that it was their business to answer the question. Though the world in 2019 could hardly be seen as a laissez-faire paradise, a common cry has been a call for different institutions to plan, more solidly, from the *top down*. Technological transitions of the sort that are now typically advocated for (from the "green" economy to central bank digital currencies) indeed presuppose experts picking a technology. Yet the prevailing view seems not to be content with only industrial policies. The very nature of the economic system should change, moving from "shareholder" to "stakeholder" capitalism.

One element that differentiates this approach from previous waves of interventionism is that it goes hand in hand with a genuine revision of the political vocabulary. Think of the very locution "the Great Reset," which acquired currency thanks to Professor Klaus Schwab, the influential founder and president of the WEF. The very use of those words implied (a) that the world needed a rebooting after the pandemic; (b) that such a rebooting could be done; and (c) that it could come about thanks to a specific set of policies. The discussion over these two terms includes a considerable toying with words.

The Great Reset and the Stakeholder Model

Professor Klaus Schwab is a German-born economist that most people know as a highly successful entrepreneur: he is the founder and president of the WEF, a not-for-profit foundation headquartered in Geneva, Switzerland. The WEF is most famous for its conferences, beginning with its annual Davos meeting, where business and political leaders reconvene to enjoy the company of some public intellectuals and ponder the world's future. The WEF success put Davos on the map, and made the village—ten thousand in population, in the Swiss canton of Graubünden—a household name. In 2004, Samuel P. Huntington christened the participants "Davos men…a (then) new global elite…empowered by new notions of global connectedness." They "have little need for national loyalty, view national boundaries as obstacles that thankfully are vanishing, and see national governments as residues from the past whose only useful function is to facilitate the elite's global operations."

In media accounts and in public perception, "Davos men" were at times seen as advocates of neo-liberalism, of globalization, of unfettered competition. This was a common misconception: equating the interest of companies and its moneyed classes with deregulation and competition, which most of the time, they dread. In one way, this was also quite naïve, even disingenuous: "crony capitalism," meaning a system in which private companies and the government collude, is the greenhouse of the global elites. In fact, the spirit of the Davos meeting was always to bring all "stakeholders" around the table.

In *Stakeholder Capitalism: A Global Economy that Works for Progress, People and the Planet* (written with Peter Vanham), Schwab, who coined the locution "the Great Reset," suggested that we should "use the post-Covid-19 recovery to enact stakeholder capitalism at home, and a more sustainable goal economic system all around the world." Why? And, in particular, *why now*? One would expect the aftermath of Covid-19 to see us all busy in getting back to what used to be "normalcy." The time for reform should come later, not now.

The idea of "stakeholderism" isn't new. Schwab himself has been advocating some version of it since the 1970s and is happy to provide an account of his own intellectual enterprise as a struggle against Milton Friedman. An important body of literature grew up around the theme, particularly in the field of business economics and corporate governance.

Why should stakeholder capitalism be important in the wake of the pandemic? Why should we all go for it, particularly now? Why has the discussion about it moved out of the circles of experts, to include wider sections of society?

In part, these discussions were rejuvenated by the anniversary of an article published by Milton Friedman in the *New York Times Magazine*. Fifty years later, in the midst of a pandemic that saw an enormous growth of public spending, Friedman's piece seemed the ideal starting point to launch a discussion regarding the future of business in the world's economies. But this would have been a more academic, less heated discussion. Instead, important public figures like Schwab emerged to say that "free markets, trade, and competition create so much wealth that in theory they could make everyone better off…But this is not the reality we're living in today."

Schwab is a capable intellectual entrepreneur and a sharp mind. If he believes that "there are reasons to believe a more inclusive and virtuous economic system is possible—and it could be just around the corner," this means that for him, the rethinking of the capitalist system is not necessarily more urgent because of the pandemic crisis, but such "reimagining" becomes easier, more within reach thanks to the growing role that governments have taken on during the lockdowns and other "emergency" measures. In other words, let's not let a good crisis go to waste.

Other commentators are equally strategic or more ideologically committed. Many argued that the pandemic should be considered a wake-up call for rethinking the capitalist system, traveling further on the way toward economic interventionism. This proposition can be seen in two different ways. On its face, the argument seems to have little merit. Epidemics and diseases always have been a feature of human social life, regardless of the economic system then in place. The plague of Athens killed one-quarter of the population even if "capitalist" is hardly an accurate description of the ancient Greek economy. The Black Death in the fourteenth century ravaged Europe even though the industrial revolution was yet to come.

The specific circumstances of Covid-19 can, however, be traced back to some *successes* of modern capitalism: growing urbanization and more affordable and thus more widely experienced international travel, which accelerated the spread of the disease. Developed countries were therefore at risk of being plagued with a pandemic as a result of trade and movement of people, as happened with Covid-19 coming from China to Italy and then beyond. As a matter of fact, viruses (like humans) have always traveled, albeit never quite as easily as today. The pandemic's death toll was particularly high in countries that experienced an otherwise happy byproduct of the modern economy: an aging population, which happened to be more susceptible to this particular virus.

Of course every coin has two sides, as we knew even before Covid-19. By increasing life expectancy, capitalist economies have caused an increase in the population that, as it ages, is more liable to fall ill with chronic degenerative diseases (cardiovascular, oncological, and metabolic diseases in particular). Universal health care systems, which are financially sustainable only in rich capitalist economies, are currently geared to cope with conventional diseases than with the rapid outburst of an epidemic.

The circumstances of the Covid-19 pandemic were instead interpreted by many as if Sars-Cov-2 is "a virus of globalization." In times of crisis, millenarianism is always popular, so the pandemic was seen as a revenge by a Mother Nature long exploited by humans and, thus, by capitalism. This resonated quite well with environmentalism, which has become a hegemonic force in politics.

In addition, the pandemic stress strengthened a "we're all in this together" mindset; it was interpreted by many as implying that whatever solution could be found would come out of a collective and dirigiste framework. This notion brought many to look to government with hope, as the resource of economic relief much needed after prolonged government-mandate shutdowns—precisely as it was intended to do. After all, Schwab argues, Covid-19 and migrations remind us of our shared "interconnectedness." So, although vague at best, appeals for the reform of the capitalist system happened to be attractive and entered the public debate.

Yet one should ask how well capitalism actually performed, insofar as human welfare is concerned. In the course of the twentieth century, human ecosystems more economically (and hence scientifically) developed have seen a decline of infectious diseases, with the attendant lengthening of life expectancy. During the last thirty years, worldwide communicable diseases have gone from being the cause from one-third of deaths to one-sixth. At the same time, the overall deaths from noncommunicable diseases have grown from 65 percent to 73 percent: two-thirds to three-fourths. These changes have been precisely the consequence of improvements in general hygiene, vaccinations, and pharmacological treatments made possible by the greater wealth generated by "capitalism."

Also, so-called degrowth (moving away from the capitalist growth paradigm) does not appear a promising candidate to bring about an improvement in human ecology. Typically, in productive areas where economic growth is uncertain or waning, with more unemployment and lower incomes, infectious agents circulate more easily because of lifestyles or conditions of life that are more at risk. The matter is serious, as economic crises can induce behaviors or create contexts conducive to the reemergence of infections: for example, inappropriate use of antibiotic treatments or self-harming practices (drug use or unprotected sex) that favor the transmission of infectious of infectious agents.

Yet these points seldom entered in the discussion. The demand for reforming the capitalist system increased with the pandemic. It fit a *narrative* more than a set of evidence, however questionable. It is this narrative that we shall now examine.

Return to Corporatism

Klaus Schwab has long advocated a "stakeholder model of management." He insists that a company must serve not only shareholders—that is: not only its *owners*—but all stakeholders to achieve long-term growth and prosperity. Stakeholders include the employees, but also the local authorities, suppliers, and so forth: "all those who have a stake in the economy."

Stakeholder management capitalism is at the center of a wide literature in corporate governance, not necessarily with political overtones. It is sometimes equated with so-called Rhineland capitalism. The term refers to a number of features of the business sector as it structured itself in Germany in the second half of the twentieth century. Schwab himself has referred to the Ravensburg company of his childhood as "embracing the stakeholder mindset"; at his father's factory, "everyone, from the shop floor to the corner office, had the same drive to make the company and its products a long-term success." Though Schwab has acknowledged that this may have had to do with the cultural climate of the immediate aftermath of World War II and the widely felt urge to rebuild the country, he clearly considers this mindset to relate more to the stakeholder model than with the historical circumstances.

In this "model," as it came to life in Germany, businesses finance themselves mainly through banks, instead of the stock market; businesses tend to organize themselves in federations of enterprises and join chambers of commerce; collective agreements govern the labour market; there are often overlapping company shareholdings; bigger companies need to follow the law on codetermination, *Mitbestimmung*, which allows for workers to elect representatives to the company's board. These elements make for a governance of the economy that, if we may paint its portrait with a broad brush, is more consensual than in Anglo-Saxon countries but also more cohesive, thus enjoying a certain advantage in dealing with equally cohesive trade unions and with government. That said, specific features of German capitalism still do not suffice to explain neither the ethos of stakeholderism, nor its intellectual fortune.

In a sense, stakeholder capitalism is no novelty. That a business should take its surroundings into proper consideration is a truism that can also be turned into a subversive proposition. It is a truism because any business relies on a network of cooperation, more or less narrow or wide depending on its circumstances, to make and sell its products or services. Any business has suppliers and, when planning its activity, needs somehow to accommodate their needs and wants as well. If a company, for example, sees opportunities in its future such that it must demand more of a certain component or raw material, it had better have a good relationship with its respective providers. Further, this company must be considered trustworthy and pay its suppliers regularly, the more so the more demanding it gets. On top of that, flexibility and understanding cannot hurt: as a product evolves, so its components, up to a certain extent, must evolve too: hence the cooperation between a company and its suppliers is different than the one between your mom's home cooking and the grocery store.

One way to look at the market is to consider it as an institutional device that makes possible transactions among strangers. That is our experience when confronted with the cornucopia of goods a modern economy can offer. But when it comes to producers, more often than not, a little personal interaction happens, and it had better be cordial than not. The same is obviously true for workers and "human resources." Though the relationship between employer and employees can have its tensions, the former needs the latter to be serious, committed, and devoted. Indeed, capitalism presupposes a basic alignment of interests: employer and employees are, at the end of the day, all in the same boat, insofar as the one's success enables the others'. Certainly the capitalist will try to reduce its costs, and certainly workers will agitate to increase their salaries. But ultimately, they may find agreement. It typically doesn't escape a company owner that he can catch more flies with a spoonful of honey than with a cupful of vinegar.

Therefore, that a company ought to build a certain degree of trust and reputation, that it must pay its bills, that it should tend to treat its employees with respect, is a truism. A company does not exist in a vacuum. It needs to interact constantly with a number of persons and had better treat them nicely. Advocates of stakeholder capitalism, like the economist Mariana Mazzucato, think we ought to consider, to quote Mazzucato's recent book, *The Value of Everything: Making and Taking in the Global Economy*, "the social relationships between management and employees, between the company and the community." It is what businessmen and employees do every day and what, in a fully socialized economy, the corresponding plant managers and workers habitually do not do.

In a sense, this is nothing new. Stakeholderism emphasizes, a contrario, the conflictual elements in business relationship. The workers' movement, seeing the workers as the weaker counterpart to owners of the means of production, is the most obvious example. But workers have enrolled in trade unions to gain contractual leverage and socialist revolutionaries have made a target of expropriating the owners of the means of production. The chances are good that this behavior is particularly appealing to "Davos men."

Stakeholderism thus builds on a conflictual understanding of the market economy but aims to conciliate and harmonise the contrasting interests, not to have them struggle dialectically to find an accommodation. It has, in this regard, an interesting predecessor in the "corporatist" outlook theorized and practiced by the fascist regime in Italy under Mussolini and also by the Peronistas in Argentina.

Corporatism is conceived as an attempt at social conflict therapy. It presupposes that conflicts are not a feature of life or of capitalism but rather an anomaly, a bug that can be eliminated. The therapy descends from a diagnosis: this bug manifests itself only because a peculiar institution has been adopted. Contractual freedom is destined to divide, if not the son from his father and the daughter from her mother, then surely the wage earners from the holders of the means of production. Instead of nationalizing the means of production, as socialism and communism do, corporatism besieges freedom of contract, aiming to domesticate capitalism.

Like corporatism, stakeholderism claims, in effect, to be a "third way." In his work, Klaus Schwab has defined stakeholder capitalism as "capitalism in the traditional definition of the word: individuals and private companies make up the largest share of the economy" but "the economic activities of such private actors must also be protected and guided to ensure that the overall direction of economic development is beneficial to society."

In a sense, this is not very different from the market economy in our societies, where regulation is supposed to offset problems of externalities and taxation is supposed to finance public goods that the market won't provide by itself. Yet stakeholder capitalism targets a more profound transformation. Though ownership per se remains in private hands, this idea of capitalism postulates that everybody should have "a seat at the table." In seizing ownership not de jure but de facto, it holds that companies should become responsive to other things than the intentions of owners (shareholders), which are often seen as mere whims of self-enrichment.

In this sense, then, as a doctrine, stakeholderism (as we may call it henceforth) can be subversive. Corporatism was conciliatory in the face of often grim confrontations between workers and owners at the time of its inception. Stakeholderism is not exclusively about labour relations; it claims to have a wider scope and a farther-reaching vision. This would make managers even more powerful. Directors and managers especially have a better knowledge of their company than any outsider observers, their shareholders included. In part, this is due to the fact they are experts with particular skills and who possess knowledge in some relevant areas, partially due to their familiarity with a business's daily operations. The narrowness of "shareholder value" somehow limits the scope of their decision-making. But if they ought to be responsive to a larger set of issues than merely creating value for their shareholders, their discretion, almost by definition, increases. And thus the danger.

Milton Friedman Caricatured

A key element in the contemporary reflections over politics and economics is the rediscovery of *words*. Indeed, the social works are made of words. But some contemporary trends in critical theory and postmodern thought have suggested that they are not designed for *persuading*. To persuade someone of your views, you ought to believe she has her own, and legitimately so, and that a dialogue can be fruitful: you will explain yourself better and so will she. Perhaps a point of agreement might be reached. Perhaps she changes her mind. Perhaps you do.

But if words are just the scaffolding of power, there is no dialogue possible, no persuasion. One narrative can only take the place of the other. The way in which it happens, the way in which people learn to go along with the newer paradigm rather than stick with the older, is not so much by persuasion, by patiently confronting arguments, but rather by repetition. A recent example tries to overcome the "growth paradigm." Current measures of GDP and economic growth are actually reinvigorating the stronghold of the capitalist class. Hence, "challenging the growth paradigm is not just a matter of finding more effective measurements for the present and future. It also requires retelling the past to offer a convincing set of narratives about how and why to change the contemporary world, " as Stephen Macekura notes in *The Mismeasure of Progress: Economic Growth and Its Critics*. Notice the language: the problem is not measuring economic progress better than by using GDP but to have a different narrative of the past.

For this reason, it is appropriate to look at the narrative on which support for stakeholderism is predicated. Why should we move in that direction, and why now? Such a narrative is highly unrealistic. It is, basically, predicated on the idea that capitalism utterly neglects human relationships.

One may say that love and tenderness are not the attributes most often associated with the world of business. In a sense, they should not be: the economy is part of the lives of both a single individual and society at large. Everybody is more than his job: for some, the job is dreadfully important; for others, it is a way to put food on the table. Different intentions may produce very different results, particularly as they tend to be associated with the willingness to work hard. Yet the economy is blind to them.

This argument goes back a long way. Such blindness is best observed in the daily occurrences of life: the committed nationalist who uses a cell phone at least partly made in China, the religious baker who happily serves an LGBT activist his bread without caring about his political preferences, and so forth. We are often choosy with friends, and many relationships have broken off over modest disagreements. But we aren't this way with suppliers. As Adam Smith put it: "It is not from the benevolence of the butcher, the brewer, or the baker, that we expect our dinner, but from their regard to their own interest. We address ourselves, not to their humanity but to their self-love, and never talk to them of our own necessities but of their advantages."

It is worth noting, as Maria Pia Paganelli does in *The Routledge Guidebook to Smith's Wealth of Nations*, that "Smith simply says we do not get our dinner by relying exclusively on other people's benevolence. Smith does not say we have no benevolence. We are indeed benevolent, but it is in vain to rely entirely on the benevolence of others to get dinner." Yet the champions of stakeholderism tend to assume this is not the case.

The statist Left tends to suppose that profit is inversely correlated with social values: profit is seen as a sin, a pointless and indeed evil extraction of wealth by the bosses, when the whole product of labor should go to labor alone. Nobel laureate Milton Friedman is the most straightforward advocate of such system. Friedman, in 1962 in *Capitalism and Freedom* and later in 1970 in a *New York Times Magazine* op-ed, claimed famously that "there is one and only one social responsibility of business—to use its resources and engage in activities designed to increase its profits so long as it stays within the rules of the game, which is to say, engages in open and free competition, without deception or fraud." As in Smith's butcher and brewer case, the quote is often presented out of context. In particular, it is interpreted by some as implying that companies should pursue profits no matter what. They care about paying dividends, and that's it.

This is a caricature of reality. Friedman pointed out that business should "use its resources and engage in activities designed to increase its profits." Such activities contemplate sweet talk and persuasion. A cursory glance at reality would suggest that the caring and smiling shopkeeper tends to be more successful than a gloomy one. CEOs are rightly paid to engage in "motivational" speech, as nonmonetary rewards are important too. A person who cares about the company she works for can do so with more enthusiasm and commitment. A human being who feels personally appreciated is likelier to prioritise his task over the mere requirements of a contract.

Friedman did not advise companies not to provide private welfare to employees, nor did he think that they absolutely should not finance a local museum or pay for university scholarships. He thought the decision on the part of the company's management to engage in such endeavours should be considered in light of the pursuit of profit. Paying for a university scholarship can help a company in hiring future employees whose skills match its needs even more closely than normally. Offering private welfare packages is akin to increasing an employee's salary. Financing a local museum builds public legitimacy, and prospective customers may therefore look more favourably upon a company, and thus they may be more willing to buy its products. It could well be a kind of advertisement, often of the cheaper, more cost-effective kind.

Yet all these things, Friedman argues, are legitimate insofar as they do not redound to the detriment of shareholders. How can that be the case? Consider the CEO who lazily agrees to any and all demands on the part of workers without asking for something in return. Or the CEO who values contemporary art highly and eagerly sponsors any new exhibition, thus de facto signing company checks for a personal passion (and perhaps enjoying being called a patron of the arts). The lines are blurred, and it is sometimes hard to distinguish sound business strategies from vanity. Yet CEOs and managers should at least try to make a case to their boards and shareholders that their decisions are beneficial for all.

This is the descriptive part of Friedman's famous quote: capitalism with a human face, as it were. Now let's consider the normative part of that sentence: shareholder value needs to come first, so long as the company "stays within the rules of the game." Friedman is not making profits an alternative to ethics. Most people who have expressed shock or pleasure at Friedman's article have not actually read it, and therefore have not noticed that he adds a side constraint to the manager's fiduciary duty to the shareholders: "make as much money as possible *while conforming to the basic rules of the society, both those embodied in law and those embodied in ethical custom.*" Note: "ethical customs." Ethics in Friedman's thinking trace the perimeter of the socially permissible.

Moreover, and perhaps more importantly, deception or fraud are torts. Friedman puts the emphasis upon the law. Institutional constraints—good or bad laws concerning fraud and theft and coercion—make the pursuit of profit beneficial for society. They could make it detrimental too, if cultural norms give a pass to liars or, more likely, if the government allows selected businesses to benefit from special protection of one kind or another. Heavy regulations by omnipotent functionaries are likely to yield not market innovations but crony capitalism in which a handful of beneficiaries have convenient access to the public purse. If good laws and customs and alert self-interest are in place, cheating gets caught, and effort is turned to positive-sum activities.

The Elusive Stakeholder

The connection between paying and receiving in ordinary markets is tight. Upon meeting a baker and not talking with him about of our own necessities but of his own advantage, we gain bread. We *pay* for bread. It is a quick, generally reliable process. Billions of people, every minute, trade things with each other, trading goods with their means of exchange at their disposal.

The connection between outcomes and the voting or other political expressions of desire is looser. You want a chocolate cake, you pay for it, you get it. Not so in politics. You may vote for Mr. X, but then Ms. Y wins the election. Or your favored candidate actually could win and then be forced by exigent circumstances, or by the need to build a coalition, to pursue policies that are quite different than the ones promised. Or he may simply fail.

A market economy as we know it, "shareholder" capitalism if you want to call it that, has the advantage of linearity. Were the world made up exclusively of mom-and-pop businesses, in which the owner is more or less by definition the manager, Friedman's 1970 article "The Social Responsibility of Business Is to Increase Its Profits" would have never made news. But with the intertwined development of capital markets and mass production, business grew bigger and bigger. "Corporations" are complex entities, which hardly can be understood by assuming them to be single decision-making units. Their governance is as complex as the trades in which they're engaged—which are often varied and do, indeed, involve a number of "stakeholders." Big companies can have factories and commercial representatives in a number of countries and can be involved in the production of many things, not necessarily interconnected one with the other. The individual capitalist is a rarer occurrence in our economic landscape than he used to be. He may be in charge of a mom-and-pop business or the founder of a new one. Our society recognizes and appreciates the inventive genius of the Steve Jobses and the Jeff Bezoses of this world.

As with these illustrious cases, not all new companies stay small. The modern corporations are the genuine protagonists of our economic life, and they already were when Friedman published his article. Picturing them as focusing solely on the creation of value for the shareholder is, then, partly a rough simplification of what they do: a narrative that allows the observer to make sense of an intricate web of decisions. Yet it is also a very straightforward understanding of accountability in the business world. At the top of vast and complex corporations—which are typically run by professional managers rather than their founding entrepreneurs—sits a board of directors. It picks the executive management of the company and is elected by shareholders.

The board needs to be accountable to the shareholders. It manages *their* company not by divine right, but precisely because it was picked by them—sometimes in an uncontroversial manner, sometimes after bitter corporate fights. The board, in turn, should keep the CEO in check. The problem is that clearly both the board and the CEO have far better and more accurate information about what a company actually does than do the shareholders. Their knowledge is not necessarily complete: the bigger the company, the more that directors have to rely on second-tier information. The financial crisis of 2007–2008 exposed how little top executives actually understood about the operations of some of their employees. "Geeks and suits" is now a familiar dichotomy.

Yet to assess a manager's performance, or to verify that the board of directors is doing as it promises, one should have a reference point. What are these people supposed to do? Thinking they should create value for the shareholders is a sensible answer and gives us a reliable yardstick. Accountability requires a certain degree of precision and clarity. To assess the performance of the people at the helm, we need to know which sport are they supposed to be playing.

"Shareholder value" is a simple, straightforward answer. In 2021, the otherwise very popular CEO of Danone, Emmanuel Faber, was forced to step down from the multinational food products company by so-called activist investors. Under his leadership, the Paris-based company adopted the French "entreprise à mission" framework (a version of stakeholdering), committing itself to pursue a social and environmental purpose "beyond profit." Faber was a champion of "stakeholder capitalism," and the press saw his ouster as a dispute between champions of stakeholder capitalism and a few nostalgic for traditional shareholder capitalism. As reported by the *Wall Street Journal*, the nostalgic had a very basic point: "Danone shares are up 11 percent since Mr. Faber took over in October 2014. Meanwhile, rival Nestlé stock has risen 43 percent, and Unilever PLC by 55 percent." These simple numbers provided a reliable yardstick, which is what the noble commitment to make the world a better place is clearly not.

Others, including many a "Davos man," think that *share*holder value is a thing of the past and that we should move to a more inclusive understanding of what business ought to do. This means a different concept of "accountability." A company should thus be accountable to anyone who has a stake in its production, as we have seen.

Shareholders are a group of people who clearly have a highly relevant characteristic in common—to wit, owning shares of a company, which is to say having a claim to what's left over from voluntarily paid revenues after the costs of voluntarily supplied inputs. But what about stakeholders? What, after all, *is* a "stakeholder"?

In spite of a growing body of literature on "stakeholder capitalism," the question is surprisingly hard to answer, unless one is content to say *everybody*. Is a stakeholder the neighbor who objects to a new restaurant next door on not-in-my-backyard grounds, but who certainly won't put his money where his mouth is by buying up the vacant lot to preempt the unwelcome development? Is the stakeholder merely a grouch who wants to keep things just as they are, opposing whatever new factory may come to town, insofar as he doesn't have to pay a price for keeping them away? Is the stakeholder a worker who wants to be paid for his average rather than his marginal product, and reckons that by means of threats and politics, he can achieve it?

Schwab mentions four stakeholders that are interconnected in his model and hence should act in accord: governments, civil society, companies, and the international community. This is basically an holistic model, in which nobody is left out.

Indeed, since civil society is interpreted "in its broadest sense, from unions to NGOs, from schools and universities to action groups, and from religious organizations to sport clubs," anyone with an opinion gets to be a stakeholder. There is a bit of an irony here, since advocates of stakeholderism tend to think they are holding "capitalism accountable." Accountable to *whom*? The gist of stakeholderism is moving away from the idea that managers should be accountable to the owners of their companies, to the idea that they should be responsive to other, nonfiduciary interests.

According to Schwab, the "better capitalism" should now be the one in which vague parameters such as social justice and corporate social responsibility are given the same importance as the company's balance sheet. Hence, "rather than chasing short-term profits or narrow self-interest, companies could pursue the well-being of all people and the entire planet. Companies must be freed from economic calculation." Their performance ought then to be measured not only on the basis of profits but also "nonfinancial metrics and disclosures that will be added (on a voluntary basis) to companies' annual reporting in the next two to three years, making it possible to measure their progress over time."

Indeed, according to Schwab, we should measure "any stakeholder's true value creation or destruction, not just in financial terms but also in achieving of environment, social and governance objectives." Such metrics are happily adopted by many a company, busy with virtue signaling. But they add unwarranted complications to the business of evaluating a company's performance. Since this is now the prevailing fashion, companies that decide *not* to add some new metrics to the old-fashioned capitalist ones are likely to be penalised. Businesses strive to please their prospective customers and, under the best of circumstances, have a hard time doing so. It's a process of discovery. If they are adding "nonfinancial metrics and disclosures," they are trying to please someone else. Who is this "someone else"? The nebulous "stakeholder" or the influential men behind the curtain?

Understanding what people's needs are, what to produce, under what conditions, and where, is anything but an easy task. Production decisions are the result of a whole series of assumptions, risks, and considerations of competent businessmen. Some turn out to be right, others wrong; the success of individual careers and even entire companies depends on them.

Some entrepreneurs and business leaders are sometimes right "too early," which is to say before a technology becomes profitable. This is one of the risks that private actors bear. Timing is everything in business: the fact that a particular product does not make a profit does not imply any judgment on the human or professional qualities of those who worked on it. It only means that the same means of production can be used differently and better for the benefit of society as a whole.

Old-fashioned Capitalism

"Capitalism"—or, better, the market economy—is based on profits and losses. Profits and losses signal to companies that they are doing something that consumers appreciate or don't. This data tells whether there is a "demand" for a company's services, how big, at what price. Profit, which determines shareholder value, summarizes at the margin for decision-making today about what to do tomorrow; what the millions of customers, suppliers, workers are willing to offer and accept; and taking responsibility for a company's actions rather than shouting at public meetings to persuade politicians to coerce other people. In the various markets in which people participate, they put their money where their mouths are.

The market sends a signal of profits, which accrue as economic rents to holders of stock shares, that is, to the owners of businesses, until a newer entry spoils it. Losses tell those who produce or market a certain type of goods what they need not to do—what to stop producing, where not to employ resources, what is not worth investing in.

Hence, the fact that a company makes a profit is the best guarantee that workers will be paid fairly and may even see their wages rise. A profit-oriented company also has the means to take care of the social concerns of the environment in which it operates. As a reminder, therefore, in the tumultuous years of early industrial capitalism, the great captains of industry voluntarily looked after their communities. They established schools and hospitals for their workers, for example, for which they were criticised as paternalists. How times have changed.

Of course, if a company makes less profit, not only may workers feel more precarious but also there will be less, not more, money to channel into socially approved projects. This is not only true of so-called "corporate social responsibility" (a less-profitable company won't be able to subsidise scholarship as generously as a more-profitable one) but also for public spending. Government spending needs to be financed and for that to happen, a thriving capitalist economy (as the Nordic states understand better than others) is vital. East Germany had fewer resources available for health care than West Germany.

There may be good reasons to renounce a certain path to profit. These include the fact, highlighted by Friedman, that certain actions would not conform to the basic ethical rules of the society—such as not dealing with some Latin American dictatorships as business partners for fear that whatever money the regime got would be used to finance repression of dissent; avoiding animal experimentation on household pets like cats and dogs, to which humans feel a particular attachment; or not selling cigarettes to minors. "Ordinary" ethics apply to ordinary business transactions—and it is hard to maintain that it is less-practiced in business than in government, for example.

Critics of "shareholder" capitalism consider profit in its distributive aspect. Advocates of stakeholderism tend to emphasise the issue of inequalities, viewing capitalism as disproportionately benefitting corporate owners. The issue of accountability mentioned above does not bother them very much. Property produces "rent," whereas managing a company is, after all, intellectual work. In supporting stakeholderism, one might be seen to advocate redistribution of resources from property to labour, though labour of a peculiar kind.

Further, stakeholderists seem to suppose that if the profit expressed in shareholder value is distributed to shareholders and spent by them, it will be wasted. They suppose indeed that most of individual consumption is a mere race for the pursuit of silly baubles. They suppose that the wider the scope of decision-making, the better the investment of profits will be. The memos from the choices of consumers and workers transmitted up the supply chain by markets are to be set aside, and higher-level planners are to decide what to do after wisely pondering all relevant factors, which they purport to know in their entirety. Corporate officers, when they set aside shareholder value and focus on stakeholder value, are thought to be better at spending investible funds than individual shareholders and the capital markets in which they swim.

This is a profound distrust of the individual, whose choices are seen as inferior to those of a bureaucracy, government, or corporation. If that individual is a property owner, the distrust is even bigger. As property often comes with birth and family, it is often meritless. On the other hand, you need to be brainy and thoughtful to arrive at the top of a corporation, even more so when the government owns or strongly influences it. Bureaucracy rhymes with meritocracy; property does not.

Mariana Mazzucato notes that "a *stakeholder* understanding of value denotes a very different type of finance: one that is more 'patient' and supports necessary long-term investments." In other words, a finance that bleeds money in pursuit of the intellectuals' delusions, and is prevented from learning its errors and thus unable to change course.

This is a common thought among stakeholderists. Yet, it is not clear why so-called stakeholders should be better at long-term managing than managers attending to the stock market. The long-term value is reflected in the value of the firm right now. For one thing, a price on a stock market does a better job of getting the long-term right than a committee of busybodies from outside the institution. For another, we do not think it is a good idea to give thousands of people tangentially connected to the company a vote in how it is run. Such is the notion of "democracy in the workplace," for example. As already pointed out, we know who shareholders are, like them or not. Not stakeholders, an expansible category that inevitably includes whoever manages to get hold of a megaphone. Why should people tangentially interested in a company's workings be better at apprising the "true" value of its production?

This argument is seemingly commonsensical thanks to environmental issues and the growing importance of "climate justice" in the public debate. But if a company is clearly responsible for polluting the environment, or creates substantial externalities, regulation seems a more appropriate instrument to straighten up its production. Of course, regulation needs to be grounded in facts and regulators should produce evidence for their demands. No matter how corrupt the political process is, it still is more fact oriented than vaguely defined practices concerned with how to divine the stakeholders' minds.

Conclusions

In an interview in the 1970s, Milton Friedman remarked: "It's fortunate that the capitalist society is more productive, because if it were not it would never be tolerated. The bias against it is so great that, as it is, it's got to have a five-to-one advantage in order to survive." It is hard to avoid the impression that the hostility against capitalism precedes any diagnoses about its uncertain future.

The relationship between intellectuals and the institutions of the free market is a subject that has long been investigated. After all, if there is one thing that unites all socialist movements in their various incarnations it is that they were born and established themselves as elitist movements: vanguards of a working class that was then far from fully gaining self-awareness. Yale forensic psychologist Dan Kahan, in a series of studies, found that people with high levels of numerical literacy, that is, who can read and work with data—more likely to be "experts" and "intellectuals"—are prone to manipulate data in the face of political controversy. Schematically, if you offer to one group of people who are nonliterate and to another group proficient in mathematics a set of data with which to analyze a neutral issue, such as establishing the effectiveness of a cream that cures a dermatitis, the noncompetent people will not be able to use that data and will provide irrelevant answers.

Instead, numerate people were able to use figures to correctly decide whether the cream was effective. If, however, the problem became of a politically contentious nature, i.e., if it involved immigration, gun control, climate change, use of human papilloma virus vaccines, or something in that vein, when confronted with the same data, people who were not knowledgeable took sides based on political orientation while scientists bent unfavorable data to their expectations, so that they were consistent with their bias. Polarization among them was more pronounced than that among ordinary people.

We are all biased: we tend to demand explanations that exaggerate the simplicity of causal links, that exalt the effectiveness of a single act, of a single initiative or a single man. We are not apt to understand the complexity of a bottom-up process such as the market economy. In the end, we construct the images of reality that we have matured the need for and, in times of crisis, we want problem-solvers. Experts and managers do not have necessarily biases different than ours, plus they enjoy the comfort of picturing *themselves* as the much-needed problem solvers.

The Great Reset promises "capitalism with a human face." It does not imply—or at least, it says it does not—a sharp break with the status quo; rather, it promises improvement by involving more people in the decision-making process. Giving a voice to more persons, rather than to fewer, makes a superficially attractive slogan. But stakeholderism is built on a shaky premise: an incongruous portrait of capitalism as it is. It is a powerful narrative but a flawed one.

PART VI: THE INEFFABLE

HISTORY UNDER THE GREAT RESET

BY JEREMY BLACK

History's place at the fore of culture wars is no surprise. The destruction of alternative values, of the sense of continuity, an appreciation of complexities, and of anything short of a self-righteous presentist internationalism, is central to the attempt at a 'Great Reset.' Moreover, in a variety of forms, including cultural Marxism and, particularly and very noisily at present, critical race theory, such a "reset" is part of a total assault on the past, one that is explicitly designed to lead the present and determine the future.

This assault is a long-term process that owed much to the Marxist side in the Cold War that began in 1917 and continued until the fall of the Soviet bloc in 1989–1991, but this process has been revived and given new direction in recent years. The relentlessness of the struggle; the Leninist approach; that the core true believers and committed will lead the rest; that there is to be no compromise, no genuine debate; and that the end result must be power for its own sake attacks, through prejudging groups as inherently racist, the notion of every human being having intrinsic value, a notion that is central to the Judeo-Christian tradition. In part, this revival reflects the extent to which those who were the rebels of the late 1960s are now very much in the driving seats of intellectual and cultural would-be direction, and thereby able to move from protest to proscription. Thus, the "long march through the institutions" beloved of the Left has succeeded.

In part, this was because conservatives devoted insufficient attention to trying to contest this march. In particular, the degree to which institutions and companies controlled by, and for, the "soft Left" could become the means for propaganda, indeed indoctrination, by the "hard Left," while appreciated by many right-wing commentators, was given far too little attention by conservative governments. This was true of Reagan/Thatcher/Bush Senior, all of whom understandably focused on international relations and economic affairs, including the development of neoliberalism, and then again of Bush Junior/Cameron.

Other issues thus came to the fore but so also, in a lack of adequate response to the culture wars waged by the Left, did an understandable wish not to use the power of the state in order to limit the autonomy of institutions such as museums and universities. Neither did they come up with any other solution to the problem. That approach, however, left conservatism at a serious disadvantage, one that has become increasingly apparent and one that there is still a difficulty in facing.

This situation was very much of concern before the storm of protest and aggressive virtue signalling associated with the 'Black Lives Matter' movement of 2020. However, the latter helped rapidly to drive forward the pre-existing tendency, not least by leading many organisations, institutions, and companies to endorse and adopt attitudes and policies that were at best tendentious and at worst extremely damaging to any practice of rational enquiry. Thus, a survey circulated by Oxfam in June 2021 to its staff in Britain stated that racism was deeply embedded in society and that all echelons of power, to some degree, exist to serve whiteness (whether by legacy, the presence of neocolonialism, or cultural imperialism).

Leaving aside the question of what whiteness means, and the difficulty of determining how somebody thinks, which is a crucial aspect of charges of racism, the past is defined in terms of a hostile legacy. The emphasis throughout is on whiteness and blackness in oppositional terms and with a clear primacy for both across time. This is fundamentally ahistorical as it acts to downplay all other identities and causes of tension, most notably rivalry within these supposed opposites—for example, the tribal conflicts within Africa that were the major sources of the Atlantic slave trade, and what also can be seen as tribal conflicts in Europe. Indeed, the role of tribalism is seriously downplayed by the drive for a racist dichotomy in analysis. There is an endless number of aspects of a question, and the ambition ought to be to cover as many aspects as possible, not to take one a priori.

The abandonment of any support for rational enquiry, indeed, was unsurprising, as there was an explicitly anti-Enlightenment argument at play, and notably and aggressively so with critical race theory. This theory acted to deny rationality, presenting it somehow as racist and an imperialising project, whatever that is held to mean. This theory was a deeply ironic ally for the companies and others that offered endorsement as their entire ethos was based on rational planning. In a resumption of the postmodernist hash, objectivity has become a term of abuse and objection, as has teaching in a linear fashion. The "progressive" or "woke" agenda can be advanced by such a wide coalition because all its elements have adopted the social constructivist position that facts are irrelevant or disposable. Thus, for many, history becomes part of a continuum in which gender activists can adopt the mantra of "transwomen are women" because they dismiss the fact of biology as subject to the social construct of gender. Race activists can seek to do the same. Moreover, data suggesting that the white working class faces difficulties is ignored because it does not fit with the prevailing socially constructed view that white men are the "problem" and oppress others. In the same way, history activists, a category that includes many history academics but does not deserve the designation "historians," can construct an account of the past that is not supported by evidence but is how they want it to be. If everything can be constructed on the basis of whim, history as a discipline is in real peril.

As a related point, education in the West increasingly becomes a matter of emphasising therapy and feeling better. In line with this, the desire by some academics to 'self-medicate' intellectually and feel better has become the motivator for decolonization of the curriculum. Such decolonisation is at core both political and a therapeutic initiative (larded with the language of "feeling safe"), which enables the decolonisers to feel virtuous. Critical race theory says nothing new in so far as it points, as when it was advanced in the 1970s, to an interconnectivity among many elements contributing to the historical animosity toward African Americans. More seriously, the theory has a bleak outlook and appears to state that there has been little or no progress in ameliorating racial discrimination. This is mistaken. Moreover, in applying the past to the present, the theory is misconstrued and ossified, falling into the ethnic-blame fallacy trap in its focus on retroactive, collective ethnic guilt. This was initially an American phenomenon reacting to specifically American societal and historical problems. This element makes its simple adoption in Britain and elsewhere in the West all the more problematic. In part, this adoption is the result of an increasingly monoglot and ahistorical society. Using empire to make some sort of bridge is problematic not in small part due to the "transracial" alliances involved in empire. For Britain, this was prominent in the case of slave-sellers, while the British empire in Asia was essentially an Anglo-Indian enterprise.

The wash of protest in 2020 was given concrete form by being taken on board in mission statements, hiring policies, and other such mutually supporting practices that are backed by the designation and filling of new posts. Thus, ideology was focused accordingly.

In Britain, as a result, historical issues, such as the slave trade, empire, and the reputation of Winston Churchill, have received attention to an unaccustomed degree, and history of a type was thrust into public debate. However, as an empirical basis for critique, "history wars" has scarcely been to the fore, and the situation has not changed. In particular, there is a tendency among critics, for example of empire, to write in terms of undifferentiated blocs of supposed alignment, to move freely back and forth across the centuries, and readily to ascribe causes in a somewhat reductionist fashion.

Thus, the popular historian William Dalrymple, writing in *The Guardian* on 11 June 2020, linked the continued presence in Central

London of a statue of Robert Clive, a valiant hero and key figure in the acquisition of the Indian empire, to the Brexit vote:

> a vicious asset-stripper. His statue has no place on Whitehall…a testament to British ignorance of our imperial past…. Its presence outside the Foreign Office encourages dangerous neo-imperial fantasies among the descendants of the colonisers…Removing the statue of Clive from the back of Downing Street would give us an opportunity finally to begin the process of education and atonement.

This idea, that education has to lead to atonement, captures the extent to which those writing were not interested in critical debate, nor indeed in the previous mantra of reconciliation. Moreover, it is also part of the strategy of trashing the past, that scholarship and 'education' in it have also to be found inadequate if not worse. This is a highly doctrinaire approach. And so on, for Dalrymple and others, with the usual attacks on Brexit being apparently a consequence of an imperial mentality that has never been confronted. Leave aside the extent to which Dalrymple was strong here on assertion rather than evidence, and that "Little Englanders" and specific issues of the moment, such as David Cameron's lack of popularity and widespread concerns about immigration, were of far more consequence in the 2016 referendum than any supposed hankering after empire. What, instead, you get is a running together of past and present with the modern British supposedly trapped by the past. Therefore, in this approach, the statues have to fall, and presumably the reading lists and libraries must be reordered, and, indeed, renamed. "Decolonization" becomes a catch-all that can be employed to castigate whatever is disliked and then to demand support for a purge.

Academic historians, the majority of whom ironically are clearly on the Left themselves, find they are subject, as part of history wars, not to the usual rational and empirical conventions and constraints of intellectual debate, but to an increasingly more intrusive and even controlling attitude on the part of colleagues as well as the broader world, not least some, or many, university authorities. Those who set policy in the latter do so by the finger-in-the-air method, one that senses what is fashionable among those who will affirm their prejudices. That, indeed, threatens, far more than the debate already mentioned, a closure of the space for free thought and expression. Strident demands for "antiracist" affirmation can compound the latter issue.

Given the bullying approach, tone, and stance adopted by some universities, not least anonymous denunciations, those thus attacked will be anxious. In part, this is a struggle for mastery within the Left, one parallel to that between transgender activists and feminists, but conservative academics are frequently attacked. With some universities apparently endorsing the idea that the workplace is the mission field, there is, in an echo of the nonconformist tradition, the language of impatient revivalism, as in concepts such as needing to grasp the moment, condemnation, and the endlessly reiterated language and idea of decolonisation. The claim, in the *Economist* on 10 July 2021, that American liberals are open "to a more fragmented…version of the country's past" ignores the strident orthodoxy of many on the Left. It is deeply disturbing that our once-great institutions founded on open and honest inquiry and scholarship are now merely vessels to promote orthodoxies in which the only debates are within narrowly defined arenas completely divorced of genuine scholarship. We have seen it creep into the humanities for decades and now it is deeply ensconced within the sciences as well. This all bodes very poorly for our civilisation.

The Covid pandemic, a minor one compared to past such outbreaks, has been a hugely advantageous occurrence enabling the acceleration of the current agenda. Covid has disrupted our culture and atomised our citizenry so that the vast middle is simply exhausted and distracted, an instance of the centre finding it difficult to hold. The process, already well underway before Covid, has accelerated to an astonishing degree in the past eighteen months, in part because the normal functioning of society has been seriously compromised.

History as a subject proves particularly important, as the past is used as a necessary basis for the decolonising mantra. Ludicrous claims, such as genocide by Europeans in Africa and the Americas, are repeated. Old ideas, such as world-systems theory, are taken out of storage, given a "racist" dimension, and deployed without care or context. The latter, particularly regrettable as world or global history, was a qualification of earlier Eurocentric models, and one on which much effort was expended. It proved particularly valuable in demonstrating links between civilisations and in undermining any "zero-sum-game" of cultures. Instead, empires were presented as collective undertakings in which those who were subjects had a significant role and indeed to a considerable extent agency or semi-independent action. Similar points were made about the slave trade.

There are many contextual aspects that deserve thought. The historian will note that the direction of travel, the apparent attack on white male "privilege," has little to do with the most obvious and persistent "bias" in university entry in Britain, that toward a pronounced majority of female students, and notably so in the humanities, including history. There is nothing inherently wrong with that, but it is the most pronounced feature. Among students, there is also, whether state or private schools are the issue, a middle-class background to the British undergraduate population. These are far more noticeable than any supposed "white supremacism." As far as staff is concerned, and notably so in the humanities and social sciences, the lack of "diversity" and "inclusion" are also most obviously the case as far as the representation of conservative staff are concerned as this representation is very limited and generally a case of "getting in under the radar." There are yet more demands for "diversity" training, which has become an end in itself.

Perish the thought that empire might be explained and contextualised, not only in terms of other contributions to British growth and stability, but also with reference to other empires. It is striking for example how few experts on the British Empire are able to compare its development and activities with those of non-Western empires of the period. That was an aspect of world history, but most British specialists lack the necessary range. In Britain, it seems easier to import something from America and then call it global. The American equivalent is in practice a travesty in the understanding of both the slave trade as a global phenomenon and, separately, empire.

What is possibly most striking is the apparent suspension of any real sense of critique of the new order. Maybe, debate is so beneath you when you possess all truth. Much better just to steamroll people into compliance. Debate is seen as oppressive. Those who hold contrasting views are readily dismissed and shunned: if you do not think you are a "white supremacist," which is the subtext I would suggest of the term white "privilege," that means that you are inherently guilty. If you feel uncomfortable about being accused of being a white supremacist—that means you are guilty. This is like a blatantly constructed trap, as is the reference to having "a conversation," when, of course, that is the very last thing that is intended. And notably so in terms of the past, for there is no attempt to understand the values of the past, and, without understanding, there can be scant rational discussion of it.

In practical terms, we are seeing a bringing to fruition of the attack on positivism that has been so insistent from the Left since the 1960s, an attack that is bridging from academic circles to a wider public, and with the active encouragement of the former. In particular, there was, and continues to be, a critique of subordinating both scholarship and the scholar to the evidence; and a preference, instead, for an assertion of convenient evidence that was derived essentially from theory. Empiricism from then was discarded, or at least downplayed, as both method and value, and there was a cult of faddish intellectualism heavily based on postmodernist concepts, and that despite the weakness of the latter, a weakness that is conceptual, methodological, empirical and historiographical, liberating the present from the past.

Divorcing the arts and social sciences from empirical methods meant less work for the staff and no real standards other than those of virtue signalling. This approach invited a chaos that some welcomed as such, not least with calls for revolution, but that others sought to reshape in terms of a set of values and methods equating to argument by assertion and proof by sentiment: "I feel therefore I am correct," and, in a world of calling out whatever is presented as microaggression, it is apparently oppression to be told otherwise.

It is instructive to turn to an example from a member of the academic power fashion-house, an example that could be readily replicated and notably so in Britain and the United States. You might think that the biggest problem in the teaching of humanities at British universities is how best to maintain quality and standards given the massive rise in student numbers, but you are totally wrong; for the problem, according to Catherine Hall, professor emerita of modern British social and cultural history at University College London, in a 2019 notice sent to some departments, is that "the discipline urgently needs decolonisation!"

Hall, in 2016, turned down a prize from the Dan David Foundation in Israel for her pioneering of gender history research (her subject before she moved into empire), apparently doing so due to her support for the Palestinian boycotts, divestment, and sanctions movement against that country. The British Committee for Universities of Palestine described this rejection as "a significant endorsement of the campaign to end ties with Israeli institutions," but the irony of such virtue signalling at the time of the Syrian civil war was, and remains, painful, with Russian and Iranian openly imperial ambitions at stake in that civil war.

If that point has essentially passed by the stalwarts for boycotting Israel, it tells you much about that cause and concerning "anti-imperial" history in general. Aside from displaying an antiwhite racialism, it is frequently anti-Semitic as well. Indeed, the presentation of Israel as an imperial and/or colonial power, a presentation that looks back to the Soviet wooing of Arab opinion, is in practice heavily anti-Semitic as well as lacking context. This is anti-Semitism masquerading as anti-imperialism, or more perniciously, as anti-Zionism.

So also, in terms of violence, with the emphasis on that by Western imperial powers, and the failure to give due weight to post-colonial violence, as in Haiti, or in much of Africa, most notably, but not only, Angola, Congo, Ethiopia, Ivory Coast, Liberia, Libya, Mozambique, Nigeria, Rwanda, Sierra Leone, Somalia, Sudan, and Uganda. Blaming violence on Western powers or "capitalism" is a fantasy distraction from the extent to which tribalism is a key element, as it was in the long-standing conflicts that produced the slaves sold to nonAfrican traders, and some of which continue to produce slaves held in Africa. Indeed, the role of tribalism in modern history requires more attention.

Hall's book *Macaulay and Son: Architects of Imperial Britain* (2012) provides a good example. It is a committed work as well as a scholarly one and shows all the strengths and weaknesses of such commitment. Hall explains that she became an historian of Britain and empire to explain the legacies of colonialism for the British, and that she started work on Thomas Macaulay in the wake of the "war on terror." Hall presses on to explain that she was opposed to the 2003 Iraq War "and horrified by the claim that the West had the right to assume such positions of moral certitude, apparently with no memory of past "civilising missions," key aspects of some phases of European colonialisms. This was the return of the...assumption that Britain, despite its loss of empire, could use force and legislate for those others who were stuck in barbaric times, who needed white knights to rescue them. Moral rectitude was masking new geo-political claims. Britain's shameful colonial history in Iraq, and subsequently in Afghanistan, seemed to be entirely forgotten. The discourse of liberal humanitarian intervention under the sign of gender equality was deployed unproblematically. Yet this was a reconfiguration of the arguments made by nineteenth-century imperialists—including both Macaulays—for an empire of virtue and civilisation.

For such historians, Britain becomes a country in which a malign history, notably of imperial manhood, reflects and sustains, an identity based on ethnicity, class and gender, with hierarchy and violence entwined themes.

Linked, however, to the lack of any subtlety in the drawing of links, let alone of any adequate contextualisation for imperialism, there is also a sense of "so what?" Is it surprising that leaders and intellectuals, whether or not presented as apologists, offered a view of the world in which they associated their values and interest with progress and civilisation? This is not exactly news; and, ironically but all too predictably, those today imposing their views on the past display very much the same tendency in their work, identifying values with their own concept of progress.

Hall is all too typical of the cultural warfare that is repeatedly at stake. *History Workshop* published a blog in 2019 in its learning and teaching section: Radhika Natarajan's "Imperial History Now," which claims that "calls to decolonise curricula are more than a matter of addition, subtraction, or replacement of authors and texts. Instead, they are calls to address the relationship between the forms of knowledge we value in the classroom and the inequities and violence that exist on our campuses and in the world...Decolonising the curriculum is not an end, but the beginning of a longer process of transformation."

There have of course been many similar pieces in newspapers such as the *Guardian*, the *New York Times*, and the *Los Angeles Times*, as well as online. Moreover, the 1619 Project developed by the *New York Times* gained prominence due to that newspaper's support for what was otherwise a deeply problematic account.

There is also pressure across the curriculum, in both the United States and Britain. In the former, the 1619 Project has gained excessive traction, as has critical race theory. In Britain, the situation lacks the welcome public discussion of American school meetings and state legislatures, and the process is frequently obscure, and therefore all too often settled in accordance with partisanship masquerading as professionalism.

The possibility of access to materials means that I have to emphasise the University of Exeter, where I was the senior history professor until retiring in 2020. I note, for example, proposals for "Decolonising the curriculum" in terms of "curriculum review: assessment and attainment gap; staff-student roundtables; and teacher training," the last two in practice intimidating as well as Orwellian or Maoist. On 22 July 2020, the registrar, or head of the administration, of Exeter, sent an email to staff declaring: "If you see or hear any inappropriate behaviour, and you feel able to call it out, please do so in an appropriate way. It may be that a colleague is unaware of the impact of their behaviour, and mentioning this may give them a chance to adjust their behaviour alongside allowing them space to reflect." Such "space" to "reflect" is steadily becoming tighter, but the entire exercise is reminiscent of Communist activity. Those who do not say the right things can be "called out." This "cleansing" will doubtless cause a thousand flowers to bloom as long as they are the same colour and height.

An additional trouble is that now, as apparently "silence is violence," those who remain silent will also be forced to go to mandatory "retraining" sessions. Freedom of thought and expression, as well as open enquiry, have been totally discarded. This is power at play, but, as so often, it is power masquerading as weak and suffering hardship, so that grievance becomes a necessary drive to action, a reflection of the politics of victimhood. In 2020, the Department of History at Exeter put out the following:

> As a department, we are working to decolonise the way we teach, research, and work with one another....
>
> ...We recognise that History—and the legacies of its colonial foundations—constitutes one of the ways in which some groups of people have been, and continue to be, oppressed, ignored, or abused in our societies today. In solidarity with Black Lives Matter and other decolonial and postcolonial movements around the world, we also recognise that History can be an important tool for positive social change.
>
> Racial prejudice continues to mar our discipline, from the underrepresentation of BME scholars on our reading lists and in our faculties to the day-to-day experiences of our colleagues. We recognise that the

> way we "do" History, at Exeter as elsewhere, needs to change if we are to remain relevant, and help to address chronic and systemic injustices, in our increasingly connected and interdependent global society.
>
> ...We believe these changes need to go beyond simply diversifying our reading lists and footnotes. As a group, we are working to re-think our pedagogical and research methodologies to more fully avail ourselves of the tools developed by postcolonial, anti-colonial, and decolonial scholarship, thus enabling a stronger and broader appreciation of the complexities of past societies and cultures.

To describe this approach as tendentious is polite, not least because using history to advance any sort of social change is itself problematic. In addition, the phrases used are the products of commitment rather than reasoned debate and in practice coercion as far as dissenting voices are concerned. "Needs to change if we are to remain relevant" is a classic totalitarian approach.

Moreover, not to describe such aspiration action as "culture wars" is foolish. The argument frequently expressed in 2021 that such wars were being begun and waged by Conservatives, an argument particularly seen in criticism of the British government that June, willfully ignored the extent to which they were very much a limited response to a process of at least quasi-indoctrination that was initiated and strongly pursued by self-styled radical and reformist groups, which are, in practice, revolutionary.

In part, there was the normative repetition of slogans about inherent white privilege, many linked to reductive analyses on the part of "New Left" academics keen to reduce individuals to categories and to explain people in terms of supposedly inherent thought. Most of those offering this analysis were middle-class of some type or other, so, in order to pose as helping the underprivileged the critique of redundant, imperialising, conservative whiteness suited them.

That raises, of course, the bigger question of how best, in the context of modern history, to discuss and teach imperialism, and history in general. Personal commitment does not excuse any fondness for argument by assertion and, also, without adequate qualification or sufficient caveats. Nor is such a practice acceptable simply because the author is at a major institution or is published by a leading press. Would the now standard faddish approach be allowed for junior academics, let alone students? Presumably only if they agreed with the precepts, a point that is more widely true of an approach that seeks not pluralism, but rather the apparent certainty of an apparent and imposed zeitgeist.

This is a one-dimensional history, a unidirectional account of heroes and villains. Consider, for example, a Simon Schama piece in the *Financial Times* of 10 July 2021. Aside from repeating the misleading argument that slavery was central to the American Revolution, one that is part of the more general assault on the Founding Fathers, there is a more general use of partisan language as in Britain. We find the use of partisan language: "Britain liquidated the institution of slavery itself in 1834 but on condition that obscene sums of British taxpayers' money would go to compensate former owners of the enslaved." Maybe so from today's perspective, but the payment helped bring consent without struggle, which was somewhat different to the situation in America during the Civil War, and notably once the Union moved from the suppression of rebellion to outright abolition. Schama goes on: "Come the Civil War across the Atlantic, the great majority of the British political elite, including Liberal Party leaders like Gladstone, whose family fortune was in cotton, cheered on the Confederacy." This is misleading at best. Leaving aside the decision by the British government not to intervene, sympathy for the Confederacy was despite slavery and not because of it. Such subtlety, not least in the sense of the understanding that people are complex, can hold a number of views, and defy ready labelling and explanation, is apparently beyond not only Schama but also a large number of other writers who provide a caricature of the past designed to serve a politicisation from and in the present.

More generally, there is the repeated failure to appreciate that people in the past believed that they were right for reasons that were perfectly legitimate in terms of their own times, experience, and general view of the world. Imposing anachronistic value judgments is obviously illegitimate. Religion is scarcely ever mentioned. The belief of missionaries that they were saving souls cannot just be ignored: what could be more important to them? They thought they were as right in undertaking their work as those who now want to impose their views. Saving modern souls appears to be the agenda.

Whether or not you welcome the specifics of contemporary one-dimensional history, that is history simply as propaganda. It is a world away from debate, and is fundamentally antidemocratic, as well as anti-intellectual and antiacademic. This is an appropriate matter for government concern not least as most of these institutions benefit from state money and tax-breaks.

The conventional academic spaces, the geopolitics of academic hierarchy and method, from the lecture hall to the curriculum, have all been very deliberately repurposed to this political end, and to a degree that many alumni benefactors and politicians do not appreciate. Arguing that academics have always been foolish does not capture the seriousness of the issue, nor the extent to which the changes have been actively entrenched with the strong support of university administrators. Contrary views are at best ignored but more commonly silenced, with no platforming but part of a broader pattern of no appointment, no promotion, no recognition, no grants, and so on.

And so also with public spaces, notably museums, while the statues that are unwelcome are treated not as isolated residues of allegedly outdated and nefarious glories, but a quasiliving reproach to the new order in the culture wars of the present in which there is no space for neutrality or noncommittal, or, indeed, tolerance and understanding.

In part, possibly, and as an aspect of decolonisation, the legitimacy of opposing views is dismissed, indeed discredited, as allegedly racist and anti-intellectual because there is an unwillingness to ask awkward questions and to ignore evidence which does not fit into the answer wanted and already asserted. Examples of the latter might include the extent of slavery and the slave trade prior to the European arrival in Africa; the long Muslim history of enslaving white Europeans from the late Middle Ages into the seventeenth century; or the major role of European powers and the United States in eventually ending both and at sea as well as on land. Indeed, the extension of British imperialism was frequently linked, as in Nigeria and Sudan between 1860 and 1905, with the ending of slavery.

In contrast, much of the resistance to imperialism in these areas was linked with slaving interests. This does not make imperialism or resistance "good" or "bad" but should ensure that complexity is offered when explaining the past. Complexity does not prevent the opportunity to offer judgment, but that requires a degree of contextualisation that is too often absent.

It is possible, and necessary, to debate these and other points, but debate often is not accepted by the Left if it involves questioning assumptions, including those summarised and advanced as critical race theory. However, questioning these assumptions is crucial to understanding the past, which is the key aspect of history as an intellectual pursuit, rather than as the sphere for political engagement. As such, the theory has absolutely no place other than as a proposition and one that emerged in a particular conjuncture and to specific ends.

Historians need to understand why practices we now believe to be wrong and have made illegal, such as slavery, or (differently) making children work or marrying them, were legitimate in the past. It is not enough, in doing so, to present only one side of, and on, the past simply because that is allegedly useful for present reasons. The way in which the future will view us ought to encourage caution on this point, but none of this will be encouraged under a Great Reset that is more totalitarian by its commitment.

Nor is it pertinent to refuse to recognise debate in earlier, plural societies. People in the past believed that they were right for reasons that were legitimate in terms of their own times, experiences, and general views of the world. These elements deserve consideration as part of the inherently pluralist conception of values in a democratic society.

Somewhat curiously, that conception is more present today for religious faith than for political opinion, and notably so in the West: there is more of a willingness in the West to accept religious diversity than political opinions judged unwelcome. This willingness is not seen across the West, however. Thus, freedom of religious practice in the Middle East is most clearly present in Israel, as is also the case with democracy and care for minority rights. It is interesting to consider the one-sided anti-Israeli sources of the present "debate" that are, and will be, applied to conceal these points.

Returning to the broader observation, all religions in the past had views that presentists would now find reprehensible and would wish to criminalise or, indeed, which are already illegal. This raises instructive questions about the logic of historicising the present politics of ambitious grievance, in terms eventually of an assault on religions. Alternatively, critical race theory can be seen not only as thinly veiled cultural Marxism but also as a form of cult or religion, with a strong notion of original sin for others, and no salvation for those bearing this sin. This idea of inherited sin, a morally bogus proposition and one most applied in history by anti-Semites, is widely used by those demanding some form of restitution for colonialism and slavery, again an approach that underplays the complexity of the past, as in massive African complicity in the Atlantic slave trade.

Focusing anew on empire (although the same point can be made in other respects), how then is empire to be presented in a way that does more than make sense of it largely in terms of modern values which tell us little about the past? The answer clearly will not be provided in the "decolonisation" approach, which is explicitly antithetical to academic methods in that it proclaims its engagement as its rationale. In a classic instance of Herbert Butterfield's definition of anachronism—making the study of the past a ratification or attack on the present, the past is to be used, in the form of a supposedly exemplary decolonisation, as part to an attempt to recast ideas to match an account of society designed to provide an exemplary future; or at least to defend the role of universities and the careers of particular academics.

This view of being an historian appears to be of spending their time wishing that people in the past did not think as they, in fact, did and converting this into a platform for sociopolitical activism in the present. This approach has no analytical substance, and, indeed, both threatens to dissolve the discipline and leaves the student not so much short-changed as totally cheated intellectually and pedagogically, which indeed is an aspect of a current-day civilisational malaise.

Imposing anachronistic value judgments is antithetical to the historical mindset of the scholar and is inherently transient as the fullness of time will, in turn, bring in fresh critiques of present-day values, which, possibly, also will be wrenched out of their historical context, not least by ignoring inconvenient evidence. There is a somewhat fantasist approach at present in academe in the assertion of present-day values and, even more, definitions, as if these are transcendent universals, but, maybe, that approach is part of a religious imperative in a secular milieu, one very much seen with "mission statements." It also has a corrosive effect on society and politics in general.

Leave aside, please, the temptation to observe that those who talk about teaching are frequently those who cannot do it and often do not wish to do so. While that is true, the issue of decolonisation is too serious for such points. Instead, we have a clear instance of the standard idea of capturing the institutions, and then propagating an ideology. That, indeed, is at full tilt, and notably so in the humanities and social sciences, and particularly, but not only, in the United States, Britain, and Canada. Decolonisation might sound good to some and silly to others, but it is certainly a programme, and a requirement for change, one that is authoritarian in its methods and totalitarian in its objectives. Moreover, it has become more potent due to the way in which institutions seek to determine the parameters of thought within which society is perceived.

The significance of the issue can be seen in the furore in Britain in the summer of 2021 when the government sought to offer some rather modest pushback. It was variously accused of meddling for political advantage, provoking a culture war, and so forth. In practical terms, the governmental response in Britain has been at best patchy in the extreme; in France, President Macron in 2021 was more robust in stigmatising what he has presented as a challenge to French identity.

Indeed, there is a civilisational dimension. Wallowing in the past, trolling it for grievances, and then using these grievances in trolls, is in part an opt-out from the real challenges of the present, but that is not how it is seen by its protagonists. Indeed, their view is a Great Reset that destroys capitalism and, in their terms, redresses and silences all forms of "white supremacism," a concept that is misleading other than in the racism it propounds.

Western liberals who do not see this as a serious challenge to their civilisation are foolish in the extreme. While that civilisation has always encouraged debate, which indeed is part of its strength, the type of criticism that is now at play is deliberately intended as revolutionary. It is not debate, but aims at the end of discussion, and should be treated accordingly.

This is doubly a challenge because the West, its liberal humanism, and the very concept of humane reason is under a grave threat from external changes, notably the rapid rise of the Chinese system and China's energetic attempt to propagate its views around the world. Across the world, albeit to different audiences, China's path is greatly eased by the stigmatisation of the West as racist and imperial, a stigmatisation made more damaging by the extent to which domestic audiences within leading former colonial powers are willing to endorse this approach. This approach ignores China's imperial past and present, and thus repeats the situation seen during the Cold War when such international hostility from the Soviet Union was matched by an ideological misrepresentation of the West from within by critics who subscribed to Soviet nostrums.

This situation is a clear indication of a cultural geopolitics that has important political consequences. For the West to take debate so far as to allow the trashing of its culture, institutions, civilisation, and legacy is very serious, and a situation about which history provides many warnings. Indeed, it is precisely because of this danger that the entire issue cannot be seen as solely or simply "academic," let alone "historical." Instead, it is history as a key facet of society and civilisation, notably of identity, value, legitimacy, and motivation, that emerges clearly. Doubtless it is for these reasons that the assault on history is so pronounced, and not least the attempt to annex it to particular ideologies and politics. Those in the West who adopt this practice may not see themselves as totalitarians, but that is what they are, and their approach is designed to make society easier to mould by subjugating it to a set of propositions that are then to be enforced. This approach is compatible neither with a democratic present nor with a civilisation based on debate and rights.

DUELING FAITHS: SCIENCE AND RELIGION UNDER THE GREAT RESET

BY RICHARD FERNANDEZ

Science and the Great Reset

Perhaps the fairest approach to the role of science in the Great Reset is to let its founders describe it. According to the book *COVID-19: The Great Reset*, cowritten by Klaus Schwab (one of the concept's proponents) and Thierry Malleret, technology has created a world crisis through unmanaged complexity. The coronavirus, they argue, is a product of the collision between a complex global world and nature, which has exposed the human habitat to unknowable dangers.

Although many pundits have mischaracterized the Covid-19 pandemic as unforeseeable, in reality, it was totally predictable, a white-swan event, to use a term popularized by statistician and author Nassim Taleb in *The Black Swan* "that would eventually take place with a great deal of certainty" because policy-makers were trying to apply the linear and predictable methods of classical science to a highly interconnected and complex global system. Something was bound to bring down the house of cards and Covid-19 was it.

Yet Schwab and Malleret's solution to this crisis of complexity is to prescribe more technology and complexity. "The containment of the coronavirus pandemic will necessitate a global surveillance network capable of identifying new outbreaks as soon as they arise, laboratories in multiple locations around the world that can rapidly analyze new viral strains and develop effective treatments, large IT [information technology] infrastructures so that communities can prepare and react effectively, appropriate and coordinated policy mechanisms to efficiently implement the decisions once they are made, and so on."

All this will be orchestrated by government. "The COVID-19 pandemic has made government important again. Not just powerful again (look at those once-mighty companies begging for help), but also vital again." And it will require really big government, which the authors see as correcting the recent swing to the private sector.

> One of the great lessons of the past five centuries in Europe and America is this: acute crises contribute to boosting the power of the state.... World War II, for example, led to the introduction of cradle-to-grave state welfare systems in most of Europe...Already and almost overnight, the coronavirus succeeded in altering perceptions about the complex and delicate balance between the private and public realms in favor of the latter.

Bureaucracy will work this time around because corrupt governments will be made virtuous by necessity. "Changing course will require a shift in the mindset of world leaders to place greater focus and priority on the well-being of all citizens and the planet." In what is really the philosophical core of their book, Schwab and Malleret argue that we must become enlightened or die:

> The pandemic has forced all of us, citizens and policy-makers alike, willingly or not, to enter into a philosophical debate about how to maximize the common good in the least damaging way possible.... The pandemic brought them to a boil, with furious

> arguments between opposing camps. Many decisions framed as "cold" and rational, driven exclusively by economic, political and social considerations, are in fact deeply influenced by moral philosophy—the endeavor to find a theory that is capable of explaining what we should do.... Since the pandemic started, it has provoked furious debates about whether to use a utilitarian calculus when trying to tame the pandemic or to stick to the sacrosanct principle of sanctity of life.

The Great Reset is like an Anonymized Religious Movement

Creating a morally guided war-footing bureaucracy to remake the world is quite an undertaking. As a BBC summary of the Great Reset concept noted with British understatement, it is less an engineering manual than a sweeping vision. "The scope is huge—covering technology, climate change, the future of work, international security and other themes—and it's difficult to see precisely what the Great Reset might mean in practice."

At the very least it will mean specifying the moral code that will guide the enterprise; a compass defining what is "holy, sacred, absolute, spiritual, divine, or worthy of especial reverence...or attitudes towards the broader human community or the natural world," to quote *Encyclopedia Britannica*'s definition of religion. Since the only way to solve the pandemic problem is to solve *everything*, the Great Reset becomes a blank check to do everything deemed *good* while avoiding *evil*. The obvious problem is identifying what is good and evil.

It would seem the first place to look for answers would be in our civilizational legacy, particularly in the great religions with millennia of evolutionary experience in trying to resolve these issues. These religions have evolved in the forge of schism, persecution, social collapse, and even pestilence, and hence their doctrines possess an evolutionary toughness that ideologies like political correctness have yet to demonstrate.

In fact, this was the way it used to be, but using the great religions as moral reference is problematic for the giant bureaucracies that need to create their own absolute justifications for their expansive agendas. Without a time-tested belief system to fall back on, governments must find a source of legitimacy to rearrange—i.e., "reset"—the world.

The most popular candidate for the next holy writ is science. After all, popular culture often assumes science can make the moral choices for us, an expectation often associated with the phrase "trust the science."

After all, if science tells us the "truth" about the natural world, why can't the "experts" also have the last word on moral questions such as whether and when to disconnect life-support systems and whether molecular biologists should be free to unravel the entire human genome without any intervention. Why can't science tell us what virtue is?

It's already being invoked. Preventing "climate change," for Schwab and Malleret, is not only "more respectful of Mother Nature" (more virtuous) but is also scientific. The new rule is that following science *is virtue*. In place of the prophets, you have the experts.

However, many scientific aspects of the climate models are disputed. When Steven Koonin, a former undersecretary at the Department of Energy in the Obama administration, revealed that some consensus-supporting climate scientists had serious doubts about the supposedly "settled science," global warming advocates simply argued that it didn't matter.

Yet the particulars do matter, especially in complex systems like a planetary climate. Any actual plan to prevent climate change almost certainly will involve geoengineering, in which details matter because even small mistakes can lead to vastly different outcomes. Write Drs. Neil Craik and Wil Burns in a recent joint paper, "Geoengineering and the Paris Agreement," prepared for the Centre for International Governance Innovation in Canada:

> In order to meet the Agreement's objective (outlined in article 2), of keeping global average temperature increase "well below" 2°C above pre-industrial levels while pursuing efforts to limit that increase to 1.5°C, it is likely that significant carbon dioxide removal (CDR) will be required. Almost all of the modelled scenarios for achieving the 2°C objective include a significant deployment of one carbon dioxide removal option, bioenergy with carbon capture and storage (BECCS), towards the middle and end of the century.

Being "respectful of Mother Nature" boils down to funding giant engineering projects. For example, the *Independent* has described plans to dim the sun by shooting particulates into the upper atmosphere:

> Plans to geo-engineer the atmosphere by blocking out sunlight have been floated before, but an experiment launched next year by Harvard researchers will be the first to test the theory in the stratosphere. The team will use a balloon suspended 12 miles above Earth to spray tiny chalk particles across a kilometer-long area, with the intention of reflecting the Sun's rays away from the planet. In doing so, they will attempt to replicate on a small scale the eruption of Mount Pinatubo in the Philippines in 1991.

Readers who might be worrying about what could go wrong with dimming the sun or mimicking a cataclysmic volcanic eruption should recall that Schwab and Malleret wrote their Great Reset book months before Joe Biden publicly acknowledged that the coronavirus epidemic might have originated in a Chinese lab. When one recalls that the 1977 H1N1 pandemic that killed seven hundred thousand people in Central Asia probably resulted from another Chinese lab accident, there exists the possibility that science itself might be a source of a catastrophe.

If scientists who meant well accidentally killed seven hundred thousand people, then our confidence in science cannot be absolute because when it comes to complex systems—as Schwab and Malleret themselves have noted—minor errors can have huge consequences. Our ability to predict what viruses and dimming the sun will do is limited.

Since the facile equivalence between virtue and science is not always guaranteed, it is not sufficient to "trust the science," but we must "trust and verify."

Science Cannot Tell Us What Is Virtuous

Most people are familiar with the philosophical distinction between ends and means. Because extreme ends impel extreme means, communities are usually careful about declaring the equivalent of war. War justifies actions that would never be countenanced in peace. If you are really out to save the planet, then dimming the sun is a reasonable risk.

Can we get such imperative ends from science? It may come as a shock to a generation taught to equate science with progress that it is silent on intrinsic values. Science will equally make an electric toaster or an electric chair. Science itself doesn't care whether humanity survives or not. It concerns itself with anticipating the outcomes consequent to certain physical arrangements. The moral values of those outcomes must be supplied from elsewhere. Ever since Newton, science has consciously restricted itself to constructing mathematical models that can usefully predict observable phenomena. If governments want science to prophesy on morals, it will be a silent prophet.

As Edward R. Dougherty wrote in his 2016 book *The Evolution of Scientific Knowledge from Certainty to Uncertainty*, "The epistemology of modern science begins to mature with Newton. The structure is relational, its form is mathematical…The mathematical structure represents a precise, inter-subjective, and operational form of knowledge…*Hypotheses non fingo*—'I frame no hypotheses.' In three words, Newton changes man's perspective on himself and the universe, a change more profound than the one brought about by Copernicus because it is a fundamental change in what it means to know."

Newton effectively said he wasn't going to explain things in terms of philosophical meaning and human understanding. What is gravity? "Hypotheses non fingo." He simply presented a mathematical system that describes how this phenomenon we call gravity behaves. At a stroke, science left the subject of "ends" to philosophy, religion, and politics to concern itself strictly with "means."

The silence of science on human ends creates serious problems for those who would invoke it to justify totally remaking the world. Science cannot by itself explain why humanity ought to exist as opposed to deliberately choosing its own extinction to allow other species to thrive. It is from the more human sources of religion, politics, and ideology that the ultimate objects of the Great Reset must derive. As Blaise Pascal said, "The heart has its reasons, which reason does not know."

The Science of Complex Systems Imposes Risks on Long-term Planners

But even the Newtonian dream of forecasting physical phenomena has problems justifying policies prospectively. Science's inability to accurately predict complex systems is the most troublesome. "The epistemological challenges confronting the 21st century," says Dougherty, "are the most severe since the dawning of the seventeenth century. They arise from a desire to model complex systems that exceed human conceptualization ability." While the term science evokes certitude, exactness and perfection in the popular press, the reality is that twenty-first-century problems are probabilistic and some may actually exceed human comprehension.

> There was a profound enigma lurking in the thinking of Galileo and Newton. It was genius to declare that knowledge of Nature is constituted within mathematics,

> not within human categories of understanding; yet, as long as the mathematical laws were consistent with human cognition, the full implication of this thinking lay hidden. The advent of quantum mechanics in the first part of the 20th century brought it to light: a theory may be preposterous from the perspective of human intelligibility but lead to predictions that agree with empirical observation—and therefore be scientifically valid. Man can possess knowledge beyond the limits of his physical understanding.

Richard Feynman famously warned against looking for human categories of intelligibility in the physical sciences. Regarding quantum physics, he said: "It is not a question of whether a theory is philosophically delightful, or easy to understand, or perfectly reasonable from the point of view of common sense. The theory of quantum electrodynamics describes Nature as absurd from the point of view of common sense. And it agrees fully with experiment. So I hope you can accept Nature as she is—absurd."

Models are all the scientific understanding we have but there are limits. We simply can't model complex phenomena like the climate, the biosphere, and human society with the exactitude necessary to take precisely calculated high-stakes risks.

Nor can we bet the farm on models without accepting that we might get it wrong. One of the most recent and dramatic demonstrations of model limits was the Covid-19 forecast by British government scientific adviser Neil Ferguson that proved grossly inaccurate. "We're building simplified representations of reality. Models are not crystal balls," Ferguson explained. He may know that, but the public—even politicians—may have thought otherwise.

A survey by *Nature* magazine reported that "more than 70 percent of researchers have tried and failed to reproduce another scientist's experiments, and more than half have failed to reproduce their own experiments." The phenomenon even has a name: the replication crisis.

If the Great Reset is anything, it is "interaction-dominant." Biological, environmental, and social systems are hard to predict because they are sensitive to small differences in starting conditions (latent variables) and perturbations in their elements. A latent variable is exterior to the model but since complex phenomena like the climate, biosphere, or society cannot be isolated from the outside influences, there is always something uncontrolled that can affect the initialization. Further randomness is introduced by perturbation. In genetic networks, for example, there is some probability a gene will switch values due to random variation in the amount of mRNA and protein produced. One might be able to predict a simple system of billiard balls on a table yet fail to forecast the life trajectories of identical twins because of the difference in complexity.

The impact of uncertainty has prompted some scholars to warn against attempting goals like altering the course of nature or changing the genetic destiny of humanity in favor of far more limited and more easily foreseeable goals—managing the risk in engineering. As Dougherty notes, they propose "a course of action based on integrating existing partial knowledge with limited data to arrive at an optimal operation on some system, where optimality is conditioned on the uncertainty regarding the system."

In layman's language, instead of making one big visionary bet, we should learn as we go along using Bayesian techniques (hindsight) to estimate the risks and benefits of the next possible step based on the most recent experience. But the limits of science's predictive powers with respect to complex systems mean some element of human or religious judgment must remain to deal with the incalculable—unless we can eliminate the human factor altogether.

Can We Avoid These Predictive Limits Using Artificial Intelligence?

One of the suggested solutions to the inability of the human mind to control complex systems is to delegate the task to a kind of superintelligence. Humanity could then rely on a technological oracle or genie to provide the knowledge and wisdom to remake the world. We could get our moral code from robots.

Collective Superintelligence

In a way, we already do. The most familiar kind of superintelligence is collective: governments, corporations, technical megaprojects—the proposed governance structures of the Great Reset. All are examples of collective superintelligence whose institutional capacity is supposed to overcome individual limitations. When the media says "believe in the consensus," they usually mean deference to the authority of official collective superintelligence. However, human experience has revealed to most of us the limitations of collective intelligence. Collective superintelligence failed to anticipate the fall of the U.S.S.R., 9/11, Brexit, and Covid-19 itself. Aware of these limits, most Western democracies have constitutional safeguards to prevent them from undertaking overly ambitious ends because they know from historical experience how awry they can go.

Machine Superintelligence or AI

The other potential approach to controlling complex systems is through artificial intelligence, the notion that through some algorithm, mapping of the whole human brain into electronics, or evolutionary self-programming, we can create an oracle that can spit out the answer.

Because such systems are intentionally designed to go beyond human understanding, they create "what's known as the control problem," Susan Schneider, director at the Center for the Future Mind, has explained. "It is simply the problem of how to control an AI that is vastly smarter than us."

We could take our moral code from machine AI but only on the basis of faith. Taking men out of the loop includes politicians also, as presidents sometimes forget. Governments would be like morons trying to peer-review Einstein. Morons would have to treat him like a black box without any real power to critique, much as elected officials do today when receiving "expert advice" on Covid-19.

Will Knight of the *MIT Technology Review* has described the problems associated with the new machine learning techniques. "Last year, a strange self-driving car was released onto the quiet roads of Monmouth County, New Jersey…The car didn't follow a single instruction provided by an engineer or programmer. Instead, it relied entirely on an algorithm that had taught itself to drive by watching a human do it…But it's also a bit unsettling, since it isn't completely clear how the car makes its decisions…. But what if one day it did something unexpected—crashed into a tree, or sat at a green light?… you can't ask it: there is no obvious way to design such a system so that it could always explain why it did what it did."

The heart of the dilemma is that to solve the problem of modeling complex systems that the Great Reset aspires to control, one has to resort to mechanisms of equal complexity that can't be understood either without a leap of faith.

Perverse Instantiation

That leap of faith may take us to places we never actually wanted to go. As Oxford professor Nick Bostrom has put it, politicians bent on controlling nature and humanity through technologies they cannot even understand are "like children playing with a bomb."

Superintelligences, whether of the AI or collective kind, eventually can adopt end goals of their own devices. They could pursue their own goals in ways their creators had not originally intended. They could "wake up" and take on lives of their own. We could wind up on the pilgrimage to perdition.

The technical term for this is *perverse instantiation.* Our "genie" may take us not where we intend to go but where it reckons is good for us. It can maximize some variable but ignore a consideration the programmers forgot to mention because we as humans *assume it*. If we set AI the goal of minimizing coronavirus infection, it could perversely instantiate the solution of a police state and extreme movement restriction. Even Schwab and Malleret recognize that a project to remake the world unintentionally could result in a surveillance state:

> Surveillance technology is developing at breakneck speed, and what seemed science-fiction 10 years ago is today old news. As a thought experiment, consider a hypothetical government that demands that every citizen wears a biometric bracelet that monitors body temperature and heart-rate 24 hours a day. The resulting data is hoarded and analyzed by government algorithms. The algorithms will know that you are sick even before you know it, and they will also know where you have been, and who you have met. The chains of infection could be drastically shortened, and even cut altogether. Such a system could arguably stop the epidemic in its tracks within days. Sounds wonderful, right?
>
> The downside is, of course, that this would give legitimacy to a terrifying new surveillance system. If you know, for example, that I clicked on a Fox News link rather than a CNN link, that can teach you something about my political views and perhaps even my personality. But if you can monitor what happens to my body temperature, blood pressure and heart-rate as I watch the video clip, you can learn what makes me laugh, what makes me cry, and what makes me really, really angry.... corporations and governments start harvesting our biometric data *en masse*...Imagine North Korea in 2030, when every citizen has to wear

> a biometric bracelet 24 hours a day. If you listen to a speech by the Great Leader and the bracelet picks up the tell-tale signs of anger, you are done for.

As Bostrom emphasizes, the first time you'll know you're in jail is when the door clangs shut behind you.

Orthogonality

There is also the danger the superintelligence we set over us may aspire to something we cannot even anticipate—such as becoming a god or world dictator, for example. As Nick Bostrom points out, *any* combination of technology and morality is possible. It is not the case that smart always leads to good. "Intelligence and final goals are orthogonal: more or less any level of intelligence could in principle be combined with more or less any final goal." Absent a special effort to shape our super-endeavor's ends, it may adopt some unpredictable or reductionistic final goal similar to China's, Russia's or the Woke West's.

The Value-loading Problem

How do we choose which politics, philosophy, ideology, or religion we should load into our world-transformative Great Reset? According to Bostrom, there is no available consensus set of human values or religious precepts even in the West:

> No ethical theory commands majority support among philosophers, so most philosophers must be wrong. It is also reflected in the marked changes that the distribution of moral belief has undergone over time, many of which we like to think of as progress. In medieval Europe, for instance, it was deemed respectable entertainment to watch a political prisoner being tortured to death. Cat-burning remained

> popular in sixteenth-century Paris. A mere hundred and fifty years ago, slavery still was widely practiced in the American South, with full support of the law and moral custom.
>
> When we look back, we see glaring deficiencies not just in the behavior but in the moral beliefs of all previous ages. Though we have perhaps since gleaned some moral insight, we could hardly claim to be now basking in the high noon of perfect moral enlightenment. Very likely, we are still laboring under one or more grave moral misconceptions. In such circumstances to select a final value based on our current convictions, in a way that locks it in forever and precludes any possibility of further ethical progress, would be to risk an existential moral calamity.

Liberal early twenty-first-century beliefs, upon whose bearings we are asked to set our fateful course, are unlikely to prove the final writ. It is humbling to recall that eugenics was once regarded as consensus "enlightened" thinking in the United States. California's Asexualization Act of 1909 authorized the involuntary sterilization of certain groups of people, including inmates of state hospitals, life-sentenced prisoners, and repeat offenders. Its advocates were often personally well-meaning and included many prominent scientists, including:

- David Starr Jordan: Founding president of Stanford University and chairman of the American Eugenics Commission, vice-president of the American Society for Social Hygiene, and vice president of the Eugenics Education Society of London.
- Lewis Terman: Creator of the IQ test, and member of eugenics group the Human Betterment Foundation. A school in Palo Alto California, Terman Middle School, was named after him until it was renamed in 2018.
- Robert Andrews Millikan: Director of the Norman Bridge Laboratory of Physics at the California Institute of Technology

> (Caltech) in Pasadena, California, winner of the Nobel Prize for Physics, and member of the Human Betterment Foundation.

It is sometimes presumed that woke values and political correctness will be universally acceptable and enduring in an *End of History and the Last Man* way. Yet a time traveler from Woodstock 1969 would find 2021 an alien place. Even before the pandemic, public resistance to globalism was potent enough to touch off Brexit and the election of Donald Trump. Some critics think the Great Reset is just the same globalism warmed over. "No, the World Economic Forum is not involved in a conspiracy to remake the world," said one critical article on the website Spiked. "In truth, what is conspiratorially referred to as 'the great reset' represents regressive ideas that have been taking hold in Western societies for a very long time…all of this thinking has been around for decades, and is clearly formulated in the ideology of environmentalism and climate protection. None of it is new."

It will be resisted domestically. "Donald Trump became the political vehicle for the American people's resentment of an overweening, corrupt ruling class. Trump's invaluable contribution to the Republic was to lead Americans publicly to disrespect that class," wrote the late Angelo Codevilla. Perhaps more importantly, those values will be resisted internationally by China, which has advanced its own arc of history and declared the willingness to impose it. "In April," noted the *Wall Street Journal* in June 2021, "China's cyberspace regulator launched an online platform and a telephone hotline for the public to denounce…statements that criticize party leaders and policies or deny 'advanced socialist culture.'"

China is arguably second only to the U.S. in scientific progress, with spacecraft on Mars and a developed biotechnology industry, yet it has a very different code of ethics from that of the West. According to the *New York Post* (July 12, 2021), China is suspected to be engaged in banned experiments on human beings:

> The World Health Organization issued new recommendations Monday on human genome editing,

> calling for a global registry to track "any form of genetic manipulation" and proposing a whistle-blowing mechanism to raise concerns about unethical or unsafe research. The U.N. health agency commissioned an expert group in late 2018 following a dramatic announcement from Chinese scientist He Jiankui that he had created the world's first gene-edited babies.

The Chinese Communist Party also has long been accused by dissidents of sanctioning the harvesting of organs from certain groups.

Beijing's response to the climate change agenda is a perfect example of both moral orthogonality and perverse instantiation. As the *Guardian* reported on June 29, 2021:

> China, India, Indonesia, Japan, and Vietnam plan to build more than 600 coal-power units, even though renewable energy is cheaper than most new coal plants. The investments in one of the most environmentally damaging sources of energy could generate a total of 300 gigawatts of energy—enough to power the U.K. more than three times over—despite calls from climate experts at the U.N. for all new coal plants to be cancelled.

China's contribution to the green agenda has been to manufacture cheap solar panels with coal plants and slave labor. It is a classic case of perverse instantiation, maximizing one isolated variable—solar panels—at the expense of implicit assumptions. Movies have been made about "blood diamonds" mined in Africa. But few realize that their green batteries also come from child labor in the Congo.

Advanced technological states need not morally resemble each other. They could be extremely alien and diverge radically from those of the proponents of the Great Reset, due to different historical backgrounds. Perhaps the Chinese Communist Party has the right to taunt the West in this way: evolution, the "survival of the fittest" is scientific. Where else did we get the idea that evolution favors the good guys but from the religious conjectures of the heart?

Winston Churchill reminded us long ago that science can be light or dark depending on what it is used for,[20] that technique by itself is free of content. Noam Chomsky, realizing that technology most likely explained the apparent absence of other intelligent life in the universe, quoted biologist Ernst Mayr's plaint: "intelligence is a lethal mutation." Simply relying on technology without wisdom has not been enough since the Atomic Age.

The Threat of a Singleton: The Great Reset

The only predictable aspect of the value-loading problem is that political factions will vie to create the new religion that controls it, that the Great Reset will set off a power struggle over its agenda. Historically, all-encompassing endeavors have created their own official ideology and ruthlessly persecuted rivals. Among the most familiar instances are:

- The French Revolution's Cult of Reason. The Cult of Reason was France's first established state-sponsored secular religion, intended as a replacement for Catholicism. Since it proved difficult to completely sate the transcendental instincts of the public with bare atheism, Robespierre "created a new cult which believed the creation of the universe was an act of a 'supreme being' and that human souls are immortal, but that humans are responsible for their own actions and destinies—these are

20 "But if we fail, then the whole world, including the United States, including all that we have known and cared for, will sink into the abyss of a new Dark Age made more sinister, and perhaps more protracted, by the lights of perverted science." An excerpt of Winston Churchill's "Finest Hour" speech delivered to the House of Commons on June 18, 1940.

not acts of God. He called this 'The Cult of the Supreme Being' and decreed it the new state religion."

- The Bolshevik's' antireligious campaign. The Soviets famously tried to destroy Russian Orthodox Christianity and replace it with atheism and materialism. "More than 85,000 Orthodox priests were shot in 1937 alone. In the period between 1927 and 1940, the number of Orthodox Churches in the Russian Republic fell from 29,584 to less than 500."
- The Nazi Kirchenkampf or "church struggle." In 1937 Heinrich Himmler wrote, "We live in an era of the ultimate conflict with Christianity. It is part of the mission of the SS to give the German people in the next half century the non-Christian ideological foundations on which to lead and shape their lives." They were working on a religion compounded of paganism and the occult before this was cut short by defeat in 1945.
- China's antireligious campaign. "Religious controls have been part of communist practice since the foundation of the People's Republic of China," wrote Azeem Ibrahim in *Foreign Policy*. "As a result, churches split into "patriotic" associations, officially sanctioned if frowned upon...Government officials have been asked to compile more details of worshippers, feeding into discrimination in employment, especially in official posts. All children under age 18 have been strictly prohibited from attending any kind of religious education."

The motive for suppression in each case is similar: to kill the rival religion; to remove the obstacle to the total commitment and faith required to remake the world. Thus, there were always capitalist roaders blocking the path of the locomotive of history, Untermenschen taking up much-needed Lebensraum, deniers endangering the climate. Can wokeness afford to brook a rival?

Information, and the Modern Search for God

The silence of science on metaphysics means the quest to answer the ultimate questions will continue unabated. The woke obsession with becoming a religion in itself underscores the importance of the metaphysical enterprise. As through history, the great religions will adapt to the new bureaucratic challenge by taking up new technologies and assimilating emerging insights. Just as they enlisted writing, mathematics, architecture, and philosophy into their past endeavors, religions are certain to adopt the latest technologies to pursue and disseminate their inquiries into the ultimate questions.

On a practical level, they have already made the move into virtual space. Perhaps the most famous example is jihadists and the internet. "Before the Taliban took Afghanistan, it took the internet," writes the Atlantic Council. National Public Radio warns that the Christian "American Taliban" are not far behind: beware "QAnon: The Alternative Religion That's Coming to Your Church."

The most implacable online foe of the Chinese Communist Party is the Falun Gong, a new religious movement founded by Li Hongzhi in China in the early 1990s. "Since 2016, the Falun Gong-backed newspaper has used aggressive Facebook tactics and right-wing misinformation to create an anti-China, pro-Trump media empire," wrote the *New York Times*. None of this should be surprising. One of the things that religion, taken as a whole, does well is preserve dissent. The history of religion is the archive of heresy.

On a substantive level, religious thought is likely to be energized by the possibility that information may be the fundamental basis of reality. For most of the twentieth century, matter has occupied the basement of the universe and information was merely derived from it. However, twenty-first-century physics theories have tended toward reversing the primacy of matter. Now it is information that is regarded as forming the bedrock and matter that is emergent. Not only are models all that human scientists have, as Newton observed, but models may be all that even nature has. Information realism is potentially an upheaval fully as great as the emergence of quantum mechanics a century ago. Bernardo Kastrup in *Scientific American* says,

> To some physicists, this indicates that what we call "matter," with its solidity and concreteness—is an illusion; that only the mathematical apparatus they devise in their theories is truly real...Indeed, according to information realists, matter arises from information processing, not the other way around. Even mind—psyche, soul—is supposedly a derivative phenomenon of purely abstract information manipulation.

The fact that information can interact with biological structures, including human brains through the new discipline of quantum biology, raises the possibility that consciousness is networked in some way. Whether this paradigm will prosper and what its effect will be on the doctrine and development of religions is beyond the scope of this chapter to anticipate. But at the very least, it will open the search by religions and science for structures in this information universe.

Is there a hierarchy of consciousness? Orders of higher intelligence? Some will seek in such structures the explanation to the Fermi Paradox, named after physicist Enrico Fermi's observation that if other intelligent life existed in the galaxy, its civilization would be detectable by now. Perhaps the reason we do not find aliens in outer space is because we should be looking for superintelligences in the information universe around us. The idea would not be completely novel. One of the fourteen points in logician Kurt Gödel's proof of God is "there are other worlds and rational beings of a different and higher kind." Of course, the great religions already anticipated a hierarchy of angels and demons since antiquity.

The flag of exploration has already been planted on the shores of this new world. In the field of virtual reality, Google is seriously and deliberately working toward building a civilization ruled by machine superintelligence with humans in a supporting role only. It is Google's equivalent of SpaceX's Mars Project. One wants to reach another planet; the other wants to climb the next rung on the information-universe hierarchy.

The two efforts will probably combine to give religions of the mid- to late twenty-first century a character we scarcely imagine today. At a minimum, it would give religions—new and old—additional means of expression and, with the opening of outer space, an unlimited refuge from persecution. At maximum, it will endow religions with a potentially new source of revelation, a way to confirm, extend, or repudiate beliefs. The possibilities are many, and some even wondrous, but everything presumes humanity will survive into the future.

Lessons for the Sorcerer's Apprentice

The world is in not-inconsiderable peril from those who would remake it. The University of Cambridge Centre for the Study of Existential Risk has begun to develop a research agenda for global catastrophic biological risks. In fact, it may soon be possible to engineer even more dangerous pathogens than Covid-19: more infectious and more fatal.

The Prophets Are Armed

Religions have long acted as a brake against the domination of the world by any single ideological force. This is rooted in self-preservation because each religion must compete against other faiths to survive. *But primarily against other faiths*, as there has been little religious competition with actual science to create mathematical models of the universe for over a century. The reality on the ground has been to keep theology and science separate. What's new is the emergence of comprehensive new ideologies, of which the Great Reset is but one, disguising their moral and eschatological agendas with the rhetoric of science and invading the realm of religion.

One such new religion, which has been called the church of woke, is sworn to the destruction of racism, traditional gender roles, and sinful fossil fuels. Rather than being driven by perpetually tentative, necessarily experimental science, it is propelled by posited moral certainties and therefore the facts must follow as best they can. These types of churches, which base themselves in bureaucracies, aspire to become civil religions in which the arguments from authority approximate the edicts of the divine.

Several civic religions of this sort are likely to arise, one in the U.S. and Western Europe and another in China at the minimum, each with radically different moral codes yet ironically claiming the same legitimacy in science. It is possible to have two or more versions of the Great Reset ostensibly rooted in the same expertise. For example, there are two sets of climate change goals and two versions of the Covid-19 origin story, the Chinese and the Western, yet despite the differences, they alike claim a scientific basis for their moral and operational goals.

Such quasireligions are a challenge not only to humanity's philosophical and moral legacy but also to the intellectual integrity of science itself. Unlike faiths that feel themselves accountable to some higher power, or in the case of science, to empirical validation, these unelected hierophants, cynically fronting for economic interests who will benefit from their projects, are willing to boldly transform the world, come what may.

Aware of the dangers inherent in a bureaucracy convinced of its own infallibility, some scientists have warned against doing anything global or irreversible with powerful technologies without being very careful. Kevin Esvelt, an American biologist involved with the development of gene-drive technology who focuses on bioethics and biosafety, noted that gene drives make it possible to replace whole populations for good. "The technique relies on the gene-editing tool CRISPR [Clustered regularly interspaced short palindromic repeats] and some bits of RNA to alter or silence a specific gene or insert a new one" so that all descendants are clones of the altered parents.

Esvelt, who was among the first to build a CRISPR-based gene drive, saw how potentially dangerous a genetic engine that could exterminate whole populations could be. Esvelt therefore invented a way to localize genetic engineering called a daisy chain control system. "Imagine you have a chain of daisies, and at each generation you remove the one on the end. When you run out, the daisy chain drive stops," Esvelt explained.

Such an approach emphasizes localization and reversibility rather than global transformation. It stresses local decision-making instead of governance by some United Nations intergovernmental panel. It adopts this approach because it is too dangerous to put government in charge of complex systems to change the world.

But individual scientists cannot fight organized political dogmas without support from competing belief systems in order to not be beaten down. At a recent National Science Foundation meeting, grant applicants found they had to pass four hurdles. Three were conventionally scientific and academic. The fourth was "Diversity and Culture of Inclusion" (DCI). You can't fight City Hall. To prevent one collective superintelligence from dominating the world, it must face stiff and spirited competition from others.

Creating Competition Among Collective Intelligences

Only in this way can the search for meaning develop in a healthy way. Not only should our engineering evolve gradually, but as Bostrom argues, so should our final religious and moral goals. This could prevent the emergence of a singleton, the new Moloch. This means the intrinsic elements that go into major biotechnological, AI, and social engineering projects always should be negotiated among the greatest possible number. AI theorist Eliezer Yudkowsky thinks humanity's long-term goals should evolve slowly. "[We] should be conservative about saying 'yes,' and listen carefully for 'no.'"

In other words, humanity's religious goals should evolve incrementally rather than in sweeping, discontinuous great leaps forward. They should be negotiated rather than proclaimed by advocates, however well-meaning or credentialed. However, no one should be under the illusion that such evolution or negotiation will be a polite process. It will be as bitterly contested as any religious war in history between the truest of believers over issues each side regards as more important than life itself.

Diverse Ways to Listen to the Heart's Reasons

From humanity's beginning, people have been reverse-engineering the messages pouring down from the stars in the hopes of deducing not only the "what" of things but also the "why." Like cryptographers trying to piece together the design of some unseen coding machine from the signals it produces, humanity has labored long and sometimes fruitlessly. Perhaps our species ultimately will fail before the challenges of complexity or prove unable to discern a God too great for it to grasp. But for so long as humanity survives, it will keep on trying. In any case, history argues that this is more a task for the artists and creators than the scientists.

The one thing we must not do is stop on some arbitrary answer provided by a government panel or adopt some faith supplied by ideologues. Rather, we must test limited propositions against the actual experience of civilization step by little step. In this, we should be guided by a sense of limits as much as by the lure of possibilities.

This is how we left the cave and most likely how we will eventually reach the stars. But if we do not watch our steps, instead of a great flowering, we will enter the age of the singleton. In place of a Great Reset, there will be a Great Diktat. A project that seeks to remake the world according to a single vision imposes a global-risk externality. The uncertainties inherent in complexity and the risks associated with an ideological singleton are too great for humanity to wager everything on a single throw of millenarian enthusiasm. Our primary defense against the rise of a singleton is intellectual diversity. No one entity should self-appoint itself as morally righteous.

Still Only the Beginning for Science and Religion

The late mathematician and physicist Freeman Dyson, one of the architects of modern particle physics and a researcher of nuclear reactors, nuclear-powered space travel, astronomy, astrobiology, climate-change skepticism, and futurism, was a commentator on religion as well. His acceptance speech on being awarded the 2000 Templeton Prize for science and religion sums up the case against imposing a single plan and vision on humanity. Maximum diversity is the key to survival because we are never sure which of many strategies is finally going to work.

> Perhaps the universe is constructed according to a principle of maximum diversity. The principle of maximum diversity says that the laws of nature, and the initial conditions at the beginning of time, are such as to make the universe as interesting as possible. As a result, life is possible but not too easy. Maximum diversity often leads to maximum stress. In the end we survive, but only by the skin of our teeth...

"Maximum stress" lies ahead but it can't be helped if we are to preserve diversity and avert the singleton. Dyson reminds us that asking questions and accepting that we may never fully know the answers is less dangerous than bureaucratic certitude and ideological dogma:

> Both as a scientist and as a religious person, I am accustomed to living with uncertainty. Science is exciting because it is full of unsolved mysteries, and religion is exciting for the same reason. The greatest unsolved mysteries are the mysteries of our existence as conscious beings in a small corner of a vast universe. Why are we here? Does the universe have a purpose? Whence comes our knowledge of good and evil? These

> mysteries, and a hundred others like them, are beyond the reach of science. They lie on the other side of the border, within the jurisdiction of religion....

Scientists and common humanity may be accustomed to uncertainty, but people aspiring to remake the world often profess more certitude than they actually have. This leads to the underestimation of risk in social restructuring projects, climate engineering, and bioengineering—all hallmark undertakings of the Great Reset. The potential for overreach in viral "gain of function" research, population movement control, and public health mandates is greatest in those convinced they are doing the Lord's work, atheist or not. They can get in over their heads because they are the adults in the room, the anointed ones, the experts.

To counter the hubris of kings, it helps to bear in mind the very real possibility, if not probability, that God exists. As Dyson points out, humanity is merely discovering the rules, not making them.

> The universe shows evidence of the operations of mind on three levels. The first level is elementary physical processes, as we see them when we study atoms in the laboratory. The second level is our direct human experience of our own consciousness. The third level is the universe as a whole...Our minds may receive inputs equally from atoms and from God. This view of our place in the cosmos may not be true, but it is compatible with the active nature of atoms as revealed in the experiments of modern physics. I don't say that this personal theology is supported or proved by scientific evidence. I only say that it is consistent with scientific evidence....

Dyson says "our minds may receive inputs equally from atoms and from God" but only if we are listening to the signal and haven't handed over our minds to the authority of the fact-checkers:

> The message is simple. "God forbid that we should give out a dream of our own imagination for a pattern of the world." This was said by Francis Bacon, one of the founding fathers of modern science, almost four hundred years ago. Bacon was the smartest man of his time, with the possible exception of William Shakespeare. Bacon saw clearly what science could do and what science could not do. He is saying to the philosophers and theologians of his time: look for God in the facts of nature, not in the theories of Plato and Aristotle. I am saying to modern scientists and theologians: don't imagine that our latest ideas about the Big Bang or the human genome have solved the mysteries of the universe or the mysteries of life.

Western political leaders, after watching their carefully planned global New World Order collapse from unpredictable events like Covid-19, are ill-advised to save it through an even more controlling recovery process called the Great Reset. This recovery requires state powers so vast that they must be sustained by a cultlike moral imperative legitimized by "science."

Since Newton, however, science has gotten out of the business of metaphysics and moral pronouncements. This leaves unscrupulous bureaucrats free to actively subordinate or suppress both traditional values and the great religions in order to push their fantastic vision through. The great faiths, survivors of millennia of competitive evolution and no strangers to persecution, are likely to respond in effective and surprising ways we cannot even begin to imagine. We are, after all, mere mortals, not gods.

If Western political leaders try to remake the world on the basis of political certainties, they are likely to unleash disastrous results from complex systems they cannot control. Only an approach humble enough to absorb natural feedback will allow humanity to evolve the moral ground upon which to stand higher and to rise not on the tiptoes of pride but of wonder.

The hardest stories to end are tales that can have no ending. The only way a human author can finish them is to lay down the pen after his allotted time and hope—nay, know—that the pages will be taken up with a continuation more marvelous than he could have imagined. Here our chapter ends, or rather, it begins.

"WHAT AN ARTIST DIES IN ME!"

BY MICHAEL WALSH

Or so the Emperor Nero was supposed to have said, just before one of his freedmen helped him drive a dagger through his throat in the year 68 A.D. Too afraid to die a noble Roman by his own hand, declared a public enemy by the Senate, his castrated transsexual catamite, Sporus, by his side, the last of the Julio-Claudians went to Hades piteously declaiming what a loss to the world his death would be.

We remember Nero[21] today primarily as the man who fiddled, or rather played upon the lyre and sang, while Rome burned as he pondered some architectural improvements. As the man who murdered his own mother (Agrippina the Younger, the model for all scheming momsters), as well as two of his wives—Octavia, the daughter of Emperor Claudius, and the pregnant Poppaea, who formerly had been married to one of his closest friends, Otho, who later briefly succeeded him as emperor. And as the man who threw the early Christians to the lions, when he wasn't covering them in pitch and setting them ablaze as human torches, according to some hostile accounts.

But we remember him still, despite his notorious reputation as a sexual deviant, even by Roman standards, a matricide, an uxoricide, and the unworthiest descendant of the line of Mark Antony

21 For an indelible portrait of Nero and his time, Henryk Sienkiewicz's 1896 novel, *Quo Vadis*, is indispensable.

and Germanicus, a category that also includes the stiff competition of Caligula. He considered himself, however, a great poet, musician, singer, and actor, who spent much of the period 66–67 A.D. in Greece, where he competed in the Olympic Games as both an actor and a charioteer. And his last words, more poignant and delusional than most, tell us how he saw himself. He was not just the emperor, a demigod, and the absolute monarch of a still-expanding empire: he was a bard and a singer.

The nexus between art, religion, and power is an ancient one, dating back to the wellsprings of humanity. To the seer and the shaman were given tribal standing; the man of insight and ability won leadership. The talent to conceive and draw big game on the walls of caves—three-dimensional objects in two-dimensional space—was tantamount to summoning them to the slaughter. To evoke the as-yet-unborn Schopenhauer, the world was both will and representation, and it would take millennia of scientific and philosophical advancement to try—imperfectly—to separate them.

The path from *reification* to the middle step of representation—objectification—led, perhaps paradoxically in the eyes of modern "feminists," to more abstract concepts of beauty, with their attendant webs of nuance, recollections, desires, hopes, dreams. Writing in his book, *Beauty*, the late Sir Roger Scruton noted, "Metaphors make connections which are not contained in the fabric of reality but created by our own associative powers. The important question about a metaphor is not what property it stands for, but what experience it suggests." This was the next step in the creation of art,[22] because at root, art is about beauty and nothing but beauty. No matter how brutal the art may be, how coarse and even nihilistic, beauty in a free society is always present by its absence, the standard against which the emptiness of evil is measured. The corruption of art is therefore an act of the purest evil. Small wonder that totalitarian movements

22 Throughout this essay, I will be using the term "art" to encompass all the arts, not simply painting and sculpture.

such as the Great Reset[23] fear its power and must co-opt and destroy its independence.

The Greeks had Mount Parnassus, sacred to both Apollo and Dionysus and their attendant arts, and perhaps the home of the Muses as well. Later, pedagogues developed the notion of the Gradus ad Parnassum, denoting the steps to mastery novices must take as they ascend to the peak of artistic attainment. And, as noted in my Introduction, the great German novelist Thomas Mann synthesized these themes and many more in 1924 his masterpiece, *The Magic Mountain*—located, as fate would have it, in Davos, Switzerland, in the heart of the Swiss Alps, which also happens to be the locus of the World Economic Forum's annual celebration of obscene wealth and unbounded ambition—a fitting locale for our latter-day emperors.

However, instead of encountering Mann's indelible cast of characters at the Berghof sanatorium—the scalding intellectual Naphta; the rationalist, secular freemason Settembrini; the seductive hot kitten, Clawdia Chauchat of the Kirghiz eyes; and the despotically exotic Mynheer Peeperkorn—we find waiting for us instead the clinical dispassion of Klaus Schwab, as Teutonic in mien and accent as the character of Dr. Szell in *Marathon Man.* We half expect him to ask us, "Is it safe?" But he has other queries in his book, *COVID 19: The Great Reset*, cowritten with Thierry Malleret:

> Many questions came to mind, like: Might the pandemic give birth to better selves and to a better world? Will it be followed by a shift of values? Will we become more willing to nurture our human bonds and more intentional about maintaining our social connections? Simply put: will we become more caring and compassionate…?

---

23 Swiss-based, it echoes in its ethos some of the tenets of the Swiss Calvinism of Zwingli and the French-born Calvin (Cauvin) himself, principally the fundamental depravity of human beings and the doctrine of predestination.

> At the beginning of *The Decameron*, a series of novellas that tell the tale of a group of men and women sheltered in a villa as the Black Death ravaged Florence in 1348, Boccaccio writes that: "fathers and mothers were found to abandon their own children, untended, unvisited, to their fate". In the same vein, numerous literary accounts of past pandemics, from Defoe's *A Journal of The Plague Year* to Manzoni's *The Betrothed*, relate how, so often, fear of death ends up overriding all other human emotions...The COVID-19 pandemic has unequivocally shown us all that we live in a world that is interconnected and yet largely bereft of solidarity between nations and often even within nations.
>
> Put in the simplest possible terms: if, as human beings, we do not collaborate to confront our existential challenges (the environment and the global governance free fall, among others), we are doomed. Thus, we have no choice but to summon up the better angels of our nature.

The evocation of Lincoln by a Bismarckian plutocrat with dreams and delusions of moral grandeur—a Bond villain without the pussy or the charm—is rich. But here we have the voice not just of Schwab and his fell barbarian fellows but of Hofrat Behrens himself, the sanatorium's director, in whose best interest it is for him not to cure his patients but to keep them there, treating them indefinitely, until they are finally either "well" or dead. Indeed, like many physicians, Behrens sees human beings only as carriers of disease who must be dealt with sternly in the greater interests of humanity—a description that also fits Schwab and his colleagues perfectly, since they view human beings as carbuncles upon the earth, despoilers of the environment, and dumb animals that need to be tamed and cured; no wonder they so eagerly seized upon the Covid panic to unleash their programs of quarantine and lockdown. That few leave the Berghof under their own steam is hardly mentioned: for most, the only way out is feet first.

In this view, widely shared by totalitarians who see themselves as do-gooders, something is very wrong with humanity, the universality and stubborn persistence of Covid-19 has vividly illustrated that, and therefore now something must be done. Human beings are, literally, fatally flawed and it is up to their betters to conduct them to the grave with as little fuss and trouble as possible. Were Schwab a woman, he might most strongly resemble Nurse Ratched from Ken Kesey's masterpiece, *One Flew Over the Cuckoo's Nest* (1962), who enters a room "with a gust of cold" and sports painted fingers "like polished steel… like the tip of a soldering iron."

Hans Castorp's moral triumph in *The Magic Mountain* is to finally depart of his own volition, to be killed by a professional in the war instead of by a quack in a white coat. It's the closest to heroism he can get, and it provides a model for all of us as we confront the deep core of inhumanity at the black heart of the Great Reset.

Artists are a threat to the hive mind of the collective; there's a reason we have the word "iconoclastic." From earliest times, a conquering civilization has destroyed both the religious symbols and the art of its victims (often the same thing) in order to impose a new world order upon a prostrate land. One need only think of the destruction of the Bamiyan Buddhas by the Muslim Taliban in Afghanistan in 2001 as "idols"—which in fact they were, as well as towering works of pre-Islamic art. Islam understands the threat that art, a potent form of heresy, poses to dogmatic faith.

This might, at this historical juncture, seem to be a controversial statement in light of the murderous history of the twentieth century. But to prize the present and the immediate past, which are transitory things, over the extended past that made us and the indefinite future into which we are inexorably heading is short-sighted, and the root of many of modernity's problems. We are like a great ship in the midst of battle, badly damaged and listing to port, but not completely lost yet.

We can yet rouse ourselves if only to continue the fight as long as we can and pass along the fruits of our struggle to the next generations.

It may seem at first glance odd to conflate warfare with art, but consider: the history of art in all its manifestations—pictographs, sculpture, poetry, storytelling, the theater, film—is often congruent with the history of warfare, or at least violence. One of the formative myths of early Rome is the so-called Rape of the Sabines (the word *raptio* in Latin is better translated as "abduction" of "kidnapping"). The event has been the subject of many a work of art, but let Giambologna's *Abduction of a Sabine Woman* stand in for all:

Carved from a single, imperfect block of marble, Giambologna's commemoration of a seminal if apocryphal moment in early Roman history remains one of the glories of the Italian Renaissance. Housed in the Loggia dei Lanzi in Florence, and designed to be viewed from any angle, or even circumnavigated by the viewer, the statue of three naked figures seems to leap from the earth, spiraling upward from the defeated older Sabine man, the husband, conquered by the younger, more virile Roman, who erotically embraces the woman even as she twists away, her left arm upraised to the heavens. The past, the present, and the tantalizing future are all represented here, frozen in kinetic motion. Rome, we know, will prosper; the Sabines will disappear; the ripe woman, her children yet unborn, is eternal.

Take any view of it you wish: brute force, sexual ecstasy, the Hegelian dialectic in action, the word of structural Marxism nearly made flesh, or the law of the jungle. In the *Abduction of a Sabine Woman*, Giambologna gives us a picture of cultural rape as self-preservation, an act of violence as transfiguration, the adumbrated sexual act as both agony and ecstasy.

Great art doesn't care about correctness, moral, political, or otherwise. It goes straight to the bedrock of human emotion upon which our social order is founded. There are exceptions to every rule, and art's job is to find them. The reason that great works of art, of all kinds, are so potent is that they can embrace a world of complexity in a single image—and while we may not know precisely what the artist intended, we all know exactly what the artist intended.

In this instance, the Giambologna sculpture depicts an episode from the mid-eighth century B.C., recounted in Livy's *History of Early Rome*: short of women, their marriage proposals turned down by neighboring tribes fearful of growing Roman power, the Roman founder and leader Romulus invited the Sabine and other neighboring families—men, women, and children—inside his fledgling city to celebrate a religious festival. At a prearranged signal, however, the Roman men "dashed in all directions to carry off the maidens who were present," with the most beautiful girls designated for the nascent Roman nobility.

> The abducted maidens were quite as despondent and indignant. Romulus, however, went round in person, and pointed out to them that it was all owing to the pride of their parents in denying right of intermarriage to their neighbors. They would live in honorable wedlock, and share all their property and civil rights, and—dearest of all to human nature—would be the mothers of freemen. He begged them to lay aside their feelings of resentment and give their affections to those whom fortune had made masters of their persons. An injury had often led to reconciliation and love; they would find their husbands all the more affectionate because each would do his utmost, so far as in him lay to make up for the loss of parents and country. These arguments were reinforced by the endearments of their husbands who excused their conduct by pleading the irresistible force of their passion—a plea effective beyond all others in appealing to a woman's nature.

When, sometime later, the Sabine men attacked Rome in order to get their women back, and actually captured the citadel, they taunted the Romans with the cries of, "We have conquered our faithless hosts, our cowardly foes; now they know that to carry off maidens is a very different thing from fighting with men." As the fighting intensified, however, it was suddenly brought to a halt by the intervention of the abducted women, who interposed themselves between the warring men: "Turn your anger upon us; it is we who are the cause of the war, it is we who have wounded and slain our husbands and fathers. Better for us to perish rather than live without one or the other of you, as widows or as orphans."

And so peace was made. The two warring nations became one state, centered in Rome. Observes Livy: "The joyful peace, which put an abrupt close to such a deplorable war, made the Sabine women still dearer to their husbands and fathers, and most of all to Romulus himself."

And this is where beauty comes in. There are few sculptures more perfect in their intertwining of human forms, more dramatic in their conflict, more erotic in their intent—we know from Livy what is going to happen to the beautiful Sabine woman and what her reaction, however politically incorrect by today's standards, is going to be. The overall effect is one of sheer beauty. As Sir Roger notes of beauty in general, it "can be consoling, disturbing, sacred, profane; it can be exhilarating, appealing, inspiring, chilling. It can affect us in an unlimited variety of ways. Yet it is never viewed with indifference: beauty demands to be noticed; it speaks to us directly like the voice of an intimate friend."

The abduction of the Sabines is roughly contemporaneous with the cornerstone of Western art and literature, Homer's *Iliad*, which should come as no surprise to any student of history. For the *Iliad* is both a war story—its very first word is "Rage" *(mēnin)*—and a love story; indeed, multiple love stories that take place within history's first war story. Achilles's famous wrath is provoked by the loss of a beautiful woman; not Helen of Troy, but Briseis, a captured slave girl, whom he must surrender to Agamemnon, the commander of the Greeks, and a man for whom he has nothing but contempt. Frustrated in love, Achilles has no weapon at his disposal with which to counter Agamemnon except the withdrawal of his martial services. Brave

Achaeans must die in their hundreds or thousands so that Achilles can maintain his pique and his honor, but the visceral brutality of the conflict is offset by its beauty—the beauty of Helen and Briseis, the beauty of Achilles's closest friend, Patroclus (whose death triggers an even greater rage than the loss of Briseis), to the final beauty of aged, doomed Priam, come to take the mangled body of his beautiful son, Hector, the breaker of horses, back to Troy after Achilles's malicious and unforgivable act of desecration.

This transitory moment of generational reconciliation finally slakes Achilles's uncontrollable fury and, as we later understand from other sources, dooms him to death from Paris's fatal arrow. It is, however, his choice. As the hero himself, says: "Either, if I stay here and fight beside the city of the Trojans, my return home is gone, but my glory shall be everlasting; but if I return home to the beloved land of my fathers, the excellence of my glory is gone, but there will be a long life left for me, and my end in death will not come to me quickly."

In other words, at least as far back as 750 B.C., the Poet sang of many things, but revealed that his themes were twinned, his subject one. That the beauty of human beings, and their deaths by dismemberment and butchery in warfare, are inseparable. Presence and absence as representation and will. And thus the basic truths of the everlasting human condition were limned at the start.

It is important to note at this point that the *Iliad* and its companion, the *Odyssey*, are at least contemporaneous with and likely even older than most of the Hebrew scriptures that form the basis of the Jewish Bible[24] and the Christian Old Testament. Homer's myths, and humanistic truths, antedate the monotheism of Judaism, Christianity, and Islam—each one in turn regarded as a heretical distortion of its antecedents. Monotheism, however, has itself distorted our view of other faiths (and thus other arts, and other truths), and in particular of the Greco-Roman gods—who in any case simply embody in their

---

24 The earliest surviving Pentateuch manuscript in Hebrew is the Codex Leningradensis of 1008 A.D. although we have portions both in Greek translation and in Hebrew that antedate it by centuries.

various manifestations and impersonations the many moods of the vengeful, censorious, jealous, arbitrary, prescriptive, proscriptive God of the Old Testament[25]—minus, of course, their rampant sexuality. Locating the origins of Western civilization in the Bible is therefore incorrect, although its texts had an effect equal to that of classical antiquity on Western art.

Art has evolved precisely to deal with this problem. The best of Western art engages religion—since, at root, they both spring from the same worshipful impulse—without dogmatism or even judgmentalism. This is why religion tends to condemn nonconformist art as heretical, blasphemous, or otherwise offensive, even though those qualities are part of its mission. Art asks of religion questions it would prefer not to answer—indeed, cannot answer if it is to remain true to its dogma. Art both celebrates and threatens Holy Writ—which is why Writ has so desperately sought to absorb it and compel it to theological or political uses.

That said, there is plenty of ecclesiastical and sacred art; a walk through any major art gallery proclaims as much. Western music can trace its written existence back to the medieval monks and the neumes of Gregorian chant notation, although the modal chants themselves are even older. During the classical period, composers such as Mozart and Haydn churned out masses by the bushel; and prior to them, J. S. Bach had spent most of his career working in and writing for the Lutheran church, which resulted in the towering masterpieces of musico-religious-dramatic art, the *St. Matthew Passion* of 1727, and the *Mass in B minor* of 1749, one of his last works. Even

25 The second-century Christian gnostic/heretic Marcion of Sinope, whose principal work was done in Rome, argues that the captious Hebrew God and the loving Christian God the Father are two different entities. Certainly, literarily and artistically, they are. His contemporary Valentinus also believed in a lesser god the creator (the *demiurge,* akin to the Jewish God of Abraham), outranked by the real God the Father of the Christians.

Beethoven, not a man given to overt religiosity, composed the *Missa Solemnis.*[26]

Yet religious art succeeds or fails not on its dogmaticism but on its intrinsic artistic qualities, including novelty and beauty. The vast bulk of the masses by Bach, Mozart, Haydn, Schubert, and others are largely forgotten or unperformed today, having served their utilitarian purposes in much the same way as the *Tafelmusik* ("table music") of Telemann did during the Baroque.

It is not enough for the sacred to simply be sacred; often, the profane can be made sacred as well. One of the most popular tunes of the late Middle Ages and early Renaissance, "L'homme Armé," turns up time and again in Ordinary masses of the Burgundian School (Josquin des Prez, Pierre de la Rue, Guillaume Dufay) as a cantus firmus running throughout the composition as its melodic foundation. Its lyrics are worth pondering in our context here:

> *L'homme armé doibt on doubter.*
> *On a fait partout crier*
> *Que chascun se viegne armer*
> *D'un haubregon de fer.*
> *L'homme armé doibt on doubter.*
> The armed man should be feared.
> Everywhere it has been proclaimed
> That each man shall arm himself
> With a coat of iron mail.
> The armed man should be feared.

Here again, we see the unity between the spiritual and the martial that so often characterizes Christian art from the creation of the Holy Roman Empire under Charlemagne through the nineteenth century; like so much of Europe, it died face down in the mud of Flanders'

---

26 Another example might be the "Heiliger Dankgesang" movement of the Op. 132 string quartet, a "song of thanksgiving" to God for having recovered from a serious illness.

Fields during World War I. But Christian theologians from the time of St. Augustine had been describing the moral parameters of the just war. Bloodshed qua bloodshed was not, in itself, objectionable as long as the objective was beneficial. Thus we have the celebratory Christian epic poems of the era, including *La chanson de Roland* (1115), *Gerusalemme liberata* of Tasso (1581) and *The Siege of Sziget* by Miklós Zríny (1651), all consciously modeling themselves after the Homeric sagas and Virgil's *Aeneid.*

The sacred, of course, could even more easily be made profane, most easily by placing it in a diabolical context. The transformation of Berlioz's idée fixe, the melody representing the Beloved in his programmatic *Symphonie fantastique,* from virginal radiance to whorish repellence is one of the best examples in the orchestral literature.

And sometimes the two combine. The agonized, tortured faces and poses of Christ on the Cross in their many representations, particularly by the German artists of early Renaissance, such as Matthias Grünewald and Lucas Cranach, attest to that. Where the Italian painters transfigured their sacred subject, the Germans were more interested in him as a man, not a god. Indeed, one might say that Bach's *Matthew Passion* is the musical embodiment of the Passion depicted by the earlier generation of visual artists, with the terrible agony of the Passion redeemed at the end by Joseph of Arimathea's healing aria, "Mache dich, mein Herze, rein."

The blending of art with faith and fatherland worked well for a very long time—certainly from Charlemagne to the Somme (a mere 150 miles apart on the map). But there it ended. While fatherland was lost for some but not for all, faith took a beating from which it never recovered. The Christian God (or gods, depending on one's degree of gnosis) finally collapsed of their own (as the ascendant Marxists would say) internal contradictions. The Jewish God, or demiurge to some of the early Christians, remained a distinctly minority pursuit. Art in celebration of either/all of them vanished. Enter atheistic, or at least virulently agnostic, Settembrinian humanism.

Art is dangerous—at least it is when you're doing it right. Art, and its manifestation in religion, is the twin sister to science: a way of understanding mankind, which is, after all, the proper study of man. The fetishization of ideologized "science" has long been characteristic of gullible societies, and the proper response has always been mockery. Mozart's opera, *Cosi fan tutte* (1790), lampoons the fad for mesmerism and its theories of animal magnetism when the maid Despina produces a giant magnet and pretends to cure the lovesick "Albanians" of poisoning. A century and a half later, the Soviets were extolling the genius of Trofim Lysenko, whose crackpot theories of genetics and agriculture, enforced at gunpoint, led to the imprisonment and execution of dissenters.

The Schwabians, however, will brook neither mockery nor contradiction. From the outbreak of the "pandemic" in 2020, they have pushed steadily for ever-greater and ever-tightening control of the institutions of democratic societies—in the name of "science" and, more important, "compassion." The pandemic, writes Schwab, "has forced all of us, citizens and policy-makers alike, willingly or not, to enter into a philosophical debate about how to maximize the common good in the least damaging way possible. First and foremost, it prompted us to think more deeply about what the common good really means. Common good is that which benefits society as a whole, but how do we decide collectively what is best for us as a community?"

Needless to say, these are issues with which the arts have long dealt. Indeed, there cannot be a "community" without an audience, which is to say, fellow human beings who come together voluntarily in communion with each other to share a religious, artistic, or social experience. That's not the meaning of "community" in the lexicon of the "progressive" Left, which prefers to define the word by shared, largely immutable and typically Marxist characteristics such as race (which they also deny exists), sex (which they are similarly certain is arbitrarily "assigned at birth" and thus changeable, and class. "Community" to the social justice warriors is viewed as an entity, rather than a collection of individuals freely associating. It's a grimly deterministic, malignant parody of Calvinism on an industrial scale. In such hands, art shorn of its potency and individuality becomes a cudgel of conformity instead of a weapon of change.

As it happens, in my capacity as the classical music critic of *Time Magazine* at the end of its glory days, I was lucky enough to spend the period between 1985 and 1991 in and out of the German Democratic Republic (the former East Germany) and the Union of Soviet Socialist Republics, now once again simply Russia. The potency of art as propaganda was manifest in both the D.D.R. and the U.S.S.R., where huge posters honored the leaders and exhorted the people, where works of musical and the plastic arts were commissioned, performed, and displayed in honor of the never-ending revolution *pour encourager les autres*.

Poets, composers, actors—those who conformed to the regime's strictures prospered. In East Germany, one thinks immediately of the playwright Bertolt Brecht and the actor Gustaf Gründgens, whose career—he was considered the finest Faust of his day—had also flourished under the National Socialists as one of the "Gottbegnadeten" (those "blessed by God"). Sergei Prokofiev left Russia in 1918, first for the U.S., then Germany and finally Paris as he pursued his career as a concert pianist and composer but returned to the Soviet Union in 1936. His great compatriot Dmitri Shostakovich remained in his homeland and even composed part of his Symphony No. 7, the "Leningrad," in that city in 1941, near the beginning of its nine-hundred-day siege by the Wehrmacht. Its premiere there in March 1942 was both a propaganda victory for the beleaguered Soviets and an international sensation, with famous conductors vying with each other to give the work its free-world premiere (Toscanini won).

Shostakovich's controversial memoir, *Testimony*, was published by his putative amanuensis, Solomon Volkov, in 1979. In it, the composer frankly discusses the terror of his life under Stalin and his hatred of the Leader and Teacher, which he poured into several sardonic and unforgettable musical portraits, most notably in the ferocious scherzo of the Symphony No. 10 (1953). Since Shostakovich had twice been denounced publicly by Stalin, this is entirely believable. "Without party guidance," he said after the dictator's death in 1953, "I would have displayed more brilliance, used more sarcasm, I could have revealed my ideas openly instead of having to resort to camouflage." The memoir was turned into a memorable 1988 film by British director Tony Palmer starring Ben Kingsley as Shostakovich.

During my time in the Soviet Union, in Moscow and Leningrad (now once again St. Petersburg) I took in as many concerts and operas as I could, including Kirill Molchanov's *The Dawns are Quiet Here* (in Russian: *Zori Zdes Tikhie*), written in 1973 to celebrate the Red Army in the Great Patriotic War, principally focusing on a squad of female antiaircraft gunners posted on the Russian-Finnish border. Undistinguished musically, the opera was typical of Soviet socialist-realistic art of its time—art exemplified by the head of the Soviet Composers Union, Tikhon Khrennikov, who had been one of Shostakovich's chief persecutors both in 1936 and 1948, when the great composer was officially denounced for "formalism."

I met Khrennikov in 1986 in Moscow under somewhat fraught circumstances: during an interview at the Composers Union in advance of his planned visit to Houston later that year, I was pressing him on the Resolution of 1948 (something I had been warned not to mention). Pointing to the portraits of Prokofiev and Shostakovich on the walls, I inquired how he had the gall to sit beneath pictures of men whose careers and lives he had tried to ruin.

My state-provided translator gulped and hesitated. He looked like he wanted to slide underneath the long, formal meeting table. I told him to go ahead. He did.

Khrennikov, a bullet-headed Slav, absorbed the question—and then blew his top. He began pounding the table, à la Khrushchev but with his bare hand, and shouted, "How dare you ask me about that?" or words to that effect. His squad of retainers (one of them, I recall, had a dueling scar running down his face) shifted uneasily as they awaited my answer.

"As a courtesy," I replied. "Because when you come to America, that's the first question the musical press is going to ask you, and I wanted you to be prepared for it."

A pause—and then a big smile. Hugs and Soviet-style kisses all around. From then on, the active member of both the Central Committee of the Communist Party and the Supreme Soviet of the U.S.S.R. and I were best friends, and no ticket in Moscow was too tough for me to cadge. Ballets and stage works depicting raw-boned Soviet farm girls and heroic tractor-factory employees followed, but I can't recall a note of the music. The one work I do remember was Yuri Shaporin's dazzling opera, *The Decembrists*, a musical depiction of an 1825 revolt against the Tsar. Shaporin worked on his protorevolutionary masterpiece off and on from 1920, but was constantly withdrawing and revising it, mindful of what was happening to Shostakovich and Prokofiev and fearful of what Stalin might think. The opera finally premiered at the Bolshoi Theatre in Moscow in June of 1953—three months after Stalin's death on March 5 of that year, by coincidence the same day Prokofiev died.

Such is the life of the artist under totalitarianism of any stripe. The Russians and East Germans had it easy: they only had to be attuned to the whims of a few powerful men and their network of informers, snitches, and rats.[27] In today's "cancel culture," anyone can denounce anyone via social media at any time, quickly assemble a virtual mob, and almost instantly remove the victim's source of livelihood. Their offense need not have been committed against political Holy Writ or party line dogma—who today even knows what "formalism"[28] was?—but against anything deemed by the mob to be "problematic."

Today's totalitarianism is, in other words, far more than simple governmental proscription. Rather, it has expanded to become societal, with right-think constantly pushed by both social and mainstream

---

27 For details, see the 2006 film, *The Lives of Others*, directed by Florian Henckel von Donnersmarck, about life under the East German Stasi.

28 Music for music's sake, in contrast with Soviet "realism," in which the music or drama contained a political message.

media. Journalists whose forebears prided themselves on their independence now, like courtiers in the Nero's palace, curry favor—not just with the boss but with his wives and mistresses, the Praetorian Guard, powerful senators and generals, with anyone who can feed these geldings scraps of gossip and disinformation with which to advance their careers and enforce unanimity of thought.

What effect this might have on art should be obvious: few artists have the spine or stamina of Shostakovich, willing insofar as possible to "push boundaries" (a favorite cliché among the stunning and brave practitioners of total orthodoxy) and yet remain relatively viable within an algorithmic system which elevates literal-mindedness to a cardinal principle. So entrenched is "transgressive" art that the creative community now bears more than a little resemblance to the sham battles between Union and Unanimity in the "Orison of Sonmi-451" chapters of David Mitchell's brilliant 2004 novel, *Cloud Atlas.* Even those who think they are rebels in fact are in fact being manipulated by government power designed to present the illusion of debate, disagreement and, when necessary, outright rebellion.[29]

One of the hallmarks of the modern, cultural-Marxist Left is its desire for postrevolutionary stasis. I have often compared their aggressive philosophy to the Brezhnev Doctrine, which held as axiomatic that any territory acquired for international Communism, once acquired, must forever remain Communist. In this, godless Communism was theologically similar to monotheistic Islam, which has a similar attitude regarding its conquests in the *dar-al-Harb*. That neither dogma has proved accurate in practice fails to dissuade the true believers from their moral certitude, however.

Like Stalin's order to the defenders at Stalingrad, "Not one step back," avant-garde progressives suddenly develop an affection for the derrière, so to speak, once they have staked out captured turf. The

29 The 2012 film adaptation defensibly omits this final realization on Sonmi's part. The audience has become so invested in her parlous slavery, dramatic escape, heroic defiance, and her tragic death that it would have negated the movie's overall tone and message.

idea of a rollback or a reconquista never seems to occur to them as being within the realm of possibility. For years, decades, their own artists have derided, attacked, and assaulted the cultural and moral norms of the society they wish to besiege—a society that, mind you, has sheltered, protected, and nurtured them with its own laws. But once ascendant, Herbert Marcuse's doctrine of "repressive tolerance" comes into play, which is to say that "tolerance" is delisted from the cardinal virtues and becomes just another quaint luxury the new society can no longer afford if it is to survive.

A world of stasis is, of course, a dead world, and that is the lee shore on which the Davoisie hopes to ground us. The target land mass may be Fiji or it may be Skull Island; no one really has any way of knowing. A good seaman tries to avoid losing control of his sails to avoid the collision; a shipwrecked castaway has only hope, the cruelest of all the so-called theological virtues. Communism, meanwhile, has a one hundred percent track record of foundering upon the perfectly visible and avoidable rocks of reality.

The Great Reset's gambit is to mask and cloak itself, like an obedient handmaiden, in good intentions while stealing you blind and enslaving you. It positively radiates concern for its billions of fellow men even as it consigns them to indefinite house arrest. Advocating the fiscal lunacy of so-called Modern Monetary Theory, for example, Schwab and Malleret write:

> These are unprecedented programmes for an unprecedented situation, something so new that the economist Carmen Reinhart has called it a "whatever-it-takes moment for large-scale, outside-the-box fiscal and monetary policies". Measures that would have seemed inconceivable prior to the pandemic may well become standard around the world as governments try to prevent the economic recession from turning into a catastrophic depression. Increasingly, there will be calls for government to act as a "payer of last resort" to

> prevent or stem the spate of mass layoffs and business destruction triggered by the pandemic.

In fact, "stimulus" is what the Great Reset purports to be all about. Vast deficit spending will inexorably lead to an "explosion of creativity among start-ups and new ventures in the digital and biotechnological spaces." But it's the arts, they argue, that could really take off with just a little more privation and solitary confinement:

> The same may well happen in the realms of science and the arts. Illustrious past episodes corroborate that creative characters thrive in lockdown. Isaac Newton, for one, flourished during the plague. When Cambridge University had to shut down in the summer of 1665 after an outbreak, Newton went back to his family home in Lincolnshire where he stayed for more than a year. During this period of forced isolation described as *annus mirabilis* (a "remarkable year"), he had an outpouring of creative energy that formed the foundation for his theories of gravity and optics and, in particular, the development of the inverse-square law of gravitation....
>
> A similar principle of creativity under duress applies to literature and is at the origin of some of the most famous literary works in the Western world. Scholars argue that the closure of theatres in London forced by the plague of 1593 helped Shakespeare turn to poetry. This is when he published "Venus and Adonis," a popular narrative poem in which the goddess implores a kiss from a boy "to drive infection from the dangerous year." A few years later, at the beginning of the 17th century, theatres in London were more often closed than open because of the bubonic plague. An official rule stipulated that theatre performances would have to be cancelled when the deaths

> caused by the plague exceeded 30 people per week. In 1606, Shakespeare was very prolific precisely because theatres were closed by the epidemic and his troupe couldn't play. In just one year he wrote "King Lear," "Macbeth," and "Antony and Cleopatra."
>
> The Russian author Alexander Pushkin had a similar experience. In 1830, following a cholera epidemic that had reached Nizhny Novgorod, he found himself in lockdown in a provincial estate. Suddenly, after years of personal turmoil, he felt relieved, free and happy. The three months he spent in quarantine were the most creative and productive of his life. He finished *Eugene Onegin*—his masterpiece—and wrote a series of sketches, one of which was called "A Feast During the Plague."

It takes some gall to argue that Newton, Shakespeare, and Pushkin were the beneficiaries of the plague; one might just as well argue that their equals, or betters, perished anonymously. But Schwab and his profoundly uncreative and dead-souled ilk clearly prefer the mortuary and the graveyard to the hustle and bustle of the rialto, where free men act in their own best interests—and thus in their "community's"—with like-minded others. Although art has indubitably benefited from enlightened and benign patronage, no one but a well-fed jailer could argue that privation and punishment is a recipe for artistic success.

True, there is often a fine line between patronage and propaganda, as artists have known for centuries. Medieval and Renaissance art is replete with renderings of the patron on a portion of the canvas, either rapt in prayer or as a bystander to momentous but anachronistic events he could not possibly have witnessed. As history it is perhaps risible but as an economic transaction it is unexceptionable. Composers throughout the eighteenth and nineteenth centuries routinely dedicated their works to various nobles. Other sought employment in the service of the church, as Bach did, or the local prince, as Haydn did with the Esterházy family. Many of Beethoven's compositions are dedicated to various noble noggins—and Beethoven was a revolutionary democrat who violently erased the "Eroica" symphony's inscription to Napoleon after the Little Corporal was proclaimed Emperor of the French: "So he is no more than a common mortal!" Beethoven is supposed to have exclaimed to his student, Ferdinand Ries, as he expunged the dedication with such force that he tore through the manuscript's title page. "Now, too, he will tread under foot all the rights of Man, indulge only his ambition; now he will think himself superior to all men, become a tyrant!"

The "Rights of Man," of course, is an at least oblique reference to the French Revolution and to the British-born Thomas Paine's 1791 book of that name (the "Eroica" was written in 1803). Paine, an inveterate troublemaker and passionate advocate of the revolutionary position no matter where he found himself (he was also a leading figure in the American Revolution) recorded the rights as declared by the National Constituent Assembly in 1789; the first, an homage to, and a hopeful improvement upon, Rousseau, reads: "Men are born and remain free and equal in rights. Social distinctions can be founded only on the common good."

It's also the name of the merchant ship from which the title character is removed and impressed aboard a warship aptly named the HMS *Bellipotent* in Herman Melville's final novella, *Billy Budd*, which is set in 1797 during the Napoleonic Wars. Benjamin Britten turned it into an opera in 1951; "Farewell, to you forever, old *Rights o'Man*," sings Billy as he leaves the commercial vessel for his doom. Echoes upon echoes—but this is how culture is built and maintained. We stand upon the shoulders of giants,[30] now under attack by the Lilliputians of Davos.

---

30 Sometimes that can be disconcerting. "You have no idea how it feels to hear the tramp of a giant like Beethoven behind you," snapped Brahms, who was so intimidated by his illustrious predecessor that it took him years to finally premiere his first symphony. When a critic pointed out the resemblance of the main theme of its finale to the last movement of Beethoven's Ninth, Brahms replied: "Any ass can see that."

Which is not to say that Beethoven wished to be a propagandist for Napoleon the revolutionary. Like Goethe, Beethoven was unique, a one-off, a self-contained creative volcano who loved but never married, who went deaf but defied his disability by force of will to become even greater than he might have been otherwise, who eschewed privilege but remained steadfastly in business for himself, with all the sharp practices that entailed in order to keep a roof over his head and the chamber-pot out of his piano's innards. A fighter to the end, Beethoven raised a defiant fist to the heavens as a thunderclap and a flash of lightning punctuated his last moment on earth. Or so the legend goes.

Mozart, for his part, failed in his attempts to secure a steady job with either church or state; he was hustling a Broadway-style German-language musical (*The Magic Flute*) at the same time he was writing an old-fashioned Italian opera seria on a classical theme, *La Clemenza di Tito,* and died immediately thereafter with the Requiem still unfinished. Meanwhile, his literary bête noire, Antonio Salieri, was getting all the good gigs, at least according to the playwright Peter Shaffer[31] in his play and, later, film, *Amadeus.*

Perhaps Schwab is partially correct in his implication that some suffering is good for the soul and the art, but matching an artist's external circumstances to his creative moods is generally a fool's errand, although it suits a cloddish pragmatist's need for an explanation of such things as Tchaikovsky's Pathetique Symphony or Gustav Mahler's congenital orchestral unhappiness. But Beethoven's misery was, despite his unsuccessful love life, primarily physical: at his death he had likely been suffering from cirrhosis of the liver with high levels of lead in his system for at least a decade. A professional to the end, he wrote his late-period masterpieces for the piano and the string quartet in spite of his pain, not because of it.

Surely Schwab and the Resetters would not want to find themselves in the position of the Prisoner in Luigi Dallapiccola's serialist

---

31 Inspired by Pushkin, who wrote a speculative play on the subject, and Rimsky-Korsakov, who set it to music in 1898. Shoulders of giants.

opera, *Il prigioniero* (1949), set not coincidentally during the Spanish occupation of the Netherlands, a period that also inspired Beethoven in both the "Egmont" Overture[32] and his opera, *Fidelio.*

A product of the composer's wartime experiences, and composed originally for a hour-long radio performance, *Il prigioniero*—based on a story by the nineteenth-century French symbolist writer Auguste Villiers de l'Isle-Adam called "The Torture by Hope"—is one of the essential works of twentieth-century art. Languishing like Beethoven's Florestan in a dank dungeon, the prisoner discovers one night that his cell door has been left open, giving him a chance to at least emerge into the prison yard where he encounters none other than the Dostoyevskian figure of the grand inquisitor,[33] who—calling him *fratello* (brother)—gently disabuses him of any notions of escape and instead evokes the shade of Dante with the line, "*La speranza... l'ultima tortura....*"

Hope, as every inquisitor knows, is the final torture of the condemned man. The prisoner's last words, uncertain but fatalistic, echo as the curtain falls: "*La libertà?*" "Freedom?" What a contrast to Florestan's magnificent Act II prison aria in *Fidelio*, which moves from abject despair to overwhelming, certain victory, to the triumphant power of his defiant shout of "Freiheit!"

Freedom? *La libertà*? *Freiheit*?" These are the canapés the Davoisie—the crowned heads of dying dynasties, the nouveau riche of a modern *Decameron*, the Silicon Valley technocrats holed up on the *Magic Mountain*—dangle before us, like the prisoner's tantalizingly unlocked cell.

Ah, but this is not a "rescue opera" the Resetters will say, and there is no offstage Leonore, the faithful wife, waiting in the wings to save the day. What the Dr. Strangeloves of Davos, so contemptuous of freedom, have forgotten are Florestan's final words in his aria, in which

---

32 The anthem of the Hungarian Revolution against the Soviets in 1956. *Pace* Mark Twain, history not only rhymes, it repeats. *Pace* Marx, the second time can also be tragic.

33 Who also appears in Verdi's opera, *Don Carlos*. More shoulders, more giants.

he apotheosizes Leonore as "my angel, my wife, who will lead me to freedom, to the kingdom of God." Sexless, passionate, aging men of power, prestige, and privilege—in the end, they have nothing to fall back upon except their own frustration, bitterness, impotence, and hatred for the hoi polloi. In their hearts, they are all Grand Inquisitors, men of authority but no character, who cannot withstand the sunlight of freedom—God's kingdom.

That kingdom is best ruled by priests and artists, not kings and business tycoons. Yes, there are times when the artists and priests converge, confuse, and confound. Evil Nero, the descendant of some of the greatest men of antiquity, a man of ultimate if transitory authority who mistook infamy for fame, one whose art and music died with him but whose sordid memory lingers on, was nevertheless justified in his own valedictory, even as the wen of ancient Rome still partly lay in ashes and the slave's dagger severed his jugular. And that impulse is something the likes of Schwab, Britain's Prince Charles, and their confreres will never understand, because the transcendental, no matter how misguided, will always elude the pedestrian.

In the year 1643, in France, the Sun King assumed the throne. The Age of Exploration was well underway. The English civil war raged. The Thirty Years' War was nearing an end. And in the sovereign state of Venice, La Serenissima, the Italian composer Claudio Monteverdi premiered the last of his works in a new art form called, fittingly, *opera* (works). Its name: *L'incoronazione di Poppea.* Its main characters: the beautiful Poppaea Sabina, soon to be called the Augusta, whose favorite saying was that she hoped she would die before she got old; and the man born Lucius Domitius Ahenobarbus and ended up as Nero Claudius Caesar Augustus Germanicus—or, simply, Nero.

Its final, ravishing duet, "Pur ti miro" ("I adore you, I embrace you, I desire you"), Poppea and Nerone (performed today by a woman or a countertenor, *castrati* being largely unavailable, except among the progressive gender dysphorics) sing of their undying love. No matter that Nero has killed his mother and made his marriage to Poppaea possible by eliminating the prior Mrs. Nero, Claudia Octavia. No matter that we know the marriage will last only three years, when Nero will kick Poppaea and her unborn child to death in a fit of pique, and then marry again, taking not only Statilia Messalina to wife but an emasculated boy made up to look, and function, exactly like the dead Poppaea.

We know the tragic ending but they don't—and it doesn't matter. In this radiant moment, one of history's greatest monsters is resurrected as a lovesick hero, transformed not by dramatic fiat but by the otherworldly power of Monteverdi's music, which makes us forget history and be carried along by an alternate reality we briefly prefer to believe. The artist Nero fancied himself is thus given immortality—but not absolution—in the field in which he most desired it.

Art, like the Christ figure, has conquered death. This is its power, which cannot be reset. This is why religious and secular authorities fear it, seek to diminish it, try to co-opt it, reduce it to a grubby economic transaction, send it to a prison camp, hang it. Like Boccaccio's Decameronians, holed up in a fashionable villa to avoid the Black Death but with absolutely no storytelling ability, they await and encourage the collapse of contemporary civilization so that they might improve it, along with their own fortunes. That artists subscribe, consciously or not, to the Nietzschean doctrine of eternal recurrence never seems to occur to them; even if they've never read *Cloud Atlas,* perhaps they should harken to the sextet by Vyvyan Ayrs.

Artists neither mourn nor celebrate their subjects; rather, they exhibit their own power to resurrect the dead or summon the nonexistent to squalling life, whether their characters are sacred or profane. Profoundly indifferent to morality, yet completely human, art exists on its own terms, open to all to inspect, embrace, imitate, or reject. From the Roman Empire to the seventeenth-century Venetian court; from the Zauberberg a hundred years ago to Davos Dorf today, many have tried to geld it or beat it into submission, but art and artists will always have the last word. There is no Reset, neither by gods nor bonzes, but there is always rebirth. And that is forever the province of the glory, jest, and riddle of the world—Man.

CONTRIBUTORS

Michael Anton is a lecturer in politics at Hillsdale College's Washington, D.C., campus. He served on the National Security Council in both the Trump and George W. Bush administrations. He is the author of three books: *The Suit* (as "Nicholas Antongiavanni"), *After the Flight 93 Election*, and *The Stakes*. His scholarly work includes articles on Xenophon, Machiavelli, and Montesquieu. He writes frequently for the *Claremont Review of Books*, *American Greatness*, and the *American Mind*. He is also a senior fellow of the Claremont Institute and was educated principally at the Claremont Graduate School.

Salvatore Babones is a political sociologist at the University of Sydney. His short book *The New Authoritarianism: Trump, Populism, and the Tyranny of Experts* was named "Best on Politics 2018" by the *Wall Street Journal*. Salvatore is the author or coauthor of seven other books and dozens of academic papers. His academic research focuses on globalization and world society theory, but he has also published articles on autonomous vehicle futures in *Forbes*, *Foreign Policy*, and other popular venues.

Conrad Black was the principal owner of many newspapers, including the *Daily Telegraph* and *Spectator* in the UK, the *Chicago Sun-Times*, the *Jerusalem Post*, and most of the newspapers in Australia and Canada, including the *National Post*, which he founded. He writes on American Greatness, the *New York Sun*, the *Epoch Times*, and at the *National Post* every week, and frequently appears on other sites in the U.S. and U.K. He has written extensive biographies of Franklin D. Roosevelt, Richard Nixon, and Donald Trump. His books include *A Strategic History of the U.S.*, *Flight of the Eagle*, and *Rise to Greatness: The History of Canada*. He has been a member of the British House of Lords as Lord Black of Crossharbour since 2001.

Jeremy Black, Emeritus Professor of History at the University of Exeter, is a prolific lecturer and writer, the author of more than one hundred books concerning aspects of eighteenth-century British, European, and American political, diplomatic, and military history. He has also published on the history of the press, cartography, warfare, culture, and on the nature and uses of history itself. He has lectured extensively in Australia, Canada, Denmark, France, Germany, Italy, New Zealand, and the U.S.A., where he has held visiting chairs at West Point, Texas Christian University, and Stillman College. He was appointed to the Order of Membership of the British Empire for services to stamp design.

Angelo Codevilla was born near Milan, Italy, emigrated to the United States in 1955, and was educated at Rutgers, Notre Dame, and the Claremont Graduate School. He was a longtime professor of International Relations at Boston University, a fellow of Stanford's Hoover Institution, and Senior Fellow of the Claremont Institute. His long service to the United States government included stints as a Naval officer, foreign service officer, eight years as staff director of the Senate Intelligence Committee, and service on the Reagan transition team and in President Reagan's National Security Council. His many books include *Informing Statecraft*, *The Character of Nations*, *Advice to War Presidents*, *The Ruling Class*, and a forthcoming volume on the statesmanship of John Quincy Adams. Professor Codevilla died in September 2021 shortly after completing this project.

Janice Fiamengo is a retired Professor of English at the University of Ottawa who lives in Vancouver, B.C., with her husband, poet and songwriter David Solway. For five years, she hosted the *Fiamengo File*, a YouTube series on *Studio Brule* about the fraud of academic feminism and its impact on Western culture. In 2018, she edited and introduced *Sons of Feminism: Men Have Their Say*, a collection of personal essays.

Richard Fernandez is an Australian software developer and writer. He comments mostly on current events on his weblog, the *Belmont Club*, but occasionally contributes to publications like the *Wall Street Journal*. He is occasionally interviewed on radio shows. He is the author of one novel, *No Way In*, and coauthor of privacy pricing model, *Open Curtains*, in collaboration with George Spix. Originally from the Philippines, Richard was active for many years in the anti-Marcos underground and, in the subsequent government, worked in a staff capacity for the government panel negotiating a peace agreement with Islamic insurgents in Mindanao. He worked as a forestry consultant before focusing on software development.

David P. Goldman is deputy editor of *Asia Times*, where he has written the *Spengler* column since 2000, and a Washington Fellow of the Claremont Institute. His books include *How Civilizations Die* (2011), *It's Not the End of the World, It's Just the End of You* (2011), and *You Will Be Assimilated: China's Plan to Sino-Form the World* (2020). He publishes in the *Wall Street Journal, Claremont Review of Books, First Things, Tablet Magazine, Law & Liberty*, PJ Media, and many other venues. He has been the global head of fixed income research at Bank of America and the global head of credit strategies at Credit Suisse, among other senior positions in finance. He has won *Institutional Investor* magazine's award for General Strategy, one of the highest honors in investment research.

Victor Davis Hanson is a senior fellow in classics and military history at the Hoover Institution, Stanford University, a recipient of the

National Humanities Medal and the Bradley Prize, and the author most recently of *The Dying Citizen* (Basic Books 2021).

Martin Hutchinson was born in London, brought up in Cheltenham, England, and has lived in Singapore, Croatia, London, suburban Washington, and since 2011 in Poughkeepsie, NY. He was a merchant banker for more than twenty-five years before moving into financial journalism in 2000. He earned his undergraduate degree in mathematics from Trinity College, Cambridge, and an MBA from Harvard Business School. He is the author of *Britain's Greatest Prime Minister* (Lutterworth Press, 2020); *Great Conservatives* (Academica Press, 2004); and, with Professor Kevin Dowd, *Alchemists of Loss* Wiley (2010).

Roger Kimball is the editor and publisher of the *New Criterion* and president and publisher of Encounter Books. He is the author of several books, including *Tenured Radicals: How Politics Has Corrupted Our Higher Education*, and *The Long March: How the Cultural Revolution of the 1960s Changed America*, and is a regular columnist for *American Greatness*, the *Epoch Times*, and the *Spectator*.

Alberto Mingardi is Director General of the Italian free-market think tank, *Istituto Bruno Leoni* in Milan; he is also associate professor of the history of political thought at the International University of Languages and Media University (IULM). Mingardi has authored or edited several books, including *The Myth of the Entrepreneurial State* (2020) with Deirdre N. McCloskey. His commentaries have appeared in major Italian newspapers, and he frequently appears on Italian radio and television. Internationally, his opinion pieces have also been published by the *Wall Street Journal*, the *Washington Post*, and the *Financial Times*.

Douglas Murray is an author and journalist based in Britain. His books include *The Sunday Times* No. 1 bestseller *The Strange Death* *of Europe: Immigration, Identity, and Islam* (2017), and *The Madness of Crowds: Gender, Race, and Identity*. He has been Associate Editor at *The Spectator* magazine since 2012 and has written regularly there, as well as for other publications including the *Wall Street Journal*, the *Times*, the *Sunday Times*, the *Sun*, the *Mail on Sunday*, the *Telegraph*, the *New York Post*, and the *National Review*. A regular guest on the BBC and other news channels, he has also spoken at numerous universities, parliaments, the O2 Arena, and the White House.

James Poulos creates and advises brands and enterprises at the intersection of technology, media, and design. He is the cofounder and executive editor of the *American Mind* at the Claremont Institute and the author of *Human, Forever* and *The Art of Being Free*. His work has appeared in the *Claremont Review of Books*, *Le Figaro*, *National Affairs*, the *New York Times*, and the *Washington Post*, among many other publications. He holds a PhD in government from Georgetown University and a BA in political science from Duke University, and is a fellow at the Center for the Study of Digital Life. He lives on the edge of Los Angeles.

Harry Stein, a former Lefty who wised up, is the author of twelve books, among them *How I Accidentally Joined the Vast Right-Wing Conspiracy (and Found Inner Peace)*, *No Matter What…They'll Call This Book Racist*, *Hoopla* and the conservative comic novels *Will Tripp: Pissed Off Attorney at Law* and *Will Tripp Goes Hollywood*. In his former life a regular contributor to the *New York Times Magazine*, *Playboy* and *Sport*, and the creator of *Esquire*'s Ethics column, among the most popular features in that magazine's history. He is currently a contributing editor to *City Journal* and the editorial director of Calamo Books.

John Tierney is a contributing editor to *City Journal*, which has published his reporting throughout the Covid-19 pandemic. He is the coauthor, with the social psychologist Roy Baumeister, of *The Power* *of Bad: How the Negativity Effect Rules Us and How We Can Rule It* and *Willpower: Rediscovering the Greatest Human Strength.* During more than two decades at the *New York Times*, he was a science columnist, an Op-Ed columnist, and a staff writer for the *New York Times Magazine.* His articles have been published in dozens of newspapers and magazines, and his books have been translated into more than twenty languages.

Michael Walsh was for sixteen years the classical music critic and a foreign correspondent for *Time Magazine*, for which he wrote cover stories on James Levine, Andrew Lloyd Webber, and Vladimir Horowitz on the occasion of the pianist's 1986 return to his native Russia. He is the author of sixteen books of both fiction and nonfiction, including *The Devil's Pleasure Palace* (2015), *The Fiery Angel* (2018), and *Last Stands* (2020). His novel *And All the Saints*, an "autobiography" of the Prohibition era–gangster Owney Madden, won the 2004 American Book Award for fiction. He is the editor of the-Pipeline.org.